PSYCHOLOGY OF EMOTIONS, MOTIVATIONS AND ACTIONS

# SOCIAL ANXIETY

# PERCEPTIONS, EMOTIONAL AND TRIGGERING SYMPTOMS AND TREATMENT

# PSYCHOLOGY OF EMOTIONS, MOTIVATIONS AND ACTIONS

Additional books in this series can be found on Nova's website
under the Series tab.

Additional e-books in this series can be found on Nova's website
under the e-book tab.

# SOCIAL ANXIETY

# PERCEPTIONS, EMOTIONAL AND TRIGGERING SYMPTOMS AND TREATMENT

## EFROSINI KALYVA
### EDITOR

NOVA BIOMEDICAL

*New York*

For permission to use material from this book please contact us:
Telephone 631-231-7269; Fax 631-231-8175
Web Site: http://www.novapublishers.com

**NOTICE TO THE READER**

The Publisher has taken reasonable care in the preparation of this book, but makes no expressed or implied warranty of any kind and assumes no responsibility for any errors or omissions. No liability is assumed for incidental or consequential damages in connection with or arising out of information contained in this book. The Publisher shall not be liable for any special, consequential, or exemplary damages resulting, in whole or in part, from the readers' use of, or reliance upon, this material. Any parts of this book based on government reports are so indicated and copyright is claimed for those parts to the extent applicable to compilations of such works.

Independent verification should be sought for any data, advice or recommendations contained in this book. In addition, no responsibility is assumed by the publisher for any injury and/or damage to persons or property arising from any methods, products, instructions, ideas or otherwise contained in this publication.

This publication is designed to provide accurate and authoritative information with regard to the subject matter covered herein. It is sold with the clear understanding that the Publisher is not engaged in rendering legal or any other professional services. If legal or any other expert assistance is required, the services of a competent person should be sought. FROM A DECLARATION OF PARTICIPANTS JOINTLY ADOPTED BY A COMMITTEE OF THE AMERICAN BAR ASSOCIATION AND A COMMITTEE OF PUBLISHERS.

Additional color graphics may be available in the e-book version of this book.

**Library of Congress Cataloging-in-Publication Data**

Social anxiety : perceptions, emotional and triggering symptoms and treatment / editor, Efrosini Kalyva.
       pages cm
   Includes index.
    ISBN: 978-1-62808-396-5 (hardcover)
    1. Social phobia. 2. Anxiety--Social aspects.  I. Kalyva, Efrosini.
   RC552.S62S629 2013
   616.85'225--dc23
                                        2013024372

*Published by Nova Science Publishers, Inc. † New York*

# Contents

| | | |
|---|---|---|
| **Preface** | | **vii** |
| **Chapter I** | Variations in the Assessment of Social Anxiety<br>*Kathy Sexton-Radek and Reyna Schwartz* | **1** |
| **Chapter II** | Perception of Autonomic Arousal in Social Anxiety: Mechanisms and its Role As a Maintaining Factor<br>*Margit Gramer* | **19** |
| **Chapter III** | Enhancing Help and Treatment-Seeking Behaviors among Adolescents and Young Adults with Social Anxiety Disorder (Social Phobia)<br>*Suela Sulo and Maya Ramic* | **31** |
| **Chapter IV** | Family Influences of Children's Social Anxiety during Early Adolescence<br>*Cheryl Buehler and Bridget B. Weymouth* | **49** |
| **Chapter V** | The Role of Family Factors in Social Anxiety:<br>A Review of Empirical Findings and Implications for Treatment<br>*Ourania Founta* | **71** |
| **Chapter VI** | Social Anxiety and Substance Use<br>*Erika Melonashi* | **91** |
| **Chapter VII** | Social Anxiety in the School Setting for Students with Autism Spectrum Disorders<br>*Efrosini Kalyva and Vlastaris Tsakiris* | **127** |
| **Chapter VIII** | Social Anxiety and HIV/AIDS: Psychological Well-Being and Intervention Effectiveness<br>*Miltiadis Stefanidis, Charilaos Liampas,*<br>*Fotis Katimertzopoulos, Vlad Dediu, Christina Zintro,*<br>*Victoria Georgieva, and Aleksandar Ilievski* | **141** |

**Chapter IX**      Barriers to Medication Adherence among Chronic Heart Failure
                    Patients in Greece                                              **157**
                    *Paraskevi Theofilou Konstadina Griva and Sophia Zyga*

**Chapter X**       Social Anxiety Disorder: The Role of Cognitive Behavioral
                    Therapy                                                         **183**
                    *Stavros Simitsis,*
                    *Klearchos Konstantinos Stamatoulakis,*
                    *Valeria Strigkou, Kyriaki Avramidou,*
                    *Nikolaos Drouboulas-Theodoridis*
                    *and Pagona Papadimitriou*

**Index**                                                                           **203**

# Preface

Social anxiety or social phobia has become increasingly common in contemporary societies due to the increased isolation in impersonal living environments and the weakening family ties that leave many individuals feeling withdrawn and estranged.

In this book, Sexton-Radek et al. provide a comprehensive review of contemporary research on the ways of assessing social anxiety and conclude that a specific analysis of the studies in the areas of social anxiety measurement revealed the strength of the studies in classification and identification of outcome. A revision of these standardized measures will be needed once the new DSM is released.

Margarit Gramer examines the suggestion that perception and subsequent dysfunctional appraisal of somatic sensations might be a major determinant of negative self-evaluations in socially anxious individuals. Emphasis is placed on the role of autonomic arousal in the development of social phobia. Her review provides an overview of the current state of knowledge in this area and tries to delineate pathways between interoceptive sensitivity and the maintenance of the disorder.

Given the increasing numbers of young people suffering from social anxiety disorder, Suela et al. aim to process and understand social anxiety disorder from the point of view of a young person affected by it as well as from the point of view of experts familiar with this population. Their writing style is direct and accessible so that readers can benefit from it the most. They review various available treatments and recommendations for social anxiety, emphasizing that it is a disorder and not a character flaw.

Special reference in this book is made to the impact of family on the development and maintenance of social anxiety in children on a both theoretical and practical level. Buehler et al examines the influences of three family factors (child-related marital conflict, marital hostility, and parents' psychological intrusiveness) on youths' social anxiety during early adolescence. Their main finding is that child-related marital conflict is instrumental in two-parent families for shaping social anxiety in children. Founta explores the family's role on the development and maintenance of social anxiety from a theroretical perspective and proposes ways to overcome dysfunctional family relationships.

Social anxiety is also discussed in the terms of different groups of individuals that have unique characteristics. Melonashi reviews the role of social anxiety in the development of substance use/abuse and social anxiety and provides a discussion of both theoretical frameworks (e.g., cognitive affective theories, social learning theories) as well as relevant empirical studies in trying to understand this relationship. Kalyva et al refer to the social anxiety experienced by individuals with autism spectrum disorders and propose various ways to help them deal with this anxiety providing also many practical real-life examples. Stefanidis et al refer to the stigmatization that increases the social anxiety of individuals with HIV/AIDS and there is specific reference to the psychological impact of social anxiety as well as the role of culture in the effectiveness of implemented interventions. Theofilou et al conduct an empirical study to demonstrate the impact of social anxiety on medication adherence of patients with chronic heart failure.

Finally, Simitsis et al review extensively cognitive behavioral training and other relevant effective treatment or intervention techniques to deal with social anxiety. This chapter concludes this book that is dedicated to social anxiety and provides an interesting insight from different perspectives. The diverse cultural, training and practical background of the authors adds a critical and interdisciplinary flavor to the book.

*Dr Efrosini Kalyva, Psychologist*
*SEERC, Thessaloniki, Greece*

In: Social Anxiety
Editor: Efrosini Kalyva

ISBN: 978-1-62808-396-5
© 2013 Nova Science Publishers, Inc.

*Chapter I*

# Variations in the Assessment of Social Anxiety

### *Kathy Sexton-Radek[1],* and Reyna Schwartz[2]*
[1]Elmhurst College, Elmhurst, IL, US
[2]The Chicago School, Chicago, IL, US

## Abstract

An overview of the measurement of Social Anxiety is provided. A review of the literature using PsychLit and combinations of search terms (same as keywords) yielded one hundred and seventy-eight studies from the last five years. Studies were excluded if they were not empirical, were a masters dissertation project, not in English. Fifty-nine studies met the criteria and were reviewed.

**Keywords**: Social Anxiety Disorder, Social Phobia, Gender and Social Anxiety, Age and Social Anxiety, Treatment of Social Anxiety, Measurement of Social Anxiety

## Variations in the Assessment of Social Anxiety

Social anxiety disorder (SAD) is estimated to be common; however, 5% of individuals with SAD seek treatment (Feldman and Rivas-Vasquez, 2003). The general prevalence is 10-15% in the community and 5-7% in primary care (Ballenger, Davidson, Lecrubier, Nutt, Bobes, Beidel, Ono and Westenberg, 1998). Additionally, individuals with SAD symptoms do not always come to the attention of health care providers. Thus, the experience of symptoms is coupled with the handicapping conditions of their existence such as under employment, unemployment, dissatisfaction with relationships, and difficulty in relationships than normal. While the characteristic symptom pattern of SAD is anxiety in social and

---

* Corresponding author: Kathy Sexton-Radek, E-mail: ksrsleep@aol.com.

performance situations, the individual with SAD is believed to escape detection by the health professional as "shyness" attributes are considered.

However, the individual with SAD in situations where they feel they will be scrutinized or evaluated. The subtypes of public speaking, using a public rest room or eating or writing in front of others. SAD also occurs co-morbidly, usually major depressive disorder or panic disorder. Research studies have identified that 45% of patients with panic disorder with or without agoraphobia also have SAD (Feldman and Rivas-Vasquez, 2003). Additionally, SAD has co-morbidities with irritable bowel disorder, post-traumatic stress disorder, specific phobias, stuttering, and benign essential terror.

It has been reported from an assessment of 437 twin pairs that 42% of the variance in fear of a negative situation (Stein, Jang, and Lively, 2002). Behavioral inhibition has been described as a temperamental trait that demonstrates fear, avoidance and quiet restraint when exposed to novel situations (Langer, Bergman, and Piacentini, 2010). Parenting styles have been identified of low affection, warmth, restrictedness, using shame as discipline and over concern with opinions of others sufficient to influence their children to develop apprehensions of novel situations Ollendick and Hirshfeld-Becker, 2002). It is estimated that 44-58% of adults with SAD indicated an early childhood experience of peer rejection (Stemberger, Turner, Beidel, and Calhoun, 1995).

## Psychometric Issues

Recently empirical support of the validity of the *Fear of Positive Evaluation Scale* which solidifies the concept of evaluation as conflictual for the social anxiety disorder individuals was identified (Weeks, Heimberg, Rodebaugh, Goldin, and Gross, 2012). Previous studies have supported the empirical basis of the negative evaluation scale, thus, it is the evaluation that is feared, not the valence of the evaluation.

The social anxiety disorder, when used as a diagnosis of childhood symptoms, has been distinguished by subtype using multi-trait, multi-method models of construct validity measurement (Langer et al., 2010). Further, researchers identified in an investigation of maternal/paternal agreement of preschoolers' anxiety that statistically significant indices of congruency for both the measures was found (Edwards, Rapee, and Kennedy, 2010).

Reported findings of congruence from a structural equation modeling to classification of behavioral inhibition and vulnerability factors leading to the development of social anxiety has been identified (Muris, vanBrakel, Arntz, and Schouten, 2011).

Additional psychometric support in terms of scale internal consistency and validity of the *Social Phobia and Anxiety Inventory of Children – Parent Report* to classification of social anxiety was supported (Muris et al., 2011). The *Screen for Child Anxiety Related to Emotional Disorders (SCARED)* was found to be both reliable and valid and generalizable to classification factors of social anxiety in a multicultural sample (Essau, Anatassiou-Hadjicharalambous, and Muñoz, 2013).

A final evidence point of the psychometric strength of current measures and their relationship to the classification system is found in investigation (Ogliari, Scaini, Kofler, Lampis, Zanoni, Pesenti-Gritti, Spatala, Battaglia, and Beidel, 2012). The *Social Phobia and Anxiety Inventory for Children (SPAI-C)* was found to be a reliable and valid instrument to identify child patients with social phobia.

## Social Anxiety Measures

In Table 1, the commonly used measures to diagnose social anxiety are listed. In Table 2, a shorter list of instruments is listed that measure social anxiety and are commonly used in treatment interventions with social anxiety disorder. With the projected May, 2013 release date of the *Diagnostic and Statistical Manual V* (DSM-V- APA, 1994), updates to these studies are anticipated.

# Early Detection of Social Anxiety

Longitudinal studies of social anxiety onset have indicated a prediction of first use of alcohol, tobacco, and marijuana (Marmorstein, Loeber, and Stouthamer-Loeber, 2010). This evidence that early onset of symptoms places the individual at risk for seeking means to alter their state (i.e., "self-medicate"). Using the social functioning scale from the World Health Organization Disability Assessment Scale, researchers found a correspondence to participants' responses on the Brief Social Phobia Scale (Chudleigh, Naismith, Blaszczynski, Hermens, Hodge, and Hickie, 2011). The results indicated that in those at risk for severe disorders such as psychosis, elevation in social phobia and depression symptoms were also measured. Thus, with severe pathology onset in late adolescence/young adulthood, the interruption (or perturbance), developmentally, of social phobia functioning was identified. The *Liebowitz Social Anxiety Scale* was used as an outcome measure to distinguish improvement from treatment from CBT and internet-based CBT. The correct, statistically significant identified clusters of patients improvement in both groups was of a significant magnitude and did not distinguish the groups (Hedman, Anderson, Ljotsson, Anderson, Rück, Mörtberg, and Lindefores, 2011).

Highly socially anxious college students were identified by a cut off score on the Social Phobia Scale before undergoing a substance abuse (alcohol) intervention. Those participants in this grouping that did not seek intervention for their social anxiety also had poor substance abuse intervention results (Terlecki, Buckner, Larimer, and Copeland, 2011). Matched utility of measures of social anxiety to focus and respondent. With the new DSMV classification system, their schema may change somewhat but still appears to be clinically valuable (Velting, Setzer, and Albano, 2004). This work is captured in Table 3 (Velting et al., 2004). Newer research in the area of phenotype pattern with the collection of environmental, neuropsychological, nutritional and biological factors as they related to social anxiety disorder symptoms (Salum, 2011). The *Screen for Children and Adolescent Emotional Related Disorders (SCARED)* amongst other measures was used to identify social anxiety symptomology patterns. This data building on the foundation has been established in a cross-sectional analysis of social fears in school aged children that lead to socially anxious adolescents (Garcia-Lopez, Hidalgo, Beidel, and Turner, 2008; Garcia-Lopez, Ingles, and Garcia-Fernandez, 2008). In this study, the Social Phobia Inventory, with its strong psychometric properties, identified symptomatic levels equivalent to the social anxiety diagnosis (Johnson, Inderbitzen-Nolan, and Anderson, 2006). The generalizability of the *Social Interaction Anxiety Scale* was tested and found support in both clinical and analogue samples (Rodebaugh, Woods, Heimberg, Liebowitz, and Schneier, 2006).

**Table 1. Rating Scales Available for Use in Social Anxiety Disorder (SAD)**

| |
|---|
| SAD Symptoms Checklist for Adults: |
| Liebowitz Social Anxiety Scale (Liebowitz, 1987) |
| Liebowitz Social Anxiety Scale – Self-Report (Fresco et al., 2001) |
| Social Phobia Inventory (Connor et al., 2000) |
| Mini Social Phobia Inventory (Connor et al., 2001) |
| SAD Symptoms Checklist for Children or Adolescents: |
| Liebowitz Social Anxiety Scale for Children and Adolescents (Masia et al., 1999) |
| Social Anxiety Scale for Children – Revised (LaGrece et al., 1993) |
| Social Anxiety Scale for Adolescents (Sturner et al., 2002) |
| Social Phobia and Anxiety Inventory for Children (Beidel et al., 1995) |
| Functional Impairment or Disability Scale: |
| Liebowitz Self-Rated Disability Scale (Schneir et al., 1994) |
| Reilly Work Productivity and Impairment (Reilly et al., 1993) |
| Social and Occupational Functioning Assessment Scale (APA, 1994) |
| Sheehan Disability Scale (Leary, 1983) |
| Quality of Life or Psychological Well-Being Scales: |
| Schwartz Outcome Scale – 10 (Blais et al., 1999) |
| Quality of Life Inventory (First et al., 2000) |
| Short Form 36-Item (Ware et al., 1992) |

**Table 2. Scales used in Cognitive Behavior Therapy Approaches to Manage Social Anxiety**

| |
|---|
| Social Phobia Inventory (Connor et al., 2000) |
| Mini-SPIN |
| Anxiety Disorders Interview Schedule for DSM-IV: Lifetime Version (DiNardo et al., 1994) |
| Structured Clinical Interview for DSM-IV-TR Axis I Disorders – Patient Edition (First et al., 2000) |
| Social Interaction Anxiety Scale (SIAS) |
| Social Phobia Scale (SPS) (Hart et al., 1999) |
| Brief Fear of Negative Evaluation Scale (BFNE) (Leary, 1983) |
| Subtle Avoidance Frequency Examination (SAFE) |
| Behavior Test (Standing in line at grocery store, assertive situation such as returning an unwanted item) |
| Social Anxiety Session Change Index (SASC II) (Hayes et al., 2008) |

Results from item response analyses of the Social Phobia Scale indicate a distinction between socially anxious and controls response styles (Peters, Sunderland, Andrews, Rapee, and Mattick, 2012). Specific scales, such as the *Unhelpful Thoughts and Beliefs about Stuttering (UTBAS) Scale* have been found to be valid in criterion-related studies with standards such as the *Social Phobia Scale.*

The *Clinical Global Impressions (CGI) Scale* has been found to be useful in the measurement of social anxiety disorder over trial (i.e., treatment sessions), as compared to the *Liebowitz Social Anxiety Scale* and other measures (Hedges, Brown, and Shwalb, 2008).

## Table 3. Measures of Child Anxiety Disorders and Related Constructs

| Measure | Focus | Respondent(s) |
|---|---|---|
| Interview | | |
| Anxiety Disorders Interview Schedule for DSM-IV | Anxiety, mood and externalizing disorders, with screens for learning and developmental disorders, substance abuse, eating disorders, psychotic symptoms, and somatoform disorders | Child and parent |
| Broad self-report measures of anxiety | | |
| Revised Children's Manifest Anxiety Scale | General levels of anxiety with three clinical subscales (Worry Concentration, Physiological Arousal) and I validity scale (Lie scale) | Child |
| State-Trait Anxiety Inventory for Children | State and trait levels of general anxiety | Child |
| Multidimensional Anxiety Scale for Children | Physical anxiety (tense/restless and somatic/autonomic), harm avoidance (perfectionism and anxious coping behaviors), social anxiety (humiliation fears and performance anxiety), and separation anxiety | Child |
| Screen for Child Anxiety Related Emotional Disorders | Panic disorder, generalized anxiety disorder, separation anxiety disorder, social phobia, and school phobia | Child and parent |
| Self-report measures of specific anxiety constructs | | |
| Fear Survey Schedule for Children-Revised | Specific fear sensitivities | Child and parent |
| Social Phobia and Anxiety Inventory for Children | Social anxiety and avoidance | Child |
| Social Anxiety Scale for Children-Revised | Social anxiety and avoidance | Child and parent |
| Penn State Worry Questionnaire for Children | Severity of worry | Child |
| Self-report measures of related constructs | | |
| School Refusal Assessment Scale | Motivating and maintaining factors of school refusal behavior | Child and parent |
| Child Anxiety Sensitivity Index | Aversion to somatic forms of anxiety | Child |
| Fear and Avoidance Hierarchy | Top 10 feared and avoided situations, ideographic to the child | Child and parent |

Validity has been determined for the *Anxiety Disorder Diagnostic Questionnaire (ADDQ)* (Norton and Robinson, 2010). Approximately 45% of the variance due to social anxiety disorder symptoms was determined using this scale. An evaluation of the ability of online and paper-pencil administration of the *Social Interactions Anxiety Scale* and *Social Phobia Scale* found adequate reliability and validity at both modalities (Hirai, Vernon, Clum, and Skidmore, 2011).

The integration of psychophysiological measures in assessment of social Anxiety is recommended. Because the fear and uneasiness is hypothesized to occur while reacting to the moral, evaluative, social situation it is assumed that initially sympathetic autonomic nervous system activity ensues.

Variability is heart rate, indicating increased vagal tone and parasympathetic activity in more severe conditions once identified, may improve diagnosis of Social Anxiety Disorder (Thomas, Aldao, and De Los Reyes, 2012).

Cell phones (calls received only) were utilized to sample real time ratings of emotion in socially anxious adolescents versus controls (Tan, Forbes, Dahl, Ryan, Siegle, Ladouceur, and Silk, 2012).

The findings of this innovative study revealed no significant difference between the groups in momentarily reporting of emotions. The *Emotion Regulation Interview* was utilized to summarize the times the person engaged in situation selection, situation modification, attention deployment, and response modulation. Training in this interview method served to establish reliability amongst the interviewers (r = .62 - .77) (Tan et al., 2012). The interview method had convergent validity (r = .55) with the *Liebowitz Social Anxiety Scale*.

A *cognitive assessment* technique was utilized to quantify the number and valence (positive or negative) of statements representing the socially anxious thought content. Public speaking anxiety responded better to treatment while social interactions measures were more valid. The *Social Interaction Self-Statement Test* and the *thought listing* (production methods were compared in terms of *state of mind ratio* (number of positive thoughts divided by the sum of positive plus negative self-statements). Little convergent validity between the two measures was found (Sturner, Bruch, Haase, and Amica, 2002).

Table 4 provides details regarding the measures used to assess a variety of anxiety symptoms in both youth and adults. Research journal articles that evaluated the validity and reliability of anxiety measures were reviewed and compiled into the current table. Assessment instruments included self-report measures, parent-report measures, clinician administered interviews, and physiological indicators of anxiety.

Many of these measures were normed on individuals across the United States, along with various countries in Europe and South America. Table 4 gives an exhaustive list of different assessments that can be used to either assess specific anxiety disorders, or anxiety symptoms that may overlap with other psychiatric disorders or an individual's overall functioning.

# Summary

Results from the review of the Psychological Literature identified several psychometrically strong, useful measures. Examples of the application of such measures to instructive studies provided support for the utility of common measures. A specific analysis of the studies in the areas of social anxiety measurement revealed the strength of the studies in classification and identification of outcome.

The proposed changes to the diagnosis of Social Anxiety with the DSM-V will lead to restandardization of these sound measures.

**Table 4. Psychometric Properties of Commonly Used Assessments of Social Anxiety**

| Author | Sample Characteristics | Assessment |
|---|---|---|
| Werner, Goldin, Ball, Heimberg, and Gross (2011) | N= 48 Social Anxiety Disorder; 33 Control; *M age*= 33 years, 50.6% male, 55.5% Caucasian, 30.8% Asian | Emotion Regulation Interview (ERI); reliability (*r* =.62 to .77); validity (*r* =.21 to.55) Likert scale<br><br>Liebowitz Social Anxiety Scale (LSAS-SR; avoidance subscale), 24 items 4-point Likert scale<br><br>Response Styles Questionnaire (RSQ), 22 items 4-point Likert scale<br><br>Emotion Regulation Questionnaire (ERQ; cognitive reappraisal scale), 8 items 7-point Likert scale<br><br>Emotion Regulation Questionnaire—Self Efficacy (ERQSE), 8 items 7 point Likert scale |
| Norton and Robinson (2010) | N= 146 undergraduate students, *M* Age 22.41 years, 84.9% female, 28.1% Caucasian 21.2% Asian, 19.9% African American;<br><br>N= 94 outpatients, *M* Age= 31.72, 59.8% female, 58.7% Caucasian, 16.3% Hispanic 8.7 % African American | Anxiety Disorder Diagnostic Questionnaire (ADDQ), 9-point Likert scale; internal consistency (α =.833 and .851)<br><br>Panic Disorder Severity Scale (PDSS), 7 items 5-point scale<br><br>Beck Anxiety Inventory (BAI), 21 items 1996).<br><br>Social Phobia Diagnostic Questionnaire (SPDQ), 25-items<br><br>Brief Fear of Negative Evaluation scale (BFNE), 12 items<br><br>Yale-Brown Obsessive Compulsive Scale (Y-BOCS), 10 items<br><br>Padua Inventory—Washington State University Revision (PI-WSUR), 39 items<br><br>Generalized Anxiety Disorder Questionnaire for DSM-IV (GDAQ-IV), 9 items<br><br>Penn State Worry Questionnaire (PSWQ), 16 items<br><br>Post-Traumatic Stress Scale (PSS) Self-Report, 17 items<br><br>Posttraumatic Checklist (PCL), 17 items<br><br>Anxiety Disorders Interview Schedule for DSM-IV (ADIS-IV), 9-point Likert scale |
| Garcia-Lopez, Hidalgo, Beidel, Olivares, and Turner (2008) | N= 1931 high school students in Spain, *M* age = 15.57 years, 54% female, | Social Phobia and Anxiety Inventory-Brief (SPAI-B), 16 items 5-point Likert scale, internal consistency (α =.92), test-retest reliability (*r* =.60), concurrent validity (*r* >.60)<br><br>Social Phobia and Anxiety Inventory (SPAI; Social Phobia subscale), 32 items 7-point Likert scale;<br><br>Social Anxiety Scale for Adolescents (SAS-A), 22 items 5-point scale |

**Table 4. (Continued)**

| Author | Sample Characteristics | Assessment |
|---|---|---|
| Schneier et al. (1994) | N=17 Generalized Social Anxiety Disorder, *M* age = 31.1, 64.7% male, 58.9% Caucasian, 23.5% African American, 17.6% Asian; N= 13 Healthy Control, *M* age = 30.9, 53.8% male, 61.5% Caucasian, 15.4% African American, 23.1% Asian | Anxiety Disorder Diagnostic Questionnaire (ADDQ), internal consistency ($\alpha$ = .833 to .851) |
| Johnson, Inderbitzen-Nolan, and Anderson (2006) | N= 174 students; *M* age = 14.7 years, 56.9% female, 92% Caucasian, 4% Asian | ADIS-IV: C semi structured diagnostic interview ($\kappa$ = .82 to.95); SPIN, 17 items 5-point Likert scale, test-retest reliability ($r$ =.78 to .89), internal consistency ($\alpha$ = .82 to .94); SPAI-C, 26 items 3-point scale, internal consistency ($\alpha$ = .95); test-retest reliability ($r$ =.86); SAS-A, 18 items 5-point Likert scale, test-retest reliability ($r$ = .54-.78), internal consistency ($\alpha$ =.76 to .91) |
| Ogliari, Scaini, Kofler, Lampis, Zanoni, Present-Griti, et al. (2012) | N= 228 elementary school children in Milan, *M* age = 9.4 years, 53.9% female | Positron emission topography |
| Essau, Anastassiou-Hadjicharalambous, and Munoz (2013) | N= 1072 school children in Cyprus, *M* age = 14.7 years, 57.7% female, 98% Caucasian | Screen for Child Anxiety Related Emotional Disorders (SCARED) 41 items 3-point Likert scale, internal consistency( $\alpha$ =.92), test-retest reliability ($r$ = .84); Strengths and Difficulties Questionnaire (SDQ), 25 items 3-point Likert Scale, internal consistency ($\alpha$ = .73); Columbia Impairment Scale (CIS) 13 items, 5-point Likert scale, internal consistency ($\alpha$ =.81); Youth Self-Report (YSR), list of 118 specific problems 3-point scale; internal consistency ($\alpha$ = .94) |

| Author | Sample Characteristics | Assessment |
| --- | --- | --- |
| Iverach, Menzies, Jones, O'Brian, Packman, and Onslow (2011) | N= 140 adults seeking treatment for stuttering in Australia, *M* age = 32.0 years, 77.9% male | Unhelpful Thoughts and Beliefs About Stuttering (UTBAS I, II, III), 66 items each 5-point scale; internal consistency ($r > .80$); convergent validity ($r = .49-.64$)<br>The Endler Multidimensional Anxiety Scales—Trait (EMAS-T), 60 items 5-point Likert scale<br>The Fear of Negative Evaluation Scale (FNE), 30 True-False items<br>The State–Trait Anxiety Inventory—Trait (STAI-T), 20 items 4-point Likert scale |
| Edwards, Rapee, Kennedy, and Spence (2010) | N= 764 children in Australia, *M* age = 3.9 years, 50.3% female, 85.5% Caucasian, 12.9% Other;<br>N= 764 mothers *M* age = 35.81 years;<br>N= 418 fathers *M* age = 38.09 years | Preschool Anxiety Scale–Revised (PAS-R), 30 items 5-point Likert scale, internal consistency ($\alpha > .70$), construct validity ($r = .62$ and .70);<br>Short Temperament Scale for Children (STSC; Approach subscale), internal consistency ($\alpha = .90$);<br>SDQ (parent version; emotional symptoms (ES), hyperactivity-inattention (HI), and conduct problems (CP) subscales), internal consistency ($\alpha = .47$ to .77);<br>Anxiety disorders interview schedule for DSM–IV, parent version (ADIS–P), semi-structured interview, 9-point scale; inter-rater reliability (kappas =.56 to .89) |
| Kashdan and Steger (2006) | N = 97 university students, *M* age = 19.75 years, 65.9% female | Social Phobia and Anxiety Inventory for Children (SPAIC); 26 items 3-point Likert Scale, convergent validity ($R^2 = .50$), internal consistency($\alpha = .89$);<br>Screen for Child Anxiety Related Emotional Disorders (SCARED); 41 items, internal consistency ($\alpha = .87$) |
| Rodebaugh, Woods, Heimberg, Liebowitz, and Schneier (2006) | N = 445 clients at anxiety disorder clinics, *M* age =33.84 years, 46% female, 73% Caucasian, 12 % African American, 6% Hispanic;<br>N = 1689 students, *M* age = 19.28 years, 70% female, 44% Caucasian, 27% African American, 7% Asian | Screen for Child Anxiety Related Emotional Disorders (SCARED); internal consistency ($\alpha = .92$), test-retest reliability ($r = .84$) |

**Table 4. (Continued)**

| Author | Sample Characteristics | Assessment |
|---|---|---|
| Terlecki, Buckner, Larimer, and Copeland (2011) | N = 52 heavy drinking undergraduate students, M age = 20.38 years, 67.9% male, 90.6% Caucasian | The Social Phobia Scale (SPS) and the Social Interaction Anxiety Scale (SIAS), 20 items 5-point Likert scale, internal consistency ($\alpha$ = .91); Spielberger Trait Anxiety Inventory (STAI), internal consistency ($\alpha$ = .87). |
| Hiya, Fernandez, Nakamura, Chorpita, and Daleiden (2006) | N = 176 caregivers, M age = 38.65 years, 80% mothers, 29% Asian, 27% multiethnic, 26% biracial, 13% Caucasian; N = 158 children, M age = 11.53 years, 55% female, 44% multiracial, 28% biracial, 17% Asian, 6% Caucasian | Preschool Anxiety Scale, 30 items 5-point Likert scale, internal consistency ($\alpha$ = .72 to.92), construct validity (all zs > 5) |
| Weeks, Heimberg, Rodebaugh, Goldin, and Gross (2012) | N = 226 adult patients at anxiety clinics, M age = 32.12 years, 47.8% female, 57.1% Caucasian; N = 42 non-anxious control, M age = 32.93 years, 52.4% female, 52.76% Caucasian | Social Interaction Anxiety Scale (SIAS), 19 items 6-point Likert scale, internal consistency ($\alpha$ = .89); Fear of Negative Evaluation Scale, 5 items 5-point Likert scale, construct validity (r = .56) |
| Peters, Sunderland, Andrews, Rapee, and Mattick (2012) | N = 456 patients with social phobia in Australia participating in a RCT examining online clinician assisted CBT, M age= 39.09 years, 41.8% male N = 446 patients with social phobia in Australia participation in treatment trials at the Emotional Health Clinic, M age = 34.15 years, 51.6% male; N = 137 community volunteers M age = 35.76 years, 42.3and male; N = 164 undergraduate students, M age = 20.54, 29.8 % male | SIAS-6/SPS-6, 6 items each, 5-point Likert scale; construct validity (r>.88); SIAS/SPS, 20 items each, 5-point Likert scale, internal consistency ($\alpha$ > .90), test–retest reliability (r > .91); Brief Fear of Negative Evaluation (bFNE), 12-items, 5-point scale; Depression Anxiety Stress Scales—21-Item Version (DASS- 21), 21 statements, 4-point scale |

| Author | Sample Characteristics | Assessment |
|---|---|---|
| Hirai, Venon, Clum, and Skidore (2011) | N = 514 university students, $M$ age = 20.2 years, 64.2 % female, 71.6% Caucasian, 5.6% Asian, 5.3% Hispanic, 3.7% African America | The Social Phobia Scale (SPS), 20 items 5-point Likert scale, internal consistency ($\alpha$ = .87-.94), test-retest reliability ($\alpha$ = .66 to.93), convergent validity ($\alpha$ = .54 to .69); The Social Interaction Anxiety Scale (SIAS), 19 items 5-point Likert scale, internal consistency ($\alpha$ = .92 and .93) |
| Blais et al. (1999) | N = 3000 psychiatric outpatients, $M$ age = 38.5 years, 60.6% female, 87.4% Caucasian, 4.5 % African American, 2.6% Hispanic; N=1800 candidates for bariatric surgery, $M$ age = 42.3 years, 82.7% female, 80.8% Caucasian, 7.7% African American, 6.1% Hispanic | Social Phobia and Anxiety Inventory for Children (SPAI-C), 26-items 3-point Likert scale, test-retest reliability ($r$ = .63 to .86), internal consistency ($\alpha$ =.95), convergent validity ($r$ = .63); Social Phobia and Anxiety Inventory for Children- Parent Report (SPAI-C-P), 26 items 3-point Likert scale, internal consistency ($\alpha$ = .93); Child Behavior Checklist (CBCL), 113 items, internal consistency ($\alpha$ =.97), test-retest reliability ($r$ =.94) |
| Hedman, Andersson, Ljotsson, Andersson, Ruck, Mortberg, et al. (2011) | N = 126 participants who met criteria for Social Anxiety Disorder, $M$ age = 35.3 years, 35.7% female | Fear of Positive Evaluation Scale (FPES), 10 items 10-point Likert scale, internal consistency ($\alpha$ =.83to.85), test-retest reliability ($r$ = .80); Anxiety Disorders Interview Schedule for DSM-IV-Lifetime Version (ADIS-IV-L); Liebowitz Social Anxiety Scale, 24 items 4-point Likert scale, internal consistency ($\alpha$ =.96); Social Interaction Anxiety Scale (SIAS) 20 items 5-point Likert scale, internal consistency ($\alpha$ =.89); Social Phobia Scale (SPS), 20 items 5-point Likert Scale, internal consistency ($\alpha$ = .92); Brief Fear of Negative Evaluation Scale-Straightforward Items (BFNE-S) 12 items, internal consistency ($\alpha$ =.91) |
| Watanbe, Furkawa, Chen, Kinoshita, Nakano, Ogawa, et al. (2010) | N= 57 outpatients diagnosed with SAD in Japan, $M$ age = 32.5 years, 52.6% female | Social Phobia Scale (SPS), 20 items 4-point Likert scale; Social Interaction Anxiety Scale (SIAS), 20 items 4-point Likert scale |

**Table 4. (Continued)**

| Author | Sample Characteristics | Assessment |
|---|---|---|
| Chorney and Morris (2008) | N = 757 adolescents, Age range 15-18 years, 67.8% Hispanic | Dating Anxiety Scale for Adolescents (DAS-A), 21 items 5-point Likert scale, convergent validity ($r = .73$) |
| Heinrichs and Hofmann (2005) | N= 58 individuals with Social Phobia, $M$ age = 34.7 years, 64 % male | Social Phobia and Anxiety Inventory (SPAI); Self-Statements During Public Speaking Questionnaire (SPSS), 10 items 6-point Likert scale; Social Interaction Self-Statement Test, 30 items 5-point Likert scale; Thought listing task |
| Chudleigh, Naismith, Blaszcynski, Hermens, Hodge, and Hickie (2011) | N = 20 at-risk individuals for psychosis, $M$ age = 20.75 years, 55% male; N = 20 first episode psychosis individuals, $M$ age = 22.05 years, 65% male; N = 20 non-psychiatric controls, $M$ age = 22.0 years, 50% male | Depression Anxiety Stress Scale (DASS), 21 items; Brief Social Phobia Scale (BSPS), 18 items |
| Tan, Forbes, Dahl, Ryan, Siegle, Ladouceur, et al. (2012) | N = 65 anxious youth, $M$ age = 10.90 years; N = 65 healthy control, $M$ age =10.41 years | Schedule for Affective Disorders and Schizophrenia in School-Age Children- Present and Lifetime version (K-SADS-PL); Ecological momentary assessment (EMA) |
| Kashdan and Collins (2010) | N = 38 community residents, $M$ age = 26.9 years, 52.6% male; 81.6% Caucasian | Self-Consciousness Scale, 17 items 4-point Likert scale, internal consistency ($\alpha > .82$); Ecological momentary assessment (EMA) to monitor everyday emotions and experiences |
| Morrison, Amir, and Taylor (2011) | N = 21 socially anxious undergraduate students, $M$ age = 21.0 years, 85.7% female; N = 19 non-anxious control, $M$ age = 21.3 years, 78.9% female | Strait-Trait Anxiety Inventory (STAI), internal consistency ($\alpha$ =.91, 93); Liebowitz Social Anxiety Scale-Self Report (LSAS-SR), internal consistency ($\alpha$ =.92) |

| Author | Sample Characteristics | Assessment |
|---|---|---|
| Thomas, Daruwala, Goepel, and Reyes (2012) | N = 40 families with adolescents- 20 socially anxious youth and 20 community control, M age = 15.15 years, 65% female, 60% African American, 32.5% Caucasian, 12.5% American Indian | Subtle Avoidance Frequency Examination (SAFE), 32 items 5-point Likert scale, internal consistency ($\alpha$ =.89); Multidimensional Anxiety Scale for Children (MASC), 39 items 4-point Likert scale, internal consistency ($\alpha$ = .87) |
| Langer, Wood, Bergman, and Piacentini (2010) | N = 174 children undergoing diagnostic evaluation at a university clinic, M age = 11.61 year, 54% male, 77% Caucasian, 5% Asian, 4% Hispanic, 4% African American | ADIS for DSM-IV: C/P, semi-structured interview 9-point Likert scale, interrater reliability ($\kappa$ =.82 to.96), test-retest reliability ($\kappa$ =.80 to .92); Multidimensional Anxiety Scale for Children (MASC) 39 items 4-point Likert scale, internal consistency ($\alpha$ =.64 to .82) MASC-Parent Report (MASC-P), 39 items 4-point Likert Scale, internal consistency ($\alpha$ =.68 to.85) |
| Garcia-Lopez, Ingles, and Garcia-Fernandez (2008) | N = 2543 students in Spain, M age = 13.9 years, 51.7% male | Social Phobia and Anxiety Inventory (SPAI), 45 items |
| Marmorstein, White, Loeber, and Stouthamer-Loeber (2012) | N = 503 male children, M age = 6.2 years, 56.4% African American | Child Behavior Checklist (CBCL), Youth Self Report (YSR), Teacher Report Form (TRF)-, reliability ($\alpha$ =.60 and.61) |
| Salum, Isolan, Bosa, Tochetto, Teche, Schuh, et al. (2011) | N = 2457 students in Brazil, M age = 12.8 years | Screen for Children and Adolescent Emotional Related Disorders-Child version (SCARED-C), 41 items |
| Naragon-Gainey, Watson, and Markon (2009) | N = 350 university students, M age = 19.2 years, 76.6% female, 90% Caucasian, 5.4% Asian, 2.3% African American, 1.7% Hispanic; N =204 psychiatric outpatients, M age = 44.0 years, 68.5% female, 92% Caucasian, 2% Asian, 2% African American | Inventory of Depression and Anxiety Symptoms (IDAS), 5-point Likert scale, internal consistency ($\alpha$ =.80) Phobic Stimuli Response Scales (PSRS), 4-point Likert scale, internal consistency ($\alpha$ =.88) Social Interaction Anxiety Scale (SIAS), 5-point Likert scale |

**Table 4. (Continued)**

| Author | Sample Characteristics | Assessment |
|---|---|---|
| Sturner, Bruch, Haase, and Amico (2002) | N = 133 undergraduate students, M age = 19.6 years, 53.4% female | The Social Interaction Self-Statement Test, 30 items, internal consistency ($\alpha$ =.84 and .92)<br>Interaction Anxiousness Scale (IAS), 15 items 5-point Likert scale, internal consistency ($\alpha$ =.89), test-retest reliability ($\alpha$ =.80), validity ($\alpha$ =.88)<br>Affect Balance Scale (ABS), 40 items 5-point Likert scale, internal consistency ($\alpha$ =.95 and .94)<br>Timed Behavior Checklist for Performance Anxiety (TBCL), 13 behavioral coding categories, inter-rater reliability ($\alpha$ =.80-.94) |
| Lesniak-Karpiak, Mazzocco, and Ross (2003) | N = 29 females with Turner syndrome, M age = 9.57 years and 16.51 years;<br>N = 21 females with Fragile X, M age = 10.14 years and 17.21 years;<br>N = 34 female control group, M age = 9.91 years and 15.29 years | Child Behavior Checklist (CBCL)<br>Revised Children's Manifest Anxiety Scale (RCMAS)<br>Social Phobia and Anxiety Inventory (SPAI)<br>Social Phobia and Anxiety Inventory for Children (SPAI-C) |
| Muris, Brakel, Arntz, and Schouten (2011) | N = 124 children identified as behaviorally inhibited in The Netherlands, M age = 6.6 years, 53.2% female, 97% Caucasian;<br>N = 137 control children in The Netherlands, M age = 6.6 years, 58.3% female, 97% Caucasian | Behavioral Inhibition Instrument (BII), 8 items 4-point Likert scale, internal consistency ($\alpha$ >.80), test-retest reliability ($r$ =.77)<br>Attachment Style Questionnaire (ASQ)<br>Modified EMBU (Egna Minnen Betra¨ffende Uppfostran, which is Swedish for My memories of upbringing), 40 items 4-point Likert scale<br>Screen for Child Anxiety Related Emotional Disorders (SCARED), 4 point scale<br>Life Experiences Survey (LES), 57 items 3-point scale<br>Dominic- R, assess 7 DSM-II-R disorders in youth<br>Spielberger State –Trait Anxiety Inventory (STAI; Dutch translation), 20 items 4-point scale |

# References

American Psychiatric Association. (1994). *Diagnostic and statistical manual of mental disorders* (4th Ed., text revision). Washington, DC: Author.

Ballenger, J. C., Davidson, J. R., Lecrubier, Y., Nutt, D. J., Bobes, J., Beidel, D. C., Ono, Y., and Westenberg, H. C. (1998). Consensus statement on social anxiety disorder from the international consensus group on depression and anxiety. *Journal of Clinical Psychiatry,* 59, 54-60.

Beidel, D. C., Turner, S. M. and Morris, T. L. (1995). A new instrument to assess childhood social anxiety and phobia: The Social Phobia and Anxiety Inventory for Children. *Psychological Assessment,* 1, 73-79.

Blais, M. A., Lenderking, W. R., Baer, L., deLorell, A., Peets, K., Leahy, L., and Burns, C. (999). Development and initial validation of a brief mental health outcome measure. *Journal of Personality Assessment,* 73, 359-373.

Chorney, D. B. and Morris, T. L. (2008). The changing face of dating anxiety: Issues in assessment with special populations. *Clinical Psychology, Science and Practice,* 15, 228-238.

Chudleigh, C., Naismith, S. L., Blaszczynski, A., Hermens, D. F., Hodge, M. A., and Hickie, I. B. (2011). How does social functioning in the early stages of psychosis relate to depression and social anxiety? *Early Intervention in Psychiatry,* 5, 224-232.

Connor, K. M., Davidson, J. R., Churchill, L. E., Sherwood, A., Foa, E., and Weisler, R. H. (2000). Psychometric properties of the Social Phobia Inventory (SPIN) New self-rating scale. *British Journal of Psychiatry,* 1716, 379-386.

Connor, K. M., Kobak, K. A., Churchill, L. E., Katzelnick, D., and Davidson, J. R. (2001). Mini-SPIN: A brief screening assessment of generalized social anxiety disorder. *Depression and Anxiety,* 14, 137-140.

DiNardo, P. A., Brown, T. A. and Barlow, D. H. (1994). *Anxiety disorders interview schedule for DSM-IV – Lifetime Version (ADIS-IV-L).* San Antonio, TX: Psychological Corporation.

Edwards, S. L., Rapee, R. M. and Kennedy, S. J. (2010). The assessment of anxiety symptoms in pre-school-aged children: The Revised Preschool Anxiety Scale. *Journal of Clinical Child and Adolescent Psychology,* 39(3), 400-409.

Essau, C. A., Anatassiou-Hadjicharalambous, X. and Muñoz, L. (2013). Psychometric properties of the Screen for Child Anxiety Related Emotional Disorders (SCARED) in Cypriot. *European Journal of Psychological Assessment,* 29, 19-27.

Feldman, L. B. and Rivas-Vasquez, A. R. (2003). Assessment and treatment of social anxiety disorder. *Professional Psychology: Research and Practice,* 34, 396-405.

First, M. B., Spitzer, R. L., Gibbon, M., and Williams, J. (2000). *Structural clinical interview for DSM-IV-TR axis I disorders – patient edition (SCID-IIP).* New York, NY: Biometrics Research Department.

Fresco, D. M., Coles, M. E., Heimberg, R. G., Liebowitz, M. R., Hami, S., Stein, M. B., and Goetz, D. (2001). The Liebowitz Social Anxiety Scale: A comparison of the psychometric properties of self-report and clinician-administered formats. *Psychological Medicine,* 31, 1024-1035.

Garcia-Lopez, L. J., Hidalgo, M. D., Beidel, D. C., and Turner, S. (2008). Brief form of the Social Phobia and Anxiety Inventory (SIAS-B) for adolescents. *European Journal of Psychological Assessment, 24*, 150-156.

Garcia-Lopez, L. J., Ingles, C. J. and Garcia-Fernandez, J. M. (2008). Exploring the relevance of gender and age differences in the assessment of social fears in adolescence. *Social Behavior and Personality, 36*, 385-390.

Hart, T. A., Jack, M., Turk, C. L., and Heimberg, R. G. (1999). Issues for the measurement of social anxiety disorder (social phobia). In: H. G. M. Westenberg and J. A. Den Boer (Eds.) *Focus on psychiatry: Social anxiety disorder.* (pp.133-135). Amsterdam: Syn-Thesis Publishers.

Hayes, S. A., Miller, N. A., Hope, D., Heimberg, R. G., and Juster, H. R. (2008). Assessing client progress session-by-session in the treatment of social anxiety disorder: The Social Anxiety Session Change Index. *Cognitive and Behavioral Practice, 15*, 203-211.

Hedges, D. W., Brown, B. L. and Shwalb, D. A. (2008). A direct comparison of effect sizes from the clinical global impression-improvement scale to effect sizes from other rating scales in controlled trials of adult social anxiety disorder. *Human Psychopharmacology and Clinical Experience, 24*, 35-40.

Hedman, E., Anderson, G., Ljotsson, B., Anderson, E., Rück, C., Mörtberg, E., and Lindefores, N. (2011). Internet-based cognitive behavior therapy vs. cognitive behavioral group therapy for social anxiety disorder: A randomized controlled non-inferiority trial. *PLOS ONE, 6*, 1-10.

Heinrichs, N. and Hofmann, S. G. (2005). Cognitive assessment of social anxiety: A comparison of self-report and thought listing methods. *Cognitive Behavior Therapy, 34*, 3-15.

Hirai, M., Vernon, L. L., Clum, G. A., and Skidmore, S. T. (2011). Psychometric properties and administration measurement invariance of social phobia symptom measures: Paper-pencil vs. internet administration. *Journal of Psychopathological Behavioral Assessment, 33*, 470-479.

Hiya, C., Fernandez, S. N., Nakamura, B. J., Chorpita, B. F., and Daleiden, E. L. (2006). Parental assessment of childhood social phobia: Psychometric properties of the Social Phobia and Anxiety Inventory for Children – Parent Report. *Journal of Clinical Child and Adolescent Psychology, 35*, 590-597.

Iverach, L., Menzies, R., Jones, M., O'Brian, S., Packman, A., and Onslow, M. (2011). Further development and validation of the Unhelpful Thoughts and Beliefs about Stuttering (UTBAS) scales: Relationship to anxiety and social phobia among adults who stutter. *International Journal of Language Communication Disorder, 46*, 286-299.

Johnson, H. S., Inderbitzen-Nolan, H. M. and Anderson, E. R. (2006). The Social Phobia Inventory: Validity and reliability in an adolescent community sample. *Psychological Assessment, 18*, 269-277.

Kashdan, T. B. and Collins, R. L. (2010). Social anxiety and the experience of positive emotion and anger in everyday life: An ecological momentary assessment approach. *Anxiety, Stress and Coping, 23*, 259-272.

Kashdan, T. B. and Steger, M. F. (2006). Expanding the topography of social anxiety: An experience-sampling assessment of positive emotions, positive events, and emotional suppression. *Psychological Science, 17*, 120-128.

La Greca, A. M. and Stone, W. L. (1993). Social Anxiety Scale for Children-Revised: Factor structure and concurrent validity. *Journal of Clinical Child Psychology*, 22, 17-27.

Langer, D. A., Bergman, R. L., Piacentini, J. D. (2010). A multitrait-multimethod analysis of the construct validity of child anxiety disorders in a clinical sample. *Child Psychiatry and Human Development*, 41, *549-561.*

Leary, M. R. (1983). A brief version of the Fear of Negative Evaluation Scale. *Personality and Social Psychology Bulletin*, 9, 371-375.

Lesniak-Karpiak, K., Massocco, M. M., and Ross, J. L. (2003). Behavioral assessment of social anxiety in females with Turner or Fragile X Syndrome. *Journal of Autism and Developmental Disorders*, 33, 55-67.

Liebowitz, M. R. (1987). Social phobia. *Modern Problems of Pharmacopsychiatry*, 22, 141-173.

Marmorstein, N. R., Loeber, R. and Stouthamer-Loeber, M. (2010). Anxiety as a predictor of age at first use of substance and progression to substance use problems among boys. *Journal of Abnormal Child Psychology*, 38, 211-224.

Masia, C. L., Hofmann, S. G., Klein, R. G., and Liebowitz, M. R. (1999). *The Liebowitz Social Anxiety Scale for Children and Adolescents (LSAS-CA).* (Available form Carrie L. Masia, PhD., NYU Child Study Center, 550 First Avenue, New York, NY 10016).

Morrison, A. S., Amir, N. and Taylor, C. T. (2011). A behavioral index of imagery ability in social anxiety. *Cognitive Therapy and Research*, 35, 326-332.

Muris, P., vanBrakel, A. M., Arntz, A., and Schouten, E. (2011). Behavioral inhibition as a risk factor for the development of childhood anxiety disorders: A longitudinal study. *Journal of Child and Family Studies*, 20, 157-170.

Naragon-Gainey, K., Watson, D. and Markon, K. (2009). Differential relations of depression and social anxiety symptoms to the facets of extraversion/positive emotionality. *Journal of Abnormal Psychology*, 118, 299-310.

Norton, P. J. and Robinson, C. M. (2010). Development and evaluation of the Anxiety Disorder Diagnostic Questionnaire. *Cognitive Behavior Therapy*, 39, 137-149.

Ogliari, A., Scaini, S., Kofler, M. J., Lampis, V., Zanoni, A., Pesenti-Gritti, P., Spatala, C. A. M., Battaglia, M., and Beidel, D. C. (2012). Psychometric properties of the Social Phobia and Anxiety Inventory for Children (SPAI-C): A sample of Italian school-aged children from the general population. *European Journal of Psychological Assessment*, 28, 51-59.

Ollendick, T. H. and Hirshfeld-Becker, D. R. (2002). The developmental psychopathology of social anxiety disorder. *Society of Biological Psychiatry*, 51, 44-58.

Peters, L., Sunderland, M., Andrews, G., Rapee, R. M., and Mattick, R. P. (2012). Development of a short form Social Interaction Scale (SIAS) and Social Phobia Scale (SPS) using nonparametric items response theory: The SIAS-6 and the SPS-6. *Psychological Assessment*, 24, 66-76.

Reilly, M. C., Zbrozek, A. S. and Dukes, E. M. (1993). The validity and reproducibility of a work productivity and activity impairment instrument. *Pharmacoeconomics*, 4, 353-365.

Rodebaugh, T. L., Woods, C. M., Heimberg, R. G., Liebowitz, M. R., and Schneier, T. R. (2006). The factor structure and screening utility of the Social Interaction Anxiety Scale. *Psychological Assessment*, 18, 231-237.

Salum, C. A., et al. (2011). The multidimensional evaluation and treatment of anxiety in children and adolescents: Rationale, design, methods and preliminary findings. The Protaia Project Special Report, Anxiety Disorders Program for Child and Adolescent

Psychiatry (PROTAIA), Hospital de Clinicas de Porto Alegre (HCPA), Universidad
    Federal de Rio Grande de Sul (UTRGS), Porto Alegre, R, Brazil.
Schneier, F. R., Heckelman, L. R., Garfinkel, R., Campeas, R., Fallon, B. A., Gitow, A., et al.
    (1994). Functional impairment in social phobia, *Journal of Clinical Psychiatry*, 55, 322-
    331.
Stein, M. B., Jang, K. L. and Lively, W. J. (2002). Heritability of social anxiety-related
    concerns and personality characteristics: A twin study. *Journal of Nervous and Mental
    Diseases*, 190, 219-224.
Stemberger, R., Turner, S., Beidel, D., and Calhoun, K. (1995). Social phobia: An analysis of
    possible developmental factors. *Journal of Abnormal Psychology*, 104, 526-531.
Sturner, P. J., Bruch, M. A., Haase, R. F., and Amica, K. R. (2002). Convergent validity in
    cognitive assessment of social anxiety: Endorsement versus production methods in
    deriving states of mind ratio. *Cognitive Therapy and Research*, 26, 487-503.
Tan, P. Z., Forbes, E. E., Dahl, R. E., Ryan, N. D., Siegle, G. J., Ladouceur, C. D., and Silk, J.
    S. (2012). Emotional reactivity and regulation in anxious and non-anxious youth: A
    cellphone ecological momentary assessment study. *Journal of child Psychology and
    Psychiatry*, 53, 197-206.
Terlecki, M. A., Buckner, J. D., Larimer, M. E., and Copeland, A. L. (2011). The role of
    social anxiety in a brief alcohol intervention for heavy-drinking college students. *Journal
    of Cognitive Psychotherapy: An International Quarterly*, 25, 7-21.
Thomas, S. A., Aldao, A. and De Los Reyes, A. (2012). Implementing clinically feasible
    psychological measures in evidence-based assessments of adolescent social anxiety.
    *Professional Psychology: Research and Practice*, 43, 510-519.
Thomas, S. A., Daruwale, S. E., Goepel, K. A., and De Los Reyes, A. (2012). Using the
    subtle avoidance frequency examination in adolescent social anxiety assessments. *Child
    Youth Care Forum*, 41, 547-559.
Velting, O. N., Setzer, N. J. and Albano, A. M. (2004). Update on and advances in assessment
    and cognitive-behavioral treatment of anxiety disorders in children and adolescents.
    *Professional Psychology: Research and Practice*, 35, 42-54.
Ware, J. E. and Sherbourne, C. D. (1992). The MOS 36-item short-form health survey (SF-
    36): conceptual framework and item selection. *Medical Care*, 30, 473-483.
Watanabe, N., Furukawa, T. A., Chen, J., Kinoshita, Y., Nakano,Y., Ogawa, S., Funayama,
    T., Ietsugu, T., and Noda, Y. (2010). Change in quality of life and their predictors in the
    long-term follow-up after group Cognitive Behavioral Therapy for Social Anxiety
    Disorder: A prospective cohort study. *BMC Psychiatry*, 10, 81-93.
Weeks, J. W., Heimberg, R. G., Rodebaugh, T. L., Goldin, P. R., and Gross, J. J. (2012).
    Psychometric evaluation of the fear of positive evaluation scale in patients with social
    anxiety disorder. *Psychological Assessment*, 24, 301-312.
Werner, K. H., Goldin, P. R., Ball, T. M., Heimberg, R. G., and Gross, J. J. (2011). Assessing
    emotion regulation in social anxiety disorder: The Emotion Regulation Interview.
    *Journal of Psychopathy and Behavioral Assessment*, 33, 346-354.

In: Social Anxiety
Editor: Efrosini Kalyva

ISBN: 978-1-62808-396-5
© 2013 Nova Science Publishers, Inc.

# Chapter II

# Perception of Autonomic Arousal in Social Anxiety: Mechanisms and its Role As a Maintaining Factor

## *Margit Gramer*[*]

Department of Psychology, University of Graz, Austria

## Abstract

Cognitive models suggest that perception and subsequent dysfunctional appraisal of somatic sensations might be a major determinant of negative self-evaluations in socially anxious individuals. Research on potential mechanisms of biased interoceptive awareness in social anxiety is limited. Processes that seem to be involved are superior interoceptive accuracy and attentional focus, whereas there is little evidence that perceived arousal might have a basis in actual physiological responses. The present review gives an overview of the current state of knowledge in this area and tries to delineate pathways between interoceptive sensitivity and the maintenance of the disorder.

**Keywords**: Social anxiety, perceived arousal, interoceptive accuracy, self-focus, perception of performance, post-event processing

## Introduction

Psychophysiological research on the effects of trait social anxiety in evaluative task conditions has produced very consistent results for *perceived* physiological arousal, with socially anxious individuals experiencing a greater intensity of symptoms both during

[*] Corresponding author: Dr. Margit Gramer, Karl-Franzens Universität Graz, Department of Psychology, Universitätsplatz 2A-8010 Graz, Austria. Tel.: +43 316 380 5130; Fax: +43 316 380 9808; E-mail address: margit.gramer@uni-graz.at.

anticipation of (Gramer, Schild and Lurz, 2012) and confrontation with social stressors (Anderson and Hope, 2009; Edelman and Baker, 2002; Gerlach, Mourlane, and Rist, 2004; Gramer et al.; Grossman, Wilhelm, Kawachi, and Sparrow, 2001; Mauss, Wilhelm, and Gross, 2003; 2004; Mulkens, de Jong, Dobbelaar, and Bögels, 1999; Thibodeau, Gomez-Perez and Asmundson, 2012). However, with few exceptions (Gerlach et al.; Gramer et al.), these group differences in perceived arousal were accompanied by equivalent *objective* physiological responses (i.e. cardiovascular activation). Furthermore, there is some evidence that heightened subjective distress in socially anxious individuals might be accompanied by reduced cardiovascular activation (Gramer and Saria, 2007; Gramer and Sprintschnik, 2008; Larkin, Ciano-Federoff, and Hammel, 1998). These findings seem to suggest that objective and perceived arousal in trait social anxiety might have a basis in different mechanisms.

Beginning with the pioneering work of Obrist (1981) there has been convincing evidence that cardiovascular activity in evaluative task conditions might be the result of effort and task engagement rather than affective arousal. In particular, research by Wright and coworkers (Wright, 1996; Wright and Kirby, 2001) indicates that effort in demanding performance situations is proportional to experienced task difficulty as long as success is perceived as possible and worthwhile. In situations exceeding perceived coping ability, attenuated cardiovascular activation might be observed. In agreement with these postulations Gramer and coworkers (Gramer and Saria, 2007; Gramer and Sprintschnik, 2008) found socially anxious individuals to exhibit heightened cardiovascular activity in moderately demanding social situations (e.g. speech tasks with low evaluative threat) and to reduce their task engagement and cardiovascular activity under high evaluative threat. Thus, the observed lack of differential physiological reactivity or reduced reactivity of socially anxious individuals might result from abandonment of effort in situations exceeding perceived coping ability.

As regards perceived physiological arousal, some psychophysiological researchers (e.g. Mauss et al., 2004; Mulkens et al., 1999) have suggested that these subjective experiences might have a basis in cognitive processes rather than actual physiological effects. In this respect, cognitive behavioral models of trait social anxiety (Clark and Wells, 1995; Rapee and Heimberg, 1997) assume that a specific attentional bias might play a major role in intensifying interoceptive experiences of socially anxious individuals. In particular, Clark and Wells postulate that situations with potential for negative evaluation trigger a shift of attention toward detailed self-monitoring of internal anxiety states. Interoceptive information provided by self-focus is then interpreted as evidence of actual or impending failure to make a favorable outward impression which further exacerbates symptoms of anxiety.

Heightened self-focused attention is considered to be a general characteristic of individuals with psychological disorders (Ingram, 1990) and there is consistent empirical evidence that self-focus is associated with trait social anxiety, both from questionnaire studies (for a review see Bögels and Mansell, 2004) and probe-detection paradigms that compared attention to interoceptive versus external probes (Deiters, Stevens, Hermann and Gerlach, 2013; Mansell, Clark and Ehlers, 2003; Pineles and Mineka, 2005).

Anxiety disorders and anxiety-related phenotypes such as anxiety sensitivity also seem to be characterized by heightened cardiac accuracy, i.e. awareness of actual heartbeat (for a review see Domschke, Stevens, Pfleiderer and Gerlach, 2010). Interoceptive accuracy might be an alternative explanation for heightened perceptions of physiological symptoms in socially anxious individuals. This review will give an overview of the present state of knowledge on the role of perceived physiological arousal in trait social anxiety. It begins with an evaluation of potential mechanisms contributing to increased self-reports of physiological sensations.

Then, causal effects of perceived arousal on state anxiety and negative self-perceptions are discussed and pathways between interoceptive experiences and the maintenance of the disorder are delineated.

# Mechanisms of Enhanced Perceived Physiological Arousal in Social Anxiety

## Self-Focused Attention

There is little psychophysiological research on the causal effects of self-focused attention in social anxiety. Studies that experimentally manipulated attentional focus mainly evaluated effects on state anxiety and perceptions of performance. Considering that there is substantial coherence between experienced anxiety and perceived physiological arousal (Mauss et al., 2004; Thibodeau et al., 2012), data on state anxiety might also be an important source of information. Research in this area has produced inconsistent results. Several studies suggest that self-focused attention may exacerbate state anxiety (Bögels and Lamers, 2002; Woody, 1996; Woody and Rodriguez, 2000; Zou, Hudson and Rapee, 2007). With one exception (Zou et al.), the detrimental effects of self-directed attention were not specific for participants with high social anxiety, though. Individuals with high and low levels of trait social anxiety were affected by attention manipulation. Some studies found no evidence for a causal role of self-focus. One of them (Bögels, Rijsemus and de Jong, 2002) evaluated the effect of self-focus on both state anxiety and perceived physiological arousal, the other study (Panayiotou and Vrana, 1998) was confined to state anxiety. These discrepant results may partly be an effect of different types of self-focus manipulation. Studies that did obtain a detrimental effect of self-focus on state anxiety utilized instructions to direct attention towards internal self-relevant stimuli, whereas studies which failed to observe an effect manipulated self-focus by placing a mirror or video camera in front of participants. A meta-analysis by Mor and Winquist (2002) found instructions to have a stronger effect on negative affect compared to mirror/video manipulations.

Research on the effects of self-directed attention also has to consider the aspect of *direction of causality*. Negative affect and arousal perceptions may not only be a consequence of self-directed attention, they may also cause increased attention to the self. There is some evidence that negative mood may induce self-focused attention (Salovey, 1992; Wood, Saltzberg and Goldsamt, 1990). As regards physiological arousal, several authors found false heart rate feedback to strengthen self-focus (Makkar and Grisham, 2012; Wells and Papageorgiou, 2001) and Wegner and Giuliano (1980) observed a similar effect for exercise-induced arousal. These findings might suggest a cyclical relationship (Mor and Winquist, 2002). When socially anxious individuals enter a social situation with evaluative features the experience of anxiety and physiological arousal may trigger enhanced self-focus and self-focus in turn may further intensify interoceptive experiences.

Overall, these data do not seem to provide strong support for the assumption that differences in perceived physiological arousal between high and low socially anxious individuals might be the result of attentional bias.

Focusing attention on the self in social situations may increase state anxiety and perceived arousal, but it seems to have this effect in both high and low socially anxious individuals. Considering that socially anxious individuals were found to show a stronger tendency towards self-focus when they have the possibility to allocate their attention freely (Deiters, et al., 2013; Mansell, Clark, and Ehlers, 2003; Pineles and Mineka, 2005) they nonetheless might experience the negative effects of self-focus more strongly. There is some indication, though, that differences in self-directed attention between high and low socially anxious individuals might be confined to stressor anticipation (Deiters et al.) and Woody (1996) found a self-focus manipulation to increase state anxiety in socially phobic individuals only in a passive task condition but not during active speech. Together, the present state of results lends some support to the explanation that attention to internal experiences might partly be involved in perception of physiological arousal. Considering the lack of specificity and variability of results, other mechanisms might contribute to greater reporting of physiological arousal in socially anxious individuals. Superior interoceptive accuracy has been suggested as possible additional solution in this respect (Kroeze, van den Hout, Haenen and Schmidt, 1996).

## Interoceptive Accuracy

Research on interoceptive accuracy in anxiety disorders has mainly been guided by the hypothesis that better perception of physiological symptoms might increase the probability of misinterpretations of somatic cues (Domschke et al., 2010; Stevens et al., 2011). Most studies have concentrated on the cardiovascular system and assessed cardiac accuracy, or awareness of how fast the heart is beating. Several methods have been developed to measure cardiac accuracy. A paradigm developed by Schandry (1981) requires participants to silently count their heartbeats during specified time intervals. This result is then compared to actual heartbeats and a percentage mean error score is calculated (e.g. Pollatos, Traut-Mattausch, Schroeder and Schandry, 2007a). Another approach requires participants to compare externally generated signals to the rhythm of their heartbeats (e.g. Schneider, Ring, and Katkin, 1998). This discrimination task was found to be rather difficult for untrained individuals and it is assumed that this method might prevent the detection of differential effects (Domschke et al.). There is some evidence that cardiac accuracy might be related to differences in cardiovascular activation. Heartbeat detection was found to be improved in situations that elicit heightened cardiovascular reactivity due to physical or emotional stress, compared to less demanding conditions such as rest periods (e.g. Anthony et al., 1995; Pollatos, Herbert, Kaufmann, Auer, and Schandry, 2007b; Stevens et al., 2011). Furthermore, interoceptive accuracy seems to intensify emotional experiences independent of physiological activation. Thus, the lack of coherence between perceived and objective cardiovascular arousal may partly reflect individual differences in cardiac accuracy (Wiens, Mezzacappa and Katkin, 2000).

Research on anxiety disorders has mainly utilized the heartbeat counting paradigm. It has provided rather consistent evidence for increased cardiac accuracy in individuals with heightened anxiety sensitivity, trait anxiety and panic disorder (for a review see Domschke et al., 2010), and cardiac awareness was found to mediate the relationship between trait anxiety and perceived arousal during presentation of unpleasant pictures (Pollatos et al., 2007a).

Only two studies have assessed heartbeat perception in social anxiety. One of them (Stevens et al., 2011) found high socially anxious individuals to exhibit better heartbeat perception during a rest period and anticipation of a speech stressor. The other study (Anthony et al., 1995) assessed cardiac awareness after a period of exercise and noted no differences between high and low socially anxious individuals. However, self-reported anxiety over heart-related cues was positively correlated with accuracy in heart beat estimation. Overall, perceptual differences between individuals with anxiety disorders and controls were not a function of differing levels of actual cardiovascular arousal (e.g. Richards and Bertram, 2000; Stevens et al.).

This preliminary evidence suggests that interoceptive accuracy might have a role in differential perceived arousal. Further research on trait social anxiety is necessary, though. In this respect it should also be noted that performance on the heartbeat counting task might be determined by processes other than interoceptive sensitivity. A study by Ring and Brener (1996) found that pre-experimental beliefs about the effects of different postural and exercise manipulations on heart rate were an important determinant of counted heart rates, in addition to processing of actual cardiac activity.

Furthermore, pre-experimental beliefs were related to actual heart rate. Applying this result to research on social anxiety, it might be conceived that physiological experiences during periods of heightened anxiety provide a basis for the formation of expectations about physiological responses. These expectations in turn may then be a major determinant of perceived arousal in anxiety eliciting social conditions. There is also some evidence that research in this area may benefit from including anxiety sensitivity, a variable that increases the negative valence of anxiety experiences (Reiss, Peterson, Gursky, and McNally, 1986). This construct shows moderate associations with measures of anxiety-related psychopathology, including social anxiety (Anderson and Hope, 2009; Deacon and Abramowitz, 2006; Thibodeau et al., 2007), and it is consistently related to enhanced cardiac awareness (e.g. Richards and Bertram, 2000; Stewart, Buffett-Jerrot, and Kokaram, 2001). Findings by Thibodeau et al. suggest that anxiety sensitivity may partly explain exaggerated perceptions of arousal and state anxiety in socially anxious individuals.

# Effects of Perceived Arousal on State Anxiety and Negative Self-Perceptions

Anxiety patients are considered to rely heavily on internal response information when they evaluate the threatening character of a situation. This "ex-consequentia reasoning" or emotional reasoning (Arntz, Rauner, and van den Hout, 1995) is conceptualized as a key maintaining factor in cognitive models of trait social anxiety (Clark and Wells, 1995; Rapee and Heimberg, 1997).

Empirical evidence from different sources seems to support the importance of internal cues. Research based on correlational designs observed a relationship between retrospective ratings of perceived physiological arousal and overestimation of anxious appearance in socially anxious, but not in low anxious individuals (Mansell and Clark, 1999). Furthermore, ratings of perceived arousal, but not objective arousal, were found to mediate the relationship between social anxiety and post-task appraisals of coping efficiency (Gramer et al., 2012).

Research that tried to evaluate the causal effect of perceived arousal has produced inconsistent results with respect to the specificity of emotional reasoning. Most of these studies used false feedback regarding an increase or decrease in heart rate to manipulate interoceptive information. The feedback was provided either prior to or during exposure to a social task. Information concerning an increase in heart rate provided *prior* to task exposure was found to lead to heightened state anxiety and negative self-ratings of performance in socially anxious individuals (Papageorgiou and Wells, 2002; Wells and Papageorgiou, 2001). Interoceptive information did not affect low anxious individuals and effects were independent of objective arousal (Papageorgiou and Wells). Online feedback provided *during* task exposure produced more varied results. Several studies found false feedback concerning an increase in heart rate to elicit heightened state anxiety and more negative performance perceptions regardless of level of social anxiety (Makkar and Grisham, 2012; Wild, Clark, Ehlers, and McManus, 2008). One study utilized public vs. private online feedback of veridical heart rate and observed heightened state anxiety and greater worrying about heart rate in socially anxious individuals during public feedback (Gerlach et al., 2004). Feedback conditions had no differential effects in low anxious individuals.

An explanation of these inconsistencies in the specificity of feedback effects has to consider that interoceptive feedback was found to influence self-directed attention (Makkar and Grisham, 2012; Wells and Papageorgiou, 2001). Furthermore, self-focus was observed to mediate the negative effects of interoceptive feedback on state anxiety and performance appraisals (Makkar and Grisham). As suggested by Wild et al. (2008), the salience of online interoceptive feedback may provoke a shift of attention to internal stimuli in all participants. Whereas feedback provided prior to task exposure or situations that allow to allocate attentional resources freely may be more likely to elicit differential effects in self-focus. This interpretation does not seem to correspond to results obtained for feedback of veridical heart rate (Gerlach et al., 2004). However, social demands were rather moderate in this study, (participants were seated and had to appear relaxed while being evaluated) which may have made heart rate information less important for low anxious individuals. An explanation based on self-focus as mechanism implicates that high *and* low socially anxious individuals are characterized by emotional reasoning when attention is drawn to anxiety symptoms (Makkar and Grisham). In this respect, Arntz et al. (1995) found normal controls to infer danger only on the basis of objective information, but not on the basis of anxiety response information. This study utilized scripted information, though. Further research is necessary to clarify this point.

# Perceived Physiological Arousal and the Maintenance of the Disorder

According to the model of Clark and Wells (1995) the effects of state anxiety, perceived physiological arousal and related negative self-perceptions may extend beyond the social situation. Individuals with social phobia are considered to engage in a detailed post-task review of social interactions which is guided by experiences and self-perceptions that were processed during the event. There is consistent empirical evidence for enhanced negative post-event processing in social anxiety (for a review see Brozovich and Heimberg, 2008).

As regards the role of perceived physiological arousal, both correlational studies (Kiko et al., 2012; Laposa and Rector, 2011; Mellings and Alden, 2000) and research on causal effects (Makkar and Grisham, 2012) have observed an impact of interoceptive experiences on the intensity of post-event processing. In this respect, it should also be noted that socially anxious individuals seem to be characterized by a memory bias for anxiety-related physiological symptoms (Ashbaugh and Radomsky, 2009; Mellings and Alden) which may enhance the influence of perceived arousal on post-task rumination. Empirical evidence from different sources suggests that self-focused attention might have a major role in this process. As indicated above, self-focus may enhance the awareness of interoceptive experiences (e.g. Bögels and Lamers, 2002; Woody and Rodriguez, 2000; Zou, Hudson and Rapee, 2007) and there is also some evidence that instructions to pay attention to feelings and body sensations during a conversation may instigate greater negative post-event processing (Gaydukevych and Kocovski, 2012). Furthermore, Makkar and Grisham found self-focus to mediate the effect of perceived physiological arousal on post-event rumination.

The majority of research on determinants of post-event processing has focused on performance perceptions. In keeping with postulations by Clark and Wells (1995) negative self-appraisals of performance were found to be significantly related to post-event rumination (Abbott and Rapee, 2004; Dannahy and Stopa, 2007) and several studies suggest that performance perceptions may mediate the relationship between social anxiety and post-task rumination (Gramer et al., 2012; Perini, Abbott and Rapee, 2006). One study has also indicated a causal role of performance perceptions in post-event rumination by manipulating self-appraisals via feedback (Zou and Abbott, 2012). The importance of negative self-appraisals is further supported by the observation that an improvement of self-perceptions after cognitive behavioral treatment goes along with less negative post-event processing (Abbott and Rapee). In this respect, it should also be noted that post-task rumination was found to maintain or even to worsen negative performance evaluations (Abbott and Rapee, 2004; Brozovich and Heimberg, 2011; Cody and Teachman, 2011). Thus, rumination may be elicited by negative self-appraisals but, when activated, it may in turn reinforce this negative mental representation (Abbott and Rapee). Taken together, both perceived arousal and performance perceptions seem to describe pathways to enhanced post-task rumination. However, as discussed above, several experimental studies have established a causal role for perceived physiological arousal in the formation of negative performance perceptions (Makkar and Grisham, 2012; Papageorgiou and Wells, 2002; Wild et al., 2008). In light of this evidence, a sequential model might be conceived in which perception of interoceptive information influences self-appraisals of performance, which then lead to enhanced negative post-task rumination.

# Conclusion and Further Directions

Overall, this selective review seems to support the central role of perceived physiological arousal for emotional and cognitive processes in trait social anxiety. However, it has also revealed several areas that are in need of further research. Foremost, the role of interoceptive accuracy for perceived arousal needs to be clarified.

At present there is no information available whether expectations about physiological responses (see Ring and Brener, 1996) might be an additional, or eventually stronger, determinant of interoceptive accuracy and/or perceived arousal in socially anxious individuals. Further studies on the potential mediating (Thibodeau et al., 2007) or moderating influence of anxiety sensitivity also seem to be of importance in this respect. As regards the causal role of self-focused attention for perceived physiological arousal, examination of a cyclical relationship (Mor and Winquist, 2002) between perceived arousal and self-focus over time may promote understanding. The same applies to the relationship between negative performance perceptions and post-task rumination. To date, research on perceived physiological arousal has paid little attention to the fact that there is substantial coherence between state anxiety and perceived physiological arousal (Mauss et al., 2004; Thibodeau et al., 2012). A study by Kiko et al. (2012) suggests that perceived physiological symptoms might no longer predict post-task rumination when state anxiety is controlled for statistically. Future research on the role of perceived arousal in self-evaluations of socially anxious individuals should include state anxiety to evaluate the specific contribution of perceived physiological arousal more clearly.

# References

Abbott, M. J. and Rapee, R. M. (2004). Post-event rumination and negative self-appraisal in social phobia before and after treatment. *Journal of Abnormal Psychology,* 113, 136-144.

Anderson, E. R. and Hope, D. A. (2009). The relationship among social phobia, objective and perceived physiological reactivity, and anxiety sensitivity in an adolescent population. *Journal of Anxiety Disorders,* 23, 18-26.

Anthony, M. M., Brown, T. A., Craske, M. G., Barlow, D. H., Mitchell, W. B., and Meadows, E. A. (1995). Accuracy of heartbeat perception in panic disorder, social phobia, and nonanxious subjects. *Journal of Anxiety Disorders,* 9, 355-371.

Arntz, A., Rauner, M. and van den Hout, M. (1995). If I feel anxious, there must be danger": Ex-consequentia reasoning in inferring danger in anxiety disorders. *Behaviour Research and Therapy,* 33, 917-925.

Ashbaugh, A. R. and Radomsky, A. S. (2009). Interpretations of and memory for bodily sensations during public speaking. *Journal of Behavior Therapy and Experimental Psychiatry,* 40, 399-411.

Bögels, S. M. and Lamers, C. T. J. (2002). The causal role of self-awareness in blushing-anxious, socially-anxious and social phobics individuals. *Behaviour Research and Therapy,* 40, 1367-1384.

Bögels, S. M. and Mansell, W. (2004). Attention processes in the maintenance and treatment of social phobia: hypervigilance, avoidance and self-focused attention. *Clinical Psychology Review,* 24, 827-856.

Bögels, S. M.; Rijsemus, W. and De Jong, P. J. (2002). Self-focused attention and social anxiety: The effects of experimentally heightened self-awareness on fear, blushing, cognitions, and social skills. *Cognitive Therapy and Research,* 26, 461-472.

Brozovich, F. and Heimberg, R. G. (2008). An analysis of post-event processing in social anxiety disorder. *Clinical Psychology Review, 28*, 891-903.

Brozovich, F. and Heimberg, R. G. (2011). The relationship of post-event processing to self-evaluation of performance in social anxiety. *Behavior Therapy, 42*, 224-235.

Clark, D. M. and Wells, A. (1995). A cognitive model of social phobia. In: R. G. Heimberg, M. R. Liebowitz, D. A. Hope, and F. R. Schneier (Eds.), *Social phobia: Diagnosis, assessment, and treatment* (pp. 69-93). New York: Guilford Press.

Cody, M. W. and Teachman, B. A. (2011). Global and local evaluations of public speaking performance in social anxiety. *Behavior Therapy, 42*, 601-611.

Dannahy, L. and Stopa, L. (2007). Post-event processing in social anxiety. *Behaviour Research and Therapy, 45*, 1207-1219.

Deacon, B. and Abramowitz, J. (2006). Anxiety sensitivity and its dimensions across the anxiety disorders. *Anxiety Disorders, 20*, 837-857.

Deiters, D. D., Stevens, S., Hermann, C., and Gerlach, A. L. (2013). Internal and external attention in speech anxiety. *Journal of Behavior Therapy and Experimental Psychiatry, 44*, 143-149.

Domschke, K., Stevens, S., Pfleiderer, B., and Gerlach, A. L. (2010). Interoceptive sensitivity in anxiety and anxiety disorders: An overview and integration of neurobiological findings. *Clinical Psychology Review, 30*, 1-11.

Edelmann, R. J. and Baker, S. R. (2002). Self-reported and actual physiological responses in social phobia. *British Journal of Clinical Psychology, 41*, 1-14.

Gaydukevych, D. and Kocovski, N. L. (2012). Effect of self-focused attention on post-event processing in social anxiety. *Behaviour Research and Therapy, 50*, 47-55.

Gerlach, A. L., Mourlane, D. and Rist, F. (2004). Public and private heart rate feedback in social phobia: a manipulation of anxiety visibility. *Cognitive Behaviour Therapy, 33*, 36-45.

Gramer, M., Schild, E. and Lurz, E. (2012). Objective and perceived physiological arousal in trait social anxiety and post-event processing of a prepared speaking task. *Personality and Individual Differences, 53*, 980-984.

Gramer, M. and Saria, K. (2007). Effects of social anxiety and evaluative threat on cardiovascular responses to active performance situations. *Biological Psychology, 74*, 67-74.

Gramer, M. and Sprintschnik, E. (2008). Social anxiety and cardiovascular responses to an evaluative speaking task: the role of stressor anticipation. *Personality and Individual Differences, 44*, 371-381.

Grossman, P., Wilhelm, F. H., Kawachi, I., and Sparrow, D. (2001). Gender differences in psychophysiological responses to speech stress among older social phobics: congruence and incongruence between self-evaluative and cardiovascular reactions. *Psychosomatic Medicine, 63*, 765-777.

Ingram, R. E. (1990). Self-focused attention in clinical disorders: review and a conceptual model. *Psychological Bulletin, 107*, 156-176.

Kiko, S., Stevens, S., Mall, A. K., Steil, R., Bohus, M., and Hermann, C. (2012). Predicting post-event processing in social anxiety disorder following two prototypical social situations: State variables and dispositional determinants. *Behaviour Research and Therapy, 50*, 617-626.

Kroeze, S., van den Hout, M., Haenen, M.-A., and Schmidt, A. (1996). Symptom reporting and interoceptive attention in panic patients. *Perceptual and Motor Skills*, 82, 1019-1026.

Laposa, J. M. and Rector, N. A. (2011). A prospective examination of predictors of post-event processing following videotaped exposures in group cognitive behavioural therapy for individuals with social phobia. *Journal of Anxiety Disorders*, 25, 568-573.

Larkin, K. T., Ciano-Federoff, L. M. and Hammel, D. (1998). Effects of gender of observer and fear of negative evaluation on cardiovascular reactivity to mental stress in college men. *International Journal of Psychophysiology*, 29, 311-318.

Mansell, W. and Clark, D. M. (1999). How do I appear to others? Social anxiety and processing of the observable self. *Behaviour Research and Therapy*, 37, 419-434.

Mansell, W., Clark, D. M. and Ehlers, A. (2003). Internal versus external attention in social anxiety: an investigation using a novel paradigm. *Behaviour Research and Therapy*, 41, 555-572.

Makkar, S. R. and Grisham, J. R. (2012). Effects of false feedback on affect, cognition, behavior, and postevent processing: The mediating role of self-focused attention. *Behavior Therapy*, in press.

Mauss, I. B., Wilhelm, F. H. and Gross, J. J. (2003). Autonomic recovery and habituation in social anxiety. *Psychophysiology*, 40, 648-653.

Mauss, I. B., Wilhelm, F. H. and Gross, J. J. (2004). Is there less to social anxiety than meets the eye? Emotion experience, expression, and bodily responding. *Cognition and Emotion*, 18, 631-662.

Mellings, T. M. B. and Alden, L. E. (2000). Cognitive processes in social anxiety: the effects of self-focus, rumination and anticipatory processing. *Behaviour Research and Therapy*, 38, 243-257.

Mor, N. and Winquist, J. (2002). Self-focused attention and negative affect: A meta-analysis. *Psychological Bulletin*, 128, 638-662.

Mulkens, S., de Jong, P. J., Dobbelaar, A., and Bögels, S. M. (1999). Fear of blushing: fearful preoccupation irrespective of facial coloration. *Behaviour Research and Therapy*, 37, 1119-1128.

Obrist, P. A. (1981). *Cardiovascular Psychophysiology: A Perspective*. New York: Plenum. Papageorgiou, C., and Wells, A. (2002). Effects of heart rate information on anxiety, perspective taking, and performance in high and low social-evaluative anxiety. *Behavior Therapy*, 33, 181-199.

Panayiotou, G. and Vrana, S. R. (1998). Effect of self-focused attention on the startle reflex, heart rate, and memory performance among socially anxious and nonanxious individuals. *Psychophysiology*, 35, 1-9.

Perini, S. J., Abbott, M. J. and Rapee, R. M. (2006). Perception of performance as a mediator in the relationship between social anxiety and negative post-event rumination. *Cognitive Therapy and Research*, 5, 645-659.

Pineles, S. L. and Mineka, S. (2005). Attentional bias to internal and external sources of potential threat in social anxiety. *Journal of Abnormal Psychology*, 114, 314-318.

Pollatos, O., Herbert, B. M., Kaufmann, C., Auer, D. P., and Schandry, R. (2007b). Interoceptive awareness, anxiety and cardiovascular reactivity to isometric exercise. *International Journal of Psychophysiology*, 65, 167-173.

Pollatos, O., Traut-Mattausch, E., Schroeder, H., and Schandry, R. (2007a). Interoceptive awareness mediates the relationship between anxiety and the intensity of unpleasant feelings. *Journal of Anxiety Disorders,* 21, 931-943.

Rapee, R. M. and Heimberg, R. G. (1997). A cognitive-behavioral model of anxiety in social phobia. *Behaviour Research and Therapy,* 35, 741-756.

Reiss, S., Peterson, R. A., Gursky, D. M., and McNally, R. J. (1986). Anxiety sensitivity, anxiety frequency and the prediction of fearfulness. *Behaviour Research and Therapy,* 24, 1-8.

Richards, J. C. and Bertram, S. (2000). Anxiety sensitivity, state and trait anxiety, and the perception of change in sympathetic nervous system arousal. *Journal of Anxiety Disorders,* 14, 413-427.

Ring, C. and Brener, J. (1996). Influence of beliefs about heart rate and actual heart rate on heartbeat counting. *Psychophysiology,* 33, 541-546.

Salovey, P. (1992). Mood-induced self-focused attention. *Journal of Personality and Social Psychology,* 62, 699-707.

Schandry, R. (1981). Heartbeat perception and emotional experience. *Psychophysiology,* 18, 483-488.

Schneider, T. R., Ring, C. and Katkin, E. S. (1998). A test of the validity of the method of constant stimuli as an index of heartbeat detection. *Psychophysiology,* 35, 86-89.

Stevens, S., Gerlach, A. L., Cludius, B., Silkens, A., Craske, M. G., and Hermann, C. (2011). Heartbeat perception in social anxiety before and during speech anticipation. *Behaviour Research and Therapy,* 49, 138-143.

Stewart, S. H., Buffett-Jerrott, S. E. and Kokaram, R. (2001). Heartbeat awareness and heart rate reactivity in anxiety sensitivity: A further investigation. *Anxiety Disorders,* 15, 535-553.

Thibodeau, M. A., Gomez-Perez, L. and Asmundson, G. J. G. (2012). Objective and perceived arousal during performance of tasks with elements of social threat: The influence of anxiety sensitivity. *Journal of Behaviour Therapy and Experimental Psychiatry,* 43, 967-974.

Wegner, D. M. and Giuliano, T. (1980). Arousal-induced attention to self. Journal of *Personality and Social Psychology,* 38, 719-726.

Wells, A. and Papageorgiou, C. (2001). Social phobic interoception: effects of bodily information on anxiety, beliefs and self-processing. *Behaviour Research and Therapy,* 39, 1-11.

Wiens, S., Mezzacappa, E. S. and Katkin, E. S. (2000). Heartbeat detection and the experience of emotions. *Cognition and Emotion,* 14, 417-427.

Wild, J., Clark, D. M., Ehlers, A., and McManus, F. (2008). Perception of arousal in social anxiety: Effects of false feedback during a social interaction. *Journal of Behavior Therapy and Experimental Psychiatry,* 39, 102-116.

Wood, J., Saltzberg, J. and Goldsamt, L. (1990). Does affect induce self-focused attention? *Journal of Personality and Social Psychology,* 58, 899-908.

Woody, S. R. (1996). Effects of focus of attention on anxiety levels and social performance of individuals with social phobia. *Journal of Abnormal Psychology,* 105, 61-69.

Woody, S. R. and Rodriguez, B. F. (2000). Self-focused attention and social Anxiety in social phobics and normal controls. *Cognitive Therapy and Research,* 24, 473-488.

Wright, R. A. (1996). Brehm's theory of motivation as a model of effort and cardiovascular response: In: P. M. Gollwitzer and J. A. Bargh (Eds.), *The psychology of action: Linking cognition and motivation and behavior* (pp. 424-453). New York: Guilford.

Wright, R. A. and Kirby, L. D. (2001). Effort determination of cardiovascular response: an integrative analysis with applications in social psychology. In: M. Zanna (Ed.), *Advances in experimental social psychology* (vol. 33, pp. 255-307). San Diego, CA: Academic.

Zou, J. B. and Abbott, M. J. (2012). Self-perception and rumination in social anxiety. *Behaviour Research and Therapy,* 50, 250-257.

Zou, J. B., Hudson, J. L. and Rapee, R. M. (2007). The effect of attentional focus on social anxiety. *Behaviour Research and Therapy*, 45, 2326-2333.

In: Social Anxiety                    ISBN: 978-1-62808-396-5
Editor: Efrosini Kalyva            © 2013 Nova Science Publishers, Inc.

*Chapter III*

# Enhancing Help and Treatment-Seeking Behaviors among Adolescents and Young Adults with Social Anxiety Disorder (Social Phobia)

## *Suela Sulo[1,*] and Maya Ramic[2]*

[1]James R. & Helen D. Russell Institute for Research & Innovation;
[2]Department of Psychiatry, Advocate Lutheran General Hospital, Park Ridge, Illinois, US

## Abstract

Social anxiety disorder (social phobia) is recognized as the most prevalent among all anxiety disorders. It affects a significant number of adolescents and young adults at a crucial developmental stage in life, when social interactions become an important part of one's identity. Difficulties in social adjustment easily become misinterpreted as deficiencies in one's character and greatly affect one's quality of life. This chapter focuses specifically on adolescents and young adults affected by social anxiety disorder and how the very nature of this disorder creates an obstacle in help and treatment seeking behaviors for this population. Our goal for this chapter is to process and understand social anxiety disorder from the point of view of a young person affected by it as well as from the point of view of experts familiar with this population. We also attempt to present this information in a mindful way for those who read it so that it is accessible to those who could benefit from it the most – the young people. Although we present various available treatments and recommendations for social anxiety disorder, we place an equal emphasis on the importance of how these interventions are delivered to be most beneficial to the focused population. Finally, the uniqueness of our approach lies in recognizing and encouraging utilization of strengths one possesses to cope with the weaknesses encountered. And above all, we emphasize that social anxiety is a disorder and not a character flaw.

* Corresponding author: Suela Sulo, suelasulo@gmail.com.

**Keywords**: social anxiety disorder/social phobia, adolescents, young adults, help and treatment seeking

> "Other people's opinion of you does not have to become your reality."
>
> *Les Brown*

In a recent article published in the Journal of School Nursing (*entitled "Speaking up: Teens voice their health information needs"*), after conducting focus groups with 101 students aged 13-17 years old in Illinois, United States, the authors outlined the many health concerns the students reported and the emphasis they placed on the need for accessible, high quality, and personally relevant information. Apart from highlighting the importance of taking an active role in learning about their health, the students who were interviewed preferred to access information directly from qualified individuals and reliable resources. The need for privacy and relationships that would make them develop feelings of comfort, trust, and respect were also highlighted (Smart, Spreen Parker, Lampert, & Sulo, 2012).

The participating students in this study were not asked to report if they were diagnosed with any mental disorders or social anxiety disorder (social phobia) in particular. While this limits the applicability of the findings to adolescents and young adults diagnosed with social anxiety disorder, the findings made us consider the importance of examining and confirming whether the elements voiced by the participating students can be used by health care providers, parents, teachers, and important others for helping adolescents and young adults with social anxiety. The findings of this study are revisited in the chapter, in order to answer an important question, that of how should the help and treatment seeking behavior of adolescents and young adults with social anxiety be interpreted and whether there are certain strategies that can be used to promote a more proactive approach to help seeking and treatment.

Mojtabai, Olfson, and Mechanic (2002) suggested that unmet need for mental health care is a serious public health concern. Meeting this need requires expanding our attention beyond psychopathology in considering various evaluations and decisions that affect help seeking. The authors also highlighted the importance of attitude and behavior change strategies in reducing the gap between need and care. In the Time magazine article, entitled *"The upside of being an introvert (and why extroverts are overrated)"*, which was published in 2012, Tokyo's Time magazine bureau chief, Bryan Walsh stated: *"I'm happy to be an introvert, but that's not all I am"*. Taking pride in being an introvert, Walsh outlined the common characteristics of introverts, identified famous introverts, and most importantly, provided promising advice supporting the utilization of the full potential instead of letting ones' temperaments control them.

In her book, *"Quiet: The power of introverts in a world that can't stop talking"*, Susan Cain demonstrates via numerous examples that our current cultural stereotypes prefer extroverts over introverts. Furthermore, the introverts often get the message that there is something wrong with them. She describes many strong characteristics of introverts such as the ability to form close relationships one-on-one and their dedication and ability to concentrate on a task until mastered. Cain (2013) strives to show that, among many, there are two qualities in particular that are characteristic of introverts – they like to be alone and enjoy being cooperative. In her words, "studies suggest that many of the most creative people are

seeking is the quality of the information presented. Improving overall levels of literacy in the population in general is key to enhancing people's capability to make health choices, whilst appropriate health literacy can help individuals to make best use of health services, adopting healthy lifestyles, and/or taking an active role for addressing the social determinants of their health (Nutbeam & Kickbusch, 2000). Considering that many individuals tend to use the internet as a source of obtaining information, not only for diagnoses and treatment but for obtaining confirmatory and self-diagnostic information as well (van Ameringen et al., 2010), the importance of improved health literacy is fundamental to helping adolescents and young adults in gaining knowledge about their diagnosis, available sources of health, and treatment options. While individuals with social anxiety may exhibit greater feelings of comfort and self-disclosure when socializing online than communicating face to face, lower quality of life and higher levels of depression have been reported for such individuals (Weidman et al., 2012). Also, although socially anxious internet participants have reported to have learned new information about their disorder and available treatments on the internet, the internet usage had only at certain occasions led them to actually take actions such as seeking psychotherapy or medication. The authors suggested that this might be due to both these options still requiring a good deal of face to face interaction (Erwin et al., 2004). The need and importance of having websites with high quality information on social phobia has already been recognized as the quality of information has been qualified as poor (Khazaal et al., 2008).

It is important to acknowledge that while the internet can be used for learning about social anxiety and its treatment, it might not necessarily enhance the willingness or readiness of individuals with social anxiety to take actions for receiving treatments based on what they learn (Erwin et al., 2004). All these findings signify the importance of not just relevant information but also about the health literacy aspect of the materials incorporated into the different self-help seeking websites. Health literacy refers to ones' ability to gain access to, understand, and use information in order to promote and maintain good health (Nutbeam, Wise, Bauman, Harris, & Leeder, 1993). The need for improved mental health information has been recognized as much of the mental health information most readily available to the public is ambiguous and it might significantly hold back adolescents and young adults' recognition of their symptoms, appropriate help seeking, and the acceptance of evidence based mental health care (Jorm, 2000). The use of the Internet will likely become an increasingly integral component of mental health clinical practice (e.g., it could be used in primary care settings as a preliminary screening tool). In their report, van Ameringen et al. (2013) emphasized the need for improving the usability and quality of the Internet based interventions or interactions. In particular, the authors recommend using an Internet screener evaluating a link with a telephone or Internet-based "live chat" with a health care professional. We can see the appeal of the internet as a trusted resource that could promote autonomous decision making.

## Available Treatments and Recommendations

Adolescents and young adults with social anxiety are reluctant to initiate social interactions due to a fear of others' negative perceptions of them. This persistent fear diminishes their help seeking behaviors in general (Horsch, 2006), including help seeking behavior for symptoms of social anxiety itself (Roness, Mykletun, & Dahl, 2005). As a result, they live a life of persistent discomfort and avoidance of new life experiences. Increasing help and treatment seeking behavior in these individuals involves understanding the world from their perspective in order to find interventions they will not shy away from.

Our goal in this section is to provide the readers with a variety of available choices of successful interventions that already exist to alleviate discomforts associated with experiencing social anxiety. Most importantly, we aim to present these interventions from a point of view that demonstrates validation and understanding of life with social anxiety so that these recommendations will feel acceptable to those with social anxiety. Perhaps if we show that we validate their experience with social anxiety, they will in turn be open to our expertise regarding this condition.

The experts familiar with adolescents and young adults affected by mental health disorders have been able to offer great insight into understanding social anxiety, which assisted us in formulating multiple approaches we hope will enhance help and treatment seeking behavior. These strategies utilize the understanding of how these individuals perceive and interact with their environment and people in it. We attempt to use this understanding to reach young individuals with information regarding social anxiety and raise their awareness as well as provide information regarding treatment and special considerations that go along with accepting the treatment.

Common characteristics of individuals with social anxiety are that they avoid new, stimulating, and dynamic situations because they feel overwhelmed by them. They also avoid being in or actively participating in group settings because of increased possibility of being scrutinized by others. On the other hand, they find one-on-one interactions more comfortable and easily engaging because there is no fear of observers' scrutiny. They feel more at ease and calm in a familiar, stable environment, where there is no need of scanning and processing the surroundings - they are secure regarding where they are and whom they are with.

We propose that the most effective approach of enhancing help seeking behavior in these individuals is by offering recommendations and highlighting situations that involve one-on-one interactions with familiar individuals and in a familiar setting. If an intervention takes place in a group setting, we recommend that it be done incorporated in a parallel activity to provide the intervention indirectly without much scrutiny of an individual.

First and foremost, the parents have a very important role in recognizing the impact of social anxiety on their adolescent and young adult children, considering previous findings suggesting that parental control, modeling, and acceptance of anxious behavior leads to increased anxiety in their children (Festa & Ginsburg, 2011; Wood, McLeod, Sigman, Hwang, & Chu, 2003) and a parent-child dyad is key to improving outcomes for social anxiety disorder in the youth (Ollendick & Benoit, 2012). Also, adolescents and young adults have reported that the main source of intended help for a social anxiety or other mental health disorders (Jorm, Wright, & Morgan, 2007).

Importantly, Kennedy, Rapee, and Edwards (2009) demonstrate that an intervention focused on teaching parents on how to use anxiety reducing strategies (such as graded exposure, contingency management, and parent anxiety management) results in decreasing risk of developing social anxiety in anxious children. Because the children with social anxiety are reluctant to reach out, it is important that the parents initiate this discussion in an empathic, validating, and supportive way. For example, the parents can be mindful to use everyday situations to model coping with a socially awkward situation – using mature strategies or demonstrating problem-solving abilities to empower the youth. In addition, parents can reach out for reinforcement in this task to trusted and capable teachers, who in turn can aid in this first step of awareness as they have most consistent contact and communication with both parents and students.

Familiar and trusting role models such as teachers/educators play an important role in enhancing awareness and approach to social anxiety (Benton, 2004). However, in order to utilize their help, they must have the ability to recognize avoidant behaviors, educational and social role functioning impairments in the youth. It is not difficult to imagine that quiet or withdrawn students often get overlooked by the teachers/educators, as the socially anxious students avoid noticeable behavior and rarely draw attention to themselves. For example, devoted students and athletes often spend significant amounts of time on solitary activities. What may seem a dedicated or disciplined individual can in fact be a socially anxious individual who has masked his/her anxiety with a socially acceptable coping strategy of avoiding social situations, activity, and participation. These students may have achieved their goal of remaining undetected, while teachers may have failed to recognize their social fears.

In his article, "*Shyness and academe*", Thomas Benton, a self-described introvert, uses his understanding of the social anxiety and shares his approach with students that he recognizes as shy. One of the strategies Benton (2004) described is the creation of an internet discussion board for students to interact with questions and comments regarding course material. He also reports making himself available for one-on-one student meetings because he recognized increased level of comfort and communication during these private meetings.

It is likely that a similar approach would increase help and treatment seeking behavior regarding social anxiety itself, where the youth have an anonymous forum to engage in discussion and ask questions regarding social anxiety, raising awareness, and learning about available treatments. In this case, the website can be developed into a forum that is private and easily accessible at leisure, without the pressure of reaching out and interacting with another person. This way, the need for seeking relevant information in a flexible manner can be met.

While the use of different internet websites may be helpful, it is important to guide them to a website that provides relevant and high quality information. It is recommended that the website/forum be overseen and maintained by a mental health professional who can provide information, facilitate discussion, and create engaging communication so that the participants feel that they are in contact with a knowledgeable, dedicated, and empathic individual – the desired characteristics that enhance information and help seeking behavior as outlined by Smart and colleagues (2012).

Unconventional methods of therapy such as animal assisted therapy and art therapy should not be overlooked when considering treatment for social anxiety because they provide an opportunity for individuals to become comfortable in a social setting without the pressure of direct social interaction. Barker and Dawson (1998) have reported that animal assisted therapy significantly reduced rates of anxiety in hospitalized psychiatric patients. Pet therapy may involve learning to interact and form a trusting and affectionate relationship with an animal. In her article, Young (2012) describes dog therapy decreasing test associated anxiety in students. These studies demonstrate that interactions with animals helps reduce anxiety and promote feelings of support and safety in situations where one may feel fearful, uncertain or scrutinized, as students do during the test, similar to how individuals with social anxiety feel on a daily basis. Gress (2003) outlines that interaction between people and farm animals builds confidence and social skills, and that trust develops as these interactions build relationship overcome shyness.

On a different note, The Kent Center for Human and Organizational Development therapy staff organized an Expressive Art Therapy Group (The Kent Center, 2013; for more information, http://www.thekentcenter.org/), which allows for incremental self-disclosure through nonverbal art expression free from scrutiny and criticism.

Along these lines, we are recommending that youth with social anxiety would benefit from activities that take place in a social setting without drawing attention to self; activities that come to mind are many such as swimming, tennis, being a member of a band or choir. These activities can serve as a start point for future social interactions, as it is well known and recommended that desensitization is a useful strategy in alleviating symptoms of social anxiety where the adolescents and young adults with social anxiety gradually increase their social activities. For coping and overcoming shyness, Carducci (2009) recommends that reading self-help books, attending shyness seminars, and seeking therapy should be tried before (not after) the use of forced extraversion. We agree with the recommendations of Carducci as we believe that socially anxious adolescents and young adults may not be willing to exhibit extraversion unless they do not recognize the need for self development.

Studies show that socially anxious youth have poorer peer acceptance and that they are well aware of this. They also have the tendency to choose friends that are socially anxious; thus failing to expand their network of friendship or gaining popularity. As a result of creating friendships with socially anxious individuals, they impact negatively each other anxiety levels (Van Zalk, Van Zalk, Kerr, & Stattin, 2011).

The youth have self-reported that in comparison to their non-anxious peers, they are less popular, do not have as many friends, and have a general feeling that other peers do not like them (Greco & Morris, 2005; Kingery, Erdley, Marshall, Whitaker, & Reuter, 2010). Festa and Ginsburg (2011) report that of the many peer predictors affecting youth's social anxiety (e.g., friendship quality, support, validation), peer's acceptance level was the strongest predictor. Therefore, our recommendation is encouraging academic environments to adopt utilization of already established strategies that organize an academic social environment into pre-set social framework. One such concept is that of academic families and peer-pairing utilized by some colleges such as Wells College. In this process, an academic family is automatically formed consisting of members representing each of the academic years – creating a sense of belonging and breaking of divisive barriers without any individual having to initiate effort to reach out socially and seek approval or acceptance, an intervention which eases a transition process associated with the academic experience (for more information, visit http://minerva.wells.edu/slife/sttrads.htm).

Awareness of social anxiety in adolescents and young adults can be enveloped by ongoing wide-spread familiar messages to this population of substance abuse and its associated risks. Many adolescents and young adults use substances to alleviate the discomforts of social anxiety. Additionally, substance abuse temporarily leads to more socially desirable and acceptable extroverted behavior. These are good reasons to put forth the effort into dangerous maladaptive coping of social anxiety, which inevitably leads to general negative impact on one's physical and mental health.

One of the most effective and strongly recommended interventions for social anxiety is psychotherapy as it focuses on fostering insight through interpretation of the core of patient's symptomatology. Psychotherapy captures the one-on-one interaction in a private and regular setting, which is an acceptable framework for people with social anxiety. Both in person and internet based cognitive-behavioral therapy (CBT) have been reported to be the most effective for adolescents and young adults with social anxiety (Buckner & Schmidt, 2009; Hedman, Ljótsson, & Lindefors, 2012; Heimberg, 2002; Seekles, Cuijpers, van de Ven, Penninx, Verhaak, Beekman, et al., 2012). Through a systematic review of the literature, Hoifodt, Strom, Kolstrup, Eisemann, and Waterloo (2011) suggested that when CBT for anxiety disorders (and depression) is delivered in primary care, especially including computer or internet-based self-help program is potentially more effective than usual care and could be delivered effectively by primary care therapists.

There are many explanations supporting the effectiveness of CBT with socially anxious individuals. Stein and Stein (2008) summarized the supportive arguments presented by different researchers. The authors suggested that components of CBT include psychoeducation, progressive muscle relaxation, social skills training, imaginal and in-vivo exposure, video feedback, and cognitive restructuring. Also, for the most part, CBT entails a time-limited collaboration between clinician and patients, is focused on the present, and aims to teach patients the behavioral and cognitive skills that will enable them to function effectively (Heimberg, 2002; Stein & Stein, 2008). Additionally, CBTs for social anxiety concentrate on the relationship between dysfunctional belief systems and behavioral avoidance. Use of self-help literature oriented toward a cognitive behavioral approach (Schneider, 2006) has also been reported to benefit these individuals.

All these techniques are key for adolescents and young adults with social anxiety who are more likely to generate either negative or neutral images of themselves during anxiety provoking and non-threatening imaginary situations respectively as well as see oneself from an observer's perspective (Hackmann, Surawy, & Clark, 1998; Morrison et al., 2011). However, it is important to note that CBT might be particularly effective for individuals at the mild (and sometimes moderate) end of the spectrum of social anxiety (Harden, 2012).

We recommend that in severe and debilitating cases of social anxiety, medication management may be recommended with the understanding that it may be temporary and in combination with other therapies. Also, the privacy of this intervention to alleviate symptoms may be appealing to individuals with social anxiety. Effective classes of medications include selective serotonin-reuptake inhibitors (SSRIs), serotonin and norepinephrine reuptake inhibitors (SNRIs), monoamine oxidase inhibitors, benzodiazepines, and anticonvulsants. However, while these medications are reported to be effective, well tolerated, and safe, they require close monitoring by a physician due to potential serious side-effects (Schneier, 2011; Simon, Worthington, Doyle, Hoge, Kinrys, Fischmann et al., 2004; Stein, Fyer, Davidson, Pollack, & Wiita, 1999; Stein, Ipser, & van Balkom, 2009).

Even though medication treatment can be life-changing, we are aware that many individuals with social anxiety will not seek it and utilize its benefits. Possibly they are reluctant because their view is that accepting the need for medication symbolizes that there is something wrong with them. We would like to introduce a new concept of thinking about medication use by emphasizing that anti-anxiety medication does not change one's personality. In fact, it enables individuals to express their personality and engage with their surrounding by removing the unwanted anxiety that often prevents people from feeling free to simply be themselves.

Social anxiety has a persistent course and symptoms severity fluctuates (Beesdo-Baum et al., 2012). Therefore, it is important that patient's preference, the severity of presenting symptoms, the degree of functional impairment, psychiatric and substance-related comorbidity, as well as long-term treatment goals should be considered when selecting the appropriate treatment approach (Bruce & Saeed, 1999).

Chronicity and continuity are frequent characteristics of social anxiety; therefore, early detection of this disorder is important (Memik et al., 2010). However, adolescents and young adults have been found to have a low correct identification of social anxiety (Reavley & Jorm, 2011), which in turn will decrease their likelihood of seeking help or accepting the need for treatment. These findings highlight the need for educating this population about the disorder, its symptoms or core features, the importance of seeking professional help, information about reliable sources of help and how to apply self-help interventions.

Particularly in adolescence, social anxiety disorder is difficult to be recognized and differentiated from age-appropriate social awkwardness (Schneider, 2006). We recommend that parents, teachers, peers, and important others of socially anxious adolescents are educated on how to differentiate the two. Health care or mental health providers can play a crucial role on educating socially anxious adolescents and young adults as well as their parents, teachers, and important others.

We believe that the common ground of all recommended strategies lies in interventions that are delivered in an empathic, indirect, and incremental manner. It is also very important to encourage this population to familiarize themselves with their strengths as they are all too aware of their perceived weaknesses, and to begin to restructure their sense of self.

# Conclusion

Continuing to investigate and understand the barriers that adolescents and young adults with social anxiety experience towards help and treatment seeking as well as what strategies health care and mental health professionals should consider in order to meet the needs of such individuals is key for the establishment of better outcomes for all parties.

We believe that fostering positive thoughts and perceptions of oneself among the socially anxious youth is the first step someone can take in order to start the 'social enhancement journey'. However, we recognize that fostering positive attitudes about oneself among such individuals is a long-term process. Also, individual efforts might not guarantee effective help seeking behaviors of more positive perceptions. We think that a combination of different strategies and approaches to help seeking behaviors and treatments may be more successful.

It is important that all of us recognize that these individuals can learn how to perceive themselves positively by relying on others acceptance of them. In addition, the socially anxious youth as well as their family members and important others need to be acquainted with the appropriate sources of help and the process of accessing them (Jorm et al., 2007) for themselves or their children, friends, students, and/or important others.

Our hopes are that the recommended interventions could reach a broader audience. We hope to reach practitioners in their endeavor as they undertake an important task in treating these individuals and provide them with more effective tools for self-help. We hope that researchers will utilize our recommendations in formulating new studies to evaluate their efficacy. And finally, and most importantly, we are writing for the socially anxious adolescents and young adults who need to be validated in their journey of recognizing, accepting, and overcoming the discomforts associated with their condition. We do not take credit in formulating these recommendations. Instead, we hope that this chapter provides a good source of information that could help them understand the full spectrum of social anxiety condition and engage in help and treatment seeking behaviors.

While all the recommendations may sound generally effective, failing to consider someone's cultural or ethnic background and the greater environment may result in being the undoing of putting the recommended strategies into practice. Evidence supports that social anxiety is directly impacted by social standards and role expectations that are culture dependent exists (Hofmann, Asnaani, & Hinton, 2010). In their article "*Culture & risk taking in adolescents' behaviors*", Christopherson and Jordan-March (2004) suggested that health care professionals may benefit from being culturally competent and in doing so, they need to recognize traditional cultural values, and to acknowledge personal attributes of adolescents. Therefore, it is important that health care providers and other supportive individuals consider carefully the cultural, racial, and ethnic background as well as provide culturally competent services to the adolescents and young adults with social anxiety.

Although we are sensitive that cultural behavioral differences may exist, our hope is that our recommendations can be applied across various cultural and ethnic backgrounds. This way, people who are affected by social anxiety do not have to suffer in silence as a result of their socially anxious behaviors being overlooked due to the overlap with various cultural norms or attitudes.

Finally, paraphrasing Walsh's statements, we hope that you have come to understand that although your temperament may define you as a socially anxious individual, you do not have to be controlled by it. Instead, find something or someone that motivates you to push beyond the boundaries of your nerves, and enhances your drive to overcome your fears. So, do not let social anxiety define who you are.

# References

American Psychiatric Association. (2000). *Diagnostic and statistical manual of mental disorders, text revision* (DSM-IV-TR) (4th ed.). USA: American Psychiatric Publishing Inc.

Andersson, G. (2012). Guided internet treatment for anxiety disorders. As effective as face-to-face therapies? *Studies in Health Technology and Informatics, 181*, 3-7.

Barker, S.B., & Dawson, K.S. (1998). The effects of animal-assisted therapy on anxiety ratings of hospitalized psychiatric patients. *Psychiatric Services, 49*, 797-801.

Beesdo, K., Bittner, A., Pine, D.S., Stein, M.B., Hofler, M., Lieb, R., et al. (2007). Incidence of social anxiety disorder and the consistent risk for secondary depression in the first three decades of life. *Archives of General Psychiatry, 64*, 903-912.

Beesdo-Baum, K., Knappe, S., Fehm, L., Hofler, M., Lieb, R., Hofmann, S.G., & Wittchen, H.U. (2012). The natural course of social anxiety disorder among adolescents and young adults. *Acta Psychiatrica Scandinavica, 126*, 411-425.

Benton, T. H. (2004). *Shyness and academe*. The Chronicle of Higher Education. Retrieved from http://chronicle.com/article/ShynessAcademe/44632/ on 3/12/2013.

Book, S.W, & Randall, C.L. (2002). Social anxiety disorder and alcohol use. *Alcohol Research & Health, 26*, 130–135.

Book, S. W., Thomas, S.E., Dempsey, J.P., Randall, P.K., & Randall, C.L. (2009). Social anxiety impacts willingness to participate in addiction treatment. *Addiction Behavior, 34*, 474-476.

Bruce, T.J., & Saeed, A. A. (1999). Social anxiety disorder: A common, underrecognized mental disorder. *American Family Physician, 60*, 2311-2320.

Burstein, M., Ameli-Grillon, L., & Merikangas, K. R. (2011). Shyness versus social phobia in US youth. *Pediatrics, 128*, 917-25.

Buckner, J. D., & Schmidt, N. B. (2009). A randomized pilot study of motivation enhancement therapy to increase utilization of cognitive-behavioral therapy for social anxiety. *Behavior Research & Therapy, 47*, 710-715.

Cain, S. (2013). *Quiet: The power of introverts in a world that can't stop talking.* New York: Broadway.

Carducci, B. (2009). What shy individuals do to cope with their shyness: A content analysis and evaluation of self-selected coping strategies? *The Israel Journal of Psychiatry and Related Sciences, 46*, 45-52.

Chak, K., & Leung, L. (2004). Shyness and locus of control as predictors of internet addiction and internet use. *CyberPsychology & Behavior, 7*, 559-570.

Chartier-Otis, M., Perreault, M., & Belanger, C. (2010). Determinants of barriers to treatment for anxiety disorders. *Psychiatric Quarterly, 81*, 127-138.

Christopherson, T. M., & Jordan-Marsh, M. (2004). Culture and risk taking in adolescents' behaviors. *MCN, The Journal of Journal of Maternal/Child Nursing, 29*, 100-105.

Coles, M.E., & Coleman, S. (2010). Barriers to treatment seeking for anxiety disorders: Initial data on the role of mental health literacy. *Depression & Anxiety, 27*, 63-71.

Erwin, B.A., Turk, C.L., Heimberg, R.G., Fresco, D.M., & Hantula, D.A. (2004). The Internet: home to a severe population of individuals with social anxiety disorder? *Anxiety Disorders, 18*, 629–646.

Essau, C.A., Conradt, J., & Petermann, F. (1999). Frequency and comorbidity of social phobia and social fears in adolescents. *Behavior Research & Therapy, 37*, 831-843.

Fehm, L., Beesdo, K., Jacobi, F., & Fiedler, A. (2008). Social anxiety disorder above and below the diagnostic threshold: Prevalence, comorbidity and impairment in the general population. *Social Psychiatry and Psychiatric Epidemiology, 43*, 257-265.

Festa, C. C., & Ginsburg, G. S. (2011). Parental and peer predictors of social anxiety in youth. *Child Psychiatry and Human Development, 42*, 291-306.

Greco, L. A., & Morris, T. L. (2005). Factors influencing the link between social anxiety and peer acceptance: Contributions of social skills and close friendships during middle childhood. *Behavior Therapy, 36*, 197-205.

Gren-Landell, M., Tillfors, M., Furmark, T., Bohlin, G., Andersson, G., & Svedin, C.G. (2009). Social phobia in Swedish adolescents. *Social Psychiatry and Psychiatric Epidemiology, 44*, 1-7.

Gress, K. (2003.) Animals helping people. People helping animals. Interview by Shirley A. Smoyak. *Journal of Psychosocial Nursing and Mental Health Services, 41*, 18-25.

Hackmann, A., Surawy, C., & Clark, D. M. (1998). Seeing yourself through others' eyes: A study of spontaneously occurring images in social phobia. *Behavioural and Cognitive Psychotherapy, 26*, 3–12.

Harden, M. (2012). Cognitive behaviour therapy - incorporating therapy into general practice. *Australian Family Physician,* 41, 668-71.

Hedman, E., Ljótsson, B., & Lindefors, N. (2012). Cognitive behavior therapy via the Internet: a systematic review of applications, clinical efficacy and cost-effectiveness. *Expert Review of Pharmaeconomics & Outcomes Research,* 12, 745-764.

Heimberg, R. (2002). Cognitive-behavioral therapy for social anxiety disorder: Current status and future directions. *Biological Psychiatry,* 51, 101-108.

Hofmann, S.G., & Asnaani, A., & Hinton, D.E. (2010). Cultural aspects in social anxiety and social anxiety disorder. *Depression & Anxiety,* 27, 1117-1127.

Hoifodt, R. S., Strom, C., Kolstrup, N., Eisemann, M., & Waterloo, K. (2011). Effectiveness of cognitive behavioral therapy in primary health care: A review. *Family Practice,* 28, 489-504.

Horsch, L. M. (2006). Shyness and informal help seeking behavior. *Psychological Reports,* 98, 199-204.

Jorm, A.F. (2000). Mental health literacy: Public knowledge and beliefs about mental disorders. *The British Journal of Psychiatry,* 177, 398-401.

Jorm, A. F., Wright, A., & Morgan, A. J. (2007). Where to seek help for a mental disorder? National survey of the beliefs of Australian youth and their parents. *The Medical Journal of Australia,* 187, 556-560.

Kennedy, S. J., Rapee, R. M., & Edwards, S. L. (2009). A selective intervention program for inhibited pre-school aged children of parents with an anxiety disorder: Effects on current anxiety disorders and temperament. *Journal of the American Academy of Child and Adolescent Psychiatry,* 48, 602-609.

Kessler, R. C., McGonagle, K. A., Zhao, S., Nelson, C. B., Hughes, M., Eshleman, S. et al. (1994). Lifetime and 12-month prevalence of DSM-III-R psychiatric disorders in the United States: Results from the national comorbidity survey. *Archives of General Psychiatry,* 51, 8-9.

Khazaal, Y., Fernandez, S., Cochand, S., Reboh, I., & Zullino, D. (2009). Quality of web-based information on social phobia: A cross sectional study. *Depression & Anxiety,* 25, 461-465.

Kingery, J. N., Erdley, C. A., Marshall, K. C., Whitaker, K. G., & Reuter, T. R. (2010). Peer experiences of anxious and socially withdrawn youth: An integrative review of the developmental and clinical literature. *Clinical Child and Family Psychology Review,* 13, 91-128.

Memik, N.C., Sismanlar, S.G., Yildiz, O., Karakaya, I., Isik, C., & Agaoglu, B. (2010). Social anxiety level in Turkish adolescents. *European Child & Adolescent Psychiatry,* 19, 765–772.

Merikangas, K. R., Avenevoli, S., Acharyya, S., Zhang, H., & Angst, J. (2002). The spectrum of social phobia in the Zurich cohort study of young adults. *Biological Psychiatry,* 51, 81-91.

Marom, S, & Hermesh, H. (2003). Cognitive behavior therapy (CBT) in anxiety disorders. *Israel Journal of Psychiatry & Related Sciences,* 40, 135–144.

Mojtabai, R., Olfson, M., & Mechanic D. (2002). Perceived need and help-seeking in adults with mood, anxiety, or substance use disorders. *Archives of General Psychiatry,* 59, 77-84. Morrison, A. S., Amir, N., & Taylor, C.T. (2011). A behavioral index of imagery ability in social anxiety. *Cognitive Therapy Research,* 35, 326-332.

National Institute of Mental Health. (2007). *Anxiety disorders*. National Institute of Health Publication No. 06-3879.

Nutbeam, D., & Kickbusch, I. (2000). Advancing health literacy: A global challenge for the 21st century. *Health Promotion International, 15*, 183-184.

Nutbeam, D., Wise, M., Bauman, A., Harris, E., & Leeder, S. (1993). *Goals and targets for Australia's health in the year 2000 and beyond*. Sydney: Department of Public Health, University of Sydney.

Ollendick, T. H, & Benoit, K. E. (2012). A parent-child interactional model of social anxiety disorder in youth. *Clinical Child and Family Psychology Review, 15*, 81-91.

Pasche, S. (2012). Exploring the comorbidity of anxiety and substance use disorders. *Current Psychiatry Reports, 14*,176-81.

Ranta, K., Tuomisto, M. T., Kaltiala-Heino, R., Rantanen, P., & Marttunen, M. (2013). Cognition, imagery and coping among adolescents with social anxiety and phobia: Testing the Clark and Wells model in the population. *Clinical Psychology & Psychotherapy [Epub]*.

Reavly, N. J., Cvetkovski, S., Jorm, A. F., & Lubman, D. I. (2010). Help-seeking for substance use, anxiety and affective disorders among young people: Results from the 2007 Australian National Survey of Mental Health and Wellbeing. *Australian and New Zealand Journal of Psychiatry, 44*, 729-735.

Reavley, N.J., & Jorm, A.F. (2011). Young people's recognition of mental disorders and beliefs about treatment and outcome: Findings from an Australian national survey. *Australian and New Zealand Journal of Psychiatry, 45*, 890-898.

Roness, A., Mykletun, A., & Dahl, A. A. (2005). Help-seeking behaviour in patients with anxiety disorder and depression. *Acta Psychiatrica Scandinavica, 111*, 51-58.

Scealy, M., Philips, J.G., Stevenson, R. (2002). Shyness and anxiety as predictors of patterns of internet usage. *CyberPsychology & Behavior, 5*, 507-515.

Schneider, F.R. (2006). Social anxiety disorder. *The New England Journal of Medicine, 355*, 1029-1036.

Schneier, F.R, Johnson, J., Hornig, C.D., Liebowitz, M. R., & Weissman, M. M. (1992). Social phobia: Comorbidity and morbidity in an epidemiologic sample. *Archives of General Psychiatry, 49*, 282–288.

Seekles, W. M., Cuijpers, P., van de Ven, P., Penninx, B. W., Verhaak, P. F., Beekman, A. T. et al. (2012). Personality and perceived need for mental health care among primary care patients. *Journal of Affective Disorders, 136*, 666-674.

Simon, N. M., Worthington, J. J., Doyle, A. C., Hoge, E. A., Kinrys, G., Fischmann, D. et al. (2004). An open-label study of levetiracetam for the treatment of social anxiety disorder. The *Journal of Clinical Psychiatry, 65*, 1219-1222.

Smart, K. A., Spreen Parker, R., Lampert, J., & Sulo, S. (2012). Speaking up: Teens voice their health information needs. *The Journal of School Nursing, 28*, 379-388.

Sonntag, H., Wittchen, H.U., Hofler, M., Kessler, R.C., & Stein, M.B. (2000). Are social fears and DSM-IV social anxiety disorder associated with smoking and nicotine dependence in adolescents and young adults? *European Psychiatry, 15*, 67-74.

Stein, M. B., Fuetsch, M., Muller, N., Hofler, M., Lieb, R., Wittchen, H. (2001). Social anxiety disorder and the risk of depression: A prospective community study of adolescents and young adults. *Archives of General Psychiatry, 58*, 251-256.

Stein, M. B., Fyer, A. J., Davidson, J. R. T., Pollack, M. H., & Wiita, B. (1999). Fluvoxamine treatment of social phobia (social anxiety disorder): A double-blind, placebo-controlled study. *American Journal of Psychiatry, 156,* 756-760.

Stein, M. B., & Gorman, J. M. (2001). Unmasking social anxiety disorder. *Journal of Psychiatry & Neuroscience, 26,* 185-189.

Stein, D. J., Ipser, J. C., & van Balkom, A. J. (2009). P*harmacotherapy for social anxiety disorder (Review).* The Cochrane Library, 1. Retrieved from http://www.usafp.org /Word_PDF_Files/Annual-Meeting-2012-Syllabus/FPIN%20-%20Medication%20for %20Social%20Anxiety%20Disorder(Optimized).pdf on 3/17 /2013.

Stein, M. B., & Stein, D. J. (2008). Social anxiety disorder. *The Lancet, 371,* 1115-1125.

The Kent Center. (2013). *Art therapy group helps kids with social phobia & other mental health disorders can't find an author.* Retrieved from The Kent Center for Human and Organizational Development http://www.thekentcenter.org/Newsletter-Winter-2013.pdf on 3/1/2013

Schneier, F. (2011). Pharmacotherapy of social anxiety disorder. *Expert Opinion on Pharmacotherapy, 12,* 615-625.

Titov, N., Andrews, G., Johnston, L., Schwencke, G., & Choi, I. (2009). Shyness programme: Longer term benefits, cost-effectiveness, and acceptability. *Australian and New Zealand Journal of Psychiatry, 43,* 36-44.

Valkenburg, P.M., & Peter, J. (2009). Social consequences of the internet for adolescents: a decade of research. *Current Directions in Psychological Science, 18,* 1–5.

van Ameringen, M., Mancini, C., Simpson, W., & Patterson, B. (2010). Potential use of internet-based screening for anxiety disorders: A pilot study. *Depression & Anxiety, 27,* 1006-1010.

Van Zalk, N., Van Zalk, M., Kerr, M., & Stattin, H. (2011). Social anxiety as a basis for friendship selection and socialization in adolescents' social networks. *Journal of Personality, 79,* 499-526.

Walsh, B. (2012). *The upside of being an introvert (and why extroverts are overrated).* Time Magazine. Accessed on 2/14/2013 from http://www.time.com/time/magazine/article /0,9171,2105432,00.html.

Wang, P. S., Lane, M., Olfson, M., Pincus, H. A., Wells, K. B., & Kessler, R.C. (2005). Twelve month use of mental health services in the United States. *Archives of General Psychiatry, 62,* 629-640.

Weidman, A.C., Fernandez, K.C., Levinson, C.A., Augustine, A.A., Larsen, R.J., & Rodebaugh, T.L. (2012). Compensatory internet use among individuals higher in social anxiety and its implications for well-being. *Personality and Individual Differences, 53,* 191–195.

Wells College (n.d.). *Student life traditions.* Retrieved from http://minerva.wells. edu/slife/sttrads.htm on 3/15/2013.

Wittchen, H. U., Stein, M. B., & Kessler, R. C. (1999). Social fears and social phobia in a community sample of adolescents and young adults: Prevalence, risk factors and co-morbidity. *Psychological Medicine, 29,* 309-323.

Wood, J. J., McLeod, B. D., Sigman, M., Hwang, W. C., & Chu, B. C. (2003). Parenting and childhood anxiety: theory, empirical findings, and future directions. *Journal of Child Psychology and Psychiatry,* 44, 134-51.

Wu, P., Goodwin, R.D., Fuller, C., Liu, X., Comer, J.S., Cohen, P., et al. (2010). The relationship between anxiety disorders and substance use among adolescents in the community: Specificity and gender differences. *Journal of Youth and Adolescence,* 39, 177-188.

Young, J. S. (2012). Pet-Therapy: Dogs de-stress students. *Journal of Christian Nursing,* 29, 217-21.

Zimmermann, P., Wittchen, P. U., Hofler, M., Pfister, H., Kessler, R., & Lieb, R. (2003). Primary anxiety disorders and the development of subsequent alcohol use disorders: A 4-year community study of adolescents and young adults. *Psychological Medicine,* 33, 1211-1222.

In: Social Anxiety                                                ISBN: 978-1-62808-396-5
Editor: Efrosini Kalyva                                     © 2013 Nova Science Publishers, Inc.

*Chapter IV*

# Family Influences of Children's Social Anxiety during Early Adolescence

### *Cheryl Buehler* and *Bridget B. Weymouth*

Human Development and Family Studies, University of North Carolina, Greensboro, US

## Abstract

Influences of three family factors on youths' social anxiety during early adolescence were examined in a community-based sample of 416 two-parent families. Family predictors were child-related marital conflict, marital hostility, and parents' psychological intrusiveness with the child. Child-related marital conflict and youth social anxiety were interrelated at the beginning of adolescence. Across early adolescence, a process cascade emerged with marital hostility and child-related marital conflict during 6th grade connected to greater parental intrusiveness during 7th grade. Parental intrusiveness was then associated with greater youth social anxiety during 8th grade. Longitudinal change-oriented analyses revealed a different pattern from the prospective cascade pattern. Child-related marital conflict during 6th grade was associated with higher concurrent social anxiety symptoms (daughters only) and with decreases in social anxiety symptoms across time for both daughters and sons. Family influences, child-related marital conflict in particular, were instrumental in two-parent families for shaping social anxiety in children.

**Keywords:** Adolescence, marital conflict, psychological control, psychological intrusiveness, social anxiety, triangulation

## Introduction

Creating and refining social skills that promote healthy relationships with peers and nonfamilial adults is a central developmental task for youth during early adolescence

---

* Corresponding author: Cheryl Buehler, cabuehle@uncg.edu.

(Englund, Levy, Hyson, & Sroufe, 2000). Social anxiety, importantly, may impede developmental progress in creating and maintaining these important social relationships. Although youths' social worlds expand during this developmental period, family remains a primary socialization influence (Clarke-Stewart & Dunn, 2006), particularly specific familial processes constituting marital relations and parenting (Engles, Dekovic, & Meeus, 2002; Kouros, Cummings, & Davies, 2010).

The purpose of this study was to examine the associations among select family factors and youths' social anxiety symptoms during early adolescence. These patterns of associations were compared across daughters and sons to examine whether girls and boys experience differential vulnerabilities.

We analyzed three waves of annual data from 416 two-parent families. This was a community-based sample of families, rather than a clinical sample, and the longitudinal research design allowed for the examination of three types of associations. First, we examined contemporaneous associations when youth were entering adolescence (6th grade). Second, we examined prospective associations between family factors during 6th and 7th grades, and youths' social anxiety during 8th grade.

Finally, we examined change-oriented associations between family factors during 6th grade and changes in youths' social anxiety during middle school (6th through 8th grades). Given the focus of the study was on youths' social anxiety specifically, all analyses controlled for youths' general internalizing problems during 6th grade to help minimize selection and confounding effects.

# Background

## Youths' Social Anxiety

For the present study, we defined social anxiety as feelings of nervousness, insecurity, and avoidance with peers and adults in social interactions and settings. These symptoms connote fear of negative evaluation, internalized emotional dysregulation, and problematic relational skills with peers and adults. A developmental systems perspective of social anxiety was used in this study, and therefore we focused on symptoms that range from mild to more severe. A developmental systems approach also embeds the experience of social anxiety in the literatures that examine youth well-being and social skills over time (Lerner, Theokas, & Bobek, 2005; Smetana, Campione-Barr, & Metzger, 2006).

The creation and maintenance of relationships with peers and adults outside of familial and kin relationships is an important developmental task during early adolescence. As such, it is not surprising that research on the etiology of social fears suggests that the average age of onset of serious symptoms of these psychosocial difficulties is during adolescence (Hudson & Rapee, 2000).

Although the current study adopted a developmental definition of social anxiety and employed a community-based sample of youth and their families, it is important to note that experiences of social anxiety also can be examined using a more clinically-oriented emphasis that conceptualizes this type of distress within the literatures on psychopathology during adolescence (Cummings, Davies, & Campbell, 2000). Research conducted from this perspective often is situated in the study of social phobia, and includes examinations of the etiology and course of shyness, self-consciousness, and peer neglect, in addition to social anxiety (Hudson & Rapee, 2000).

Thus, the results from this study have important implications for both developmental and clinical scholars and practitioners.

## Family Factors

Research is not extensive, but social anxiety symptoms during adolescence seem to be associated with parents' social phobia/anxiety (Lieb et al., 2000), youth behavioral inhibition during childhood (Chronis-Tuscano et al., 2009), peer victimization (Siegel, La Greca, & Harrison, 2009), and over controlling or intrusive parenting (Lewis-Morrarty et al., 2012). Given the relative paucity of research and the importance of family functioning as a socialization locus during early adolescence, we focused on family correlates/antecedents of youths' social anxiety symptoms by examining associations with marital conflict and intrusive parenting.

*Marital conflict.* Two aspects of marital conflict were examined in this study: child-related marital conflict and marital hostility. *Child-related marital conflict* includes spouses' disagreements about child-rearing and triangulating children in marital disputes. Conceptually, some scholars have included child-related disagreements and triangulation as dimensions of marital conflict (Grych & Fincham, 1993), whereas others have conceptualized these experiences as dimensions of coparenting (Teubert & Pinquart, 2010). Regardless of how these constructs are situated within the family system, we hypothesize that child-rearing disagreements and triangulation are two important aspects of child-related marital conflict that may be associated with youths' social anxiety symptoms during early adolescence. Although the central marital construct of interest in this study is child-related marital conflict, *marital hostility* (i.e., overt expressions of verbal and physical aggression) also is examined in order to control for the co-occurrence of overt and covert forms of marital conflict.

Theoretically, child-related marital conflict, defined by childrearing disagreements and triangulating children in marital disputes, is very salient to children, increasing their attention toward marital interactions and elevating their perceptions of self-relevance given parental disputes may concern children's behavior or involve children as allies or mediators (Grych & Fincham, 1990). It also may threaten children's sense of emotional security within the family system (Davies & Cummings, 1994). From clinically-oriented family systems perspectives, triangulation and coalitions formed via children's involvement in marital disputes constitute boundary violations within the family that place children at risk for emotional distress (Bowen, 1978; Minuchin, 1985). Compared with more overt forms of processing marital disagreements that include verbal and physical aggression, triangulation is part of a more covert set of family processes that indirectly address marital disagreements and may be more passive aggressive in nature (Buehler et al., 1998).

These theoretical explications of child-related marital conflict, however, have not addressed the potential links with children's social fears. As such, in this study, we extend potential implications for child well-being beyond general emotional distress and internalized problems to include social anxiety symptoms during early adolescence as children's social worlds expand.

*Parents' psychological intrusiveness.* Based on earlier work by Schaefer (1965) and Steinberg (1990), Barber (2002, p. 15) conceptualized parents' psychological control as "behaviors that are intrusive and manipulative of children's thoughts, feelings, and attachments to parents. These behaviors appear to be associated with disturbances in psychoemotional boundaries between the child and parent, and hence with the development of an independent sense of self and identity." Similar in constitutional nature to triangulation, parents' psychological intrusiveness represents a set of relatively indirect, covert processes that violate the child's sense of self and feelings of efficacy.

Thus, theoretically, parental intrusiveness may foment social fears and avoidance, undermining youths' perceived competency in relationships with peers and nonfamilial adults. This is important during the transition into adolescence because youth increasingly must independently navigate these nonfamilial social relationships. Parental intrusive may stifle this independence and may undermine experiences that enhance youths' feelings of social efficacy and self-confidence.

## Family Factors and Youths' Social Anxiety Symptoms: Empirical Foundations

*Child-related marital conflict.* The strongest empirical support for the potential importance of a link between child-related marital conflict and youths' social anxiety comes from a recent meta-analysis focused on coparenting, as well as a few longitudinal studies of children's internalizing problems or social relations during late childhood and early adolescence. Teubert and Pinquart (2010) conducted a meta-analysis of 59 studies that examined coparenting and some aspect of child well-being. Three of the four aspects of coparenting have relevance for our study. Based primarily on results from cross-sectional studies, children's internalizing problems were associated with triangulation (.21; 19 effects), childrearing agreement (-.20; 6 effects), and conflict/hostility (.19; 29 effects). They also found that coparenting factors were associated with child internalizing problems, controlling for general marital quality and parenting behaviors.

Although scarce and not focused specifically on youths' social anxiety symptoms, a link between child-related marital conflict and youth emotional distress or problems with peers also has been found in longitudinal studies. Cui, Donnellan, and Conger (2007) found reciprocal, positive associations between childrearing disagreements and youths' depressive symptoms across three years of early adolescence. Kouros et al. (2010) found that increases in marital conflict over time were associated with children's social problems at age 12 through increases in externalizing problems during childhood. Using data from the same project used in the current study (Family Life Project, FLP), Buehler and Welsh (2009) found that triangulation into parents' marital disputes was associated with increases in youths' internalizing problems during early adolescence, controlling for marital hostility, parental harshness toward the child, and changes in youth externalizing problems. Finally, also using data from the FLP, Buehler, Franck, and Cook (2009) found that triangulation was associated with greater peer rejection two years later, controlling for marital hostility.

Although most theories and research focused on child-related marital conflict suggest deleterious associations with child well-being, two studies with samples of young children have found support for the alternative hypothesis (see review by Majdandzic, de Vente,

Feinberg, Aktar, & Bögels, 2012). These two studies found a negative association between parents undermining one another in parenting and child anxiety (Belsky, Putnam, & Crinc, 1996; Davis, Schoppe-Sullivan, Mangelsdorf, & Brown, 2009). Majdandzic et al. suggested that this negative association may characterize families with a highly reactive infant.

*Parents' psychological intrusiveness.* Clinically-oriented research has suggested a link between overinvolved or intrusiveness parenting and childhood anxiety (Bruch & Heimberg, 1994; Hudson & Rapee, 2000). This link has been supported in cross-sectional, developmental research and has held even when other aspects of parenting have been controlled (Barber, Olsen, & Shagle, 1994; Benson, Buehler, & Gerard, 2008; Krishnakumar, Buehler, & Barber, 2003; Stone, Buehler, & Barber, 2002). A recent meta-analysis indicated that autonomy granting (inverse effects) and over involvement (positive effects) were the strongest parental correlates with childhood anxiety (McLeod, Wood, & Weisz, 2007).

Although a link between parents' psychological intrusiveness and children's internalizing problems has been established, the causal direction is unclear. Over a one to three-year period, some studies have found that child internalized distress predicts increases in parents' psychological intrusiveness over time (Rogers, Buchanan, & Winchel, 2003; Wijsbroek, Hale, Raaijmakers, & Meeus, 2011). Others have found linkages between parents' psychological intrusiveness and decreases in son's self-confidence (Conger, Conger, & Scarmella, 1997), and increases in daughter's anxiety/depression (Pettit, Laird, Dodge, Bates, & Criss, 2001).

Furthermore, very few of these studies examined social anxiety, specifically, which may be an important qualification because Loukas (2009) found differential effects; W1 depressive symptoms were associated with increases in maternal psychological intrusiveness a year later whereas W1 social anxiety symptoms were associated with decreases in intrusiveness. As such, depressive symptoms and general anxiety should be examined separately from youths' social anxiety and controlled for in the analyses.

## The Present Study

Given these theoretical and empirical foundations, we tested two central hypotheses. First, controlling for marital hostility and youth general internalizing problems, we hypothesized that child-related marital conflict is associated with youths' higher levels of social anxiety symptoms, concurrently and over time. We also hypothesized that child-related marital conflict during 6th grade is associated with increases in youths' social anxiety symptoms from 6th through 8th grade (during middle school). Given Davies and Lindsey (2004) have noted the potential vulnerability of marital conflict for girls, we also hypothesized that these associations are stronger for daughters than for sons. Second, controlling for marital hostility and youth general internalizing problems, we hypothesized that parents' psychological intrusiveness with their child partially mediates the association between child-related marital conflict and youths' social anxiety symptoms. Data from a community-based sample of 416 families were analyzed using structural equation modeling (SEM). Three waves of annual data were collected when youth were in 6th, 7th and 8th grades.

# Method

## Sampling Procedures and Characteristics

The sample was taken from a larger study of the effects of marital conflict on the transition from childhood into adolescence. For the larger study, 6th grade youth in 13 middle schools in a large, geographically diverse county in the southeastern United States were invited to participate. Children in 6th grade were selected because they are beginning the transition from childhood into adolescence. Ninety-six percent of the teachers participated. Youth received a letter during homeroom inviting their participation. Two additional invitations were mailed directly to parents. Consent forms were returned by 71% of the youth/parent(s) and 80% of these youth received parental permission to complete a questionnaire on family life during school. This resulted in a sample of 2,346 6th grade youth. The sample was representative of families in the county on race, parents' marital status, and family poverty status (contact the author for details using county census information).

Families for the present study of two-parent families were recruited from the larger sample of youth using the following criteria: parents were married or long-term cohabitants and no stepchildren were in or out of the home. Stepfamilies were not included for three reasons: (a) stepfamilies have complex structures that differ from ever-married families and a careful study would need to include adequate sample sizes of these various structures to conduct group comparisons; (b) data would need to be collected regarding birth parent-child relations as well as stepparent-child relations in order to understand the findings accurately; and (c) funds were inadequate to collect data from both stepparents and nonresidential birth parents.

Of the 1131 eligible families from the larger study, 416 (37%) agreed to participate. Primary reasons given for nonparticipation included time constraints and/or an unwillingness for one or more family members to be videotaped (observations not utilized in the present study). This response rate was similar to that in studies that have included 3 or 4 family members and have used intensive data collection protocols (e.g., NSFH-34%; Updegraff et al., 2004-37%). Using information from the initial youth survey for selection analyses, eligible participating families were similar to eligible nonparticipating families on all study variables, suggesting minimal selection bias. (Contact corresponding author for statistical details from the multivariate and univariate analyses of variance.)

At wave 1 when youth were in the 6th grade (W1), they ranged in age from 11 to 14 ($M =$ 11.86, $SD = .69$). There were 211 daughters (51%). In terms of race, 91% of the families were European American and 3% were African American. This 3% is lower than the percentage of married African American couples with their own children younger than 18 in the county (5%) and in the United States (7.8%) (U.S. Census, 2000, Table PCT27 of SF4). The average level of parents' education in this sample was an associate's degree (2 years of college). Parents' educational attainment was similar to that of European American adults in the county who were older than 24 (county mean category was some college, no degree; U.S. Census, 2000, Table P148A of SF4). The median level of 2001 household income for families in this study was about $70,000, which was higher than the median income for married-couple families in the county ($64,689 inflation-adjusted dollars through 2001, U.S. Census, 2000, Table PCT40 of SF3).

To further demonstrate the utility of this sample for the present study, the distributions of marital hostility and adolescents' internalizing problems at W1 (6$^{th}$ grade) were compared to norms and national distributions. The prevalence of physical marital aggression in the present sample (6.7%) was comparable to rates found in the 1985 National Survey of Family Violence (NSFV; 3.4%) and 1994 National Survey of Families and Households (NSFH; 6.4%) (Straus & Gelles, 1986; Sweet & Bumpass, 2005). The amount of verbal aggression in the sample (78.4%) was comparable to that found in the 1985 NSFV (75%). Using the Child Behavior Checklist-YSR (Achenbach, 1991c), the percentage of youth in the present sample who scored in the clinical range on self-reported internalizing problems was 15% ($M$ raw score = 10.96, $SD$ = 7.62) which was comparable to that reported by Achenbach ($M$ raw score = 11.70, $SD$ = 7.8).

## Data Collection Procedures

Youth completed a questionnaire during school. They had as much time as needed to finish, and several trained assistants and the study director were available to answer questions. After completion, students were treated to a pizza party. Family members (i.e., mothers, fathers, youth) also were mailed a questionnaire and asked to complete it independently. The completed questionnaires were collected during a home visit. Parents and youth completed another brief questionnaire during the home visit. This second questionnaire contained the most sensitive information (e.g., marital hostility) and a researcher's presence ensured privacy.

As part of the longitudinal research design, assessments were conducted again a year later (W2), and two years later (W3). Most youth were in 7$^{th}$ grade at W2 (Mean age = 12.84, $SD$ = .68), and in 8$^{th}$ grade at W3 (Mean age = 13.83, $SD$ = .67). Data collection procedures were similar for each wave. Family members were mailed a questionnaire and asked to complete it independently.

The completed questionnaires were collected during a home visit. Parents and youth completed another questionnaire during the home visit. There were 366 participating families at W2 and 340 families at W3 (82% retention of W1 families). Attrition analyses using MANOVA were conducted using the W1 data and there were no differences between the retained and attrited families on any of the study variables. For example, we grouped variables into sets based on content and reporter, and analyzed the data using multivariate analysis of variance (MANOVA). Five MANOVAs were estimated that included variables for the present study, and none of the multivariate $F$s were statistically significant (.64 - 1.60). Thus, there was little evidence of attrition bias. Families were paid $100 for their participation in W1, $120 for W2, and $135 for W3.

## Measurement

*Youth social anxiety symptoms.* Youth social anxiety symptoms was a latent construct with two manifest variables. Youths' social anxiety symptoms were measured at each of the three waves using youth reports on questionnaire items taken from the fear of negative evaluation and social avoidance subscales of the Social Anxiety Scale for Children-Revised

(SASC-R; La Greca & Stone, 1993). For both subscales, youth indicated the frequency of social experiences using a 5-point response format (1 = *not at all* to 5 = *all the time).* A sample item from the fear of negative evaluation subscale was "I worry about what other kids think of me." A sample item from the social avoidance subscale was "I feel shy around kids I don't know." Cronbach's alpha for the fear of negative evaluation subscale in waves 1 through 3 was .90, .91, and .91, respectively. Cronbach's alpha for the social avoidance subscale was .81, .82, and .84, respectively.

*Child-related marital conflict.* Child-related marital conflict was a latent variable with two manifest indicators. *Childrearing disagreements* was measured using youth reports on seven questionnaire items that asked about the content of their parent's disagreements. Four items came from the content subscale of the Children's Perceptions of Interparental Conflict (CPIC; Grych et al., 1992). A sample item was "My parents' arguments are usually about something I did." Two items came from Ahron's (1983) interparental disagreements measure. We also asked youth "How many of the disagreements between your mom and dad have to do with you or one of the other children in your family?" Item responses were standardized and averaged; higher score represented more frequent disagreements. Cronbach's alpha was .78.

*Triangulation into parents' disputes* was measured using seven questionnaire items. Two items were adapted from the CPIC (Grych et al., 1992), and five items were used from the covert conflict scale developed by Buehler et al. (1998). A sample item was "When your mom and dad disagree, how often do they try to get you to side with one of them?" The response scale ranged from 1 (never) to 4 (very often). Items were averaged (α = .79), and higher scores represented greater triangulation. Evidence of construct validity in 13 samples across eight countries was provided by Bradford et al. (2004).

*Marital hostility.* Marital hostility was a latent variable with two manifest indicators: wife's report of her own behavior and of her spouse's behavior, and husband's report of his own behavior and of his spouse's behavior. The questionnaire measure was an 18-item measure of interparental hostility (Buehler, Benson, & Gerard, 2006). A sample item was "I tell my spouse to shut up." Items were averaged and higher scores represented greater marital hostility. The response format ranged from 1 (*never*) to 5 (*always*), and Cronbach's alpha was .90 for wife reports and .91 for husband reports.

*Parents' psychological intrusiveness.* Intrusiveness was a latent variable with two manifest indicators: youth and mother reports of mother's behavior toward the child, and youth and father reports of father's behavior toward the child. Youth completed 11 items that addressed psychological intrusiveness (eight from Barber, 1996 and three from Bogenschneider, Small, & Tsay, 1997) regarding each parent. Questions regarding mother and father were in separate sections of the questionnaire to minimize halo effects. A sample item was "My mom is always trying to change how I think or feel about things." The response format ranged from *not like her* (1) to *a lot like her* (4). Cronbach's alpha was .77 for W1 youth report of mother and .74 for youth report of father. Alphas at W2 (7th grade) were .81 and .83, respectively. Parents completed the same eleven items, rephrased to reflect their appraisals of their own behavior toward their child. Cronbach's alpha was .66 at W1 and .64 at W2 for the maternal report measure, and .65 at W1 and .69 at W2 for the paternal report measure. For the current study, youth and mother reports of mother's behavior were averaged within wave to measure mothers' psychological intrusiveness. Youth and father reports of father's behavior also were averaged within wave to measure fathers' psychological intrusiveness.

*Youth internalizing problems.* Parental reports of youths' internalizing problems during 6th grade were assessed using the Child Behavior Checklist (1991). Cronbach's alpha was .82 for mothers' reports of their child and .85 for fathers' reports. Mother's and fathers' reports were averaged to create the measure of parents' reports of the youths' internalizing problems during 6th grade. The summary score was used as a control variable in all analyses to adjust for selection and confounding effects.

## Analytic Procedures

Descriptive statistics were calculated using SPSS (version 20). Hypotheses were tested using structural equation modeling (AMOS, version 20). The first set of cross-sectional analyses focused on constructs measured at the beginning of adolescence (6th grade). The second set of prospective analyses employed predictors during 6th grade and youth's social anxiety during 8th grade. The third set of change-oriented analyses were based on predicting change in social anxiety scores across three waves of data collection during middle school - 6th, 7th, and 8th grades. This set of analyses began with estimating an unconditional growth curve (i.e., no predictors other than time) of youth social anxiety symptoms during early adolescence. The adequacy of each model was evaluated using the chi-square statistic and two fit indices. A nonsignificant chi-square indicated a good model fit. Because of the relatively large sample size, however, a significant chi-square was expected and two additional fit indices were examined (Byrne, 2001). The CFI ranges from 0 to 1.00 with a cutoff of .95 or higher indicating a well-fitting model and .90 indicating an adequate fit (Byrne, 2001; Hu & Bentler, 1999). Root mean square error of approximation (RMSEA) values below .05 indicate good model fit and values between .06 and .08 indicate an adequate fit (Browne & Cudeck, 1993; Byrne, 2001). The moderating effects of youths' gender were examined using multiple-group SEM. This was done by first estimating a model in which all of the parameters were constrained to be equal across the subsamples of sons and daughters. A second model was then estimated in which the structural parameter from the predictors to the social anxiety intercept and slope were allowed to vary across the two groups.

# Results

The means and standard deviations are shown in Table 1. The zero-order correlations between the various measures used in the structural equation models were in the expected directions and most were statistically significant.

## Family Factors and Youth Social Anxiety Symptoms – Concurrent Associations

The first analysis focused on the association between parents' child-related marital conflict and youths' social anxiety symptoms during 6th grade, controlling for marital hostility and youths' general internalizing problems (Figure 1).

**Table 1. Descriptive Statistics and Correlations Among Central Variables**

| Variables | 1 | 2 | 3 | 4 | 5 | 6 | 7 | 8 | 9 | 10 | 11 | 12 | 13 | 14 |
|---|---|---|---|---|---|---|---|---|---|---|---|---|---|---|
| Youth social anxiety | | | | | | | | | | | | | | |
| 1. Fear – 6th | - | | | | | | | | | | | | | |
| 2. Avoidance – 6th | **.71** | - | | | | | | | | | | | | |
| 3. Fear – 8th | **.42** | **.36** | - | | | | | | | | | | | |
| 4. Avoidance – 8th | **.38** | **.46** | **.77** | - | | | | | | | | | | |
| 5. Total SA – 6th | **.94** | **.91** | **.42** | **.45** | - | | | | | | | | | |
| 6. Total SA – 7th | **.50** | **.50** | **.47** | **.53** | **.54** | - | | | | | | | | |
| 7. Total SA – 8th | **.43** | **.46** | **.65** | **.66** | **.48** | **.59** | - | | | | | | | |
| Child-related marital conflict | | | | | | | | | | | | | | |
| 8. CR disagreement – 6th | **.26** | **.22** | **.16** | .11 | **.26** | **.10** | **.11** | - | | | | | | |
| 9. Triangulation – 6th | **.21** | **.21** | **.11** | **.12** | **.22** | **.13** | **.14** | **.49** | - | | | | | |
| Marital hostility | | | | | | | | | | | | | | |
| 10. MR mar. hostility – 6th | **.10** | .08 | .06 | .02 | **.10** | .08 | **.12** | **.23** | **.34** | - | | | | |
| 11. FR mar. hostility – 6th | .07 | .08 | .08 | .08 | .08 | **.11** | **.11** | **.16** | **.31** | **.60** | - | | | |
| Parental intrusiveness | | | | | | | | | | | | | | |
| 12. Mother intrusiveness – 6th | **.19** | **.19** | **.12** | **.15** | **.21** | **.16** | **.23** | **.37** | **.40** | **.23** | **.16** | - | | |
| 13. Father intrusiveness – 6th | **.20** | **.16** | **.16** | .11 | **.19** | **.12** | **.15** | **.33** | **.29** | **.22** | **.26** | **.44** | - | |
| 14. Youth internalizing problems– 6th | **.22** | **.19** | **.14** | **.15** | **.22** | **.27** | **.21** | **.17** | **.13** | **.17** | **.17** | **.27** | **.27** | - |
| M | 2.30 | 2.33 | 2.22 | 2.30 | 2.31 | 2.32 | 2.30 | -.10 | 1.42 | 1.74 | 1.75 | 1.33 | 1.29 | 6.66 |
| SD | .98 | .84 | 1.04 | .92 | .84 | .87 | .90 | .59 | .52 | .42 | .41 | .22 | .20 | 4.61 |
| Alphas | .90 | .81 | .91 | .84 | .91 | .87 | .88 | .78 | .79 | .90 | .91 | .72 | .70 | .83 |

*Note.* Fear = fear of negative evaluation; Avoidance = social avoidance; SA = social anxiety; CR disagreement was standardized; MR = mother report; FR = father report; mar. = marital. Bolded correlations are significant at $p < .05$.

The model fit was good ($\chi^2 = 11.26$, $df = 9$; CFI = .99; RMSEA = .025). The correlation between child-related marital conflict and marital hostility was .50, indicating 25% shared variance. These are related but distinct aspects of marital functioning. As hypothesized, child-related marital conflict was associated positively with youths' social anxiety symptoms. This association characterized both daughters and sons given the change in chi-square from the multiple-group analysis was not significant ($\Delta\chi^2 = 2.37$, $df = 3$, $p = .499$).

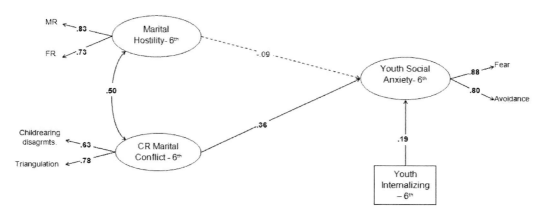

*Note.* MR = Mother report. FR = Father report. CR = Child-related. disagrmts = disagreements. Bolded estimates are significant at *p* < .05.

Figure 1.

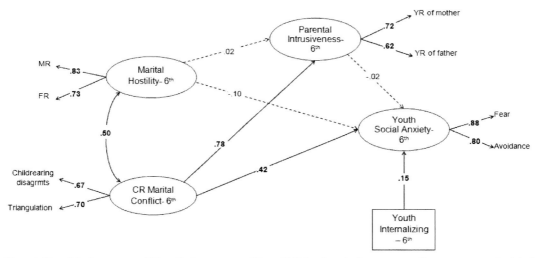

*Note.* MR = Mother report. FR = Father report. CR = Child-related. disagrmts = disagreements. Bolded estimates are significant at *p* < .05.

Figure 2.

The second concurrent analysis added parental intrusiveness as a linking mechanism (Figure 2). The model fit was good ($\chi^2$ = 43.13, *df* = 19; CFI = .97; RMSEA = .055). Child-related marital conflict was positively and strongly associated with parental intrusiveness during 6th grade. Intrusiveness, however, was not associated with youth social anxiety during 6th grade. Thus, at the beginning of adolescence, parental intrusiveness did not link child-related marital conflict and youths' social anxiety symptoms. Also note that the primary family predictor of youths' social anxiety symptoms at the beginning of adolescence was child-related marital conflict. These associations during 6th grade did not differ across daughters and sons ($\Delta\chi^2$ = 5.71, *df* = 6, *p* = .457).

## Family Factors (6<sup>th</sup> Grade) and Youth Social Anxiety Symptoms (8<sup>th</sup> Grade) – Prospective Associations

The first prospective analysis focused on the association between marital factors at the beginning of adolescence and youths' social anxiety symptoms two years later during 8<sup>th</sup> grade. The model fit was good ($\chi^2 = 23.61$, $df = 10$; CFI = .98; RMSEA = .057). Controlling for marital hostility and youths' general internalizing problems, child-related marital conflict during 6<sup>th</sup> grade was associated with higher levels of youths' social anxiety symptoms two years later during 8<sup>th</sup> grade (Figure 3).

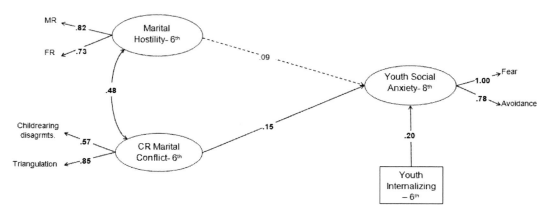

*Note.* MR = Mother report. FR = Father report. CR = Child-related. disagrmts = disagreements. Bolded estimates are significant at $p < .05$.

Figure 3.

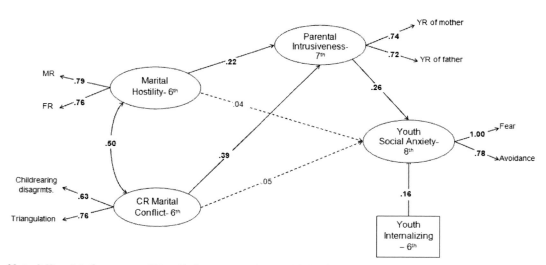

*Note.* MR = Mother report. FR = Father report. CR = Child-related. disagrmts = disagreements. Bolded estimates are significant at $p < 05$.

Figure 4.

This prospective model differed across daughters and sons ($\Delta\chi^2$ = 10.15, $df$ = 3, $p$ = .017). An inspection of the three critical ratio values indicated that the gender difference was in the path from youth internalizing problems in $6^{th}$ grade and social anxiety symptoms in $8^{th}$ grade (rather than in the paths involving the marital factors). Internalizing problems predicted later social anxiety symptoms for girls ($\beta$ = .26, $p$ < .001) but not for boys ($\beta$ = .10, $ns$).

As with the concurrent analyses, the second analysis added parental intrusiveness as a linking mechanism. In this analysis, intrusiveness during $7^{th}$ grade was included to ensure time ordering across the marital, parenting, and youth variables (Figure 4). The model fit was good ($\chi^2$ = 45.24, $df$ = 20; CFI = .97; RMSEA = .055). Both child-related marital conflict and marital hostility during $6^{th}$ grade were associated with greater levels of parental intrusiveness with their child during $7^{th}$ grade. Contrary to the findings at $6^{th}$ grade, parental intrusiveness at $7^{th}$ grade was linked with youths' social anxiety symptoms a year later during $8^{th}$ grade. Thus, parental intrusiveness during $7^{th}$ grade completely mediated the association between child-related marital conflict during $6^{th}$ grade and youths' social anxiety symptoms during $8^{th}$ grade. Including parental intrusiveness during $7^{th}$ grade also revealed the additional influence of marital hostility via the emerging significant, unique association ($\beta$ = .22, $p$ < .001). This model also differed across daughters and sons ($\Delta\chi^2$ = 14.12, $df$ = 6, $p$ = .028) because of the difference in the path from $6^{th}$ grade internalizing problems and $8^{th}$ grade social anxiety symptoms for girls and boys. The associations among marital factors, parental intrusiveness, and youth social anxiety symptoms did not differ for daughters and sons.

## Family Factors ($6^{th}$ Grade) and Changes in Youth Social Anxiety Symptoms

For these analyses, the fear of negative evaluation and social avoidance subscales were averaged into a single summary score. The first step in these analyses was to estimate the unconditional growth curve for youth social anxiety symptoms across middle school. The intercept was set at $6^{th}$ grade and the average symptom score was 2.32 (variable scaled from 1 to 5). Social anxiety symptoms, on average, were stable across early adolescence (linear slope = -.01, $p$ = .632). There were individual differences across youth in both the average symptoms in $6^{th}$ grade (variance = .37, $p$ < .001) and in the trajectories across time (variance = .04, $p$ = .027). These significant variance estimates allowed for the examination of predictors of these individual differences. Focusing first on the marital predictors, marital hostility was not uniquely associated with youth social anxiety symptoms at $6^{th}$ grade (i.e., intercept) or across time (i.e., linear slope). Child-related marital conflict during $6^{th}$ grade was a significant predictor (Figure 5). It was associated with higher levels of social anxiety symptoms during $6^{th}$ grade, but *decreases* in symptoms across time. The model fit was good ($\chi^2$ = 17.16, $df$ = 14; CFI = .99; RMSEA = .023). This model characterized both daughters and sons ($\Delta\chi^2$ = 9.73, $df$ = 6, $p$ = .136). In the last analysis, parental intrusiveness during $6^{th}$ grade also was included in the model (Figure 6). The model fit was good ($\chi^2$ = 25.12, $df$ = 24; CFI = .99; RMSEA = .011). Intrusiveness was not associated with changes in youths' social anxiety symptoms across time. This model differed for daughters and sons ($\Delta\chi^2$ = 16.31, $df$ = 8, $p$ = .038). One of the eight paths differed. Controlling for parental intrusiveness with the child, child-related marital conflict during $6^{th}$ grade was associated with daughters' social anxiety symptoms ($\beta$ = .88, $p$ < .001) but not sons' symptoms ($\beta$ = .05, $ns$).

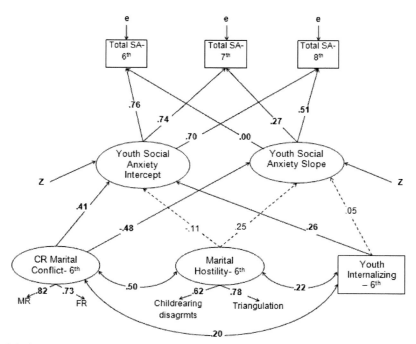

*Note.* MR = Mother report. FR = Father report. CR = Child-related disagrmts = disagreements. Bolded
estimates are significant at $p < 05$.

Figure 5.

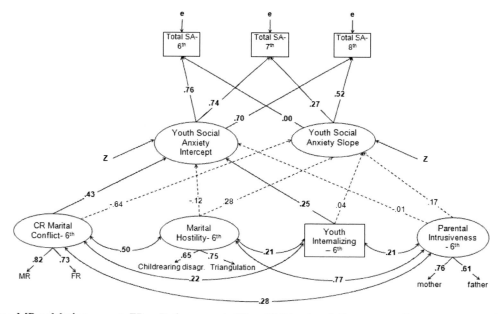

*Note.* MR = Mother report. FR = Father report. CR = Child-related disagrmts = disagreements. Bolded
estimates are significant at $p < 05$.

Figure 6.

## Summary of Results

Child-related marital conflict, parental intrusiveness with the child, and youths' social anxiety symptoms were interrelated at the beginning of adolescence. Child-related marital conflict was associated with higher levels of both intrusiveness and youth social anxiety symptoms. Intrusiveness was not uniquely associated with symptoms. These concurrent patterns of association were similar for daughters and sons.

Prospective associations differed from the concurrent associations. Both marital hostility and child-related marital conflict during $6^{th}$ grade were associated with greater parental intrusiveness with children during $7^{th}$ grade. Parental intrusiveness, in turn, was associated with greater social anxiety symptoms during $8^{th}$ grade. One of the few gender differences emerged in this analysis, with the positive association between youth internalizing problems during $6^{th}$ grade and social anxiety symptoms during $8^{th}$ grade characterizing only girls.

The change-oriented analyses of youth social anxiety symptoms highlighted the salience of child-related marital conflict. It was associated with greater symptoms during $6^{th}$ grade for daughters only and with decreases in social anxiety symptoms across time for both daughters and sons.

# Discussion

We examined youths' social anxiety symptoms during early adolescence from a developmental systems perspective. Four propositions from this theoretical orientation were utilized. First, youths' social anxiety symptoms were studied over time, given that a developmental perspective highlights the importance of both change and stability in particular developmental competencies. Second, youths' social anxiety symptoms were examined during early adolescence, a potentially critical developmental transition period (Hudson & Rapee, 2000). Third, the interdependence between social contexts was quantified by demonstrating associations between familial predictors and youths' social anxiety symptoms manifesting from interactions with peers and nonfamilial adults. Finally, the importance of distinguishing among subsystems was documented by showing unique influences from marital and parenting processes. We conceptualized youth social anxiety symptoms from a developmental perspective such that feelings of nervousness, insecurity, fear, and panic that precede or result from interaction with peers and nonfamilial adults impair the development of important social skills and social relationships.

The results from the study indicated that marital relationships and processes affect youths' feelings of social anxiety. We hypothesized that child-related marital conflict, in particular, would be associated with higher levels of youths' social anxiety symptoms during early adolescence. This hypothesis was supported, even with fairly stringent controls for marital hostility and youths' general internalizing problems. Child-related marital conflict was associated with children's concurrent feelings of social anxiety, as well as higher symptoms levels two years later. This finding replicates that by Cui et al. (2007) who studied youths' depressive symptoms during this developmental period, and extends the literature beyond a depressiogenic focus to include social fears. This finding also is particularly important because we controlled for general internalizing problems that included depressive symptoms, general anxiety, withdrawal, and somatic complaints.

The results also showed that child-related marital conflict is a unique risk factor for youth. Guided by previous research (Buehler & Welsh, 2009), marital hostility, conceptualized as verbal and physical aggression, was controlled for in analyses. This suggests that arguing about something having to do with children or involving children in disputes places them at risk for current and future feelings of social anxiety with peers and nonfamilial adults. This risk is separate and distinct from that incurred by witnessing verbal and physical aggression between parents. As such, child-related marital conflict is a unique and salient risk factor for children's development.

An implication of this finding is that practitioners need to work with parents regarding how to manage child-related conflict in ways that protect children. Important strategies may include teaching parents how to communicate with children regarding parents' responsibility for the disagreements, rather than blaming children, and how to use constructive problem solving techniques to process conflicts (Rueter & Conger, 1995). Another implication of this finding is that practitioners need to help parents learn how to manage familial boundaries so that they do not involve children in their conflicts and how to redirect children who initiate involvement in parents' disputes (Kerig & Swanson, 2010).

Child-related marital conflict also is a risk factor for youth because of its linkages with parental intrusiveness over time. Child-related marital conflict during $6^{th}$ grade was associated with intrusiveness with children during $7^{th}$ grade. Intrusiveness during $7^{th}$ grade (but not $6^{th}$ grade) was associated with higher youth social anxiety symptoms during $8^{th}$ grade. This cascade of associations during early adolescence is important for several reasons. First, it highlights the developmental nature of parental intrusiveness with children. Intrusiveness during $6^{th}$ grade, defined as parental behaviors that intrude upon and manipulate children's thoughts, feelings, and attachment to parents (Barber, 2002), was not associated with children's current or future social anxiety symptoms. Intrusiveness during $7^{th}$ grade, however, was associated with social anxiety symptoms during $8^{th}$ grade. Thus, these findings suggest a developmental window when children are between the ages of 12 and 14 in which parental intrusiveness can be particularly harmful. This is a developmental period in which children's social worlds are expanding and in which they are increasingly expected to have and desire greater independence from parents and family. This independence has both behavioral and psychological components, and is best nurtured through warm, consistent, and nonintrusive parenting (Steinberg, 2001). An implication of this finding for practitioners is that this period when children are between the ages of 12 and 14 may be a critical time to support parents as they attempt to communicate clearly with their children, stay emotionally connected to their children, and refrain from intruding upon children's psychosocial world through the use of manipulative, psychologically controlling tactics.

This process cascade of associations from child-related marital conflict to parental intrusiveness and then youths' social anxiety symptoms also is important because it may signify structuralized boundary violations within the family. These boundary violations place youth at risk for emotional and social difficulties. The structuralized, patterned nature of this cascade may suggest a need for second-order system changes. These changes are difficult to orchestrate because boundaries may be rather rigid and the family processes have served important functions over time that have been reinforced (Broderick, 1993). These changes also are difficult because the family processes constituting both child-related marital conflict and parental intrusiveness tend to be fairly indirect, covert, and passive-aggressive in nature (Stone et al., 2002). Covert family processes are often more difficult to change than overt family processes.

The cross-sectional and prospective findings highlight the risk features for children that accompany child-related marital conflict. The change-oriented, longitudinal findings suggest that child-related marital conflict may also offer children opportunities for growth. We found that controlling for the positive, concurrent association between child-related marital conflict and youths' social anxiety symptoms, conflict during 6th grade was associated with *declines* in youths' social anxiety symptoms during early adolescence. This was an unexpected finding, but follows a similar, unexpected pattern found in two studies of young children (Belsky et al., 1996; Davies et al., 2009 cited in Majdandzic et al., 2012). These studies found that unsupportive coparenting that may have included parents undermining one another was associated with lower levels of behavioral inhibition in very young children. The findings from our study indicated that experiencing child-related marital conflict may provide relational experiences that help children learn how to navigate boundary violations. These are important social skills during early adolescence when relational aggression increases among children that involves indirect tactics such as manipulating social relationships, gossiping, and exclusion (Crick, Nelson, Morales, Cullerton-Sen, Cases, & Hickman, 2001). This finding requires replication given this was the first study that examined changes *within children* in social anxiety symptoms across time.

Although parental intrusiveness was linked with higher youth social anxiety symptoms in the prospective analyses, the more consistent and robust findings associated with child-related marital conflict suggests that the emphasis on parental overcontrol as the primary family influence of children's social anxiety has been somewhat misguided. Our findings suggest that marital factors also are important, and may have stronger influences on youths' social anxiety than parenting factors. Future research and clinical interventions need to include important aspects of both marital and parental functioning.

In addition to highlighting the importance that family factors may play in shaping youths' social anxiety during early adolescence, we also found that general internalizing problems during 6th grade were associated with social anxiety symptoms during 8th grade, particularly for girls. This suggests that general problems with depression, anxiety, and behavioral inhibition during childhood may "select" children into social and relational difficulties during later developmental transitions. This pattern of children's developmental difficulties over time, particularly for girls, needs to be examined in greater detail in future research. This research should include related constructs that are useful during adolescence such as rejection sensitivity (London, Downey, Bonica, & Paltin, 2007) and relational aggression (Crick et al., 2001). Our understanding of these developmental patterns also would be strengthened by the inclusion of various aspects of youths' temperament during early childhood, so that early vulnerabilities or resiliency factors could be considered (Rubin, Burgess, & Hastings, 2002).

Although the findings from this study make innovative developmental and clinical contributions to the understanding of children's social anxiety during early adolescence, important limitations need to be considered. These family factors need to be studied within a broader context that includes risk and protective factors from additional domains, including youth, peer, and school (Gerard & Buehler, 2004). These patterns of family processes and youth development also need to be studied through a cultural lens, both within and outside of the U.S. (Bradford et al., 2004), because of the various cultural meanings attached to family processes and desired youths' social competencies during adolescence. These findings also are limited to the transitional period of early adolescence. Additional research is needed to determine whether similar processes characterize the transitional period of early adulthood.

# Conclusion

The study of social anxiety and phobia is important. We have added to the understanding of social anxiety by focusing on issues that are salient during early adolescence, a developmental period that marks the onset of social fears for many individuals. Family functioning, both marital processes and parenting, are associated with experiences of social anxiety during this developmental juncture. Child-related marital conflict, in particular, seems to be instrumental in two-parent families for shaping social anxiety in children. This deleterious influence on youths' social anxiety is important because this type of anxiety may increase difficulties in creating and maintaining valuable and needed social relationships with peers and nonfamilial adults.

# Acknowledgments

This research was supported by Grant R01-MH59248 from the National Institute of Mental Health to Cheryl Buehler. We thank the staff of the Family Life Project for their unending contributions to this work and the youth, parents, teachers, and school administrators who made this research possible.

# References

Achenbach, T. M. (1991). Integrative guide for the 1991 CBCL/4-18, YSR, and TRF profiles. Burlington, VT: University of Vermont, Department of Psychiatry.

Ahrons, C. R. (1983). Predictors of paternal involvement postdivorce: Mothers' and fathers' perceptions. *Journal of Divorce*, 6(3), 55-69. doi:10.1300/J279v06n03_05.

Barber, B. K. (1996). Parental psychological control: Revisiting a neglected construct. *Child Development*, 67, 3296-3319. doi: 10.2307/1131780.

Barber, B. K., Bean, R. L., & Erickson, L. D. (2002). Intrusive parenting: How psychological control affects children and adolescents. Washington, DC: American Psychological Association.

Barber, B. K., Olsen, J. E., & Shagle, S. C. (1994). Associations between parental psychological and behavioral control and youth internalized and externalized behaviors. *Child Development*, 65, 1120-1136. doi:10.2307/1131309.

Belsky, J., Putnam, S., & Crnic, K. (1996). Coparenting, parenting, and early emotional development. In J. P. McHale, P. A. Cowan (Eds.), Understanding how family-level dynamics affect children's development: Studies of two-parent families (pp. 45-55). San Francisco, CA: Jossey-Bass.

Benson, M. J., Buehler, C., & Gerard, J. M. (2008). Interparental hostility and early adolescent problem behavior: Spillover via maternal acceptance, harshness, inconsistency, and intrusiveness. *The Journal of Early Adolescence*, 28, 428-454. doi:10.1177/0272431608316602.

Bogenschneider, K., Small, S. A., & Tsay, J. C. (1997). Child, parent, and contextual influences on perceived parenting competence among parents of adolescents. *Journal of Marriage and the Family*, 59, 345-362. doi:10.2307/353475.

Bowen, M. (1978). Family therapy in clinical practice. New York, NY: Jason Aronson.

Bradford, K., Barber, B. K., Olsen, J. A., Maughan, S. L., Erickson, L. D., Ward, D., & Stolz, H. E. (2004). A multi-national study of interparental conflict, parenting, and adolescent functioning: South Africa, Bangladesh, China, India, Bosnia, Germany, Palestine, Colombia, and the United States. *Marriage & Family Review*, 35, 107-137. doi:10.1300/J002v35n03_07.

Broderick, C. B. (1993). Understanding family process: Basics of family systems theory. Thousand Oaks, CA: Sage Publications, Inc.

Browne, M. W., & Cudeck, R. (1993). Alternative ways of assessing model fit. In K. A. Bollen & J. S. Long (Eds.), Testing structural equation models (pp. 136-162). Newbury Park, CA: Sage.

Bruch, M. A., & Heimberg, R. G. (1994). Differences in perceptions of parental and personal characteristics between generalized and nongeneralized social phobics. *Journal of Anxiety Disorders*, 8, 155-168. doi:10.1016/0887-6185(94)90013-2.

Buehler, C., Benson, M., & Gerard, J. M. (2006). Interparental hostility and early adolescent problem behavior: The mediating role of specific aspects of parenting. *Journal of Research on Adolescence*, 16, 265-292.

Buehler, C., Franck, K. L., & Cook, E. C. (2009). Adolescents' triangulation in marital conflict and peer relations. *Journal of Research on Adolescence*, 19, 669-689. doi:10.1111/j.1532-7795.2009.00616.x.

Buehler, C., Krishnakumar, A., Stone, G., Anthony, C., Pemberton, S., Gerard, J., & Barber, B. K. (1998). Interparental conflict styles and youth problem behaviors: A two-sample replication study. *Journal of Marriage and the Family*, 60, 119-132. doi:10.2307/353446.

Buehler, C., & Welsh, D. P. (2009). A process model of adolescents' triangulation into parents' marital conflict: The role of emotional reactivity. *Journal of Family Psychology*, 23, 167-180. doi:10.1037/a0014976.

Byrne, B. M. (2001). Structural equation modeling with AMOS: Basic concepts, applications, and programming. Mahwah, NJ: Lawrence Erlbaum.

Chronis-Tuscano, A., Degnan, K., Pine, D. S., Perez-Edgar, K., Henderson, H. A., Diaz, Y., & ... Fox, N. A. (2009). Stable early maternal report of behavioral inhibition predicts lifetime social anxiety disorder in adolescence. *Journal of the American Academy of Child & Adolescent Psychiatry*, 48, 928-935. doi:10.1097/CHI.0b013e3181ae09df.

Clarke-Stewart, A., & Dunn, J. (2006). Families count: Effects on child and adolescent development. New York, NY: Cambridge University Press.

Conger, K., Conger, R. D., & Scaramella, L. V. (1997). Parents, siblings, psychological control, and adolescent adjustment. *Journal of Adolescent Research*, 12, 113-138. doi:10.1177/0743554897121007.

Crick, N. R., Nelson, D. A., Morales, J. R., Cullerton-Sen, C., Casas, J. F., & Hickman, S. E. (2001). Relational victimization in childhood and adolescence: I hurt you through the grapevine. In J. Juvonen, S. Graham (Eds.), Peer harassment in school: The plight of the vulnerable and victimized (pp. 196-214). New York, NY: Guilford Press.

Cui, M., Donnellan, M., & Conger, R. D. (2007). Reciprocal influences between parents' marital problems and adolescent internalizing and externalizing behavior. *Developmental Psychology*, 43, 1544-1552. doi:10.1037/0012-1649.43.6.1544.

Cummings, E., Davies, P. T., & Campbell, S. B. (2000). Developmental psychopathology and family process: Theory, research, and clinical implications. New York, NY: Guilford Press.

Davies, P. T., & Cummings, E. (1994). Marital conflict and child adjustment: An emotional security hypothesis. *Psychological Bulletin*, 116, 387-411. doi:10.1037/0033-2909.116.3.387.

Davies, P. T., & Lindsay, L. L. (2004). Interparental conflict and adolescent adjustment: Why does gender moderate early adolescent vulnerability? *Journal of Family Psychology*, 18, 160-170. doi:10.1037/0893-3200.18.1.160.

Davis, E. F., Schoppe-Sullivan, S. J., Mangelsdorf, S. C., & Brown, G. L. (2009). The role of infant temperament in stability and change in coparenting across the first year of life. *Parenting: Science and Practice*, 9, 143-159. doi:10.1080/15295190802656836.

Engels, R. E., Deković, M., & Meeus, W. (2002). Parenting practices, social skills and peer relationships in adolescence. *Social Behavior and Personality*, 30, 3-18. doi:10.2224/sbp.2002.30.1.3.

Englund, M. M., Levy, A. K., Hyson, D. M., & Sroufe, L. (2000). Adolescent social competence: Effectiveness in a group setting. *Child Development*, 71, 1049-1060. doi:10.1111/1467-8624.00208.

Gerard, J. M., & Buehler, C. (2004). Cumulative environmental risk and youth maladjustment: The role of youth attributes. *Child Development*, 75, 1832-1849. doi:10.1111/j.1467-8624.2004.00820.x.

Grych, J. H., & Fincham, F. D. (1990). Marital conflict and children's adjustment: A cognitive-contextual framework. *Psychological Bulletin*, 108, 267-290. doi:10.1037/0033-2909.108.2.267.

Grych, J. H., & Fincham, F. D. (1993). Children's appraisals of marital conflict: Initial investigations of the cognitive-contextual framework. *Child Development*, 64, 215-230. doi:10.2307/1131447.

Grych, J. H., Seid, M., & Fincham, F. D. (1992). Assessing marital conflict from the child's perspective: The Children's Perception of Interparental Conflict Scale. *Child Development*, 63, 558-572. doi:10.2307/1131346.

Hu, L. T., & Bentler, P. M. (1995). Evaluating model fit. In R. H. Hoyle (Ed.), Structural equation modeling: Concepts, issues, and applications (pp. 76-99). Thousand Oaks, CA: Sage.

Hudson, J. L., & Rapee, R. M. (2000). The origins of social phobia. *Behavior Modification*, 24, 102-129. doi:10.1177/0145445500241006.

Kerig, P. K., & Swanson, J. A. (2010). Ties that bind: Triangulation, boundary dissolution, and the effects of interparental conflict on child development. In M. S. Schulz, M. Pruett, P. K. Kerig, R. D. Parke (Eds.), Strengthening couple relationships for optimal child development: Lessons from research and intervention (pp. 59-76). Washington, DC: American Psychological Association. doi:10.1037/12058-005.

Kouros, C. D., Cummings, E., & Davies, P. T. (2010). Early trajectories of interparental conflict and externalizing problems as predictors of social competence in preadolescence. *Development and Psychopathology*, 22, 527-537. doi:10.1017/S0954579410000258.

Krishnakumar, A., Buehler, C., Barber, B. K. (2003). Youth perceptions of interparental conflict, ineffective parenting, and youth problem behaviors in European-American and African- American families. *Journal of Social and Personal Relationships*, 20, 239-260. doi:10.1177/02654075030202007.

La Greca, A. M., & Stone, W. L. (1993). Social anxiety scale for children—revised: Factor structure and concurrent validity. *Journal of Clinical Child Psychology*, 22, 17-27. doi:10.1207/s15374424jccp2201_2.

Lerner, R. M., Theokas, C., & Bobek, D. L. (2005). Concepts and theories in human development: Historical and contemporary dimensions. In M. H. Bornstein & M. E. Lamb (Eds.), Developmental science: An advanced textbook (5th ed.) (pp. 3-43). Mahwah, NJ: Lawrence Erlbaum..

Lewis-Morrarty, E., Degnan, K. A., Chronis-Tuscano, A., Rubin, K. H., Cheah, C. L., Pine, D. S., & ... Fox, N. A. (2012). Maternal over-control moderates the association between early childhood behavioral inhibition and adolescent social anxiety symptoms. *Journal of Abnormal Child Psychology*, 40, 1363-1373. doi:10.1007/s10802-012-9663-2.

Lieb, R., Wittchen, H., Höfler, M., Fuetsch, M., Stein, M. B., & Merikangas, K. R. (2000). Parental psychopathology, parenting styles, and the risk of social phobia in offspring: A prospective-longitudinal community study. *Archives of General Psychiatry*, 57, 859-866. doi:10.1001/archpsyc.57.9.859.

London, B., Downey, G., Bonica, C., & Paltin, I. (2007). Social causes and consequences of rejection sensitivity. *Journal of Research on Adolescence*, 17, 481-506. doi:10.1111/j.1532-7795.2007.00531.x.

Loukas, A. (2009). Examining temporal associations between perceived maternal psychological control and early adolescent internalizing problems. *Journal of Abnormal Child Psychology*, 37, 1113-1122. doi:10.1007/s10802-009-9335-z.

Majdandžić, M., de Vente, W., Feinberg, M. E., Aktar, E., & Bögels, S. M. (2012). Bidirectional associations between coparenting relations and family member anxiety: A review and conceptual model. *Clinical Child and Family Psychology Review*, 15, 28-42. doi:10.1007/s10567-011-0103-6.

McLeod, B. D., Wood, J. J., Weisz, J. R. (2007). Examining the association between parenting and childhood anxiety: A meta-analysis. *Clinical Psychological Review*, 27, 155-172. doi:10.1016/j.cpr.2006.09.002.

Minuchin, P. (1985). Families and individual development: Provocations from the field of family therapy. *Child Development*, 56, 289–302. doi:10.2307/1129720.

Pettit, G. S., Laird, R. D., Dodge, K. A., Bates, J.E., & Criss, M. M. (2001). Antecedents and behavior problem outcomes of parental monitoring and psychological control in early adolescence. *Child Development*, 72, 583-598. doi:10.1111/1467-8624.00298.

Rubin, K. H., Burgess, K. B., & Hastings, P. D. (2002). Stability and social-behavioral consequences of toddlers' inhibited temperament and parenting behaviors. *Child Development*, 73, 483-495. doi:10.1111/1467-8624.00419.

Rueter, M. A., & Conger, R. D. (1995). Antecedents of parent–adolescent disagreements. *Journal of Marriage and the Family*, 57, 435-448. doi:10.2307/353697.

Rogers, K. N., Buchanan, C. M., & Winchel, M. E. (2003). Psychological control during early adolescence: Links to adjustment in differing parent/adolescent dyads. *The Journal of Early Adolescence*, 23, 349-383. doi:10.1177/0272431603258344.

Schaefer, E. S. (1965). Children's reports of parental behavior: An inventory. *Child Development*, 36, 413-424. doi:10.2307/1126465.

Siegel, R. S., La Greca, A. M., & Harrison, H. M. (2009). Peer victimization and social anxiety in adolescents: Prospective and reciprocal relationships. *Journal of Youth and Adolescence*, 38, 1096-1109. doi:10.1007/s10964-009-9392-1.

Smetana, J. G., Campione-Barr, N., & Metzger, A. (2006). Adolescent development in interpersonal and societal contexts. *Annual Review of Psychology*, 57, 255-284. doi: 10.1146/annurev.psych.57.102904.190124.

Steinberg, L. (1990). Autonomy, conflict, and harmony in the family relationship. In S. Feldman, G. R. Elliott (Eds.), At the threshold: The developing adolescent (pp. 255-276). Cambridge, MA US: Harvard University Press.

Steinberg, L. (2001). We know some things: Parent–adolescent relationships in retrospect and prospect. *Journal of Research on Adolescence*, 11, 1-19. doi:10.1111/1532-7795.00001.

Stone, G., Buehler, C., & Barber, B. K. (2002). Interparental conflict, parental psychological control, and youth problem behavior. In B. K. Barber (Ed.), Intrusive parenting: How psychological control affects children and adolescents (pp. 53-95). Washington, DC: American Psychological Association. doi:10.1037/10422-003.

Straus, M. A., & Gelles, R. J. (1986). Societal change and change in family violence from 1975 to 1985 as revealed by two national surveys. *Journal of Marriage and the Family*, 48, 465-479. doi:10.2307/35203t.

Sweet, J., & Bumpass, L. (2005). National Survey of Families and Households. http: //www.ssc.wisc.edu/nsfh/.

Teubert, D., & Pinquart, M. (2010). The association between coparenting and child adjustment: A meta-analysis. *Parenting: Science and Practice*, 10, 286-307. doi:10.1080 /15295192.2010.492040.

Updegraff, K. A., Helms, H. M., McHale, S. M., Crouter, A. C., Thayer, S. M., & Sales, L. H. (2004). Who's the boss? Patterns of perceived control in adolescents' friendships. *Journal of Youth and Adolescence*, 33, 403-420. doi:10.1023/B:JOYO.0000037633.39422.b0.

U.S. Census Bureau. (2000a). PCT27. Family type by presence of own children under 18 years of age. Families (total), White alone, Black alone [Summary file 4]. Retrieved September 29, 2004, from http://factfinder.census.gov.

U.S. Census Bureau. (2000b). P155A. Median family income in 1999 (dollars) (White alone) [Summary file 3]. Retrieved September 29, 2004, from http://factfinder.census.gov.

U.S. Census Bureau. (2000c). P148A. Sex by educational attainment for the population 25 years and over (White alone) [Summary file 4]. Retrieved September 29, 2004, from http://factfinder.census.gov.

Wijsbroek, S. A. M., Hale, W. W., Raaijmakers, Q. A. W., & Meeus, W. H. (2011). The direction of effects between perceived parental behavioral control and psychological control and adolescents' self-reported GAD and SAD symptoms. *European Child and Adolescent Psychiatry*, 20, 361-371. doi:10.1007/s00787-011-0183-3.

In: Social Anxiety
Editor: Efrosini Kalyva

ISBN: 978-1-62808-396-5
© 2013 Nova Science Publishers, Inc.

*Chapter V*

# The Role of Family Factors in Social Anxiety: A Review of Empirical Findings and Implications for Treatment

*Ourania Founta*\*

Doctorate in Clinical Psychology, Master in Systemic and Family Psychotherapy,
Postgraduate Diploma in Clinical Supervision, Ireland

## Abstract

Social anxiety is a complex phenomenon and thus multiple pathways and factors are associated with its development. An increasing amount of evidence suggests associations between family factors and anxiety disorders, including social anxiety. This article reviews the existing literature on the role of parental child-rearing styles, parental psychopathology, family process and functioning in social anxiety. Preliminary findings from family cognitive behavioural treatment for anxiety disorders, including social anxiety, indicates that family involvement needs to be considered in the treatment of children with social anxiety.

**Keywords**: Social anxiety, social phobia, parenting, family functioning, family process, family cognitive behavioral treatment

## Definition, Diagnostic and Cultural Issues

Social anxiety disorder or social phobia is characterized by a 'marked and persistent fear of one or more social or performance situations in which the person is exposed to unfamiliar people or to possible scrutiny by others.

---

\* Email: fountao@tcd.ie.

The avoidance, anxious anticipation, or distress in the feared social or performance situation(s), interferes significantly with the person's normal routine' (APA, 2000, p.486). Generalized social phobia is characterised by extreme fear and avoidance of a broad range of social situations whereas in the specific social phobia the fear and avoidance occur in a particular context (e.g. public speaking) (Morris, 2001). The generalised sybtype is associated with greater severity than the specific phobia (Turner, Beidel, & Townsely, 1992). However, Rapee and Spence (2004) indicated that there is no consensus among researchers whether social phobia has the above distinct subtypes or not since some studies have not confirmed this distinction (e.g., Stein, Torgrud, & Walker., 2000).

Social anxiety is 'an almost universal phenomenon' since most people have occasionally experienced discomfort in a social situation (Morris, 2001). Results from community surveys (Stein et al., 2000, p.1046) indicated that social phobia is not a qualitative distinctive category but it rather 'exists on a continuum of severity with a greater number of feared situations associated with greater disability'. Rapee & Spence (2004) proposed that at the lower end of the continuum lies lack and normal levels of social anxiety followed by low levels of shyness, social fears and avoidance while at the upper end of the continuum is a marked fear of a broad range of social situations and extreme social withdrawal.

Rapee and Spence (2004) drew our attention to the cultural context within which social phobia is been conceptualized; they indicated that in non-western societies social anxiety may be expressed in different ways or that the threshold for social anxiety may be higher in these societies that externalizing disorders are constructed as more problematic than internalizing ones.

# Epidemiology, Onset, Course and Comorbidity

Lifetime prevalence estimates in western societies range from 7 to 13% (Furmark, 2002). It has been reported that social phobia is the third most common psychiatric problem in US (Kessler et al., 1994). Studies have shown that the average onset of social phobia is between early to mid adolescence (Amies, Gelder, & Shaw, 1983; Turner, Biedel, Dancu, & Keys, 1986). Social phobia, if untreated, can be lifelong, remitting and can get progressively worse (de Boer, 2000; Morris, 2001). Social phobia has been associated with suicide attempts, impaired social support and social interaction, poor employment and school performance, lower quality of life and higher service utilisation (Acarturk, de Graaf, van Straten, ten Have, & Cuijpers, 2008; Davidson, Hughes, George, & Blazer,1993). High levels of comorbidity have been reported (Morris, 2001); in particular, social anxiety disorder can co-occur with other anxiety disorders, substance alcohol misuse and affective disorders (de Boer, 2000). Social anxiety disorder can precede co-morbid disorders such as depression (Stein, Tancer, Gelernter, Vittone, & Uhde, 1990) and it has been reported that comorbid disorders began after the onset of social anxiety in 77% of the cases (Schneier, Johnson, Hornig, Liebowitz, & Weissman, 1992). Given the onset, course of social anxiety disorder and potential impact on an individual's psychological, academic and occupational functioning, identification of risk factors for the development and maintenance of social phobia as well as early intervention are required.

# Etiological Frameworks

The etiology of social anxiety remains largely unknown (Lieb et al., 2000). Ginsburg et al. (1995) underscored that anxiety disorders are complex phenomena; these disorders are multifaceted since they involve maladaptive individual processes (i.e. avoidant behavior, cognitive distortions and subjective distress) and are multidetermined since a variety of contexts (i.e. school, peer, family) can exacerbate or maintain them. Over the last decade, a number of researchers/authors have reviewed etiological factors and proposed etiological models for the development and maintenance of social anxiety disorder (Elisabeth et al., 2006; Hudson & Rapee, 2000; Morris, 2001; Rapee, 1997; Rapee & Spence, 2004). Similarly to Ginsburg et al. (1995) postulation, these researchers/theorists have suggested that there are multiple pathways and factors associated with the development and course of social anxiety. In their reviews and proposed models, the origin of social anxiety is associated with multiple factors: a) genetic factors (Fyer,1993; Kendler, Neale, Kessler, Heath, & Eaves, 1992), b) temperament (e.g. behavioral inhibition; Biederman et al., 2001; Kagan, Reznick, & Snidman, 1987), c) insecure attachment (Warren, Huston, Egeland, & Sroufe,1997) and parent/child interactions (Bruch, Heimberg, Berger, & Collins,1989; Hudson & Rapee, 2004), d) peer relationships (La Greca & Lopez, 1998) and averse social experiences (Wild, Hackmann, & Clark, 2008) e) negative life events such as sexual abuse (Magee,1999), physical abuse, marital conflict and parental psychopathology (Chartier, Walker, & Stein, 2001) including father's alcoholism, parental divorce or separation (Kessler, Davis, & Kendler, 1997), child illness (Hudson & Rapee, 2000) f) social skills deficits (Beidel, Turner, & Morris, 1999; Spence, Donovan, & Brechman-Toussaint, 1999) and g) information processing/cognitive biases (Hirsch & Clark, 2004). Rapee and Spence (2004) argued that multifinality and equifinality are constructs that can apply to an explanatory model for the development of social anxiety; this is due to the fact that only few risk factors can be specific to social anxiety and it is likely that a combination of specific risk and/or nonspecific factors contributes to the onset of social anxiety disorder.

Unfortunately, there is 'no well-articulated integrative theory of the role of the family and the socialization process in the etiology of anxiety' (Carr, 1999, p.433). Carr (1999) speculated that family transitions and family stresses can precede the onset of an anxiety disorder. He postulated that family beliefs systems can promote threat interpretation biases and maladaptive family interactions can elicit, model and reinforce anxiety-related behaviors. For instance, family members' may accommodate social avoidance behavior by accepting it as a coping strategy and modifying family routines to accompany the child to the social fearful situation; however family accommodation and its role in social phobia is underresearched (Benito & Freeman, 2011). Carr (1999) also hypothesized that in some cases a child's anxiety problem may distract their parents from addressing other serious difficulties such as marital problems and alcohol abuse. There is a lack of research from a systemic perspective on the role of family context in the development of social phobia and the impact of social phobia on the family system. For instance, it may be interesting to explore how family functioning, family member's and cultural beliefs are associated with social phobia. Most research reviewed in this paper stems from a linear epistemology whereby specific parental characteristics are associated with social phobia in children. In more recent years, researches have acknowledged the reciprocal influence of parent/child interactions on social anxiety (Rapee & Spence, 2004),but nevertheless this model focused on interactions within a dyad (mother and child or father and child) as opposed within the family as a whole.

The next sections focus on the role of family factors as portrayed in the existing literature.

# Family Factors

The first experience of socialization occurs within the family. Most individuals develop their social phobia in their early to mid adolescence which means that their family can still exert significant influence (Bogel et al., 2001). For at least these two reasons, Bogel et al. (2001) suggested that we consider the role of family factors in the development of social phobia.

Furthermore, Daniels and Plomin (1985) in an adoption study found that environmental and genetic factors can potentially contribute to the development of social anxiety. Mother's perceptions of their own levels of shyness and participation in social activities were significantly associated with their infant's shyness regardless of whether their infants grew up with them or in adoptive homes. Socially anxious children perceived their family environment as lacking cohesion and participation in social activities.

Stark et al. (1990) investigated the family functioning of 51 school children. They found that children with anxiety and depression disorders perceived their families as less democratic, less engaged in social and recreational activities, less cohesive, less supportive and more conflictual and enmeshed in comparison with nonanxious and nondepressed children. Interestingly, the mothers of anxious children perceived their family functioning in a more positive way compared with mothers of children without anxiety and depressive disorders. Hughes et al. (2008) investigated the family functioning of children with anxiety disorders, including social phobia. They found that worse family functioning was associated with worse child outcomes including anxiety disorder severity and global child functioning. Maternal and paternal anxiety and depression had adverse effects on family functioning. B oth parents of anxious children indicated worse family functioning and behavioural control, while fathers of anxious children reported significantly less affective involvement and worse problem solving skills compared to controls.

Crawford and Manasis (2001) explored familial factors affecting child treatment outcomes for anxiety disorders including social phobia; they found that family dysfunction, father's own somatic complaints and children's perception of paternal frustration were familial factors associated with worse child treatment outcomes. Ginsburg et al. (1995) postulated that parental anxiety, overcontrol, family conflict, poor family communication and problem-solving factors, lack of family cohesion, support and participation in outdoors activities can negatively influence treatment outcomes for anxiety.

# Role of Parenting

A dominant discourse emerging within the theoretical (e.g. Chorpita & Barlow, 1998) and empirical literature (e.g. Wood, McLeod, & Sigman, 2003) supports the view that there is an association between parenting and child anxiety disorders. Hudson & Rapee (2000) hypothesized that parental rearing styles, parental modeling of evaluative concerns and lack of exposure to social activities can contribute to the development of social phobia.

Reviews on the role of parenting in the development and maintenance of child anxiety disorders (McLeod, Wood, & Weisz, 1997; Rapee, 1997) have primarily identified parental overcontrol and parental rejection as factors associated with childhood anxiety. Parental modeling of anxious behavior is also linked to child anxiety (Wood et al., 2003).

# Parental Control and Parental Rejection

Parental control encompasses overprotective, restrictive behaviors which intrusively govern children activities and routines and prohibit autonomy and dependence. It is hypothesized that these parenting behaviors can potentially limit the children's exposure to new and challenging situations affecting their self-efficacy and therefore maintaining or increasing their anxiety (Chorpita & Barlow, 1998). McLeod et al. (1997) in a meta-analysis of relevant studies, including studies of social anxiety, overall found a modest association between parenting behavior and child anxiety; specifically parental control had a medium effect size (0.25) on child anxiety whereas autonomy-granting had a large effect (0.42). It is suggested that individuals with social phobia tend to experience their parents as more controlling and rejecting compared to those with panic disorder (Rapee, 1997). Rapee and Melville (1997) have found that adults with social phobia experienced their mothers as highly controlling and their fathers as engaged in less socially activities compared with controls. Bogel and Perroti (2011) have emphasized paternal influence on social anxiety. Fathers' controlling behavior during an origami task was associated with higher levels of social anxiety in 10-14 years old children; the researchers suggested that fathers' overinvolvement not only disrupted the children problem solving, but subsequently may have communicated a lack of trust on children's competencies (Greco & Morris, 2002). In another experimental study, Krohne and Hock (1991) observed that mothers of anxious children were highly controlling during a puzzle task. Hudson and Rapee (2001) investigated the relationship between rearing styles and anxiety utilizing observations of parent-child interactions during two cognitive tasks. Mothers of anxious children, including those of children with social phobia, were overinvolved and negative in their interactions compared to mothers of non-clinical groups; however mothers of oppositional children were also more intrusive in their interactions, which questions the hypothesis that parental overinvolvement is a specific pathway to social anxiety.

Rork and Morris (2009) in an observational study found that maternal overprotection was associated with children's social anxiety, while parental warmth was not associated with social anxiety. Reports on social activity were not associated with social anxiety. Maternal negative commands were strongly associated with social anxiety for boys.

Another observational study of parental child-interaction showed that parents of socially anxious children tend to use fewer verbalizations, less positive and more negative feedback compared to control group parents; the socially anxious children communicated to their parents in a similar way; the researchers hypothesized that the reinforcement of unpleasant interactions between the parents and the socially anxious children may result in children's avoidance of social interactions (Hummel & Gross, 2001). Bogel et al. (2001) hypothesized that children subjected to negative evaluations by their parents might develop a sensitivity to other's opinions and become socially anxious. Similarly, Bruch (1989) suggested that parental rejection may instill preoccupation with other's judgements which can lead to a gerenalized fear of negative evaluation and avoidance of social situations.

Bogel et al. (2006) suggested that the combination of parental control and lack of warmth can maintain anxiety. Hudson and Rapee (2000) hypothesized that overprotective parents may indirectly communicate to their children that the world is dangerous and they cannot manage to protect themselves without their parents involvement; this may instill a sense of inability to exert control over the environment. Chorpita et al. (1998) support the idea that parental overprotection can diminish the child's sense of control over events and contribute to the development of anxiety.

In a prospective longitudinal (2 year follow up) community study (Lieb et al., 2000), social phobia in adolescents was associated with parental overprotection and rejection. Knappe et al. (2009) replicated and expanded this study using a larger sample of adolescents whom they prospectively followed up over 10 years; they found that parental rearing styles of overprotection, rejection and lack of emotional warmth were risk factors for the development of offspring's social phobia.

Knapee et al. (2012) investigated separately the contributions of fathers' and mothers' parenting styles to offspring social phobia; they found that specifically maternal overprotection and paternal rejection and lack of emotional warmth was associated with offspring social phobia; paternal lack of emotional warmth affected more daughters while maternal overprotection affected similarly sons and daughters. Furthermore, they found that maternal overprotection and lower paternal warmth was associated with natal complications; they suggested that natal complications can elicit mother's overprotective behaviors, as they perceive their children as vulnerable, and father's limited emotional warmth in response to a closer mother/child dyad.

It is hypothesized that parental overprotection and lack of emotional warmth may limit children opportunities for social interactions and acquiring of social skills (Rapee & Spence, 2004). Knapee et al. (2010) suggested that lack of exposure to social situations may perpetuate social anxiety as children do not access information that can potentially challenge their anxiety provoking beliefs. They also speculated that parents of anxious children may become overinvolved in order to reduce their children's distress which may reinforce children's perceptions of the world as dangerous and uncontrollable; this can also foster threat sensitivity, increase dependence on parents and hamper autonomy.

In an experimental study (Taylor & Alden, 2006), adults with social phobia who perceived their parents as overprotective were less responsive to their partner's friendly behavior during an experiment which resulted in social rejection. Previous research has shown that socially anxious individuals can provoke negative responses by others (Meleshko & Alden, 1993) who view them as different from them due to their limited self-disclosure and overt signs of anxiety (Papsdorf & Alden, 1998). This can reinforce their negative expectations of social interactions and social avoidance perpertuating their social anxiety (Clarks & Wells, 1995). Taylor and Alden (2006) assumed that early experiences of parental overprotection may negatively influence the interpersonal behavior of people with social phobia and reinforce their social anxiety. Bogel et al. (2001) suggested that the association between parental practices and social anxiety found in retrospective studies can be influenced by interpretation and memory bias. In their cross-sectional study, they found limited evidence for the role of parental rearing styles in the development of social anxiety. Socially anxious children perceived their mothers as overprotective, while their mothers did not report overprotection. Although socially anxious children perceived their parents as more rejective and less emotionally warm in comparison to normal children, no differences were found between social anxious children and clinical control children. The researchers assumed that parental rejection and lack of emotional warmth are not specifically related to social anxiety but may be a feature in families of children with psychopathology. Furthermore, there were no significant differences reported between the mothers of socially anxious, clinical control and normal children in parental rejection, emotional warmth and overprotection.

# Modeling

It is suggested that parents can foster children anxiety through modeling of fearful or avoidant behavior or through encouraging threat interpretations (Bogel et al., 2003). Barrett et al. (1996) in an observational study found that children with anxiety disorders, including social phobia, increased their avoidance plans to a hypothetical ambiguous threat situation after family discussions. Chorpita et al. (1996) found that anxious children interpret ambiguous situations as threatening significantly more than controls and the likelihood of avoidance plans increases after family discussions. Bogels et al. (2003) found an association between parental fear, parental threat interpretation bias and children's threat interpretation bias. However, their findings did not support the hypothesis that parents can influence their children threat interpretation bias; in the contrary children interpretations of ambiguous situations were more positive following family discussions. The researchers speculated that the procedure of their experimental may have had an 'unintended effect'; by first asking the parents to consider how any child would react to the hypothetical ambiguous situations they have possible 'activated functional schemata' that have helped them afterwards in the discussion to influence their child in a positive way.

Knapee at al. (2010) argued that research indicate that key features of social phobia such as information processing bias, threat sensitivity and avoidance behavior are more likely to be transmitted through parental cognitive styles than parental rearing practices. Lester et al. (2009) have found that anxious parents interpret ambiguous situations as threatening not only in their own environment but also in their child's environment. In another study (Gifford, Reynolds, Bell, & Wilson, 2008) although mother's anxiety and child's anxiety were correlated, mother's interpretation biases and children's interpretation bias were not associated; surprisingly mother's threat interpretation was not related to their own levels of anxiety but to their child levels of anxiety and their child information biases were related to maternal anxiety. The researchers concluded that there are subtle dyadic influences between information processing and anxiety. Therefore, they argued that exposure to maternal threat interpretations may contribute to child anxiety even if parental anxiety is not present (Gifford et al., 2008).

Rapee and Melville (1997) have found that adults with social phobia experienced their mothers as highly controlling and as engaged in less social activities compared with controls; their mothers acknowledged greater control over socialization compared with mothers of the nonclinical group. Caster et al. (1999) found that socially anxious adolescents experienced their parents as being socially isolated, excessively concerned of other's opinions, ashamed of their shyness and poor performance and participating in less social activities compared to controls. In contrary, their parents' perception of the family environment and parental behaviors did not differ in comparison to parents of nonsocially anxious adolescents. These findings collaborate with previous research in which socially anxious adults recalled their parents as low in socialization and emphasizing the opinion of others (Bruch & Heimberg, 1994; Bruch et al., 1989). In Bogel's et al. (2001) cross-sectional study, the lack of family sociability, based on both parents and children's reports was related to social anxiety; however, no significant differences were found between the socially anxious and clinical control group, suggesting that the lack of family sociability is not a specific pathway to social anxiety but may characterize families of children with psychopathology. Interestingly, the parents of socially anxious children emphasized less the opinions of others than the parents of normal and clinical control group which contradicts previous findings. This could reflect social desirability bias or the parents efforts to compensate for the socially anxious children's evaluative concerns (Bogels, van Oosten, Muris, & Smuldes, 2001).

In an experimental study (Bogel, Stevens, & Majdandzic, 2010) children aged 9-11 were presented with scenarios of ambiguous social situations while their mother or father acted in a socially anxious manner or appeared socially confident. Interestingly, the father's responses significantly impacted on high socially anxious children's social anxiety and confidence. Murray et al. (2008) investigated the responses to a stranger of infants of socially phobic mothers compared to those of non-socially phobic mothers over a period of time (10 and 14 months old); they found that infants' avoidance of a stranger was predicted by mother's display of anxiety and lack of encouragement to interact with the stranger. This was in particular the case when the infants were behaviorally inhibited.

# Factors Associated with Parenting Style/Reciprocal Influence between Parent-Child Interaction

It is hypothesized that children temperament such as behavioral inhibition can elicit parental overprotection which in turn can reinforce children's social withdrawal (Rubin, Nelson, Hastings, & Asendorpf,1999). In their longitudinal study, Rubin et al. (1999) investigated the relationship between children's social fearfulness and parental beliefs about how to socialize their children. Fathers and mothers moderately agreed on their beliefs regarding their children's social wariness and their perceptions did not overall change over time. Parents who perceived their children as shy and socially fearful at age 2 were less likely to encourage their children to be independent at age 4; in contrary, children's behavioral inhibition at age 2 did not predict parental encouragement of independence at age 4. Thus, the researchers concluded that parental beliefs regarding their child's social wariness influences parental rearing style rather than the other way round.

According to Mills and Rubin (1990) parental beliefs about children's social behavior can govern the ways they foster their children's social competency and behavior. They postulated that environmental and individual factor such as social support and parental psychopathology can influence parents' perceptions and practices.

Hudson and Rapee (2002) in an observational study found that during a task mothers were overinvolved and more intrusive in their interactions with both their anxious children and their nonanxious siblings compared to controls while no differences were observed for fathers. These results may indicate that mothers' overinvolvement can be a stable parental trait occurring independently of children's anxiety. Hudson et al. (2008) in an observational study examined the cyclical interaction of children's anxiety and intrusive parental involvement. They found that mothers of children with anxiety disorder were more overinvolved in situations where their children displayed negative affect (anxiety and anger) compared to mothers of non-anxious children. Anxious mothers tended to be more intrusive in situations where their children showed anxiety and anger as opposed to situations where the children showed happiness. In contrary, nonanxious mothers were more intrusive in situations where their children showed anger. The researchers postulated that anxious mothers may have difficulty tolerating negative emotions and thus their overinvolvement occurs in specific situations in which their child experiences negative emotions. Interestingly, fathers of anxious children showed less warmth compared to fathers of non anxious children regardless of whether their children displayed positive or negative affect.

Woodruff-Borden et al. (2002) explored the interaction of anxious parents with their children and found that anxious parents appeared more withdrawn and disengaged from difficult tasks with their children than nonanxious parents. They researchers speculated that due to their own levels of distress anxious parents may not assist their children during stressful /demanding situations, which may somewhat inhibit children's learning to cope with stressors. Whaley et al. (1999) investigated the pathways for anxiety transmission by observing parent-child interactions. They found that anxious mothers were more critical, less autonomy granting, less emotionally supportive and catastrophized more in their interactions with their children in comparison to non-anxious mothers. Maternal anxiety was associated with lack of emotional warmth. Interestingly, maternal behaviors were more strongly related to child anxiety than parental anxiety. However, the most interesting findings of this study is that there were no significant differences in granting autonomy between anxious mothers with nonanxious children and nonanxious mothers with nonanxious children. In contrary, anxious mothers with nonanxious children were more autonomy granting than anxious mothers with anxious children. Thus, it appears that lower levels of granting autonomy are more evident when both mother and child are experiencing anxiety, suggesting that anxiety perhaps emerges in the pattern of their interaction.

Coparenting support refers to the extent that parents acknowledge and respect each other's parental competencies, parental decisions and parental authority and act as team (Bonds & Dawn, 2007). Bonds and Dawn (2007) found that positive marital relationship increased the level of coparenting support which in turn increased maternal warmth.

# Parental Psychopathology

Lieb et al (2010) suggested that children of parents with social phobia can be prone for developing social phobia themselves; they also found that other parental anxiety disorders, depression and parental alcohol disorders can be risk factors for social phobia in adolescents. Their findings were also confirmed in another longitudinal study; the risk for the development of offspring's social phobia increased if parents presented with psychopathology, were perceived as overprotective, rejecting and lacking of emotional warmth (Knappe, Lieb, Beesdo, Fehn, Low, & Gloster, 2009). However, the association between social phobia and the above parenting styles was independent of parental psychopathology. Knapee et al. (2012) indicated that the origins of parental overprotection, rejection and lack of emotional warmth remain unclear since parental psychopathology does not influence the relationship between rearing styles and offspring social phobia.

Lindhout et al. (2006) found significant differences in parenting rearing style between anxiety disordered parents and controls based on parent and children reports. Specifically, parents with anxiety disorders perceive their parenting style as less nurturing and more restrictive than parents without anxiety disorders; however, their children did not perceive them as more rejecting and less emotionally supportive than children of control parents; parental overprotection was the only distinctive feature between anxiety disordered parents and controls based on children reports.

# Evidence for Family Cognitive-Behavioral Therapy (CBT) treatment

Another source of evidence regarding the role of family factors in the development/maintenance of social phobia stems from research exploring the effectiveness of parental involvement in child treatment outcomes. A number of research studies have explored the effectiveness of family cognitive behavioral therapy versus individual child cognitive behavioral therapy for children with anxiety disorders. The results are mixed with some studies demonstrating the superiority of the family cognitive behavioral therapy (e.g. Barrett, Dadds, & Rapee1996) and other studies (e.g. Nauta, Scholing, Emmelkamp, Minderaa, 2003) suggesting that there are no added benefits of family cognitive behavioral therapy compared to child focused CBT (Creswell & Cartwright-Hatton, 2007; Podell & Kendal, 2010). Most of these studies have included in their samples children with a range of anxiety disorders (e.g. separation anxiety disorder, gereralized anxiety disorder, social phobia) in the same study with the exception of one study (Spence et al. 2000) which focused only on children with social phobia (Ginburg & Schlossberg, 2002). The discrepancy in the findings may be due to methodological differences of the studies including type of outcome measures, level of parental attendance and involvement, presence of parental anxiety and content as well as format of the family cognitive behavioral interventions (Podell & Kendal, 2010). In addition, some studies are conducted in university settings with no-comorbid problems reported and others in mental health settings where anxious children have also comorbit psychopathology.

In their metaanalytic review of family cognitive behavioral therapy for children with anxiety disorders, Creswell and Cartwright-Hatton (2007) concluded that this treatment seems superior to individual cognitive behavioral therapy for children with anxious parents and when the type of outcome measure is diagnostic status. However, they noted that it is less clear whether gender or age of children can moderate the efficacy of family cognitive behavioral therapy due to methodological limitations of relevant research studies (i.e. low statistical power).

Podell and Kendall (2011) investigated the relationship between parental attendance and engagement in family cognitive behavioral therapy for children with anxiety disorders including social phobia, parental psychopathology and children treatment outcome. The family cognitive behavior therapy program included 16 weekly, approximately 1 hour, sessions and it was based on a manualised family version (Howard et al.,2000) of the Coping Cat Program for anxious children (Kendall& Hedtke 2006). The fathers and mother participated as co-clients in the program. Thus, the family aspect of the program aims to challenge maladaptive parental beliefs and expectations, educate parents to use adaptive responses to their children anxiety, to support their children to master their anxiety and communicate effectively with their children. Fathers and mother's attendance and engagement in the sessions improved child treatment outcomes. Parental psychopathology was not associated with child outcomes and did not affect parental participation in the treatment. Kendall et al. (2008) in a randomised trial investigated the efficacy of individual cognitive behavior therapy, family cognitive behavior therapy and family education/support active control for children aged 7-14 with anxiety disorders including social phobia. Similarly to Podell and Kendall (2011) study, the family cognitive behavior therapy program required active participation of parents who were encouraged to use the skills learned to manage their own levels of anxiety. Therapeutic improvement was evident in all treatment conditions and gains were maintained at 1 year follow up. Individual child cognitive therapy was superior to family cognitive behavior therapy and family support/education active control based on teacher's reports on children anxiety. However, family cognitive behavior therapy was superior to the other treatment conditions when both fathers and mothers suffered from anxiety.

Wood et al. (2006) found that family cognitive behavior therapy was superior to individual cognitive behavioral therapy for youth aged 6-13 (n=42) with anxiety disorders including social phobia. The family cognitive behavior therapy program lasted over 12-16 sessions, depending on clients needs. It included exposure tasks and rewards and parents' education. Parent training targeted problematic family relational patterns and particularly intrusiveness and dependency. Parents were taught to foster their children's autonomy and self-efficacy by giving them choices, allowing them to learn from their own mistakes rather than take over and by naming and validating their emotions rather than criticizing them. They were also taught to reward their children target behaviors and to ignore behaviors that maintain their children's anxiety (i.e. reassurance seeking behaviors).

Bogel and Siqueland (2006) evaluated a family cognitive therapy program in a specialist community mental health setting. Children with anxiety disorders, including social phobia, their parents and their siblings participated in family cognitive behavior therapy; the program consisted of several stages: initial assessment and systemic formulation; at the first session the whole family discusses with the therapist their understanding of the problem and ways of overcoming it.

The treatment is then offered in 3 stages: a) didactic CBT skills sessions with the parents and child and one with the child alone targeting dysfunctional beliefs, using in vivo exposure tasks and rewards; parents are taught to help their children cope with anxiety as well as to manage their own levels of anxiety implementing CBT techniques b) parental sessions challenging their dysfuntional beliefs about the child and parenting and individual session with the child targeting maladaptive beliefs regarding their communication with their parents. They found significant improvements in children anxiety, threat interpretation in ambiguous situations, fears and dysfunctional beliefs; large improvements were observed in parental dysfunctional beliefs about children's anxiety and parental roles; only parents reported some changes in their parental rearing styles, particularly overprotection, psychological control and rejection; on the other hand, even if children did not report changes in their parental rearing style they reported improvements in family functioning. Therapeutic gains sustained over time and further improvements were noted at 1 year follow up; father's anxiety levels were significantly reduced at follow up.

The mechanisms of these changes were not investigated; however, the researchers indicated that improvement in child's anxiety may be related to changes in a) parents' dysfunctional beliefs and roles b) father's anxiety and/or c) parental skills in helping their child mastering anxiety.

Short et al. (2001) in a randomized trial investigated the efficacy of a family cognitive behavioral therapy program (FRIENDS) for children aged 6-10 and presenting with social phobia, separation and generalized anxiety disorder.

The program is tailored to the developmental needs of the children and is delivered in a group format. It combines attentional training for children's anxiety, peer support, cognitive behavioral strategies and parental training, which focuses on partner-support, problem solving/communication skills, cognitive restructuring and building social support networks. Parents are taught how to manage their own anxiety and are encouraged to reinforce their children adaptive coping strategies and to practice the skills regularly at home. The program consists of 10 sessions and two booster sessions at 1 month and 3 months following the completion of the program. The researchers found that 69% of children who completed the family cognitive behavioral program were diagnosis free compared to 6% of children on the waiting list condition and that the therapeutic gains were sustained one year later.

Cobbam et al. (1998) investigated whether parental anxiety management as an adjunct to child CBT can enhance the effectiveness of childhood focused CBT treatment for anxiety, including social phobia. Children were assigned to individual CBT and to individual CBT plus parental anxiety management treatment based on pre-treatment levels of parental anxiety. The family cognitive behavior program consisted of 10 CBT sessions and four parental anxiety management sessions. The 10 CBT sessions were identical to the individual child CBT and the parental anxiety management focused on psychoeducation about childhood anxiety and the role of the family, cognitive restructuring, relaxation and contingency management. Results from the study indicated that at short term parental anxiety management enhanced child treatment outcomes, but the gains were not sustained over 6 months and 12 months time. The researchers postulated that longer sessions for parental anxiety management may be needed; they also hypothesized that the lack of attendance of some anxious parents to the program may have influenced the results.

Spence et al. (2000) investigated the effectiveness of a social skills based cognitive behavioral program with and without parental participation for children with social phobia aged 7 to 14 years.

The integrated CBT program was delivered by psychologists and entailed 12 weeks group sessions and booster sessions at 3 months and 6 months following the completion of the program. It consisted of social skills and social problem solving training, exposure, relaxation and cognitive restructuring skills and positive self-instruction. Parental training focused on contingency management and modeling of socially proactive behaviors. Parents were prompted to encourage their children's social interactions and their application of therapy skills outside the sessions. They found that CBT with and without parental involvement was effective in reducing children's general and social anxiety compared to a waiting list condition. The improvements were maintained at 12 months follow up. Although parental involvement somewhat enhanced children 's treatment outcomes, the effect was not statistically significant. However, this may be due to the small size sample and problems of power.

Barrett et al. (1996) evaluated the effectiveness of family cognitive behavioral program for children aged 7-14 with social phobia, separation anxiety and overanxious disorder. The family behavioral program combined CBT components with parental training and was delivered over a period of 12 weeks. Parental training focused on contingency management, parental anxiety management as well as problem solving and communication skills. Results indicated that at 12 months follow up 95.6% of children allocated to the family cognitive behavioral program did not any longer meet criteria for anxiety disorder compared to 70.3% of children who completed only the CBT intervention.

The family cognitive behavioral program enhanced children's treatment outcomes across anxiety groups (i.e. social phobia, separation and general anxiety) and improvements were sustained over time. Interestingly, younger children (7 to 10 years) and females were more likely to benefit from the adjunctive to CBT family program. Barrett et al. (1998) further explored whether group family cognitive behavioral program can produce similar results to the above study. They found that both group cognitive behavioral and group cognitive behavioral plus family management program were more effective compared to the waiting list control groups and as effective as the individual intervention in Barrett et al. (1996) previous study at posttreatment and at 1 year follow up.

There was a trend for a marginal improvement in children on the group family cognitive behavioral program compared to those on the group cognitive behavioral condition. Similarly, de Groot et al. (2007) found that children with anxiety disorders, including social phobia, benefited greatly from participating in family cognitive behavioral treatment regardless of whether this was delivered in an individual or a group format. Silverman et al. (1999) reported that group cognitive behavioral therapy combined with parental sessions was effective in reducing children anxiety symptoms including social phobia. Parental sessions focused on psychoeducation, contingency management and on facilitating their children's exposure.

Nauta et al. (2003) investigated whether parent cognitive training can augment child focused CBT for children (aged 7-18) with anxiety disorders including social phobia. The study recruited children from general practitioners as well as mental health centers and included children with co-morbid problems. The parent cognitive training was delivered in 7 sessions and focused on parental thoughts, feelings and behaviors regarding their anxious children. It incorporated psychoeducation on child anxiety, behavioral advice, 'pragmatic parenting skills' and problem solving skills; parents were encouraged to promote coping behaviors and autonomy of their children while providing them with support. Children with anxiety disorders showed improvement following CBT treatment compared to wait list control. However, there were no additional benefits from the parent cognitive training. In the absence of measures/data on parental cognitions, it was not possible to ascertain whether the parents changed their cognitions, but this did not impact on child anxiety or whether the intervention was successful in changing parents' cognitions.

Bodden et al. (2008) in a study with clinically referred anxious children, found that child focused CBT was more beneficial than family cognitive behavior therapy at postreatment but this effect was no longer significant at follow up. The family CBT aimed to promote child's autonomy and included parental anxiety management and addressed parental dysfunctional beliefs about parenting and the anxious child as well as dysfunctional interactional communication patterns within the family. Parental anxiety was associated with less favorable treatment outcomes for both conditions. Surprisingly, on certain measures child focused CBT was more beneficial for children with anxious parents whereas family CBT was superior when parents did not present with anxiety disorders.

## Summary/Conclusion

Although the etiology of social phobia remains largely unknown, research suggests that the family environment can influence the development and maintenance of social phobia. In particular, parental psychopathology, parenting rearing styles, parenting modeling of social anxiety and low family sociability can be contributing factors to the development of social phobia. Preliminary research evidence suggests that family cognitive behavioral intervention can be effective for children with anxiety disorders and with social phobia.

The majority of these studies have not investigated the mechanisms of change and they did not incorporate outcome measures of family functioning, parental skills, behaviors and cognitions, which can potentially influence child anxiety. More studies are needed to focus exclusively on children with social phobia; these can explore variables that can influence treatment outcomes such as parental social phobia, format and content of intervention; interventions need to target specific family /parental factors associated with the maintenance of social phobia and relevant research needs to explore the mechanisms of therapeutic gains/changes.

## References

Acarturk, C., de Graaf, R., van Straten, A., ten Have, M., & Cuijpers, P. (1998). Social phobia and number of social fears, and their association with comorbidity, health-related quality of life and help seeking. A population-based study. *Social Psychiatry and Psychiatric Epidemiology,* 43, 273-279.

Amiens, P. L., Gelder, M. G., & Shaw, P. M. (1983). Social phobia: a comparative clinical study. *British Journal of Psychiatry,* 142, 174-179.

Barrett, P. M. (1998). Evaluation of cognitive-behavioral group treatments for childhood anxiety disorders. *Journal of Clinical Child Psychology,* 27, 459–468.

Barrett, P. M., Dadds, M. R., & Rapee, R. M. (1996). Family treatment of childhood anxiety: a controlled trial. *Journal of Consulting and Clinical Psychology,* 64, 332-342.

Barrett, P. M., Rapee, R. M., Dadds, M. M., & Ryan, S. M. (1996). Family enhancement of cognitive style in anxious and aggressive children. The FEAR effect. *Journal of Abnormal Child Psychology, 24,* 187–203.

Beidel., D.C., Turner, S. M., & Morris, T. L. (1999). The psychopathology of social phobia. *Journal of the American Academy of Child and Adolescent Psychiatry, 38,* 643-650.

Benito, K. G., & Freeman, J. (2011). Parental anxiety: how family accommodation may hinder treatment. *The Brown University Child and Adolescent Behavior Letter, 27,* 1-7.

Biederman, L., Hirshfeld-Becker, D. R., Rosenbaum, J. F., Herot, C., Friedman, D., Snidman, N., Kagan, J., & Faraone, S. V. (2001). Further evidence of an association between behavioral inhibition and social anxiety in children. *American Journal of Psychiatry, 158,* 1673-1679.

Bodden, D. H. M., Bögels, S. M., Nauta, M. H., De Haan, E., Ringrose, J., Appelboom, C., & Appelboom-Geerts, K. C. M. M. J. (2008). Child versus family cognitive-behavioral therapy in clinically anxious youth: An efficacy and partial effectiveness study. *Journal of the American Academy of Child & Adolescent Psychiatry, 47,* 1384 –1394.

Bogels, S. M., & Brechman-Toussaint, M. L. (2006). Family issues in child anxiety: attachment, family functioning, parental rearing and beliefs. *Clinical Psychology Review, 26,* 834-856.

Bogels, S. M., & Siqueland, L. (2006). Family cognitive behavioral therapy for children and adolescents with clinical anxiety disorders. *Journal of the American Academy of child and adolescent psychiatry, 45,* 134–141.

Bogels, S. M., Stevens, J., & Majdandzic, M. (2010). Parenting and social anxiety: fathers' versus mothers' influence on their children's anxiety in ambiguous social situations. *Clinical Psychology and Psychiatry, 52,* 599-606.

Bogels, S. M., & Perotti, E. C. (2011). Does Father Know Best? A Formal Model of the Paternal Influence on Childhood Social Anxiety. *Journal; of Child and Family Studies, 20,* 171–181.

Bogels, S. M., van Dongen, L., & Muris, P. (2003). Family influences on dysfunctional thinking in anxious children. *Infant and Child Development, 12,* 243-252.

Bogels, S. M., van Oosten, A., Muris, P., & Smuldres, D. (2001). Familial correlates of social anxiety in children and adolescents. *Behavior Research and Therapy, 39,* 273-287.

Bonds, D. D., & Gondoli, D. M. (2007). Examining the process by which marital adjustment affects maternal warmth: the role of coparenting support as a mediator. *Journal of Family Psychology, 21,* 288-296.

Bruch, M. A., & Heimberg, R. G. (1994). Differences in perceptions of parental and personal characteristics between generalized and nongeneralized social phobics. *Journal of Anxiety Disorders, 8,* 155–168.

Bruch, M. A., Heimberg, R. G., Berger, P., & Collins, T. M. (1989). Social phobia and perceptions of early parental and personal characteristics. *Anxiety Research, 2,* 57–65.

Carr, A. (1999). The handbook of child and adolescent clinical psychology: A contextual approach. London: Routledge.

Caster, J. B., Inderbitzen, H. M., & Hope, D. (1999). Relationship between youth and parent perceptions of family environment and social anxiety. *Journal of Anxiety Disorders, 13,* 237-251.

Chartier, M. J., Walker, J. R., & Stein, M. B. (2001). Social phobia and potential childhood risk factors in a community sample. *Psychological Medicine, 31,* 307–315.

Chorpita, B. F., Albano, A. M., & Barlow, D. H. (1996). Cognitive processing in children: Relationship to anxiety and family influences. *Journal of Clinical Child Psychology,* 25, 170–176.

Chorpita, B. F., and Barlow, D. H. (1998). The development of anxiety: the role of control in the early environment. *Psychological Bulletin,* 124, 3–21.

Clark, D. M., & Wells, A. (1995). A cognitive model of social phobia. In R. Heimberg, M. Liebowitz, D. Hope, & F. Schneier (Eds.), Social phobia, (pp. 69–93). New York: Guildford Press.

Cobham, V. E., Dadds, M. R., & Spence, S. H. (1998). The role of parental anxiety in the treatment of childhood anxiety. *Journal of Consulting and Clinical Psychology,* 66, 893–905.

Crawford, A. M., & Manassis, K. (2001). Familial predictors of treatment outcome in childhood anxiety disorders. *Journal of the American Academy of Child & Adolescent Psychiatry,* 40, 1182–1189.

Creswell, C., & Cartwright-Hatton, S. (2007). Family treatment of child anxiety:outcomes, limitations, and future directions. *Clinical Child and Family Psychology,* 10, 232–252.

Daniels, D., & Plomin, R. (1985). Origins of individual differences in infant shyness. *Developmental Psychology,* 21, 118–121.

Davidson, J. R., Hughes, D. L., George, L. K., & Blazer, D. G. (1993). The epidemiology of social phobia: Findings from the Duke Epidemiological Catchment Area Study. *Psychological Medicine,* 23, 709-718.

De Boer, J. A. (2000). Social anxiety disorder/social phobia: epidemiology, diagnosis, neurobiology, and treatment, *Comprehension Psychiatry,* 41, 405-415.

De Groot, J., Cobham, V., Leong, J., & McDermo, B. (2007). Individual versus group family focused cognitive behavior therapy for childhood anxiety: pilot randomized controlled trial. *Australian and New Zealand Journal of Psychiatry,* 41, 990-997.

Elizabeth, J., King, N., Ollendick, T. H., Gullone, E., Tonge, B., Watson, S., & Macdermott, S. (2006). Social anxiety disorder in children and youth: a research update on aetiological factors. *Counselling Psychology Quarterly,* 19, 151-163.

Fyer, A. J. (1993). Heritability of social anxiety: A brief review. *Journal of Clinical Psychiatry,* 54(12, Suppl), 10–12.

Furmark, T. (2002). Social phobia: overview of community surveys. *Acta Psychiatrica Scandinavica,* 105, 84–93.

Ginsburg, G., Silverman, W. K., & Kurtines, W. K. (1995). Family involvement in treating children with phobic and anxiety disorders: a look ahead. *Clinical Psychology Review,* 15, 457-473.

Gifford, S., Reynolds, S., Bell, S., & Wilson, C. (2008). Threat interpretation bias in anxious children and their mothers. *Cognition and emotion,* 22, 497-508.

Ginsburg, G. S., & Schlossberg, M. C. (2002). Family-based treatment of childhood anxiety disorders. *International Review of Psychiatry,* 14, 143−154.

Greco, A., & Morris, T. (2002). Parental child-rearing style and child social anxiety: Investigation of child perceptions and actual father behavior. *Journal of Psychopathology and Behavioral Assessment,* 24, 259–267.

Howard, B., Chu, B.C., Krain, A.L., Marrs-Garcia, M.A., & Kendall, P.C. (2000). Cognitive-behavioral family therapy for anxious children: Therapist manual (2nd ed.). Ardmore, PA: Workbook Publishing.

Hirsch, C., Clark, D. M. (2004). Information-processing bias in social phobia. *Clinical Psychology Review,* 24, 799-825.

Hudson, J. L., Comer, J. S., & Kendall, P. C. (2008). Parental responses to positive and negative emotions in anxious and nonanxious children. *Journal of Clinical Child & Adolescent Psychology,* 37, 303–313.

Hudson, J. L., & Rapee, R. M. (2000). The origins of social phobia. *Behavior Modification,* 24, 102-129.

Hudson, J. L., & Rapee, R. M. (2001). Parent-child interactions and anxiety disorders: an observational study. *Behavior Research and Therapy,* 39, 1411-1427.

Hudson, J. L., & Rapee, R. M. (2002). Parent-child interactions in clinically anxious children and their siblings. *Journal of Clinical Child and Adolescent Psychology,* 31, 548-555.

Hughes, A.A, Hedtke, K. A., & Kendall, P. C. (2008). Family functioning in families of children with anxiety disorders. *Journal of Family Psychology,* 22, 12-19.

Hummel, R. M., & Gross, A. M. (2001). Socially anxious children: An observational study of parent–child interactions. *Child and Family Behavior Therapy,* 23, 19–41.

Kagan, J., Reznick, J. S., & Snidman, N. (1987). The physiology and psychology of behavioral inhibition in children. *Child Development,* 58, 1459-1473.

Kendall, P. C., & Hedtke, K. A. (2006). Cognitive-behavioral therapy for anxious children: Therapist manual and workbook (3rded.). Ardmore, PA: Workbook.

Kendall, P. C., Hudson, J. L., Gosch, E., Flannery-Schroeder, E., & Suveg, C. (2008). Cognitive-behavioral therapy for anxiety disordered youth: a randomized clinical trail evaluating child and family modalities. *Journal of Consulting and Clinical Psychology,* 76, 282–297.

Kendler, K. S., Neale, M. C., Kessler, R. C., Heath, A. C., & Eaves, L. J. (1992). The genetic epidemiology of phobias in women: The interrelationship of agoraphobia, social phobia, situational phobia, and simple phobia. *Archives of General Psychiatry,* 49, 273–281.

Kessler, R. C., Chiu, W. T., Demler, O., & Walters, E. E. (2005). Prevalence, severity and comorbidity of 12-month DSM-IV Disorders in the National Comorbidity Survey Replication. *Archives of General Psychiatry,* 62, 617-627.

Kessler, R. C., Davis, C. G., & Kendler, K. S. (1997). Childhood adversity and adult psychiatric disorder in the US National Comorbidity Survey. *Psychological Medicine,* 27, 1101–1119.

Kessler, R. C., McGonagle, K. A., Zhao, S., Nelson, C. B., Hughes, M., Eshleman, S., Wittchen, H. U, & Kendler, K. S. (1994). Lifetime and 12-month prevalence of DSM-III-R psychiatric disorders in the United States. Results from the National Comorbidity Survey. *Archives of General Psychiatry,* 51, 8-9.

Knappe, S., Beesdo-Baum, K., Fehm, L., Lieb, R., Wittchen, H.-U. (2012). Characterizing the association between parenting and adolescent social phobia. *Journal of Anxiety Disorders,* 26, 608-616.

Knappe, S., Beesdo-Baum, K., & Wittchen, H.-U. (2010). Familial risk factors in social anxiety disorder: calling for a family-oriented approach for targeted prevention and early intervention. *European Child and Adolescent Psychiatry,* 19, 857–871.

Knappe, S., Lieb, R., Beesdo, K., Fehm, L., Low, N. C. P., & Gloster, A. T. (2009). The role of parental psychopathology and family environment for social phobia in the first three decades of life. *Depression and Anxiety,* 26, 363–370.

Krohne, H. W., & Hock, M. (1991). Relationships between restrictive mother-child interactions and anxiety of the child. *Anxiety Research, Journal of Clinical Child Psychology,* 17, 84-91.

La Greca, A. M., & Lopez (1998). Social anxiety among adolescents: linkages with peer relationships and friendships. *Journal of Abnormal Child Psychology,* 26, 83-94.

Lester, K. J., Fields, A. P., Oliver, S., & Cartwright-Hatton, S. (2009). Do anxious parents interpretive biases towards threat extend into their child's environment? *Behavior Research and Therapy,* 47, 170-174.

Lieb, R., Wittchen, H. R., Hofler, M., Fuetsch, M, Nat, M. R., Stein, M. B., Merikangas, K. R. (2000). Parental psychopathology, parenting styles, and the risk of social phobia in offspring: a prospective longitudinal community study. *Archives of General Psychiatry,* 57, 859-866.

Lindhout, I., Markus, M., Hoogendijk, T., Borst, S., Maingay, R., Spinhoven P, van Dyck, R., & Boer, F. (2006) . Childrearing style of anxiety-disordered parents. *Child Psychiatry and Human Development,* 37, 89–102.

Magee, W. J. (1999). Effects of negative life experiences on phobia onset. *Social Psychiatry and Psychiatric Epidemiology,* 34, 343–351.

McLeod, B. D., Wood, J. J., & Weisz, J. R. (2007). Examining the association between parenting and childhood anxiety: A meta-analysis. *Clinical Psychology Review,* 27, 155–172.

Meleshko, K. G. A., & Alden, L. E. (1993). Anxiety and self-disclosure: Toward a motivational model. *Journal of Personality and Social Psychology,* 64, 1000–1009.

Mills, R. S. L., & Rubin, K. H. (1990). Parental beliefs about problematic social behaviors in early childhood. *Child Development,* 61, 138–151.

Morris, T. L. (2001). Social Phobia. In M. W. Vasey, & M. R. Dadds (Eds.) *The development of social anxiety* (pp.435-450). New York: Oxford University Press.

Murray, L., de Rosnay, M., Pearson, J., Bergeron, C., Schofield, L., Royal-Lawson, M., & Cooper, P. J. (2008). Intergenerational transmission of social anxiety: The role of social referencing processes in infancy. *Child Development,* 79, 1049 –1064.

Nauta, M., Scholing, A., Emmelkamp, P., & Minderaa, R. (2003). Cognitive-behavioral therapy for children with anxiety disorders in a clinical setting: No additional effect of a cognitive parent training. *Journal of the American Academy of Child and Adolescent Psychiatry,* 42, 1270–1278.

Papsdorf, M., & Alden, L. (1998). Mediators of social rejection in social anxiety: similarity, self-disclosure, and overt signs of anxiety. *Journal of Research in Personality,* 32, 351-369.

Podell, J. F., & Kendal, P. C. (2011). Mothers and fathers in family cognitive behavioral therapy for anxious youth. *Journal of Child and Family Studies,* 20, 182-185.

Rapee, R. M. (1997). Potential role of childrearing practices in the development of anxiety and depression. *Clinical Psychology Review,* 17, 47 – 67.

Rapee, R. M., & Melville, L. F. (1997). Retrospective recall of family factors in social phobia and panic disorder. *Depression and Anxiety,* 5, 7 – 11.

Rapee, R. M., & Spence, S. H. (2004). The etiology of social phobia: empirical evidence and an initial model. *Clinical Psychology Review,* 24, 737–767.

Rork, K. E., & Morris, T. L. (2009). Influence of parenting factors on childhood social anxiety: Direct Observation of Parental Warmth and Control. *Child & Family Behavior Therapy*, 31, 220-235.

Rubin, K. H., Nelson, L. J., Hastings, P., & Asendorpf, J. (1999). The transaction between parents' perceptions of their children's shyness and their parenting styles. International *Journal of Behavioral Development*, 23, 937–957.

Schneier, F. R., Johnson, J., Hornig, C. D., Liebowitz, M. R., & Weissman, M. M. (1992). Social phobia: comorbidity and morbidity in an epidemiologic sample. *Archives of General Psychiatry*, 49, 282-288.

Shortt, A. L., Barrett, P. M., & Fox, T. L. (2001). Evaluating the FRIENDS Program: A cognitive-behavioral group treatment for anxious children and their parents. *Journal of Clinical Child Psychology* 30, 525–535.

Silverman, W. K., Kurtines, W. M., Ginsburg, G. S., Weems, C. F., White Lumpkin, P., & Hicks Carmichael, D. H. (1999). Treating anxiety disorders in children with group cognitive behavioral therapy: A randomized clinical trial. *Journal of Consulting and Clinical Psychology* 67, 995–1003.

Spence, S. H., Donovan, C., & Brechman-Toussaint, M. (1999). Social skills, social outcomes, and cognitive features of childhood social phobia. *Journal of Abnormal Psychology*, 108, 211-221.

Spence, S.H., Donovan, C.,& Brechman-Toussaint, M. (2000). The treatment of childhood social phobia: the effectiveness of a social skills training-based, cognitive-behavioral intervention, with and without parental involvement. *Journal of Child Psychology and Psychiatry*, 41, 713-726.

Stark, K. D., Humphrey, L. L., Crook, R, & Lewis, K. (1990). Perceived family environments of depressed and anxious children: Child's and maternal figure's perspectives. *Journal of Abnormal Child Psychology*, 18, 527-547.

Stein, M. B., Tancer, M. E., Gelernter, C. S., Vittone, B. J., & Uhde, T. W. (1990). Major depression in patients social phobia. *American Journal of Psychiatry*, 147, 637-639.

Stein, M. B., Torgrud, L. J., & Walker, J. R. (2000). Social phobia symptoms, subtypes, and severity. *Archives of General Psychiatry*, 57, 1046–1052.

Taylor, C. T., & Alden, L. E. (2006). Parental overprotection and interpersonal behavior in generalized social phobia. *Behavior Therapy*, 37, 14-24.

Turner, Samuel M., Beidel, D., C., Dancu, C.,V.,,Keys, D. J. (1986). Psychopathology of social phobia and comparison to avoidant personality disorder. *Journal of Abnormal Psychology*, 95, 389-394.

Turner, S. M., Beidel, D. C., & Townsely, R. M. (1992). Social phobia: a comparison of specific and generalised subtypes and avoidant personality disorder. *Journal of Abnormal Psychology*, 101, 326-331.

Warren, S. L., Huston, L., Egeland, B., & Sroufe, L. A. (1997). Child and adolescent anxiety disorders and early attachment. *Journal of the American Academy of Child and Adolescent Psychiatry*, 36, 637-644.

Whaley, S. E., Pinto, A., & Sigman, A. (1999). Characterizing interactions between anxious mothers and their children. *Journal of Consulting and Clinical Psychology*, 67, 826-836.

Wild, J., Hackmann, A., & Clark, D. M. (2008). Rescripting early memories linked to negative images in social phobia: a pilot study. *Behavior Therapy*, 39, 47-56.

Wood, J. J., McLeod, B. D., Sigman, M., Hwang, W.-C., & Chu, B. C. (2003). Parenting and childhood anxiety: theory, empirical findings, and future directions. *Journal of Child Psychology and Psychiatry,* 44, 134–151.

Wood, J. J., Piacentini, J. C., Southam-Gerow, M., Chu, B. C., & Sigman, M. (2006). Family cognitive behavioral therapy for child anxiety disorders. *Journal of the American Academy of Child and Adolescent Psychiatry,* 45, 314-321.

Woodruff-Borden, J., Morrow, C., Bourland, S., & Cambron, S. (2002). The behavior of anxious parents: examining mechanisms of transmission of anxiety from parent to child. *Journal of Clinical Child and Adolescent Psychology,* 31, 364–374.

In: Social Anxiety
Editor: Efrosini Kalyva

ISBN: 978-1-62808-396-5
© 2013 Nova Science Publishers, Inc.

*Chapter VI*

# Social Anxiety and Substance Use

## *Erika Melonashi**

European University of Tirana, Albania

## Abstract

The use and abuse with substances represents an important health concern. Research studies have made efforts to identify factors involved in the initiation, maintenance, and abuse with substances. Comorbidity rates between substance use disorders and psychiatric symptoms (e.g., social anxiety) suggest the involvement of the later in the etiology of the disorder. The purpose of this chapter was to critically evaluate research on the relationship between substance use/abuse and social anxiety. The chapter provides a discussion of both theoretical frameworks (e.g., cognitive affective theories, social learning theories) as well as relevant empirical studies in trying to understand this relationship. Finally, the main gaps in research are discussed, and suggestions for future studies and implications for treatment are presented.

**Keywords**: Social anxiety, substance use, initiation, maintenance, young adults

## 1. Substance Use and Abuse

Substance use and abuse are widely spread behaviors across all cultures. These behaviors have been associated with reduced life expectancy and quality of life (World Health Organization, 2011). Of all substances alcohol and tobacco are the most commonly used, while other drugs (e.g., cannabis) are less so (Rogers, 2011). The detrimental health effects of substance use and abuse have been well documented through research studies. Alcohol use has been associated with approximately 2.5 million deaths each year, i.e., about 4% of all deaths world-wide have been attributed to alcohol use only (World Health Organization,

---

* Emelonashi@yahoo.com.

2011). Research evidence has suggested that alcohol use is involved in the etiology of at least 200 diseases, while it has been identified as the primary causal factor in 60 of them. Drinking behavior has been associated with several consequences, which involve not only the individual, but also the family and society as a whole. Alcohol use has been associated with violence, child abuse and neglect, absenteeism from the workplace, road accidents, and unsafe sexual practices (Boyd, McCabe, & Morales, 2005; Cooper, 2002).

Similarly, cigarette smoking has been regarded as one of the major causes of preventable death worldwide (Taylor & Bettcher, 2000). Epidemiological studies have provided shocking estimates of the death toll attributed to smoking behavior. In their extensive study with data from 14 epidemiological sub-regions of the world, Ezzati and Lopez (2004) estimated that smoking was responsible for 4.83 million premature deaths in the world, 2.41 million in developing countries and 2.43 million in industrialized countries. Smoking behavior has been mainly related to lung cancer and heart disease but there is evidence for involvement in other illnesses too, including emphysema, bronchitis, stomach, kidney and bladder cancers, esophagus and larynx cancers, and conditions such as infertility, preterm delivery or sudden death infant syndrome (US Department for Health and Human Services, 2004).

Although not as common as smoking behavior, the prevalence of cannabis use has increased in the recent years (White, Bates, & Labouvie, 1998). The immediate negative consequences of cannabis use are reflected in the psychomotor, cognitive, emotional, and motivational aspects (White, et al., 1998). Long term effects of use comprise respiratory and brain cancers, increased risk for committing suicide, sexually transmitted diseases, accelerated or delayed entry in adult roles, impaired educational achievement etc. (Buckner, Joiner, Schmidt, & Zvolensky, 2012; Calabria, Degenhardt, Hall, & Lynskey, 2010; Darke, Duflou, & Torok, 2009; Eksborg & Rajs, 2008; Price, Hemmingsson, Lewis, Zammit, & Allebeck, 2009; White et al., 1998). Moreover, daily cannabis use has been associated to higher levels of anxiety and depression (Patton, Coffey, Carlin, Degenhardt, Lynskey, & Hall, 2006; Pedersen, 2008).

Substance users frequently tend to use more than one substance at a time, e.g., people who drink, also tend to smoke and vice-versa (Bobo & Husten, 2000; Falk, Yi, & Hiller-Sturmhofel, 2006). Indeed, research has shown that smokers are significantly more likely to smoke, when they are drinking alcohol and significant associations have been found between heavy drinking and heavy smoking behaviors (e.g., Grant, Hasin, Chou, Stinson, & Dawson, 2004; Kahler et al., 2008). Similarly alcohol drinking has been associated with cannabis use and combinations of both substances have been related to involvement in risky behaviors such as fatal accidents and unprotected, casual sex or sex with multiple partners (sexually transmitted diseases like AIDS) (Donenberg, Emerson, Bryant, & King, 2006; Poulin & Graham, 2001).

In several cases, substance use behavior degenerates towards specific disorders (e.g., alcohol use disorders, or cannabis use disorders). Substance use disorders include the abuse of and dependence on substances. Although there have been several debates as regards the conceptual distinction between abuse and dependence, the most widely accepted definition focuses on a distinction between physical/behavioral consequences (dependence) and social consequences (abuse). Thus the development of dependence on a particular substance involves the formation of tolerance and withdrawal effects, i.e., individuals continue to use the substance, to overcome the negative psychological or physical consequences of withdrawal. Substance abuse on the other hand refers to cases where individuals continue using substances despite problems in social or interpersonal domains (e.g., work, interpersonal relationships etc.) (American Psychiatric Association, 2000).

Recent studies have documented increases in rates of substance use and abuse. These fast increasing rates have been accompanied by an escalation of the corresponding healthcare costs, which has been estimated as half a trillion dollars/ year in the United States only (Rogers, 2011). Thus in a context of great personal, social, and economic burden related to substance use and abuse, it becomes important to re-evaluate existing theoretical and empirical knowledge on the issue.

# 2. Why People Use and Abuse Substances?

Several efforts have been made to understand the factors or causes influencing substance use initiation or maintenance. Research on substance use initiation has mainly focused on adolescents, an age group which faces the greatest risk for substance use and abuse (Craig & Baucum, 2002; Katz, Fromme, & D'Amico, 2000). A comprehensive review by Petraitis, Flay, and Miller (1995) has identified several theoretical frameworks trying to explain substance use initiation (smoking, alcohol, cannabis), including substance specific cognitions and emotions (cognitive-affective theories), social learning processes and social influences (including learning in families, peer groups etc.) and intrapersonal factors (age, gender, personality characteristics etc). The following theoretical discussion is largely based on this broad categorical distinction, while also providing input from recent developments in the field.

## 2.1. Cognitive-Affective Theories

Cognitive affective theories of substance use mainly focus on substance-specific perceptions and expectations (e.g., Ajzen & Fishbein, 1980). In broad terms, these theories suggest that individuals who expect substances to produce more personal benefits than costs are at higher risk of being involved in substance use. Typically, benefits of substance use include relaxation, affect regulation, improved social skills, stress management etc. (e.g., Baker, Piper, McCarthy, Majeskie, & Fiore, 2004; Tice, Bratslavsky, & Baumeister, 2001).

The 'cost-benefit' view of substance use has been further elaborated into motivation theories. Motives are viewed as the proximal pathway through which more distal factors such as anxiety or depression exert their impact. For instance, Cooper (1994) proposed four main categories of drinking motives, including enhancement (e.g., increase the enjoyment), social motives (e.g., at social gatherings), coping (e.g., escape from stress), and conformity (e.g., fitting in). Therefore, individuals might engage in alcohol drinking behavior to increase positive outcomes (enhancement and social motives) and/or minimize negative outcomes (coping and conformity) (Cooper, Russell, Skinner, & Windle, 1992). Subsequent studies have found stronger support for coping and conformity motives, as compared to enhancement and social motives (e.g., Carpenter & Hasin, 1999). In this context, the role of substance use in coping with stress has been further investigated.

Hence, according to the *tension reduction theory*, people learn to use substances (alcohol, cigarettes, cannabis) in order to relieve tension (Conger, 1956; Kushner, Sher, & Beitman, 1990). Similarly, the *stress response dampening model* suggests that individuals use substances in an effort to reduce their reactions to stressful situations (Sher & Levenson, 1982). Therefore, people would be more likely to consume alcohol when anticipating or experiencing a stressful situation (as compared to low stress situations). According to the *influential stress-coping model* of substance use, the function of substance use in those cases would mainly be emotion regulation (Kassel, Jackson, & Unrod, 2000). Thus, according to these theories, people who experience higher levels of stress, as well as those who have less effective coping strategies (e.g., cannot manage their emotions) are placed at a higher risk of using or abusing substances.

Research has provided support for the main predictions deriving from this group of theories; indeed, both alcohol and cigarettes (nicotine) are frequently used as a means of coping with stress (Wills, Sandy, & Yaeger, 2001). For instance, laboratory experiments have shown that participants who perceive higher levels of stress before or during a specific task tend to drink more alcohol (Kidorf & Lang, 1999). Moreover, survey research on smoking behavior has shown that stress, negative life events, and depression often precede smoking uptake behavior (Cohen & Lichtenstein, 1990; Glassman et al., 1990; Siqueira, Diab, Bodian, & Rolnitzky, 2000).

Building further on the above theoretical frameworks, another theoretical model has been suggested, i.e., the *self-medication model*. More specifically the self-medication hypothesis assumes that psychological problems (e.g., anxiety or depression) develop before drug or alcohol use problems and that the drug actually provides relief from the negative psychological symptoms. The positive effects of drug use enable the development of continued and ultimately problematic use, with the purpose of keeping the psychological symptoms in check. In other words, the negative reinforcement of substance use promotes the escalation of this behavior, thus increasing the risk for developing substance use disorders (Chutuape & de Wit, 1995). Therefore, differently from the previous models, the self-medication model clearly included the concept of drug dependence in an effort to understand the maintenance of substance use behavior (see Khantzian, 1985).

The self-medication model has found support both from studies with large community samples as well as from research with small treatment samples. Studies with community samples have found that a significant proportion of cases reporting anxiety symptoms also reported using alcohol (14.5%) or alcohol and drugs (4.5%) to self-medicate (Robinson, Sareen, Cox, & Bolton, 2009a, 2009b). Moreover, higher rates of substance use for self-medication purposes have been reported in treatment samples; for instance, in a study among individuals with anxiety disorders, Menary and colleagues have found rates of alcohol use for self-medication purposes, which go up to 20% (Menary, Kushner, Maurer, & Thuras, 2011). Furthermore, those individuals with anxiety disorders who self-medicated (as compared to non-self medicators) were at a significantly higher risk for developing alcohol use disorders in the following years. Indeed, the use of substances for self-medicating purposes has been also associated to other negative outcomes including a decreased quality of life, increased risk of committing suicide and decreased probability of asking for help or using formal psychological treatment (Bolton, Cox, Clara, & Sareen, 2006; Robinson et al., 2009a).

While acknowledging that self-medication might provide a fairly good explanation for substance use and abuse, it certainly does not account for all cases. Therefore an important question to address is 'Why only some individuals use substances for self-medication purposes but others do not?' Menary et al. (2011) suggest explanations in terms cognitive elements such as outcome expectancies. The term 'expectancy' refers to underlying beliefs about the effects of substances on cognition, emotions, and behavior (Burke & Stephens, 1999). These beliefs develop both from past experiences and observational learning (Del Boca, Darkes, Goldman, & Smith, 2002). Research studies suggest that expectancies provide a key element for understanding the relationship between stress, affect management, and substance use. Indeed individuals who expect substances to help them become more talkative and sociable, reduce inhibitions, or decrease anxiety levels, are also more likely to use them (Abrams & Kushner, 2004; Carpenter & Hasin; Koob & Le Moal, 1997; Lewis & O'Neill, 2000; Robinson & Berridge, 2000; Steele & Josephs, 1990). Moreover, people's beliefs about the impact of alcohol on mood and behavior have a significant impact not only on the choice of drinking or not, but also on the quantity consumed, emotional outcomes, and future behavior (Brown, Christiansen, & Goldman, 1987; Jones, Corbin, & Fromme, 2001). Furthermore, Kushner, Sher, Wood, and Wood (1994) found that men, who had strong tension reduction expectancies for alcohol, experienced the greatest reduction in anxiety during a speech task preceded by drinking. Finally, research has shown that outcome expectancies for other substances, e.g., cigarette smoking have also been related both to the initiation and maintenance of these behaviors (e.g., Johnson et al., 2008; Krisjansson et al., 2011).

To summarize, cognitive-affective theories and models suggest that substance use is the result of a cognitive appraisal process during which individuals evaluate the positive outcomes of using substances (e.g., coping with negative affect, reducing tension etc.). Positive expectancies related to substance use would be associated with greater use and an increased possibility for future abuse with substances. Cognitive models have found great empirical support and have been quite useful in understanding substance use. Nonetheless, one of the main criticisms associated with these models is their failure to consider the social aspect of substance use behavior; indeed, starting from adolescence, smoking and drinking behaviors largely occur within peer social groups (e.g., Borsari & Carey, 2001; Kobus, 2003). The impact of social factors on substance use behavior has been addressed in theories that focus specifically on social learning processes.

## 2.2. Social Learning Approach

The basic premise of the social learning approach is that individuals learn new behaviors by observing, imitating, or modeling other people's behaviors (e.g., Bandura, 1977). Therefore, according to this approach both adaptive and maladaptive behaviors, such as substance use and abuse, are learned through social processes. The observation process might directly influence behavior (i.e., imitation) or might alternatively influence beliefs about physiological, personal, and social outcomes of substance use (Bandura, 1977). For instance, if peers who smoke or use alcohol are perceived as more socially skilled, the belief that 'tobacco or alcohol improve social skills' might be established. Moreover, observation of role models also increases the self-efficacy about obtaining and using substances. Therefore, people with higher self-efficacy in obtaining and using substances would make more active efforts in this direction (Bandura, 1982, 1986).

Research into the influences of social models has identified parents and peers as two of the most influential sources. Peer relations are particularly important during adolescence, as adolescents spend significantly more time with their peers than their families (Fuligni, Eccles, Barber, & Clements, 2001). Peers might influence substance use both actively (direct offers) and passively (modeling) and studies show that adolescents' reports of substance use can be predicted by peer substance use involvement (Borsari & Carey, 2001; Curran, Stice, & Chassin, 1997). Peer pressure has been identified as a crucial factor affecting substance use in young people (Thorlindson & Bernbury, 2006) although it has been quite difficult to distinguish between peer influence and peer selection (substance users tend to associate with similar others) (Bauman & Ennet, 1996).

However, several studies have asserted that the influence of peers on substance use is mediated by a more essential factor, i.e., parenting practices (e.g., Wood, Mitchell, Read, & Brand, 2004). In fact, research examining the role of the family in health-related and risky behaviors has regarded it as the most important source of health-related behavioral patterns (Chassin & Handley, 2006; Repetti, Taylor, & Seeman, 2002; Tinsley, Lees, & Sumartojo, 2004). While peers represent the strongest risk factor for involvement in substance use, the family represents the strongest protective factor, especially in disadvantaged environments (Ary, Duncan, Biglan, Metzler, Noell, & Smolkowski, 1999; Ensminger & Juon, 1998). Parental substance use, but also more generally the quality of relationships with parents have been identified as important elements influencing substance use initiation among adolescents (McArdle, et al., 2002; Kumpfer & Bluth, 2004).

More recently, other sources of influence, such as the media have attracted research attention. Studies on smoking behavior across different cultures have found associations between marketing strategies (advertising and commercials) and changes in smoking prevalence across different demographic groups. For instance, the increasing rates of smoking among women in post-communist countries has been related to marketing strategies, which associated smoking behavior to gender equality, women's emancipation, success, and freedom (e.g., slogans such as "Test the West," "Lady's first" etc.) (Amos & Haglund, 2000; Goto, Nishimura, & Ida, 2007; Morrow & Barraclough, 2003; Morrow & Barraclough, 2010). Hence, cigarette smoking among women, which was considered as socially unacceptable during the communist regime, became a sign of emancipation and a modern lifestyle right afterwards (Zaloshnja et al., 2010).

Research on media effects highlights the need to consider a different level of analysis in the examination of social influence, i.e., the impact of social norms. The concept of social norms refers to perceptions of behavior that is approved or disapproved by others (injunctive norms) or actions that are typically performed in a social context (descriptive norms) (Ajzen, 1991; Cialdini & Sagarin, 2005; Kallgren, Reno, & Cialdini, 2000; Reno, Cialdini, & Kallgren, 1993). The relevance of norms is especially obvious in situations of uncertainty; nonetheless, even if situational uncertainty is absent, people still refer and act in accordance with social norms in order to fulfill their needs for affiliation and ensure the maintenance of a positive self-concept (Cialdini & Goldstein, 2004). Hence, descriptive as well as injunctive norms enable a more accurate understanding of social situations and provide individuals with more effective response repertoires.

Research evidence suggests that social norms are useful in understanding health behaviors including drinking and smoking. For instance, Perkins and Berkowitz (1986) in their study of college students, found a relationship between perceptions of descriptive norms for drinking and actual drinking behavior. Indeed heavy drinkers reported stronger descriptive norms favoring this behavior, i.e., they believed that most students drink as much as they drink (a false consensus effect). Similar findings have been reported about smoking behavior among adolescents; thus, the tendency to report smoking as the behavior of the majority has been related to stronger intentions to take up smoking (Henry, Kobus, & Schoeny, 2011). As regards injunctive norms, longitudinal studies have found a direct effect of social acceptability of smoking on rates of cigarette consumption, concluding that consumption decreases significantly with increased social unacceptability of smoking behavior (e.g., Alamar & Glantz, 2006).

To summarize, a large body of evidence suggests that there are important social influences on substance use, especially as regards the onset of this behavior. However, it should be noted that most research on social determinants has focused on substance use among adolescents and young adults (Katz, Fromme, & D'Amico, 2000). Indeed there is general consensus on the fact that these age groups are particularly vulnerable both to social influences in general and substance use initiation in particular (e.g., Henry et al., 2011). Nonetheless, normative influences might not be as relevant in the maintenance of substance use behavior later in life or the development of substance use disorders (Katz et al., 2000). In this context it is important to consider another source of influence on substance use and abuse, namely intrapersonal factors. The following section provides a discussion of several intrapersonal factors including age, gender, personality characteristics, and psychiatric symptoms.

## 2.3. Intrapersonal Factors

### 2.3.1. Age

As previously mentioned, adolescence has been considered as the developmental stage at greatest risk for substance use and abuse (Katz et al., 2000). These findings have been explained in terms of the particular developmental tasks of adolescence, including the quest for identity, autonomy, and independence. In this process of self-definition, adolescents experience a growing influence of the peer group (normative social influences) as opposed to an increasing distance from parents. These social factors, in conjunction with the inherent need to experiment and define oneself as a unique, independent individual have been considered to underlie the high rates of substance use among adolescents (Craig & Baucum, 2002). However, even experimental substance use during this developmental period might have important long term consequences including substance dependence, several mental health problems, and delinquency (Dawkins, 1997; Gruber, DiClemente, Anderson, & Lodico, 1996; Palmer et al., 2009).

Adolescence though, is not the only 'high risk' developmental stage. The marked independence and freedom from parental supervision accompanying young adulthood increase the risk for substance use and abuse (Katz et al., 2000). There have even been suggestions that young adults are more likely than adolescents to see themselves as invulnerable and therefore have a greater probability for engaging in risky behaviors (Millstein & Halpern-Felsher, 2002). Nonetheless, the effect of age has been often confounded with another variable, namely the educational setting (White, Labouvie, & Papadaratsakis, 2005). There is evidence that the transition from high school to college/

university is characterized by increasing levels of alcohol use, due to the greater leniency, lower control, and normalization of this behavior in college settings (Baer, Kivlahan, & Marlatt, 1995). Indeed, when controlling for educational setting, there is a tendency for a reduction in substance use with increasing age; these findings have been explained in terms of maturation processes (e.g., learning more appropriate coping behaviors) (Webb, Bray, Getz, & Adams, 2002). In addition, the achievement of important developmental milestones such as employment, stable personal relationships, marriage and children are all associated with increasing personal responsibility and reduced substance use (MacDonald & Putney, 2000; Young, Morales, McCabe, Boyd, & D'Arcy, 2005). Further evidence supporting the 'maturation process' explanation comes from cross-cultural studies in both developed and developing countries (e.g. de Lima, Dunn, Novo, Tomasi, & Reisser, 2003). However, it should be mentioned that most studies have been cross-sectional, i.e. they have used prevalence data from different age groups at the same point in time. Hence, an alternative explanation might involve cohort effects since the apparent maturation process might in fact be the result of increased substance use in the new generations (Johnston, O'Malley, & Bachman, 2006).

To summarize, most research, especially in the context of experimental substance use or substance use initiation has focused on adolescence and young adulthood (high school pupils or college students), as the two developmental stages at highest risk. Indeed studies suggest a general decrease in substance use with increasing age, which has been mainly explained in terms of maturation processes.

## *2.3.2. Gender*

Research on intrapersonal characteristics related to substance use has resulted in general consensus on the gender factor. Studies have shown that male gender is associated with higher involvement in all types of risky behaviors (Courtenay, McCreary, & Merighi, 2002; Eisenman, Dantzker, & Ellis, 2004). More specifically, Kandel (1998) concluded that male gender can be considered an important risk factor for substance use and abuse; in fact adult males display higher frequency and quantity of substance use, have higher rates of dependence than females, and are more likely to become dependent at the same levels of use (Johnson & Glassman, 1998; Kandel, 1998). Differences have been explained both in terms of biological sex characteristics and gender role socialization. For instance, physical characteristics like greater body weight, lower percentage of fat tissue, and higher mass of body water in men, reduce the effects of alcohol and increase their tolerance towards it (Angove & Fothergill, 2003). Furthermore, the lower levels of gastric alcohol dehydrogenase (digestive enzyme) in women increase their susceptibility to the effects of alcohol (McCance-Katz, Hart, Boyarski, Kosten, & Jatlow, 2005; Zilberman, Tavares, Blume, & El-Guebaly, 2003). In fact, experimental studies show that they have a significantly greater physiological response to the same amount of alcohol as compared to men; or otherwise, women need a smaller amount of alcohol than men to reach the desired physiological effect (McCance-Katz, et al., 2005). This aspect should be carefully considered especially in the process of detecting substance use problems among women (McCance-Katz, et al., 2005).

Apart from differences in biological construct, the concept of gender also inevitably comprises particular social roles and expectations associated with the specific sex (Amaro, Blake, Schwartz, & Flinchbaugh, 2001). For instance, studies have shown that men are socialized towards a more exploratory and independent behavioral style (e.g., lower levels of parental control as compared to women). Consequently, during adolescence they are more likely to participate in recreational activities involving risky behaviors (Van Etten & Anthony, 2001). More specifically, Van Etten, Neumark, and Anthony (1999) concluded that males are more likely to be exposed to drugs or have an initial opportunity for use.

Additionally, substance use is also directly related to masculine ideology (Courtenay, et al., 2002). A qualitative study among British young men suggested that alcohol consumption is still considered an important marker of masculinity (De Visser & Smith, 2007). It has been suggested that the pressure to conform to a particular masculine prototype is as much due to actual situations (concrete urges to drink) as to unspoken social conventions (Corcoran & Segrist, 1993). For instance Segrist, Corcoran, Jordan-Fleming, and Rose (2007) concluded that young men tend to overestimate the extent to which their same age peers engage in substance use. Hence, they engage in the process of normalizing this behavior and might start drinking simply because they think every real man is doing it (Prentice & Miller, 1993). On the other hand, substance use still carries greater stigma for women since it contradicts social norms of the virtuous, nurturing female role; in this way, social norms might act as important protective factors in regulating female substance use (Amaro, et al., 2001).

Even so it should be mentioned that social changes in the recent years have contributed to a reduction of the gender gap in substance use. Indeed research has shown clear links between social change (e.g., emancipation of women through joining the workforce) and an increase in the social acceptability and smoking prevalence among women in almost all Western cultures (Amos, 1996; Waldron, 1991). For instance, as norms regarding smoking in western countries have grown less and less gender-specific, the prevalence rates by gender have become very similar (e.g., Shaffey et al., 2004). Even more, there is evidence of a reversal of smoking trends of the young generation; for instance in Bulgaria smoking rates among adolescent girls are higher than rates among boys (Manolova, 2006).

To summarize, research on gender and substance use suggests that male gender represents a risk factor for substance use and abuse. Findings have been explained in terms of both biological and social factors. Nonetheless, social changes might produce reverse gender patterns as in the case of smoking behavior.

## 2.3.3. Personality Characteristics and Psychological Disorders

Several personality characteristics have been related to substance use initiation and maintenance. According to the *Multistage social* learning *model* (Simons, Conger, & Whitbeck, 1988) involvement in substance use is influenced by characteristics such as low self-esteem, high levels of emotional distress, poor social skills, a present-oriented value system etc. Moreover, studies have found links between substance use and personality traits such as high extraversion, neuroticism, and novelty seeking; substance use has been also associated with low conscientiousness and impulse control (Allen, Moeller, Rhoades, & Cherek, 1998; Chakroun, Doron, & Swendsen, 2004; Lasser et al., 2000; Swendsen, Conway, Rounsaville, & Merikangas, 2002).

As regards substance-specific research findings, there is evidence that cigarette smoking is positively related to extraversion, impulsivity, and neuroticism while negatively related to agreeableness and conscientiousness (e.g., Arai, Hosokawa, Fukao, Izumi, & Hisamich, 1997; Malouff, Thorsteinsson, & Schutte, 2006; Munafo & Black, 2007; Paunonen & Ashton, 2001; Terracciano & Costa, 2004). More recent studies have found that low conscientiousness and high neuroticism are associated not only with tobacco smoking, but also heroin, and cocaine use (e.g., Terracciano, Löckenhoff, Crum, Bienvenu, & Cost, 2008). Moreover, cannabis use has been strongly associated to high unconventionality and low conscientiousness; however, only weak relationships have been found with emotionality and negative affect (Bogg & Roberts, 2004; Gorman & Derzon, 2002). Finally alcohol drinking has been related to traits such as psychoticism, extraversion, and novelty-seeking (George, Connor, Gullo, & Young, 2010).

The main criticism on studies trying to establish relationships between personality variables and substance use has to do with their correlational nature (Terracciano et al., 2008). Indeed there is some evidence suggesting that the direction of causality might be the other way around, i.e., substance use influencing personality traits (Breslau, Novak, & Kessler, 2004; Parrott, 1998; Picciotto, Brunzell, & Caldarone, 2002). It should be noted though that this kind of interpretation might better account for adolescence and young adulthood but not later in life, since personality traits become quite stable in adulthood (e.g., Terracciano, Costa, & McCrae, 2006; Terracciano, McCrae, Brant, & Costa, 2005; Terracciano, McCrae, & Costa, 2006).

Moreover, longitudinal studies have found that personality traits indeed represent a risk factor for substance use, e.g., children and adolescents, who score low on conscientiousness but high in neuroticism and extraversion, are more likely to be cigarette smokers in adulthood (Felitti et al., 1998; Harakeh, Scholte, de Vries, & Engels, 2006; Hampson, Goldberg, Vogt, & Dubanoski, 2006; Kodl & Mermelstein, 2004). Along the same lines, research on intervention programs has provided evidence of modification of some personality variables. For instance, smoking cessation has been associated with a decrease in neuroticism scores (Breslau et al., 2004; Parrott, 1998). Similarly, interventions addressing poly-substance abusers have reported substantial declines in neuroticism and increases in agreeableness and conscientiousness after treatment (Piedmont, 2001).

Apart from personality characteristics, substance use has been also associated with several psychological disorders including anxiety and mood disorders. Epidemiological research has shown comorbidity between substance use disorders and several anxiety disorders, such as post-traumatic stress, panic disorder, and social phobia (Coffey, Read, & Norberg, 2008; Grant et al., 2004; Norton, Norton, Cox, & Belik, 2008; Tran & Smith, 2008). The results from epidemiological research have been replicated with both clinical and community based samples (Conway, Compton, Stinson, & Grant, 2006; Ross, Glaser, & Germanson, 1988). For instance, Grant and colleagues (2004) reported that 40.7% of the individuals with alcohol use disorder who asked for treatment during a 12-month period also had at least one current independent mood disorder, while more than 33% had at least one current independent anxiety disorder.

Efforts to understand the temporal order in which substance use disorders and anxiety/mood disorders appear have concluded that the later usually precede substance use disorders. In other words, anxiety and mood disorders at baseline have been associated with later onsets of substance use disorders (Wolitzki-Taylor, Bobova, Zinbarg, Mineka, & Craske, 2012). Social anxiety, relative to other types of anxiety, may be especially relevant to alcohol-related impairment; indeed the prevalence of comorbidity between social anxiety disorder and alcohol use disorders has been calculated to reach 2.4% (e.g., Book, Thomas, Smith, & Miller, 2012; Buckner et al., 2008; Schneiner et al., 2010). Individuals with comorbid alcohol use and social anxiety disorders have greater severity of alcohol dependence as compared to those without social anxiety (Bakken, Landheim, & Vaglum, 2005; Schneiner et al., 2010).

Moreover, the co-occurrence between social anxiety and alcohol-related problems is related to greater impairment than either condition alone (e.g., Schneier et al., 2010).

Similarly research on adolescents has found that those with social anxiety disorder were nearly five times more likely (than those without social anxiety) to develop cannabis dependence, after controlling for both demographic and other relevant psychiatric variables (Buckner et al., 2008; Marmorstein, White, Loeber, & Stouthamer-Loeber, 2010). Indeed social avoidance (a fundamental characteristic social anxiety disorder) has been strongly related to cannabis use and also suicidality among substance users (Buckner, Heimberg, & Schmidt, 2011; Conner, Britton, Sworts, & Joiner, 2007). Moreover research has shown that among cannabis users social anxiety interacts with craving in such a way that individuals with higher social anxiety and higher craving are more likely to use cannabis (Buckner, Crosby, Wonderlich, & Schmidt, 2011). Thus social anxiety seems to contribute not only to the etiology but also the maintenance of substance use disorders (Agosti, Nunes, & Levin, 2002; Buckner, Heimberg, Schneier, Liu, Wang, & Blanco, 2012; Tepe, Dalrymple, & Zimmerman, 2012).

To summarize, research suggests that several personality characteristics and psychological disorders might be associated with substance use and misuse. In an effort to better understand this link, one of the disorders, namely social anxiety will be discussed in more depth. The following section provides a general overview on the main features of social anxiety.

# 3. Social Anxiety

Social anxiety disorder or social phobia is a striking and constant fear of social or performance situations, which might produce embarrassment. This disorder is characterized by a permanent experience of emotional distress and negative thoughts in anticipation or during social interactions. Thus, individuals might fear exposure to unfamiliar people and are particularly anxious to being observed by others (e.g., public speech, eating in public etc) (American Psychiatric Association, 2000; Hartman, 1986; Schenkler & Leary, 1982; Weeks, Heinberg & Rodebaugh, 2008). Individuals with social anxiety disorder also rate negative social events as more likely to occur and report higher levels of distress as compared to non-anxious controls (Foa, Fraklin, Perry, & Herbert, 1996; Rheingold, Herbert, & Franklin, 2003).

The typical age of onset for this disorder is approximately 13–15 years of age, with higher rates reported in older adolescents and young adults (Ballenger et al., 1998; Chartier, Walker, & Stein, 2003; Stein & Kean, 2000). Youth with social anxiety feel unaccepted by others and report having very few friends; additionally they show particular problems in forming new friendships (La Greca & Lopez, 1998; Vernberg, Abwender, Ewell, & Beery, 1992). It should be noted though that social anxiety symptoms are much more widespread than the disorder itself; for instance, large scale research has found that 38% to 75% of the students in the United States have problems involving social acceptance, social adaptation, and social anxiety (Baum, Duffelmeyer, & Greenlan, 2001; Bryan, 2005). Nonetheless, most of them do not fulfill the criteria for being diagnosed with social anxiety disorder.

Research has found relationships between social anxiety and socio-economic status (SES), so that rates of social anxiety are higher in adolescents from lower SES (Schneiner, Johnson, Hornig, Liebowitz, & Weissman, 1992). Moreover cultural differences have been observed so that collectivistic cultures are characterized by higher social anxiety (Norasakkunkit & Kalick, 2002; Okazaki, 1997). Likewise gender differences have also been documented, as girls tend to score higher than boys in overall social anxiety (La Greca & Lopez, 1998; Wittchen, Stein, & Kessler, 1999). Gender differences have also been reported in the types of situations that provoke the greatest anxiety. For instance Turk and colleagues (1998) found that women are significantly more distressed in situations such as talking to an authority figure, acting, performing, giving a talk in front of an audience, working while being observed etc. Men on the other hand reported significantly greater distress in the use of public bathrooms or the returning of goods to a store. These gender differences have been also found in studies with adolescents (e.g., Peleg, 2004) and university students (e.g., Peleg, 2002, 2005).

Social anxiety disorder (SAD) has been related to impairment in several domains including daily activities, romantic relationships, friendships, education, employment etc. (Schneier et al., 1994). Individuals with SAD perceive themselves as 'low functioning' (as compared to those without SAD), and report low self-esteem and satisfaction in several areas including relationships with family and friends, leisure activities, school performance, job-related activities etc. (Khalid-Khan, Santibanez, McMicken, & Rynn, 2007; McCarroll, Lindsey, MacKinnon-Lewis, Campbell-Chambers, & Frabutt, 2009; Stein and Kean, 2000; Wittchen et al., 1999). Furthermore, individuals with SAD have low social support, which might be both a cause and a consequence of the disorder itself (i.e., social support impacts subsequent social anxiety, social anxiety also affects subsequent social support) (Caslyn, Winter, & Burger, 2005; Johnson, 1991; Stice & Barrera, 1995; Van Zalk, Van Zalk, Kerr, & Stattin, 2011). Finally, social anxiety disorder has been also linked to substance use and abuse (e.g., alcohol and cannabis use disorders) (e.g., Bakken et al., 2005; Book et al., 2012; Buckner et al., 2008; Schneiner et al., 2010). The following section provides a theoretical discussion of the relationship between social anxiety and substance use/abuse.

# 4. Theoretical Background: Social Anxiety and Substance Use

Among the several theories of substance use, the ones most commonly addressed to explain the relationship between social anxiety and substance use are cognitive-affective theories (including tension reduction theory, stress response dampening model, and self-medication model/hypothesis) and social learning approaches. The following sections discuss in further depth each of these approaches.

## 4.1. Cognitive-Affective Theories

The tension reduction theory provides an explanation of the relationship between social anxiety and substance use in terms of a decrease in the tension provoked by performance situations or interpersonal interactions. For instance, Conger (1956) had argued that individuals with social anxiety would use alcohol to reduce their tendency of avoiding feared social situations. Similarly the Stress Response Dampening model (Sher & Levenson, 1982) would predict that socially anxious individuals under social stress would use substances more frequently, as compared to individuals low in social anxiety (Morris, Stewart, & Ham, 2005). Finally, according to the self-medication hypothesis, substance use would reduce anxiety in socially anxious individuals, and this reduction in anxiety would produce an increased desire for future use of the substance when in social (i.e., anxiety provoking) situations (Chutuape & de Wit, 1995; Carrigan & Randall, 2003).

Research examining these theoretical models has been reviewed and classified by Morris and colleagues in the context of alcohol drinking (Morris et al. 2005). Thus, studies have been categorized into three groups; the first category includes studies which have tested the anxiolytic effects of substances for socially anxious individuals under stressful situations. This type of research has been mainly experimental and results have shown that alcohol drinking actually reduces tension, stress-response, and anxiety symptoms in laboratory settings (e.g., Abrams, Kushner, Medina, & Voight, 2001). More recent research has also shown combined anxiolytic effects of alcohol drinking and smoking behavior, as evident in psycho-physiological measures of anxiety among individuals with social anxiety (e.g., startle eye blink magnitude) (Braun, et al., 2012).

The second category of studies has focused on testing whether socially anxious individuals actually use more substances (e.g., drink more) than others in the context of social stress. Lab experiments have been also used in this context. For instance, experiments with college students have shown that participants with high trait social anxiety drink more than others, if placed under stressful conditions (e.g., Kidorf & Lang, 1999). Despite criticisms concerning the artificiality of settings and the generalizability of findings, these lab results are important in the context of establishing the link between the experience of stress and drinking behavior, among individuals with social anxiety (Morris et al., 2005).

Similar findings have been reported in experiments involving cannabis use. Buckner, Silgado, and Schmidt (2011) found that cannabis users with comorbid social anxiety were more vulnerable to cannabis use during social anxiety-provoking tasks as compared to other tasks (e.g., speech task rather vs. writing task). Along these lines, reports from individuals with comorbid social anxiety and cannabis use disorders have suggested self-medicating purposes of use (i.e., to reduce social anxiety or cope with the social situation) (Buckner, et al., 2012; Buckner, Heimberg, Matthews, & Silgado, 2012).

The third category of studies has focused on determining whether individuals with social anxiety are at a higher risk of experiencing substance use problems (e.g., alcohol disorders) as compared to others. Studies with clinical populations have demonstrated that having a social anxiety diagnosis significantly increases chances of having a comorbid alcohol use disorder (Kushner & Sher, 1993). More recently, Buckner and colleagues (2008) reported that social anxiety disorder at baseline was associated with 6.5 greater odds for cannabis dependence and 4.5 greater odds for alcohol dependence, several years later. These results were found after controlling for other confounding variables such as gender, depression, conduct disorder, and other anxiety disorders.

Along these lines, more recent research aiming to explain the relationship between social anxiety and substance use has specifically focused on moderating variables (e.g., expectancies) and cognitive processes (e.g., reduction in attention bias) involved. For instance, elaborations of the theories in terms of expectancies related to substance use, have suggested that socially anxious individuals with stronger tension reduction expectancies are more likely to use substances when experiencing tension (Goldman, Del Boca, & Darkes, 1999). Moreover, according to the avoidance coping cognitive model (an elaborated version of appraisal-disruption model, Sayette, 1993) individuals with social anxiety may be particularly vulnerable to the anxiolytic effects of alcohol because of the positive effects in reducing their attention bias to social threats (Bacon & Ham, 2010). Research studies have provided support for this theory. For instance, Stevens, Gerlach and Rist (2008) showed that individuals with social phobia who were given a drink, perceived angry faces as less threatening than controls (individuals with social phobia who did not consume alcohol). The authors suggested that the reduction in perceptions of threat might act as negative reinforcement, which contributes to the development of substance use problems. Similarly there are findings suggesting that the implicit memory bias for socially threatening words in individuals with social phobia is eliminated after alcohol drinking (Gerlach, Schiller, Wild, & Rist, 2006).

Taken together these studies suggest that coping motives seem to be inevitably involved in understanding the relationship between social anxiety and substance use. Indeed studies directly assessing motives for substance use have found significant relationships between social anxiety and coping motives but not enhancement or social motives (Windle & Windle, 2012). Moreover, coping motives have been identified as the unique mediators of the relationship between social anxiety and hazardous drinking behavior (e.g., Ham, Zamboanga, Bacon, & Garcia, 2009). Research on cannabis use has also found relationships between social anxiety and coping motives for use (e.g., coping with distressing suicidal thoughts) (Buckner, Bonn-Miller, Zvolensky, & Schmidt, 2007). Furthermore, coping motives have been found to mediate the relationship between social anxiety and cannabis use (Buckner, Schmidt, Bobadilla, & Taylor, 2006). Finally, substance use for coping motives has been associated with overall increased risk for substance use disorders (Carpenter & Hasin, 1999; Cooper Russell, Skinner, Frone, & Mudar, 1992; Thomas, Randall, & Carrigan, 2003).

To conclude, there is vast support for cognitive-affective theories, which aim to explain the social anxiety-substance use relationship in terms of coping processes, i.e., use of substances for tension reduction purposes, stress management, or self-medication. Thus it has been argued that social anxiety might indeed be considered an important risk factor for developing substance use disorders (e.g., Ham, Hope, White, & Rivers, 2002). Nonetheless, opponents of this approach have argued that social anxiety might conversely act as a protective factor from substance use, e.g., socially anxious individuals would tend to avoid the type of settings or activities that might promote substance use such as peer group affiliation (e.g., Eggleston, Woolaway-Bickel, & Schmidt, 2004). The following section discusses these contradictory claims and research findings in the context of social learning theories of substance use.

## 4.2. Social Learning Theories

Social learning and normative theories focus on the impact of social factors such as observation learning or social norms on substance use and abuse (Bandura, 1977; 1982). Considering this, it might be argued that socially anxious individuals should be rather 'immune' to social influences since they would tend to avoid those types of settings or activities that might promote substance use (e.g., parties, various social gatherings etc.) (Ham & Hope, 2005). Higgins (1997) has further argued that the great prevention focus of socially anxious individuals (e.g., the concern with avoiding mistakes and the high sensitivity of possible negative outcomes) would make them less likely to engage in risky behaviors, including substance use and abuse.

Several research studies have supported a negative relationship between social anxiety and substance use. For instance, Eggleston and colleagues (2004) found that the mean number of alcohol drinking days as well as the number of binges per week among college undergraduates were negatively correlated with social anxiety levels. The findings were interpreted in terms of avoidance coping, i.e., individuals with social anxiety avoid social situations during which alcohol might be consumed. Ham and Hope (2005) also found an inverse relationship between alcohol consumption and social anxiety among university students. Along these lines Myers and colleagues (Myers, Aarons, Tomlinson, & Stein, 2003) reported that substance use among adolescents was positively associated with negative affectivity but negatively associated with social anxiety. More recently Tomlinson and Brown (2012) study with adolescents found that drinking frequency and quantity were associated with stronger depressive symptoms but lower social anxiety levels.

These findings have been challenged by several authors who argue that they represent only part of the picture. In an attempt to integrate the contradictory findings on the relationship social anxiety-substance use Stewart and colleagues (Stewart, Morris, Mellings, & Komar, 2006) looked further into the inherent structure of social anxiety. They concluded that specific aspects of social anxiety were differentially related to drinking behavior. Thus social avoidance and distress were significantly negatively related to drinking frequency. On the other hand fear of negative evaluation/or fear of avoidance were positively related to the frequency of drinking behavior (i.e., conformity to peer pressure). Along the same lines Kashdan, Elhai, and Breen (2008) have argued that findings of a negative relationship only represent the predominantly avoidant- socially anxious individuals, who experience strong threats and avoid risky behavior. Nonetheless, positive relationships would be expected among the predominantly approach-socially anxious individuals, who perceive engagement in risky behavior as an opportunity to satisfy their curiosity, enhance their social status, and appear more attractive to others (Kashdan & Steger, 2006; Kashdan, 2007; Kashdan et al., 2008). Thus, in the second case scenario, social learning theories would predict positive relationships between social anxiety and substance use.

Indeed, especially in adolescence social anxiety has been closely related to conformity with the social group, which in many cases means involvement in risky behavior such as substance use (Buckner, Mallott, Schmidt, & Taylor, 2006; Santee & Maslach, 1982; Wright, London, & Waechter, 2010). Relationships between social anxiety and conformity drinking motives have been found in several studies with adolescents (e.g., Lewis et al., 2008). However, perceptions of social pressure (rather than actual pressure) seem to be the important element establishing the link between social anxiety and substance using behavior (e.g., Buckner et al., 2006).

Thus, individuals with high anxiety levels drink more when they perceive that most others are also drinking (descriptive norms) or are approving of drinking behavior (injunctive norms). Buckner, Ecker, and Proctor (2011) found that injunctive social norms moderated the relationship between social anxiety group status (low vs. high anxiety) and alcohol-related problems so that participants with higher anxiety levels, and stronger injunctive norms, reported the most alcohol-related problems. Conversely, high social anxiety individuals drink less than low social anxiety individuals when injunctive norms are weaker (LaBrie, Hummer, & Neighbors, 2008).

Along these lines, several studies have suggested that substance use might provide an impression management strategy for individuals with social anxiety (Sharp & Getz, 1996; Thornton, Audesse, Ryckman, & Burckle, 2006). Thus socially anxious people may be vulnerable to using alcohol to manage the impressions they wish to make on others. Indeed, Bucker and Matthews (2012) have found that the belief that others would find the participant more social and outgoing when drinking, was the only unique predictor of alcohol-related problems among individuals with high social anxiety.

To summarize, social learning models suggest that social anxiety might represent either a risk or a protective factor depending on whether the socially anxious individual is predominantly the approach or the avoidant type. However, by providing a different level of analysis Morris et al. (2005) suggest that in order to integrate the contradicting findings and reach more solid conclusions it is also important to provide an in-depth discussion of moderating variables (e.g., outcome expectancies) or third variables (situational factors and gender).

The following section represents an effort to integrate the different theoretical perspectives and research studies into providing some general conclusions.

## 4.3. Integrating Perspectives

Several authors have argued that a discussion of moderating variables (expectancies) and third variables (situational variables, gender) is necessary to explain the existence of both positive and negative relationships between substance use and social anxiety (Cooper et al., 1992; Morris et al., 2005; Tran & Haaga, 2002). In other words social anxiety might act both as a protective or a risk factor depending on outcome expectancies (e.g., tension reduction) for substance use (Ham, 2009; Ham, Zamboanga, Olthuis, Casner, & Bui, 2010). For instance, Tran, Haaga, and Chambless (1997) found a moderating role of alcohol expectancies so that high social anxiety individuals, who did not expect alcohol to reduce their anxiety in social situations, reported lower levels of drinking as compared to low social anxiety individuals. The moderating effect was situational specific; i.e., this effect was observed only for social situation expectancies but not for general tension reduction expectancies.

In this context, Wall, McKee, and Hinson (2000) have proposed the situational specificity hypothesis according to which differences in drinking behavior across contexts can be explained, in terms of the different outcome expectancies. Ham, Zamboanga, and Bacon (2011) found support for this hypothesis, as positive alcohol outcome expectancies moderated the relationship between social anxiety and alcohol drinking in convivial contexts (e.g., at a party, club, concert or celebration), but not other contexts.

The authors concluded that socially anxious young adults who hold highly positive alcohol outcome expectancies in convivial drinking contexts could be at high risk for developing alcohol-related problems. This study is in line with previous studies reporting that individuals with social anxiety drink more alcohol during social interaction tasks as compared to performance tasks (e.g., Abrams et al., 2001; Turner, Beidel, Dancu, & Keys, 1986). Indeed outcome expectancies differ across contexts and it has been suggested that abstinence from alcohol during performance tasks might be related to expectancies of negative effects on cognitive and motor functioning (e.g., MacLatchy-Gaudet & Stewart, 2001; Wall et al., 2000).

Nonetheless, research on expectancies and cannabis use has yielded quite more complicated results. For instance, Buckner and Schmidt (2009) in a study with cannabis users found that individuals with social anxiety were more likely to have negative expectancies associated to cannabis use (e.g., they associated use to cognitive and behavioral impairment). However, the authors argued that these expectancies might in fact have a positive subjective connotation for the users themselves (e.g., the cognitive impairment might be seen as a reduction in the anxiety provoking thoughts). Buckner and Schmidt (2009) also argue that a self-handicapping explanation might be plausible; in other words socially anxious individuals use cannabis because they believe that others would attribute inappropriate behavior to cannabis use and not their disorder (i.e., cannabis use as an impression management technique).

Also, in the context of smoking behavior, research has shown that outcome expectancies related to affect management, influence both smoking behavior at the time of measurement and predict future increases in smoking behavior and nicotine dependence. Nonetheless, outcome expectancies seem to represent an important risk factor on their own; indeed, their impact remains significant even when controlling for symptoms of anxiety (Heinz, Kassel, Berbaum, & Mermelstein, 2010; Henry, Jamner, & Whalen, 2012).

As regards gender, research studies have found that social anxiety is related to drinking problems for women, but not men (e.g., Buckner & Turner, 2008; Norberg, Olivier, Alperstein, Zvolensky, & Norton, 2011). Moreover, coping and conformity drinking motives seem to mediate the relationship between social anxiety and alcohol-related problems only among women (Norberg, Norton, Olivier, & Zvolensky, 2010). It has been suggested that drinking among socially anxious women might be closely related to adverse family interactions; indeed, women with social anxiety, who live in healthy, cohesive families seem to be less likely to use alcohol or develop an alcohol related disorder (Bucker & Turner, 2008).

Conversely, men with social anxiety seem to be more vulnerable to cannabis-related problems and also more likely to have a co-occurring cannabis use disorder (Buckner et al., 2011; Buckner et al., 2012). Studies have found positive associations between social anxiety and coping/ conformity motives for cannabis use among men only; in turn, these motives were mediating the relationship between social anxiety and cannabis-related problems only within this gender category. Among women, social anxiety was unrelated to cannabis problems (Norberg et al., 2011). Findings suggesting that socially anxious men might use cannabis as a means of avoidance coping (avoiding negative affect or questions by others) have been replicated in other studies (e.g., Buckner, Zvolensky, & Schmidt, 2012). Moreover, perceptions of coping skills are also involved, i.e., substance use increases with the levels of social anxiety only among individuals who perceive low coping skills (Buckner et al., 2006).

These differential findings by gender might be related to issues such as availability and access to substances (e.g., men can get easier access to cannabis through peer groups), or the diversity of the clinical picture of social anxiety for men and women (e.g., the variability in the types of anxiety provoking situations) (Peleg, 2002; 2004; 2005). Whatever the reason for these differences it is important that they are considered both in the understanding and treatment of social anxiety and substance use disorders.

To conclude, the consideration of outcome expectations, situational specificity and gender issues is very important in the context of understanding contradictory findings in the literature. Quite as important as the understanding of theoretical issues is the practical application of knowledge into specific treatment programs. The following section provides a discussion of the main treatment programs for social anxiety and substance use disorders.

# 5. Implications for Treatment

Social anxiety can contribute to the etiology, maintenance, and relapse of substance use problems and disorders (Carrigan and Randall, 2003; Morris et al., 2005; Kushner et al., 2000). Furthermore social anxiety-substance use comorbidity cases are also associated with greater overall impairment than either condition alone. Consequently the treatment of comorbid cases represents a great challenge (Buckner, Ledley, Heimberg, & Schmidt, 2008).

Several drug therapies have shown high effectiveness in reducing social anxiety symptoms, e.g., monoamine oxidase inhibitors, benzodiazepines, and selective serotonin reuptake inhibitors (SSRIs) (Book & Randall, 2002; Davidson, 1998). SSRIs such as paroxetine, have shown to be effective both in the treatment of social anxiety and comorbid social-anxiety and alcohol use disorders (Randall et al., 2001). However, it should be mentioned that although paroxetine improves social anxiety symptoms, its' direct influence on alcohol consumption rates is debatable (Carrigan & Randall, 2003). Randall and colleagues (2001) have argued that the failure to find an effect on drinking behavior is actually due to measurements in the short term only, i.e., differences in alcohol consumption might actually become statistically significant with a longer course of treatment. Nonetheless, no studies so far have tested these claims.

More recent research has shown that although paroxetine treatment might not reduce alcohol drinking overall, it seems to reduce reliance on drinking in social situations (Thomas, Randall, Book & Randall, 2008). Nonetheless, the methodology used in the study did not enable to distinguish between actual behavioral effects or subjective perceptions, i.e., it was impossible to know whether participants actually drank less in social situations or whether their self-efficacy in dealing with social situations made them believe they needed less alcohol.

Finally, the authors highlight the fact that the social anxiety treatment might have simply influenced a change in drinking motives since the frequency and quantity of drinking did not change (e.g., e.g., from social to pleasure motives) (Thomas et al., 2008).

Similar results have been reported for psychotherapy interventions (cognitive-behavioral treatment including exposure, cognitive restructuring, relaxation training and social skills training) or combined drug and psychotherapy interventions for social anxiety treatment (e.g., Book & Randall, 2002; Liappas, Paparrigopoulos, Tzavellas, & Christodoulou, 2003). Despite the scarcity of findings on positive effects of social anxiety treatment on comorbid drinking behavior, there is a need to also consider indirect influences. For instance, it has been argued that the reduction of social anxiety might be quite beneficial for individuals with comorbid social anxiety and substance use disorders, since it might enable them to engage in group therapy. Indeed successful substance use treatment frequently involves group treatment or self-help groups (e.g., Alcoholics Anonymous) and research has shown that social anxiety directly influences willingness to participate in this kind of treatments (e.g., Book, Thomas, Dempsey, Randall, & Randall, 2009).

On the other hand, the treatment of the substance use disorder (in substance use-social anxiety comorbidity cases), through psycho-social interventions such as Cognitive Behavioral Coping Skills, or Twelve-Step Facilitation has resulted in positive effects only in terms of substance use (Project MATCH Research Group, 1993; Thevos, Roberts, Thomas, & Randall, 2000). However, there is evidence showing that treatment for drinking is less effective among highly socially anxious drinkers (as compared to low social anxiety drinkers) (Terlecki, Buckner, Larimer, & Copeland, 2011). This kind of research has promoted the need to consider combined treatment both for social anxiety and substance use as an option.

Early results testing the efficacy of combined treatment have found discouraging results. For instance a study by Randall, Thomas, and Thevos (2001) documented negative effects of combined treatment; i.e., individuals assigned to both social anxiety and alcohol treatment, fared worse than individuals assigned to substance use only treatment. It has been argued that the demands of the combined treatment approach might have been too great for the participants, as suggested by the high drop-out rates. In relation to this, Morris et al. (2005) have suggested a treatment model which helps the individuals understand how the social anxiety and substance use problems are related to each other. Education on specific coping strategies for social anxiety including both positive (cognitive restructuring) and negative strategies (substance abuse) is also a necessary component. Finally the authors have argued that both attitudes and expectancies about substance use need to be challenged. Behavioral techniques such as systematic desensitization might be particularly useful as individuals are exposed to socially feared situations without drinking, smoking, or using cannabis (Morris et al., 2005).

More recently, Buckner and colleagues (2008) have reported positive effects for combined motivation enhancement therapy (for alcohol use disorders) and cognitive-behavioral therapy for social anxiety. Indeed after 19 sessions of combined therapy, their case study patient demonstrated a significant reduction both in social anxiety and alcohol-related problems. The authors explained the combined effect in terms of the chronology of the specific treatments; thus, presenting socially anxious patients with a plan for changing drinking behavior before the cognitive-behavioral treatment for social anxiety, seems to reduce the chances that patients would use drinking to relieve their anxiety. Nonetheless, Bucker et al. (2008) admit the limitations of the single case study and highlight the need to replicate findings with treatment groups, before making any strong conclusions.

To conclude it might be said that despite the great efforts and advancements in the treatment of comorbid social anxiety-substance use disorders, they still represent a great challenge. In this context, it has been suggested that efforts should be directed towards the prevention of these disorders (Kendall, Safford, Flannery-Schroeder, & Webb, 2004). Longitudinal studies have shown that interventions addressing social anxiety during adolescence might prevent the development of substance use problems related to coping motives.

Indeed, post treatment assessment (seven years later) has shown significantly less substance use among the group receiving treatment for social anxiety as compared to a normative sample. Hence, intervention at an early developmental level might be quite important to prevent the development of social anxiety-substance use comorbidy. Similarly, normative interventions at an early age (e.g., challenging maladaptive beliefs related to the approval of substance using behaviors) is also quite important both in prevention and treatment of comorbid social-anxiety substance use disorders (e.g., it has been suggested that it should be part of the standard cognitive-behavioral treatment for social anxiety) (e.g., Buckner et al., 2011).

Finally, it should be also mentioned, that most research on treatment of the social anxiety-substance use comorbidity has focused on alcohol use disorders; thus there is a need for further research to also examine treatment for comorbid social anxiety-cannabis use disorders too.

# Conclusion and Suggestions for Future Research

Substance use and abuse represent important health concerns worldwide. Among the several influences, psychiatric variables (e.g., social anxiety symptoms) have also been considered relevant in understanding the etiology and maintenance of substance use or abuse. Indeed the relationship between social anxiety and substance use disorders has been well documented in the literature. Explanations for this relationship have been mainly provided in terms of cognitive-affective theories and social learning models. Thus according to cognitive theories, individuals with social anxiety use substances mainly for coping purposes (self-medicate).

On the other hand, social learning models suggest that social anxiety might act as a risk factor for socially anxious individuals who want to approach others and be liked by them (approach-oriented socially anxious individuals), but as a protective factor for avoidant socially anxious individuals (e.g., avoid parties or social gatherings where alcohol might be consumed). Although both groups of theories have found support from empirical studies, recently efforts have been directed towards examining moderating variables or third variables that might be influencing the relationship, e.g., expectancies, situational influences etc. These studies have contributed in explaining why socially anxious individuals might use substances only under certain conditions but not others (e.g., they would drink if they believed drinking would make them more sociable at a party, but they would not drink if they believed drinking would produce cognitive or behavioral impairment before giving a speech).

Despite differences in theoretical concepts and recent developments refining theoretical constructs, it should be mentioned that both cognitive-affective and social learning theories are built on a common premise: Social anxiety develops before substance use problems and is thus involved in the etiology of these disorders. However, it has been argued that other links between social anxiety and substance use/abuse should be considered. Indeed three other hypotheses explaining this relationship have been suggested, including the possibility that: a. social anxiety symptoms appear as a consequence of substance use or withdrawal b. the two disorders are initially unrelated, but consequently interact and aggravate each other or c. they share a common etiology, be it biological or psychosocial (Lehman, Myers, & Corty, 2000). Therefore further research is needed into the etiology of the comorbidity between social anxiety and substance use disorders.

Other issues that need to be discussed and addressed in future studies have to do with gender and the use/abuse of substances. Indeed although important gender differences have been noted in the types of substances abused by socially anxious men and women (alcohol by women and cannabis by men), research has mainly focused on alcohol use disorders, while somehow ignoring cannabis use disorders.

Hence, although the few studies addressing cannabis use disorders have reported significant rates of comorbidity with social anxiety (and impairment too), alcohol abuse is still getting much more research attention. Along the same lines, research on smoking behavior and social anxiety is also quite scarce. Considering the extensiveness of smoking behavior, the increased likelihood of smokers for engaging into other risky behaviors (smoking and drinking) and the detrimental effects on health, it is important to highlight the need for further research in this direction too.

Another aspect which needs some discussion involves cultural differences. Needless to say that most research addressing social anxiety and substance use/misuse has been conducted in Western European countries and the United States, i.e., individualistic developed cultures. Nonetheless, as mentioned earlier in the chapter, research has shown that both the demographics of substance use and the patterns of social anxiety, differ by culture (collectivistic vs. individualistic). Therefore, cross-cultural research would be quite important in terms of understanding the socio-cultural factors involved in the relationship between social anxiety substance use disorders.

Finally in terms of treatment, it is quite central to mention the need for studies proposing and assessing the effectiveness of new joined treatment methods (addressing both social anxiety and substance use).

Moreover, a greater focus on preventive (well-timed) programs would be quite important. These programs should focus on critical developmental stages such as adolescence and young adulthood and would ultimately help in the creation of a healthier society both physically and psychologically.

# References

Abrams, K., Kushner, M., Medina, K., & Voight, A. (2001). The pharmacologic and expectancy effects of alcohol on social anxiety in individuals with social phobia. *Drug and Alcohol Dependence, 64*, 219–231.

Abrams, K., & Kushner, M. G. (2004). The moderating effects of tension-reduction alcohol outcome expectancies on placebo responding in individuals with social phobia. *Addictive Behaviors, 29*, 1221–1224.

Agosti, V., Nunes, E., & Levin, F. (2002). Rates of psychiatric comorbidity among U.S. residents with lifetime cannabis dependence. *The American Journal of Drug and Alcohol Abuse, 28*, 643–652.

Ajzen, I. (1991). The theory of planned behaviour. *Organizational Behaviour & Human Decision Processes, 50*, 179-211.

Ajzen, I., & Fishbein, M. (1980). Understanding attitudes and predicting social behavior. NJ: Prentice Hall.

Alamar, B., & Glantz, S. A. (2006). Effect of increased social unacceptability of cigarette smoking on reduction in cigarette consumption. *American Journal of Public Health*, 96, 1359-1363.

Allen, T. J., Moeller, F. G., Rhoades, H. M., & Cherek, D. R. (1998). Impulsivity and history of drug dependence. *Drug & Alcohol Dependence*, 50, 137-145.

Amaro, H., Blake, S. M., Schwartz, P. M., & Flinchbaugh, L. J. (2001). Developing theory-based substance abuse prevention programs for young adolescent girls. *Journal of Early Adolescence*, 21, 256-293.

American Psychiatric Association. (2000). Diagnostic and statistical manual of mental disorders, Fourth edition, Text Revision (DSM-IV-TR). USA: APA Publishing.

Amos, A. (1996). Women and smoking. *British Medical Bulletin*, 52, 74-89.

Amos, A., & Haglund, M. (2000). From social taboo to "torch of freedom": The marketing of cigarettes to women. *Tobacco Control*, 9, 3–8.

Angove, R., & Fothergill, A. (2003). Women and alcohol: Misrepresented and misunderstood. *Journal of Psychiatric and Mental Health Nursing*, 10, 213-219.

Arai, Y., Hosokawa, T., Fukao, A., Izumi, Y., & Hisamichi, S. (1997). Smoking behaviour and personality: A population-based study in Japan. *Addiction*, 92, 1023-1033.

Ary, D. V., Duncan, T. E., Biglan, A., Metzler, C. W., Noell, J. W., & Smolkowski, K. (1999). Development of adolescent problem behaviour. *Journal of Abnormal Child Psychology*, 27, 141-150.

Bacon, A. K., & Ham, L. S. (2010). Attention to social threat as a vulnerability to the development of comorbid social anxiety disorder and alcohol use disorders: An avoidance-coping cognitive model. *Addictive Behaviors*, 35, 925-939.

Baer, J. S., Kivlahan, D. R., & Marlatt, G. A. (1995). High-risk drinking across the transition from high school to college. *Alcoholism: Clinical and Experimental Research*, 19, 54-61.

Baker, T. B., Piper, M. E., McCarthy, D. E., Majeskie, M. R., & Fiore, M. C. (2004). Addiction motivation reformulated: An affective processing model of negative reinforcement. *Psychological Review*, 111, 33-51.

Bakken, K., Landheim, A. S., & Vaglum, P. (2005). Substance dependent patients with and without social anxiety disorder: Occurrence and clinical differences. A study of a consecutive sample of alcohol dependent and poly-substance-dependent patients treated in two counties in Norway. *Drug and Alcohol Dependence*, 80, 321-328.

Ballenger, J., Davidson, J. T., Lecrubier, Y., Nutt, D., Bobes, J., Beidel, D. et al. (1998). Consensus statement on social anxiety disorder from the international consensus group on depression and anxiety. *Journal of Clinical Psychiatry*, 59, 54–60.

Bandura, A. (1977). Self efficacy: Toward a unifying theory of behavior change. *Psychological Review*, 84, 191-215.

Bandura, A. (1982). Self-efficacy mechanism in human agency. *American Psychologist*, 37, 122- 147.

Bandura, A. (1986). Social foundations of thought and action: A social cognitive theory. Engiewood Cliffs NJ: Prentice Hall.

Baum, D. D., Duffelmeyer, F., & Greenlan, M. (2001). Resource teacher perceptions of the prevalence of social dysfunction among students with learning disabilities. *Journal of Learning Disabilities*, 21, 380-381.

Bauman, K. E., & Ennett, S. T. (1996). On the importance of peer influence on adolescent drug use: Commonly neglected considerations. *Addiction*, 91, 185-198.

Bobo, J. K., & Husten, C. (2000). Sociocultural influences on smoking and drinking. *Alcohol Research & Health,* 24, 225–232.

Bogg, T., & Roberts, B.W. (2004). Conscientiousness and health-related behaviors: a meta-analysis of the leading behavioral contributors to mortality. *Psychological Bulletin,* 130, 887-919.

Bolton, J., Cox, B., Clara, I., & Sareen, J. (2006). Use of alcohol and drugs to self medicate anxiety disorders in a nationally representative sample. *The Journal of Nervous and Mental Disease,* 194, 818–825.

Book, S. W., & Randall, C. L. (2002). Social anxiety and alcohol use disorder. *Alcohol Research & Health,* 26, 130-135.

Book, S. W., Thomas, S. E., Dempsey, J. P., Randall, P. K., & Randall, C. L. (2009). Social anxiety impacts willingness to participate in addiction treatment. *Addictive Behaviors,* 34, 474-476.

Book, S. W., Thomas, S. E., Smith, J. P., & Miller, P. M. (2012). Severity of anxiety in mental health versus addiction treatment settings when social anxiety and substance abuse are comorbid. *Addictive Behaviors,* 37, 1158-1161.

Borsari, B., & Carey, K. B. (2001). Peer influences on college drinking: A review of the research. *Journal of Substance Abuse Treatment,* 13, 391-424.

Boyd, C. J., McCabe, S. E., & Morales M. (2005). College students' alcohol use: A critical review. *Annual Review of Nursing Research,* 23, 179-211.

Braun, A. R., Heinz, A. J., Veilleux, J. C., Conrad, M., Weber, S., Wardle, M., et al. (2012). The separate and combined effects of alcohol and nicotine on anticipatory anxiety: A multidimensional analysis. *Addictive Behaviors,* 37, 485-491.

Breslau, N., Novak, S. P., & Kessler, R. C. (2004). Daily smoking and the subsequent onset of psychiatric disorders. *Psychological Medicine,* 34, 323-333.

Brown, S. A., Christiansen, B. A., & Goldman, M. S. (1987). The alcohol expectancy questionnaire: An instrument for the assessment of adolescent and adult alcohol expectancies. *Journal of Studies on Alcohol,* 48, 483–491.

Bryan, T. (2005). Science-based advances in the social domain of learning disabilities. *Learning Disability Quarterly,* 28, 119-121.

Buckner, J. D., Mallott, M. A., Schmidt, N. B., & Taylor, J. (2006). Peer influence and gender differences in problematic cannabis use among individuals with social anxiety. *Journal of Anxiety Disorders,* 20, 1087–1102.

Buckner, J. D., Schmidt, N. B., Bobadilla, L., & Taylor, J. (2006). Social anxiety and problematic cannabis use: Evaluating the moderating role of stress reactivity and perceived coping. *Behaviour Research & Therapy,* 44, 1007-1015.

Buckner, J. D., Bonn-Miller, M. O., Zvolensky, M. J., & Schmidt, N. B. (2007). Marijuana use motives and social anxiety among marijuana-using young adults. *Addictive Behaviors,* 32, 2238–2252.

Buckner, J. D., Ledley, D. R., Heimberg, R. G., & Schmidt, N. B. (2008). Treating comorbid social anxiety and alcohol use disorders. *Clinical Case Studies,* 7, 208-223.

Buckner, J. D., & Schmidt, N. B. (2008). Marijuana effect expectancies: Relations to social anxiety and marijuana use problems. *Addictive Behaviors,* 33, 1477–1483.

Buckner, J. D., & Schmidt, N. B. (2009). Social anxiety disorder and marijuana use problems: The mediating role of marijuana effect expectancies. *Depression and Anxiety,* 26, 864-870.

Buckner, J. D., Schmidt, N. B., Lang, A. R., Small, J. W., Schlauch, R. C., & Lewinsohn, P. M. (2008). Specificity of social anxiety disorder as a risk factor for alcohol and cannabis dependence. *Journal of Psychiatric Research,* 42, 230–239.

Buckner, J. D., & Turner, R. J. (2008). Social anxiety disorder as a risk factor for alcohol use disorders: A prospective examination of parental and peer influences. *Drug and Alcohol Dependence,* 100, 128–137.

Buckner, J. D., Crosby, R. D., Wonderlich, S. A., & Schmidt, N. B. (2011). Social anxiety and cannabis use: An analysis from an ecological momentary assessment. *Journal of Anxiety Disorders,* 26, 297-304.

Buckner, J. D., Ecker, A. H., & Proctor, S. L. (2011). Social anxiety and alcohol problems. The roles of perceived descriptive and injunctive peer norms. *Journal of Anxiety Disorders,* 25, 631-638.

Buckner, J. D., Heimberg, R. G., & Schmidt, N. B. (2011). Social anxiety andmarijuana-related problems: The role of social avoidance. *Addictive Behaviors,* 36,129–132.

Buckner, J. D., Silgado, J., & Schmidt, N. B. (2011). Marijuana craving during a public speaking challenge: Understanding marijuana use vulnerability among women and those with social anxiety disorder. *Journal of Behavior Therapy and Experimental Psychiatry,* 42, 104–110.

Buckner, J. D., Heimberg, R. G., Matthews, R. A., & Silgado, J. (2012). Marijuana-related problems and social anxiety: The role of marijuana behaviors in social situations. *Psychology of Addictive Behaviors,* 26, 151–156.

Buckner, J. D., Heimberg, R. G., Schneier, F. R., Liu, S., Wang, S., & Blanco, C. (2012). The relationship between cannabis use disorders and social anxiety disorder in the National Epidemiological Study of Alcohol and Related Conditions (NESARC). *Drug and Alcohol Dependence,* 124, 128–134.

Buckner, J. D., & Matthews, R. A. (2012). Social impressions while drinking account for the relationships between alcohol related problems and social anxiety. *Addictive Behaviors,* 37, 533-536.

Buckner, J. D., Joiner, T. E., Schmidt, N. B., & Zvolensky, M. J. (2012). Daily marihuana use and suicidality: The unique impact of social anxiety. *Addictive Behaviors,* 37, 387-392.

Buckner, J. D., Zvolensky, M. J., & Schmidt, N. B. (2012). Cannabis related impairment and social anxiety. *Addictive Behaviors,* 37, 1294-1297.

Burke, R., & Stephens, R. (1999). Social anxiety and drinking in college students: A social cognitive theory analysis. *Clinical Psychology Review,* 19, 513–530.

Calabria, B., Degenhardt, L., Hall, W., & Lynskey, M. (2010). Does cannabis use increase the risk of death? Systematic review of epidemiological evidence on adverse effects of cannabis use. *Drug & Alcohol Review,* 29, 313-330.

Carpenter, K. & Hasin, D. (1999). Drinking to cope with negative affect and DSM-IV alcohol use disorders: A test of three alternative explanations. *Journal of Studies on Alcohol,* 60, 697 – 704.

Carrigan, M., & Randall, C. (2003). Self-medication in social phobia: A review of the alcohol literature. *Addictive Behaviors,* 28, 269–284.

Caslyn, R. J., Winter, J. P., & Burger, G. K. (2005). The relationship between social anxiety and social support in adolescents: A test of competing causal models. *Adolescence,* 40, 103-113.

Chakroun, N., Doron, J., & Swendsen, J. (2004). Substance use, affective problems and personality traits: Test of two association models. *Encephale,* 30, 564-569.

Chartier, M., Walker, J., & Stein, M. (2003). Considering co-morbidity in social phobia. *Social Psychiatry and Psychiatric Epidemiology,* 38, 728–734.

Chassin, L., & Handley, E. D. (2006). Parents and families as contexts for the development of substance use and substance use disorders. *Psychology of Addictive Behaviours,* 20, 135-137.

Chutuape, M. & de Wit, H. (1995). Preferences for ethanol and diazepam in anxious individuals: An evaluation of the self-medication hypothesis. *Psychopharmacology,* 121, 91–103.

Cialdini, R. B., & Goldstein, N. J. (2004). Social influence: Compliance and conformity. *Annual Review of Psychology,* 55, 591-621.

Cialdini, R. B., & Sagarin, B. J. (2005). Principles of interpersonal influence. In T. C. Brock & M. C. Green (Eds.), Persuasion: Psychological insights and perspectives (pp.143-170). USA: Sage Publications.

Coffey, S. F., Read, J. P., & Norberg, M. M. (2008). Posttraumatic stress disorder and substance use disorder: Neuroimaging, neuroendocrine and psychophysiological findings. In S. H. Stewart & P. J. Conrod (Eds.). Anxiety and substance use disorders: The vicious cycle of comorbidity (pp. 37-58). USA: Springer.

Courtenay, W. H., McCreary, D. R., & Merighi, J. R. (2002). Gender and ethnic differences in health beliefs and behaviours. *Journal of Health Psychology,* 7, 219-231.

Cohen, S., & Lichtenstein, E. (1990). Perceived stress, quitting smoking, and smoking relapse. *Health Psychology,* 9, 466–478.

Conger, J. (1956). Reinforcement theory and the dynamics of alcoholism. *Quarterly Journal of Studies on Alcohol,* 17, 296–305.

Conner, K. R., Britton, P. C., Sworts, L. M., & Joiner, T. E., Jr. (2007). Suicide attempts among individuals with opiate dependence: The critical role of belonging. *Addictive Behaviors,* 32, 1395–1404.

Conway, K. P., Compton, W., Stinson, F. S., & Grant, B. F. (2006). Lifetime comorbidity of DSM-IV mood and anxiety disorders and specific drug use disorders: results from the National Epidemiologic Survey on Alcohol and Related Conditions. *Journal of Clinical Psychiatry,* 67, 247–257.

Cooper, M. L. (1994). Motivations for alcohol use among adolescents: Development and validation of a four-factor model. *Psychological Assessment,* 6, 117 – 128.

Cooper, M. L. (2002). Alcohol use and risky sexual behavior among college students and youth: Evaluating the evidence. *Journal of Studies on Alcohol, (Suppl. 14),* 101-117.

Cooper, M. L., Russell, M., Skinner, J., Frone, M., & Mudar, P. (1992). Stress and alcohol use: Moderating effects of gender, coping, and alcohol expectancies. *Journal of Abnormal Psychology,* 101, 139–152.

Cooper, M. L., Russell, M., Skinner, & Windle, M. (1992). Development and validation of a three dimensional measure of drinking motives. *Psychological Assessment,* 4, 123-132.

Corcoran, K. J., & Segrist, D. J. (1993). Personal expectancies and group influences affect alcoholic beverage selection: The interaction of personal and situational variables. *Addictive Behaviors,* 18, 577-582.

Craig, G. J., & Baucum, D. (2002). Human development. USA: Prentice-Hall.

Curran, P. J., Stice, E., & Chassin, L. (1997). The relation between adolescent alcohol use and peer alcohol use: A longitudinal random coefficients model. *Journal of Consulting and Clinical Psychology*, 65, 130-140.

Darke, S., Duflou, J., & Torok, M. (2009). Toxicology and circumstances of completed suicide by means other than overdose. *Journal of Forensic Sciences*, 54, 490–494.

Davidson, J. (1998). Pharmacotherapy of social anxiety disorder. *Journal of Clinical Psychiatry*, 59, 47–53.

Dawkins, M.P. (1997). Drug use and violent crime among adolescents. *Adolescence*, 32, 395-405.

Del Boca, F., Darkes, J., Goldman, M., & Smith, G. (2002). Advancing the expectancy concept via the interplay between theory and research. *Alcoholism, Clinical and Experimental Research*, 26, 926–935.

De Lima, M. S., Dunn, J., Novo, I. P., Tomasi, E., & Reisser, A. P. (2003). Gender differences in the use of alcohol and psychotropics in a Brazilian population. *Substance Use and Misuse*, 38, 51-65.

De Visser, R. O., & Smith, J. A. (2007). Alcohol consumption and masculine identity among young men. *Psychology and Health*, 22, 595-614.

Donenberg, G. R., Emerson, E., Bryant, F. B., & King, S. (2006). Does substance use moderate the effects of parents and peers on risky sexual behavior? *Aids Care*, 18, 194-200.

Eggleston, A., Woolaway-Bickel, K., & Schmidt, N. B. (2004). Social anxiety and alcohol use: Evaluation of the moderating and mediating effects of alcohol expectancies. *Journal of Anxiety Disorders*, 18, 33–49.

Eisenman, R., Dantzker, M. L., & Ellis, L. (2004). Self ratings of dependency/addiction regarding drugs, sex, love, and food: Male and female college students. *Sexual Addiction & Compulsivity*, 11, 115-127.

Eksborg, S., & Rajs, J. (2008). Causes and manners of death among users of heroin, methadone, amphetamine, and cannabis in relation to postmortem chemical tests for illegal drugs. *Substance Use & Misuse*, 43, 1326–1339.

Ensminger, M. E., & Juon, H. S. (1998). Transition to adulthood among high-risk youth. In R. Jessor (Eds.). New perspectives on adolescent risk behaviour. (pp.365-390). UK: Cambridge University Press.

Ezzati, M., & Lopez, A. D. (2004). Regional, disease specific patterns of smoking-attributable mortality in 2000. *Tobacco Control*, 13, 388–395.

Falk, D. E., Yi, H.Y., Hiller-Sturmhofel, S. (2006). An epidemiologic analysis of co-occurring alcohol and tobacco use and disorders: Findings from the National Epidemiologic Survey on alcohol and related conditions. *Alcohol Research & Health*, 29, 162–171.

Felitti, V. J., Anda, R. F., Nordenberg, D., Williamson, D. F., Spitz, A. M., Edwards, V., et al. (1998). Relationship of childhood abuse and household dysfunction to many of the leading causes of death in adults. The Adverse Childhood Experiences (ACE) Study. *American Journal of Preventive Medicine*, 14, 245-258.

Foa, E. B., Fraklin, M. E., Perry, K. J., & Herbert, J. D. (1996). Cognitive biases in generalized social phobia. *Journal of Abnormal Psychology*, 105, 433-439.

Fuligni, A. J., Eccles, J. S., Barber, B. L., & Clements, P. (2001). Early adolescent peer orientation and adjustment during high school. *Developmental Psychology*, 37(1), 28-36.

George, S. M., Connor, J. P., Gullo, M. J., & Young, R. (2010). A prospective study of personality features predictive of early adolescent alcohol misuse. *Personality and Individual Differences, 49*, 204-209.

Gerlach, A. L., Schiller, A., Wild, C., & Rist, F. (2006). Effects of alcohol on the processing of social threat- related stimuli in socially phobic women. *British Journal of Clinical Psychology,* 45, 279-295.

Glassman, A. H., Helzer, J. E., Covey, L .S., Cottier, L.B., Stetner, F., Tipp, J. E. & Johnson, J. (1990). Smoking, smoking cessation and major depression. *Journal of the American Medical Association,* 264, 1546–1549.

Goldman, M. S., Del Boca, F. K., & Darkes, J. (1999). Alcohol expectancy theory: The application of cognitive neuroscience. In K.E. Leonard, & H.T. Blane (Eds.), Psychological theories of drinking and alcoholism (pp. 203–246). New York: Guilford Press.

Gorman, D. M., & Derzon, J. H. (2002). Behavioral traits and marijuana use and abuse: a meta-analysis of longitudinal studies. Addictive Behaviors, 27, 193-206.

Goto, R., Nishimura, S., & Ida, T. (2007). Discrete choice experiment of smoking cessation behaviour in Japan. *Tobacco Control,* 16, 336-343.

Grant, B. F., Hasin, D. S., Chou, P., Stinson, F. S., & Dawson, D. A. (2004). Nicotine dependence and psychiatric disorders in the United States: Results from the National Epidemiologic Survey on Alcohol and Related Conditions. *Archives of General Psychiatry,* 61, 1107–1115.

Grant, B. F., Stinson, F. S., Dawson, D. A., Chou, P., Dufour, M., Compton, W., et al. (2004). Prevalence and co-occurrence of substance use disorders and independent mood and anxiety disorders: Results from the National Epidemiologic Survey on Alcohol and Related Conditions. *Archives of General Psychiatry,* 61, 807-816.

Gruber, E., DiClemente, R. J., Anderson, M. M., & Lodico, M. (1996). Early drinking onset and its association with alcohol use and problem behaviour in late adolescence. *Preventive Medicine,* 25, 293-300.

Harakeh, Z., Scholte, R. H., de Vries, H., & Engels, R. C. (2006). Association between personality and adolescent smoking. Addictive Behaviors, 31, 232-245.

Ham, L. S. (2009). Positive social alcohol outcome expectancies, social anxiety and hazardous drinking in college students. *Cognitive Therapy & Research,* 33, 615-623.

Ham, L., Hope, D., White, C., & Rivers, C. (2002). Alcohol expectancies and drinking behavior in adults with social anxiety disorder and dysthymia. *Cognitive Therapy and Research,* 26, 275–288.

Ham, L. S., & Hope, D. A. (2005). Incorporating social anxiety into a model of college problematic drinking. *Addictive Behaviors,* 30,127–150.

Ham, L. S., Zamboanga, B. L., Bacon, A. K., & Garcia, T. A. (2009). Drinking motives as mediators of social anxiety and hazardous drinking among college students. *Cognitive Behavior Therapy,* 38, 133-145.

Ham, L. S., Zamboanga, B. L., Olthuis, J. V., Casner, H. G., & Bui, N. (2010). No fear, just relax and play: Social anxiety, alcohol expectancies, and drinking games among college students. *Journal of American College Health,* 58, 473-479.

Ham, L. S., Zamboanga, B. L., & Bacon, A. K. (2011). Putting thoughts into context: Alcohol expectancies, social anxiety, and hazardous drinking. *Journal of Cognitive Psychotherapy: An International Quarterly,* 25, 47-60.

Hampson, S. E., Goldberg, L. R., Vogt, T. M., & Dubanoski, J. P. (2006). Forty years on: teachers' assessments of children's personality traits predict self-reported health behaviors and outcomes at midlife. Health Psychology, *25*, 57-64.

Hartman, L. M. (1986). Social anxiety, problem drinking and self-awareness. New York: Plenum Press.

Heinz, A. J., Kassel, J. D., Berbaum, M., & Mermelstein, R. (2010). Adolescents' expectancies for smoking to regulate affect predict smoking behaviour and nicotine dependence over time. *Drug and Alcohol Dependence, 111*, 128-135.

Henry, D. B., Kobus, K., & Schoeny, M. E. (2011). Accuracy and bias in adolescents' perceptions of friends' substance use. *Psychology of Addictive Behaviors, 25*(1), 80-89.

Henry, S., Jamner, L., & Whalen, C. (2012). I (should) need a cigarette: Adolescent social anxiety and cigarette smoking. *Annals of Behavioral Medicine, 43*, 383-393.

Higgins, E. T. (1997). Beyond pleasure and pain. *American Psychologist, 52*, 1280-1300.

Johnson, T. P. (1991). Mental health, social relations, and social selection: A longitudinal analysis. *Journal of Health and Social Behavior, 32*, 408-23.

Johnson, P. B., & Glassman, M. (1998). The relationship between ethnicity, gender and alcohol consumption: A strategy for testing competing models. *Addiction, 93*, 583-588.

Johnson, K. A., Zvolensky, M. J., Marshall, E. C., Gonzalez, A., Abrams, K., & Vujanovic, A. A. (2008). Linkages between cigarette smoking outcome expectancies and negative emotional vulnerability. *Addictive Behaviors, 33*, 1416–1424.

Johnston, L. D., O'Malley, P. M., Bachman, J. G., & Schulenberg, J. E. (2006). *Monitoring the Future national survey results on drug use, 1975-2005. Volume II: College students and adults ages 19-45*. UK: National Institute on Drug Abuse.

Jones, B. T., Corbin, W., & Fromme, K. (2001). A review of expectancy theory and alcohol consumption. *Addiction, 96*, 57–72.

Kahler, C. W., Metrik, J., LaChance, H. R., Ramsey, S. E., Abrams, D. B., Monti, P. M., & Brown, R. A. (2008). Addressing heavy drinking in smoking cessation treatment: A randomized clinical trial. *Journal of Consulting and Clinical Psychology, 76*, 852–862.

Kallgren, C. A., Reno, R. R., & Cialdini, R. B. (2000). A focus theory of normative conduct: When norms do and do not affect behaviour. *Personality and Social Psychology Bulletin,* 26, 1002-1012.

Kandel, D. B. (1998). Persistent themes and new perspectives in adolescent substance use: A life-span perspective. In R. Jessor (Eds.). New perspectives on adolescent risk behaviour. (pp.43-81). UK: Cambridge University Press.

Kashdan, T. B. (2007). Social anxiety spectrum and diminished positive experiences: Theoretical synthesis and meta-analysis. *Clinical Psychology Review, 27*, 348-365.

Kashdan, T. B., & Steger, M. F. (2006). Expanding the topography of social anxiety: An experience sampling assessment of positive emotions and events, and emotion suppression. *Psychological Science, 17*, 120-128.

Kashdan, T. B., Elhai, J. D., & Breen, W. E. (2008). Social anxiety and disinhibition: An analysis of curiosity and social rank appraisals, approach-avoidance conflicts and disruptive risk-taking behavior. *Journal of Anxiety Disorders, 22*, 925-939.

Kassel, J. D., Jackson, S. I., & Unrod, M. (2000). Generalized expectancies for negative mood regulation and problem drinking among college students. *Journal of Studies on Alcohol*, 61, 332–340.

Katz, E. C., Fromme, K., & D'Amico, E. J. (2000). Effects of outcome expectancies and personality on young adults' illicit drug use, heavy drinking and risky sexual behaviour. *Cognitive Therapy and Research,* 24, 1-22.

Kendall, P., Safford, S., Flannery-Schroeder, E., & Webb, A. (2004). Child anxiety treatment: Outcomes in adolescence and impact on substance use and depression at 7.4-year follow-up. *Journal of Consulting and Clinical Psychology,* 72, 276–287.

Kessler, R., Crum, R., Warner, L., Nelson, C., Schulenberg, J., & Anthony J. (1997). Lifetime co-occurrence of DSM-III-R alcohol abuse and dependence with other psychiatric disorders in the National Co-morbidity Survey. *Archives of General Psychiatry,* 54, 313–321.

Khalid-Khan, S., Santibanez, M., McMicken, C., & Rynn, M. (2007). Social anxiety disorder in children and adolescents. *Pediatric Drugs,* 9, 227-237.

Khantzian, E. (1985). The self-medication hypothesis of addictive disorders: Focus on heroin and cocaine dependence. *American Journal of Psychiatry,* 142, 1259–1264.

Kidorf, M., & Lang, A. R. (1999). Effects of social anxiety and alcohol expectancies on stress-induced drinking. *Psychology of Addictive Behaviors,* 13, 134–142.

Kobus, V. J. (2003). Peers and adolescent smoking. *Addiction,* 98, 37-55.

Kodl, M. M., & Mermelstein, R. (2004). Beyond modeling: parenting practices, parental smoking history, and adolescent cigarette smoking. Addictive Behaviors, 29, 17-32.

Koob, G. F., & Le Moal, M. (1997). Drug abuse: Hedonic homeostatic dysregulation. *Science,* 278, 52–58.

Krisjansson, S. D., Pergadia, M. L., Agrawal, A., Lessov-Schlaggar, C. N., McCarthy, D. M., Piasecki, T.M., et al. (2011). Smoking outcome expectancies in young adult female smokers: Individual differences and associations with nicotine dependence in a genetically informative sample. *Drug and Alcohol Dependence,* 116, 37–44.

Kumpfer, K. L., & Bluth, B. (2004). Parent/Child transactional processes predictive of resilience and vulnerability to substance abuse disorders. *Substance Use & Misuse,* 39, 671-698.

Kushner, M., Sher, K., & Beitman B. (1990). The relation between alcohol problems and the anxiety disorders. *American Journal of Psychiatry,* 147, 685–695.

Kushner, M. G., & Sher, K. J. (1993). Co-morbidity of alcohol and anxiety disorders among college students: Effects of gender and family history of alcoholism. *Addictive Behaviors,* 18, 543–552.

Kushner, M., Sher, K., Wood, M., & Wood P. (1994). Anxiety and drinking behavior: Moderating effects of tension-reduction alcohol outcome expectancies. Alcoholism, Clinical *and Experimental Research,* 18, 852–860.

Kushner, M. G., Abrams, K., & Borchardt, C. (2000). The relationship between anxiety disorders and alcohol use disorders: a review of major perspectives and findings. *Clinical Psychological Review,* 20, 149–171.

LaBrie, J. W., Hummer, J. F., & Neighbors, C. (2008). Self-consciousness moderates the relationship between perceived norms and drinking in college students. *Addictive Behaviors,* 33, 1529–1539.

La Greca, A., & Lopez, N. (1998). Social anxiety among adolescents: Linkages with peer relations and friendships. *Journal of Abnormal Child Psychology,* 26, 83-94.

Lasser, K., Boyd, J. W., Woolhandler, S., Himmelstein, D.U., McCormick, D., & Bor, D. H. (2000). Smoking and mental illness: A population-based prevalence study. *JAMA,* 284, 2606-2610.

Lehman, A. F., Myers, C. P., & Corty, E. (2000). Assessment and classification of patients with psychiatric and substance abuse syndromes. *Psychiatric Services,* 51, 1119–1125.

Lewis, B., & O'Neill, K. (2000). Alcohol expectancies and social deficits relating to problem drinking among college students. *Addictive Behaviors,* 25, 295–299.

Lewis, M. A., Hove, M. C., Whiteside, U., Lee, C. M., Kirkeby, B. S., Oster-Aaland, L., et al. (2008). Fitting in and feeling fine: conformity and coping motives as mediators of the relationship between social anxiety and problematic drinking. *Psychology of Addictive Behaviors,* 22, 58–67.

Liappas, J., Paparrigopoulos, T., Tzavellas, E., & Christodoulou, G. (2003). Alcohol detoxification and social anxiety symptoms: A preliminary study of the impact of mirtazapine administration. *Journal of Affective Disorders,* 76, 279–284.

Malouff, J. M., Thorsteinsson, E. B., & Schutte, N. S. (2006). The five-factor model of personality and smoking: A meta-analysis. Journal of Drug Education, *36,* 47-58.

Marmorstein, N. R., White, H. R., Loeber, R., & Stouthamer-Loeber, M. (2010). Anxiety as a predictor of age at first use of substances and progression to substance use problems among boys. *Journal of Abnormal Child Psychology,* 38, 211–224.

MacDonald, Z., & Putney, S. (2000). Illicit drug use, unemployment and occupational attainment. *Journal of Health and Economy,* 19, 1089-1115.

MacLatchy-Gaudet, H. A., & Stewart, S. H. (2001). The context-specific positive alcohol outcome expectancies of university women. *Addictive Behaviors,* 26, 31–49.

McArdle, P., Wiegersma, A., Gilvarry, E., Kolte, B., McCarthy, S., Fitzgerald, M. et al. (2002). European adolescent substance use: the roles of family structure, function, and gender. *Addiction,* 97, 329-336.

McCance-Katz, E. F., Hart, C. L., Boyarski, B., Kosten, T., & Jatlow, P. (2005). Gender effects following repeated administration of cocaine and alcohol in humans. *Substance Use and Misuse,* 40, 511-528.

McCarroll, E. M., Lindsey, E. W., MacKinnon-Lewis, C., Campbell-Chambers, J., & Frabutt, J. M. (2009). Health status and peer relationships in early adolescents: The role of peer contact, self-esteem, and social anxiety. *Journal of Child and Family Studies,* 18, 473-485.

Menary, K. R., Kushner, M. G. Maurer, E., & Thuras, P. (2011). The prevalence and clinical implications of self-medication among individuals with anxiety disorders. *Journal of Anxiety Disorders,* 25, 335-339.

Millstein, S. G., & Halpern-Felsher, B. L. (2002). Judgments about risk and perceived invulnerability in adolescents and young adults. *Journal of Research on Adolescence,* 12, 399-422.

Morris, E. P., Stewart, S. H., & Ham, L. S. (2005). The relationship between social anxiety disorder and alcohol use disorders: A critical review. *Clinical Psychology Review,* 25, 734-760.

Morrow, M., & Barraclough, S. (2003). Tobacco control and gender in South-East Asia. Part II: Singapore and Vietnam. *Health Promotion International,* 18, 373-380.

Morrow, M., & Barraclough, S. (2010). Gender equity and tobacco control: Bringing masculinity into focus. *Global Health Promotion,* 17(Suppl. 1), 21-28.

Munafo, M. R., & Black, S. (2007). Personality and smoking status: A longitudinal analysis. *Nicotine Tobacco Research, 9*, 397-404.

Myers, M. G., Aarons, G. A., Tomlinson, K., & Stein, M. B. (2003). Social anxiety, negative affectivity, and substance use among high school students. *Psychology of Addictive Behaviors, 17*, 277-283.

Norasakkunkit, V., & Kalick, S. M. (2002). Culture, ethnicity, and emotional distress measures: The role of self-construal and self-enhancement. *Journal of Cross-Cultural Psychology, 33*, 56-70.

Norberg, M. M., Norton, A. R., Olivier, J., & Zvolensky, M. J. (2010). Social anxiety, reasons for drinking, and college students. *Behavior Therapy, 41*, 555–566.

Norberg, M. M., Olivier, J., Alperstein, D. M., Zvolensky, M. J., & Norton, A. R. (2011). Adverse consequences of student drinking: The role of sex, social anxiety, drinking motives. *Addictive Behaviors, 36*, 821–828.

Norton, G. R., Norton, P. J., Cox, B. J., & Belik, S. (2008). Panic spectrum disorders and substance use. In S. H. Stewart & P. J. Conrod (Eds.). Anxiety and substance use disorders: The vicious cycle of comorbidity (pp. 81-100). USA: Springer.

Okazaki, S. (1997). Sources of ethnic differences between Asian American and White American college students on measures of depression and social anxiety. *Journal of Abnormal Psychology, 106*, 52-60.

Palmer, R. H., Young, S. E., Hopfer, C. J., Corley, R. P., Stallings, M. C., Crowley, T. J., et al. (2009). Developmental epidemiology of drug use and abuse in adolescence and young adulthood: Evidence of generalized risk. *Drug and Alcohol Dependence, 102*, 78–87.

Parrott, A. C. (1998). Nesbitt's paradox resolved? Stress and arousal modulation during cigarette smoking. *Addiction*, 93, 27-39.

Patton, G. C., Coffey, C., Carlin, J. B., Degenhardt, L., Lynskey, M., & Hall, W. (2006). Cannabis use and the mental health of young people. *The Australian and New Zealand Journal of Psychiatry, 40*, 105–113.

Paunonen, S. V., & Ashton, M. C. (2001). Big five factors and facets and the prediction of behavior. Journal of Personality and Social Psychology, 81, 524-539.

Pedersen, W. (2008). Does cannabis use lead to depression and suicidal behaviours? A population-based longitudinal study. *Acta Psychiatrica Scandinavica*, 118, 395–403.

Peleg, O. (2002). Children's test anxiety and family interaction patterns. Anxiety. *Stress and Coping, 15*, 45-59.

Peleg, O. (2004). Differentiation and test anxiety in adolescents. *Journal of Adolescence*, 27, 645-662.

Peleg, O. (2005). The relation between differentiation and social anxiety: What can be learned from students and their parents? *American Journal of Family Therapy*, 33, 167-183.

Perkins, H. W., & Berkowitz, A. D. (1986). Perceiving the community norms of alcohol use among students: Some research implications for campus alcohol education programming. *International Journal of the Addictions, 27*, 961-976.

Petraitis, J., Flay, B. R., & Miller, T. Q. (1995). Reviewing theories of adolescent substance use: Organizing pieces in a puzzle. *Psychological Bulletin, 117*, 67-86.

Picciotto, M. R., Brunzell, D. H., & Caldarone, B. J. (2002). Effect of nicotine and nicotinic receptors on anxiety and depression. Neuroreport, 13, 1097-1106.

Piedmont, R. L. (2001). Cracking the plaster cast: Big Five personality change during intensive outpatient counseling. *Journal of Research in Personality, 35*, 500-520.

Poulin, C., & Graham, L. (2001). The association between substance use, unplanned sexual intercourse and other sexual behaviours among adolescent students. *Addiction,* 96, 607-621.

Prentice, D. A., & Miller, D. T. (1993). Pluralistic ignorance of alcohol use on campus. Some consequences of misperceiving the social norm. *Journal of Personality and Social Psychology,* 64, 243-256.

Price, C., Hemmingsson, T., Lewis, G., Zammit, S., & Allebeck, P. (2009). Cannabis and suicide: Longitudinal study. *The British Journal of Psychiatry,* 195, 492–497.

Project MATCH Research Group. (1993). Project MATCH: Rationale and methods for multisite clinical trial patients to alcoholism treatment. *Alcoholism, Clinical and Experimental Research,* 17, 1130–1145.

Randall, C., Thomas, S., & Thevos, A. (2001). Concurrent alcoholism and social anxiety disorder: A first step toward developing effective treatments. *Alcoholism, Clinical and Experimental Research,* 25, 210–220.

Randall, C., Thomas, S., Thevos, A., Sonne, S., Thomas, S., Willard, S., et al. (2001). Paroxetine for social anxiety and alcohol use in dual-diagnosed patients. *Depression and Anxiety,* 14, 255–262.

Reno, R. R., Cialdini, R. B., & Kallgren, C. A. (1993). The trans-situational influence of social norms. *Journal of Personality and Social Psychology,* 64, 104-112.

Repetti, R. L., Taylor, S. E., & Seeman, T. E. (2002). Family social environments and the mental and physical health of offspring. *Psychological Bulletin, 128,* 330-366.

Rheingold, A. A., Herbert, J. D., & Franklin, M. E. (2003). Cognitive bias in adolescents with social anxiety disorder. *Cognitive Therapy and Research,* 27, 639-655.

Robinson, T. E., &. Berridge, K. C. (2000). The psychology and neurobiology of addiction: An incentive-sensitization view. *Addiction,* 95, S91–S117.

Robinson, J., Sareen, J., Cox, B., & Bolton, J. (2009a). Correlates of self-medication for anxiety disorders: results from the National Epidemiologic Survey on alcohol and related conditions. *The Journal of Nervous and Mental Disease,* 197, 873–878.

Robinson, J., Sareen, J., Cox, B., & Bolton, J. (2009b). Self-medication of anxiety disorders with alcohol and drugs: results from a nationally representative sample. *Journal of Anxiety Disorders,* 23, 38–45.

Rogers, K. (2011). *Substance use and abuse.* New York: Britannica Educational Publishing.

Ross, H. E., Glaser, F. B., & Germanson, T. (1988). The prevalence of psychiatric disorders in patients with alcohol and other drug problems. *Archives of General Psychiatry,* 45, 1023–1031.

Santee, R. T., & Maslach, C. (1982). To agree or not to agree: Personal dissent amid social pressure to conform. *Journal of Personality and Social Psychology,* 42, 690-700.

Sayette, M. A. (1993). An appraisal disruption model of alcohol's effects on stress responses in social drinkers. *Psychological Bulletin,* 114, 459-476.

Schenkler, B. L., & Leary, M. R. (1982). Social anxiety and self-presentation: A conceptualization model. *Psychological Bulletin,* 92, 641-669.

Schneiner, F. R., Johnson, J., Hornig, C. D., Liebowitz, M. R., & Weissman, M. M. (1992). Social phobia comorbidity and morbidity in an epidemiologic sample. *Archives of General Psychiatry,* 49, 282-288.

Schneier, F. R., Heckeman, L. R., Garfinkel, R., Campeas, R., Fallon, B. A., Gitow, A., et al. (1994). Functional impairment in social phobia. *Journal of Clinical Psychiatry,* 55, 332-351.

Schneiner, F. R., Foose, T. E., Hasin, D. S., Heimberg, R. G., Liu, S. M., Grant, B. F., et al. (2010). Social anxiety disorder and alcohol use disorder comorbidity in the National Epidemiologic Survey on Alcohol and Related Conditions. *Psychological Medicine,* 40, 977-988.

Segrist, D. J., Corcoran, K. J., Jordan-Fleming, M. K., & Rose, P. (2007). Yeah, I drink... but not as much as other guys: The majority fallacy among male adolescents. *North American Journal of Psychology,* 9, 307-320.

Shaffey, O., Fernandez, E., Thun, M., Schiaffino, A., Dolwick, S., & Cokkinides, V. (2004). Cigarette advertising and female smoking prevalence in Spain, 1982-1997. Case studies in International Tobacco Control Surveillance. *Cancer,* 100, 1744-1749.

Sharp, M. J., & Getz, J. G. (1996). Substance use as impression management. *Personality and Social Psychology Bulletin,* 22, 60–67.

Sher, K., & Levenson, R. (1982). Risk for alcoholism and individual differences in the stress–response-dampening effect of alcohol. *Journal of Abnormal Psychology,* 91, 350–367.

Simons, R. L., Conger. R. D., & Whitbeck. L. B. (1988). A multistage social learning model of the influences of family and peers upon adolescent substance abuse. *Journal of Drug Issues.* 15, 293-315.

Siqueira, L., Diab, M., Bodian, C., & Rolnitzky L. (2000). Adolescents becoming smokers: The roles of stress and coping methods. *Journal of Adolescent Health,* 27, 399–408.

Steele, C. M., & Josephs, R. A. (1990). Alcohol myopia: Its prized and dangerous effects. *American Psychologist,* 45, 921–933.

Stein, M. B., & Kean, Y. M. (2000). Disability and quality of life in social phobia: Epidemiological findings. *American Journal of Psychiatry,* 157, 1606-1613.

Stevens, S., Gerlach, A. L., & Rist, F. (2008). Effects of alcohol on ratings of emotional facial expressions in social phobics. *Journal of Anxiety Disorders*, 22, 940-948.

Stewart, S. H., Morris, E., Mellings, T., & Komar, J. (2006). Relations of social anxiety variables to drinking motives, drinking quantity and frequency, and alcohol related problems in undergraduates. *Journal of Mental Health,* 15, 671–682.

Stice, E., & Barrera, M., Jr. (1995). A longitudinal examination of the reciprocal relations between perceived parenting and adolescents' substance use and externalizing ehaviors. *Developmental Psychology,* 31, 322-334.

Swendsen, J. D., Conway, K. P., Rounsaville, B. J., & Merikangas, K. R. (2002). Are personality traits risk factors for substance use disorders? Results of a controlled family study. *American Journal of Psychiatry,* 159, 1760-1766.

Taylor, A. L., & Bettcher, B. W. (2000). WHO Framework Convention on Tobacco Control: A global 'good' for public health. *Bulletin of the World Health Organization*, 78, 920-929.

Tepe, E., Dalrymple, K., & Zimmerman, M. (2012). The impact of comorbid cannabis use disorders on the clinical presentation of social anxiety disorder. *Journal of Psychiatric Research,* 46, 50-56.

Terlecki, M. A., Buckner, J. D., Larimer, M. E., & Copeland, A. L. (2011). The role of social anxiety in a brief alcohol intervention for heavy drinking college students. *Journal of Cognitive Psychotherapy: An International Quarterly,* 25, 7-21.

Terracciano, A., & Costa, P. T. (2004). Smoking and the Five-Factor Model of personality. *Addiction*, 99, 472-481.

Terracciano, A., Costa, P. T., & McCrae, R. R. (2006). Personality plasticity after age 30. Personality and Social Psychology Bulletin, 32, 999-1009.

Terracciano, A., McCrae, R. R., & Costa P. T. (2006). Longitudinal trajectories in Guilford-Zimmerman Temperament Survey data in the Baltimore Longitudinal Study of Aging. The Journals of Gerontology, 61,108-116.

Terracciano, A., McCrae, R. R., Brant, L. J., & Costa, P. T. (2005). Hierarchical linear modeling analyses of NEO-PI-R scales in the Baltimore Longitudinal Study of Aging. Psychology and Aging, 20, 493-506.

Terracciano, A., Löckenhoff, C. E., Crum, R. M., Bienvenu, O. J., & Cost, P. T. (2008). Five-Factor Model personality profiles of drug users. *BMC Psychiatry, 8*, 1-10.

Thevos, A., Roberts, J., Thomas, S., & Randall, C. (2000). Cognitive behavioral therapy delays relapse in female socially phobic alcoholics. *Addictive Behaviors, 25*, 333–345.

Thomas, S. E., Randall, C. L., & Carrigan, M. H. (2003). Drinking to cope in socially anxious individuals: A controlled study. *Alcoholism, Clinical and Experimental Research, 27*, 1937–1943.

Thomas, S. E., Randall, P. K., Book, S. W., & Randall, C.L. (2008). A complex relationship between co-occurring social anxiety and alcohol use disorders: What effect does treating social anxiety have on drinking? *Alcoholism: Clinical and Experimental Research, 32*, 77-84.

Thorlindson, T., & Bernbury, J. G. (2006). Peer groups and substance use: Examining the direct and indirect effect of leisure activity. *Adolescence, 41*, 321-339.

Thornton, B., Audesse, R. J., Ryckman, R. M., & Burckle, M. J. (2006). Playing dumb and knowing it all: Two sides of an impression management coin. *Individual Differences Research, 4*, 37–45.

Tice, D. M., Bratslavsky, E., & Baumeister, R. F. (2001). Emotional distress regulation takes precedence over impulse control: If you feel bad, do it! *Journal of Personality and Social Psychology, 80*, 53-67.

Tinsley, B. J., Lees, N. B., & Sumartojo, E. (2004). Child and adolescent HIV risk: Familial and cultural perspectives. *Journal of Family Psychology, 18*, 208-224.

Tomlinson, K. & Brown, S. A. (2012). Self-medication or social learning? A comparison of models to predict early adolescent drinking. *Addictive Behaviors, 37*, 179-186.

Tran, G., Haaga, D., & Chambless, D. (1997). Expecting that alcohol use will reduce social anxiety moderates the relation between social anxiety and alcohol consumption. *Cognitive Therapy and Research, 21*, 535–553.

Tran, G., & Haaga, D. (2002). Coping responses and alcohol outcome expectancies in alcohol abusing and non-abusing social phobics. *Cognitive Therapy and Research, 26*, 1–17.

Tran, G. Q., & Smith, J. P. (2008). Co-morbidity of social phobia and alcohol use disorders: A review of psychopathology research findings. In S. H. Stewart & P. J. Conrod (Eds.). Anxiety and substance use disorders: The vicious cycle of comorbidity (pp. 59-80). USA: Springer.

Turk, C. L., Heimberg, R. G., Orsillo, S. M., Holt, C. S., Gitow, A., Street, L. L., Schneider, F. R., et al. (1998). An investigation of gender differences in social phobia. *Journal of Anxiety Disorder, 12*, 209-223.

Turner, S., Beidel, D., Dancu, C., & Keys, D. (1986). Psychopathology of social phobia and comparison to avoidant personality disorder. *Journal of Abnormal Psychology*, 95, 389–394.

U.S. Department of Health and Human Services. (2006). The health consequences of involuntary exposure to tobacco smoke: A report of the Surgeon General. Retrieved from http://www.surgeongeneral.gov/library/secondhandsmoke/report/fullreport.pdf.

Van Etten, M. L., & Anthony, J. C. (2001). Male-female differences in transitions from first drug opportunity to first use: Searching for subgroup variation by age, race, region, and urban status. *Journal of Women's Health & Gender-based Medicine*, 10, 797-804.

Van Etten, M. L., Neumark, Y. D., & Anthony, J. C. (1999). Male-female differences in the earliest stages of drug involvement. *Addiction*, 94, 1413-1419.

Van Zalk, N., Van Zalk, M., Kerr, M., & Stattin, H. (2011). Social anxiety as a basis for friendship selection and socialization in adolescents' social networks. *Journal of Personality*, 79, 499-526.

Vernberg, E. M., Abwender, D. A., Ewell, K. K., & Beery, S. H. (1992). Social anxiety and peer relationships in early adolescence: A prospective analysis. *Journal of Clinical Child Psychology*, 21, 189-196.

Waldron, I. (1991). Patterns and causes of gender differences in smoking. *Social Science Medicine*, 32, 989-1005.

Wall, A., McKee, S. A., & Hinson, R. E. (2000). Assessing variation in alcohol outcome expectancies across environmental context: An examination of the situational-specificity hypothesis. *Psychology of Addictive Behaviors*, 14, 367–375.

Webb, J., Bray, J., Getz, J., & Adams, G. (2002). Gender, perceived parental monitoring, and behavioral adjustment: Influences on adolescent alcohol use. *American Journal of Orthopsychiatry*, 72, 392-400.

Weeks, J. W., Heinberg, R. G., & Rodebaugh, T. L. (2008). The Fear of Positive Evaluation Scale: Assessing a proposed cognitive component of social anxiety. *Journal of Anxiety Disorders*, 22, 44-55.

White, H. R., Bates, M. E., & Labouvie, E. (1998). Adult outcomes of adolescent drug use: A comparison of process-oriented and incremental analysis. In R. Jessor (Eds.). New perspectives on adolescent risk behaviour (pp.15-45). UK: Cambridge University Press.

White, H. R., Labouvie, E. W., & Papadaratsakis, V. (2005). Changes in substance use during the transition to adulthood: A comparison of college students and their non-college age peers. *Journal of Drug Issues*, 35, 281-306.

Wills, T. A., Sandy, J. M., & Yaeger, A. M. (2001). Stress and smoking in adolescence: A test of directional hypotheses. *Health Psychology*, 21, 122–130.

Windle, M., & Windle, R. C. (2012). Testing the specificity between social anxiety disorder and drinking motives. *Addictive Behaviors*, 37, 1003-1008.

Wittchen, H. U., Stein, M. B., & Kessler, R. C. (1999). Social fears and social phobia in a community sample of adolescents and young adults: Prevalence, risk factors and co-morbidity. *Psychological Medicine*, 29, 309-323.

Wolitzki-Taylor, K., Bobova, L., Zinbarg, R. E., Mineka, S., & Craske, M. G. (2012). Longitudinal investigation of the impact of anxiety and mood disorders in adolescence on subsequent substance use disorder onset and vice-versa. *Addictive Behaviors*, 37, 982-985.

Wood, M. D., Mitchell, R. E., Read, J. P., & Brand, N. H. (2004). Do parents still matter? Parent and peer influences on alcohol involvement among recent high school graduates. *Psychology of Addictive Behaviors,* 18, 19-30.

World Health Organization. (2011). Global status report on alcohol and health. http://www.who.int/substance_abuse/publications/global_alcohol_report/en/index.html

Wright, D. B., London, K., & Waechter, M. (2010). Social anxiety moderates memory conformity in adolescents. *Applied Cognitive Psychology,* 24, 1034-1045.

Young, A. M., Morales, M., McCabe, S. E., Boyd, C. J., & D'Arcy, H. (2005). Drinking like a guy: Frequent binge drinking among undergraduate women. *Substance Use and Misuse,* 40, 241-267.

Zaloshnja, E., Ross, H., & Levy, D. T. (2010). The impact of tobacco control policies in Albania. *Tobacco Control,* 19, 463-468.

Zilberman, M., Tavares, H., Blume, S., & El-Guebaly, N. (2003). Substance use disorders: Sex differences and psychiatric comorbidities. *Canadian Journal of Psychiatry,* 48, 5–13.

In: Social Anxiety
Editor: Efrosini Kalyva

ISBN: 978-1-62808-396-5
© 2013 Nova Science Publishers, Inc.

*Chapter VII*

# Social Anxiety in the School Setting for Students with Autism Spectrum Disorders

*Efrosini Kalyva[1],* and Vlastaris Tsakiris[2]*
[1]The South-East European Research Centre, Thessaloniki, Greece
[2]Special Needs Educator, Thessaloniki, Greece

## Abstract

Many students with autism spectrum disorders attend inclusion or mainstream classes in an effort to promote and respect their rights to education. However, it is widely acknowledged that emphasis is placed mainly on the cognitive and not so much on the social and emotional aspects of inclusion. Therefore, many students with autism spectrum disorders experience social anxiety not only in the classroom, but also in the playground, and this anxiety is often transferred to out of school activities. Social anxiety can have serious impact on the overall wellbeing of the students with autism spectrum disorders and affect not only their quality of life but even their academic performance. The aim of this chapter is to identify potential causes of social anxiety for students with autism spectrum disorders (e.g., inadequate interpersonal conflict resolution skills, literal understanding, minimal social interaction opportunities, and stigmatization) and to suggest some interventions that could be effective in dealing with social anxiety. These interventions should be implemented with the help of teachers and parents in order to be tailored to the individual needs of every student with autism spectrum disorders and thus more likely to succeed.

**Keywords**: Autism spectrum disorders, social anxiety, inclusion, interventions

---

* Corresponding author: Efrosini Kalyva, E-mail: kalyva@city.academic.gr.

# Introduction

Individuals with autism spectrum disorders (ASD) tend to exhibit significantly higher levels of anxiety in comparison to their typically developing peers (Bellini, 2004; Gillott, Furniss, and Walter, 2001; Green, Gilchrist, Burton, and Cox, 2000; Kim, Szatmari, Bryson, Streiner, and Wilson, 2000). They have been documented to experience a broad range of anxiety symptoms - such as physiological arousal, panic, separation anxiety, and social anxiety – that may have detrimental effects on their life. Childhood anxiety is often associated with excessive worry, fear, and isolation that could lead to depression, substance abuse, suicidal ideation, and other forms of psychopathology later on in life (Tantam, 2000).

Many individuals with ASD face severe difficulties in their social interactions due to the excessive worry and distress that they feel when in the company of others. As a result, they miss on important social cues that can help them behave more properly in a social context and they have limited support from close friends (Koning and Magill-Evans, 2001). These challenges become more prominent in adolescence - when individuals with ASD struggle to meet the increased social demands - and in adulthood - when they try to cooperate with their work associates or colleagues.

# Anxiety in Autism

Gillott et al. (2001) reported that children with high-functioning autism scored higher on measures of anxiety in comparison to their typically developing peers or peers with specific learning impairments. They experience more generalized anxiety, social anxiety, separation anxiety, obsessive-compulsiveness, physical injury fears, and panic. These difficulties make them less willing to engage in social interactions and could account for their interpersonal problems.

Kim et al. (2000) found that 13.6% of the children with ASD who participated in their study scored at least two standard deviations above the mean on a measure of generalized anxiety and on the internalizing factor, which includes generalized anxiety, separation anxiety, and depression. Green et al. (2000) found that the adolescents with Asperger syndrome who comprised their sample exhibited significantly higher levels of anxiety compared to a group of adolescents with conduct disorder and this testifies to the severity of their symptoms.

An alarming finding of the same study was that one third (35%) of the adolescents with Asperger syndrome met the ICD [International Classification of Diseases]-10 criterion for generalized anxiety disorder, while 10% met the criterion for a specific phobia.

Bellini (2004) examined the prevalence and types of anxiety exhibited by adolescents with high-functioning autism and tried to identify the factors that are related to this anxiety. He confirmed the findings of previous studies that adolescents with ASD exhibit significantly higher levels of anxiety than the general population and he reported a significant association between social skill deficits and social anxiety.

A very important parameter that needs to be taken into consideration is that all the studies mentioned so far have looked at individuals with high-functioning autism who can express their anxiety. But what about individuals with low-functioning autism who do not have the means to directly communicate the anxiety they feel? How is it possible to assess the levels of anxiety that they experience and the extent to which they interfere with their social and emotional life?

# Social Anxiety

Social anxiety is defined as the manifestation of an intense fear of social situations or performance situations where it is likely to experience embarrassment. There are two distinct types of social anxiety: individuals who suffer exclusively from performance fears (such as giving a talk in public) and individuals with a broader syndrome of both performance and social interactional fears (Heimberg, Holt, Schneier, and Leibowitz, 1993; Kessler, Stein, and Berglund, 1998; Turner, Beidel, and Townsley, 1992). Since the second type of social anxiety is more complicated, it is linked to more severe impairment, longer duration or persistence of symptoms, and higher comorbidity with other forms of psychopathology, namely depression (Kessler et al., 1998).

Individuals with social anxiety–generalized tend to report increased anticipatory anxiety that is related to public performances and social interactions (APA, 2000). This anticipation may create a self-fulfilling prophecy, since the belief that they will not perform well can lead to actual poor performance (Vasey and Daleiden, 1994). Social anxiety is a quite common disorder that is estimated to occur in 3% to 13% of the general population (APA, 1994; Stein, Torgrud, and Walker, 2000), with its prevalence among individuals with ASD being less well established. One relevant study that used self-reports to measure the social anxiety of adolescents with high-functioning autism found that 49% scored above the level indicative of clinically high social anxiety (Bellini, 2004).

There seems to be a key differentiating factor between social anxiety disorder and pervasive developmental disorders (which encompasses autism spectrum disorders), according to the *Diagnostic and Statistical Manual of Mental Disorders–Fourth Edition* (*DSM-IV*; APA, 1994). This distinction is that individuals with social phobia-generalized are interested in participating in social interaction but lack the appropriate skills, whereas individuals with pervasive developmental disorder are not interested in engaging in social interactions. However, this assumption has been disputed, since there is evidence that individuals with ASD do want to get involved in social interactions but do not possess the necessary social skills (Attwood, 1998; Kalyva, 2010).

One of the greatest challenges of examining social anxiety in individuals with high-functioning ASD is that some of the symptoms of social anxiety (such as social withdrawal, preference for isolation, and lack of involvement in social situations) may overlap with some of the basic symptoms of ASD. This could lead potentially to misdiagnosis or overdiagnosis of social anxiety in individuals with ASD, especially those at the higher end of the spectrum. On the other hand, socially anxious individuals may be socially awkward and experience various difficulties with nonverbal communication and emotional expression that are characteristic of individuals with ASD (Tantam, 2000). The need for individuals with social anxiety to devise stereotyped routines and rituals to decrease their anxiety is another overlapping symptom with ASD that stresses the need for proper and timely differential diagnoses.

Kuusikko et al. (2008) examined self-reported symptoms of social and evaluative anxiety in 44 children and adolescents with high-functioning ASD and found that they tend to experience and report significantly more social anxiety symptoms than their controls. Moreover, parents reported that their children with ASD were facing more internalizing problems than parents of healthy controls.

Another interesting finding of that study was that children with ASD reported more social anxiety as they grew older, whereas typically developing children reported less social anxiety with age. This may reflect the increased awareness of individuals with ASD who enter adolescence that they lack certain social interaction skills that are instrumental in developing interpersonal relationships (such as empathy, interpersonal conflict resolution skills) (Kalyva, 2011b).

# Models of Anxiety

## Temperament

Children with behavioral inhibition are less able to regulate their own physiological arousal and this makes them more vulnerable to stressful social encounters and more likely to be adversely conditioned by negative social interactions (Biederman, Rosenbaum, Chaloff, and Kagan, 1995). Although there is no relevant research conducted with children with ASD, infants with ASD are often characterized as passive and disengaged from their environment, showing thus traits of behavioral inhibition (Butera and Haywood, 1995).

## Neurobiological Models

Impairment in the amygdala interferes with the individual's ability to relate emotionally and socially with others, significantly affecting thus emotional learning and development (Schultz, Romanski, and Tsatsanis, 2000). This is characteristic of children with ASD who become more vulnerable to overstimulation by the social interactions of caregivers that can then lead to gaze aversion and social withdrawal (Trepagnier, 1996). More evidence for the neurobiological models is presented by Kleinhans, Richards, Weaver, Johnson, Greenson, Dawson, and Aylward (2010) who examined 31 adults with Asperger syndrome and concluded that greater social anxiety was associated with increased activation in right amygdala and left middle temporal gyrus, and decreased activation in the fusiform face area in comparison to the control group.

## Developmental Pathways

Rubin and Burgess (2001) proposed that social withdrawal is the developmental gateway to social anxiety. It is likely that because of early fearful or insecure temperament the child withdraws from social interaction and has thus limited opportunities to develop adequate interpersonal skills. This social skills deficit leads to negative peer interactions that in turn increase social anxiety. Bellini (2006) suggested that a combination of social skills deficits and physiological arousal can act as significant predictor of social anxiety for young people with high-functioning ASD. A developmental hypothesis of social anxiety for ASD was proposed by Attwood (1998) who claimed that frequent peer rejection and social failure can lead to increasing anxiety about subsequent social interactions.

Tantam (2000) also suggested that social skills deficits impede the development of meaningful interpersonal relationships for individuals with ASD, creating thus feelings of anxiety and depression.

# Treatment

A very interesting qualitative study was conducted by Müller, Schuler and Yates (2008) with eighteen individuals with ASD who were interviewed in relation to the social challenges that they face and the kind of support that they need in order to overcome them. It is always interesting and important to explore the needs and beliefs of individuals who are directly involved. The researchers found that the interviewees identified the need for different kinds of supports in order to deal with their social anxiety. These supports were grouped by the researchers into four main themes (1) external supports, (2) communication supports, (3) self-initiated supports, and (4) attitudinal supports, which will be described below in more details.

*External Supports*

All the individuals with ASD who participated in the Müller et al. (2008) study emphasized the importance of externally implemented supports, which were summarized in the following five themes:

a) joint focus activities that are usually structured around a common interest such as chess, jogging, vintage Volkswagens, or disability rights and provide unique opportunities for social interaction. Being member of a group of individuals with ASD was identified as inspirational by some participants who realize that they are not alone. It should be noted, however, that not all individuals have access to such groups either due to practical issues (e.g., distance, lack of transportation) or because of social stigmatization that may prevent them from participating in such groups – if they do exist. Moreover, individuals with ASD may decide to quit the group in case that some extra social demands are placed on them in the context of the joint focus activities.

Another interesting joint activity that was described by the participants was doing something alongside others, but without actually interacting with them, such as watching a movie or studying in the library. We can also train them to use the movie that they watched or the book that they read as an incentive to initiate a discussion or another social interaction. When recalling their childhood, they identified parallel play with peers as their happiest social childhood memory. This is important for practitioners to note, since parallel play is usually considered to be a form of play that is not appropriate after a certain stage and interventions aim at changing it to cooperative or social play. Therefore, we might want to reconsider this notion and allow children with ASD to engage in more parallel play viewing it as a recreational activity for them.

b) structured social activities - such as attending the mass – that follow a certain routine and thus help individuals with ASD feel more at ease and relaxed because they know what to expect. What follows the structured activity, however, may sometimes be emotionally overwhelming. Since many things in life are unpredictable it is important to teach individuals with ASD to overcome their social anxiety using techniques such as cognitive-behavioral training that will be described later on. One adolescent girl we worked with enjoyed going to a dance class and she liked the structure that was inherent in this activity.

However, when the instructor started teaching them more free style dances and asked them to improvise she could not deal with this and she wanted to quit the group. It took a lot of work from our part to train her to become more flexible and implement some relaxation techniques to cope with change, since she did want to continue belonging to the specific group.

c) small groups and dyads were reported by most participants as their favorite medium for socializing and as an optimal educational setting, although they admitted that the presence of someone else was necessary to ensure group coherence and sustainability. The integrated play groups and the circle of friends (Kalyva, 2011a; Kalyva and Avramidis, 2005) are treatments based on these principles that have been used effectively with individuals with ASD at different stages of the spectrum. We have to mention, however, that the typically developing children who participate in these small groups or dyads often avoid socializing with children with ASD out of the intervention context. So, they will not invite them to birthday parties or to play dates and they may not even play with them during the break. This observation is food for thought regarding the actual power of these interventions to create friendships instead of occasional play dates. It is obviously something that teachers, parents, and practitioners have to work on and target during the implementation of the interventions.

d) facilitated social interactions that offer the opportunity to socialize with more socially competent peers, who tend to act as ambassadors and help them create further relationships with other people. Siblings may often be called to play this role, but although it is helpful it may put a lot of stress on the socially competent peer. Therefore, it is imperative that individuals with ASD take advantage of this help to boost their sociability but then learn to depend on themselves more and rely on their socially competent peers less. The challenges are pretty similar to the ones described in the previous paragraph.

e) observing/modeling social behaviors so that individuals with ASD can develop some scripts or copy the behaviors of other people around them in an effort to overcome their social anxiety and become more sociable. This is the whole philosophy behind some interventions such as social stories and video modeling that have been proven to be quite effective with individuals with ASD of various functioning levels (Kalyva, 2011a). It should be noted, however, that observing certain behaviors does not guarantee their accurate and effective implementation. It is quite typical of individuals with ASD to possess certain social skills that they have difficulty generalizing to other settings and individuals without specific guidance and support. Therefore, it is important to realize the need for training in natural settings where children with ASD have the chance to actually practice the social skills that they have acquired through social stories and scenarios.

## Communication Supports

Since communication has been identified as one the most prominent deficits in individuals with ASD that seems to be highly associated with social anxiety, communication supports are perceived as essential in overcoming this anxiety and the participants in the Müller et al. (2008) study have produced the three following groups:

a) alternative modes of communication that in this case do not refer to sign language or the Picture Exchange Communication System (Kalyva, 2011a) that are traditionally used with individuals with ASD who have no or very limited verbal communication skills. Here reference is made to alternative and less stressful ways of communication (both face-to-face and on the phone) where less attention is paid to non-verbal language and other emotionally loaded stimuli. An example is communication through e-mails, chat groups, listservs, forums, or online 'role-playing' clubs. It is easier for individuals with ASD to reduce the social anxiety that they feel in face-to-face interactions using these means because they have to concentrate only on the written word and not on the non-verbal context that is associated with it. However, using these means of communication exclusively can lead to even more problems in face-to-face interactions, since individuals with ASD will try to avoid the situations that are most awkward to them. A young girl with ASD started using social networking to talk to boys that she liked from her school. At the beginning she was talking about more general topics, but then these discussions became more intimate and she was involved in sexual conversations. Soon she was not able to deal with it emotionally, since the boys started teasing her at school and calling her names. They were making sexual advances on her and she did not know how to react, since she did not have to interact with a screen but with other human beings face-to-face.

b) explicit communication that refers to the inability of individuals with ASD to understand metaphors, humor, and/or irony and to their tendency to interpret everything literally. They need from the person who converses with them to speak literally, to explain everything in details and to avoid using ambiguous meanings. This can sometimes be a nuisance for typically developing individuals, especially if they are not sensitized to the individuals with ASD. Parents, teachers, or other individuals who interact with individuals with ASD should try to provide very clear and specific instructions. For example, the mother could tell her son with ASD 'First you go to your bedroom, then you open the top drawer, and last you take your red t-shirt'. By breaking down the task into smaller steps the mother facilitates her son to go through the motions and checks which part of the directions he cannot remember, offering thus extra support when needed (for example, by asking her son to repeat the steps and focusing on the part that he might have forgotten). The mother should also spell out clearly to her son what she expects of him to do and why and not assume that he can guess it because of something that she alluded to before. If she says 'I feel so tired', she should not normally expect him to infer that because mummy is tired he should get her a glass of water. The mother should make this connection explicit to her son and expect him to learn in time to make such connections with relevant targeted training.

c) instruction in the use of social cues, since many individuals with ASD have problems both interpreting and using them effectively. They need to receive explicit training on how to use body language, facial expressions, and tone of voice. We remember working with an adolescent boy with ASD who used to stroke our hand in order to show that he was feeling close to us. This behavior could easily be misinterpreted as harassment, so we had to train him how much physical contact was appropriate and in which settings. Before trying to address this behavior we wanted to know why he thought that this was a desirable way to express his feelings. He said that he had seen many movies where actors used to touch, hug, or kiss each other in order to express their affection. He was using this as a behavioral script, but he could not identify the context in which this behavior was considered to be appropriate. We also taught him alternative ways of expressing his positive feelings that did not involve physical contact (for example, by paying a compliment) and were more appropriate for same-sex interactions or for friendly interactions with the opposite-sex. We also explained to him, of course, that this behavior was totally relevant in the context of an intimate relationship with his partner. It is essential to help the individual with ASD understand why a behavior is or isn't appropriate without trying to scare him or provide him with false information.

Many individuals with ASD are actually unaware of the fact that with their verbal and/or nonverbal behavior they may offend, bore or intimidate people around them, and this is largely due to the fact that their family, teachers, friends and peers often avoid expressing and discussing their true emotions. This partly happens because in today's world people have learned that it is better to hide their emotions in order to protect themselves and so a lot of times they prefer not to say anything. This, however, does not help individuals with ASD learn the emotional consequences of their actions and they may become even more 'awkward' and 'inconsiderate'. We are working with a young boy with ASD who liked to talk constantly about his two favorite topics, trains and Toy Story. He would go on for hours without realizing that this could be tiring for people around them. What we did was show him some verbal and nonverbal social cues indicating that the other person may be bored or disinterested (e.g., look at the watch, yawn, say 'let's play something else') and identified with him other appropriate conversation topics. We also discussed with him that he could take the time when talking to someone else to find out about his interests and hobbies and make room for them as well in his planned discussion. He has learned to talk about what he likes and then to move on to the topic of the other person. At this point he uses his watch to know when to let the other person talk or to change his topic. Of course, this is not the last stage of the training, since he needs to further develop his empathy and do this spontaneously.

## Self-Initiated Supports

Most individuals with ASD have recognized the need to not rely solely on others to offer them the appropriate support, but to learn how to initiate supports on their own in order to become more independent. Participants stressed the importance of self-initiated supports, such as creative and improvisational outlets; physical and/or outdoor activity; spiritual practice and/or organized religion; mediating objects; and alone time.

a) creative and improvisational outlets are essential to help individuals with ASD overcome the stress that they experience due to their social anxiety. They choose to engage in unstructured social interactions that tend to revolve around pleasant activities, such as participating in amateur theater groups, dance or art class. The emphasis on a joint activity takes away some of the pressure that is exerted because of the very nature of interpersonal communications. It should be noted, however, that for some individuals with ASD the lack of structured and organized activities can create even more stress. One young woman with ASD told us that becoming member of a theater group helped her learn how to relax and improvise due to the exercises that she was doing. She had never realized before that it could be fun to act without being based on a script. Although it was stressful initially, she learned how to deal with these emotions effectively using the guidance of her instructor and the support of her peers. She also practiced how to coordinate her verbal and nonverbal cues in order to express her emotions without being overdramatic or minimizing the extent of her feelings.

b) physical and outdoor activities can be very relaxing for individuals with ASD who look for an outlet for their stress. One little girl with ASD was transformed according to her parents every time that she went outdoors. She seemed to enjoy the sights, the smells, and the sounds of nature and she insisted on going out as much as she could. Her parents encouraged these activities that made her happy, but we have instructed them to engage also in some of the things that she was doing and this helped them develop a more close relationship that enhanced their communication in general.

Just letting children with ASD running around free into the wilderness may be relaxing for them, but it does not help them overcome their social skills deficits.

Some other individuals with ASD participate in exercise routines that help them reduce social stress, such as hiking, running, yoga, bicycling, or swimming. The structure that is embedded in some of these sports can be very relaxing for them, while they may hang out with some of their co-athletes when the training is over. It is important to make sure that the sports that they practice are of their own choice. The parents of an adolescent boy who had come to consult us were forcing their son to participate in a skiing team and to train daily in order to become a champion. The boy liked skiing, but when his parents starting pressuring him to take it on professionally he started to become overly stressed. He did not feel comfortable spending time with his fellow athletes during their weekend practice trips and so he ended up wetting his bed at night and developing ticks. It took us a lot of effort to explain to the parents that they had to respect their son's wishes and to try to work out a plan that would work for him as well.

c) spirituality and religion may constitute a significant mechanism for coping with stress for many individuals with ASD, who might develop further their social/self-awareness according to Müller et al. (2008). We believe that this is again something that should not be forced on the individual with ASD, since one boy that they referred to us a long time ago was forced by his grandmother to attend all masses and to pray and chant all the time. He was eight and fasting regularly, while he was convinced that he was taken over by the devil and he had suffered several exorcist attempts that were not successful according to the priest. He was starving himself to be punished for his sins and the whole religious involvement had turned into an obsession with the cooperation of the wider family environment. We are aware that such cases may be extreme, but we must ensure that in exercising their spiritual or guidance role priests do not substitute the mental health professional who should be in charge of the individual with ASD with the family's participation and cooperation.

d) mediating objects that refer to some objects that individuals with ASD may carry with them to social events in order to use them as «baits» to approach others and as an excuse to initiate a social interaction, without having to resort to more dreaded verbal exchanges. A 6-year-old boy that we are treating likes to carry with him a small bag that is full of miniature figurines that his parents bought for him during a holiday abroad. These figurines are very popular among his age group and they cannot be found in Greece, so he shows them to the children that he wants to approach in social situations, such as parties, playgrounds, etc. This trick works and he is happy with it, but the main problem that he has to face is dealing with other children taking his figurines and occasionally not wanting to return them to him. He used to throw temper tantrums that drove the other children away, but he is now following some relaxation techniques to deal with his stress and he has developed some methods through scripts and role-playing to ask for his toys. It works well most of the times and when the other children do not respond his parents usually step in to save the day. However, as this boy is growing older our goal is to rely less on mediating objects and to develop other social communication skills.

e) alone time, which is something that many individuals with ASD enjoy since it gives them a chance to relax and to balance social interaction. Although it is widely accepted that individuals with ASD need this time alone, teachers and parents often try to make sure that they repeatedly engage in group activities in order to avoid solitude. We have to try not to take things to the extreme, however, and to respect their need for alone time.

Because we want to associate with other people and we get pleasure out of these interactions we automatically assume that everybody should feel the same. We remember a boy with ASD who enjoyed going to the playground, listening to music and watching other children play. He actually told us that this gave him the opportunity to observe other and try to make sense of their behaviors before joining in the activities. He realized that he had to join the activities at some point, but he needed to take this time at the beginning to settle down and to get in control. He said that his mother understood that and let him have some alone time, while his father would literally push him into joining what the other children were doing and would not have him sit at all by himself. He described how bad it felt to be forced into playing football that he did not like just because this was his father's dream – to see his son kick the ball.

## Attitudinal Supports

Most of the individuals with ASD in the Müller et al. (2008) study stressed the importance of attitudinal supports from teachers, family members and peers, including: a patient and caring attitude; tolerance of and respect for differences; and willingness to initiate social interactions, which will be analyzed below:

a) patient and caring attitudes that should be expressed by significant others in their life, such as their parents, siblings, teachers, friends, peers, and therapists. Individuals with ASD want others to be patient, caring, understanding and supportive with them and show them that they are willing to accept their different way of thinking. However, it is important for them to realize that they should also try to express similar attitudes and not use their ASD as an excuse to getting away with behaving inappropriately. An adolescent boy we worked with used to state how happy he was that his parents accepted him as he was, but when we talked about some of his behaviors that he needed to change (e.g., not swear at them and not insult them) he used to say «No, I do not have to change anything. They have to accept me as I am. I have ASD and I do not have to be polite. It is one of the symptoms». Of course, we had to explain to him that he had to respect also that his parents had feelings that he should not hurt intentionally and that this understanding relationship should be bidirectional.

b) tolerance of differences is associated with the previous parameter and many individuals with ASD believe that others should be considerate and accepting of their different way of thinking. This can significantly help them alleviate the social anxiety that they experience in social interactions. They feel less threatened and so they can behave more naturally and without feeling constrained by strict social rules. However, it is difficult many times to gain the acceptance of others when the individuals with ASD have not yet fully realized their actual way of thinking and embraced their diversity. We were working with an adolescent girl with high-functioning ASD who wanted to know why she was attending therapies and why she had so many difficulties making friends. She had overheard during a hospital visit that she has Asperger syndrome, but her parents refused to further discuss it with her. This made her feel strange, increased her social anxiety and decreased her self-esteem. We explained to her parents that this was not a healthy attitude and tried to make them realize what would be the potential consequences of continuing to behave in this way. Then we started talking to the girl about Asperger as a different way of thinking that informs her behaviors and social skills and this relieved her greatly of the stress that she was experiencing. Once she realized that she started explaining to others why she was different and this made them more willing to interact with her.

c) willingness of other people to initiate social interaction with individuals with ASD and to overcome any stereotypical or stigmatizing attitudes to become their friends. We have already mentioned that although there are quite a few interventions that successfully target social skills deficits, they rarely lead to the creation of real friendships. Typically developing individuals will not take the initiative to contact the individual with ASD, to invite them to different social activities and to discuss with them their actual problems. They may respond positively to the initiatives of individuals with ASD, but this relationship is usually not bidirectional. A lot of work is needed both on individual and on group/societal level to help people understand and embrace the diverse way of thinking and acting of individuals with ASD.

*Cognitive Behavioral Training*

One of the therapies that have been most effective with individuals with social anxiety disorder is Cognitive Behavioral Training (CBT), which usually employs a combination of exposure and cognitive therapy (Heimberg and Becker, 2002). Cardaciotto and Herbert (2004) used CBT with an adult with social anxiety disorder who had comorbid Asperger syndrome (high-functioning ASD). The aim of the treatment was to reduce fear and to promote engagement in social situations. This would be accomplished through training in starting, continuing and closing conversations, meeting new people, dating, and assertiveness. The training lasted for 14 weeks and a variety of methods were used – including role-playing, cognitive restructuring and homework assignments. Following intervention, the client showed lees anxiety symptoms and an improvement in social skills – such as appropriate eye contact and conversational skills. We are also using CBT training, especially the emotional thermometer (for more details see Kalyva, 2011a) with individuals with high-functioning ASD and the improvement is remarkable when treating their social anxiety. However, since CBT requires a basic level of understanding and communication, it is not very effective with individuals with ASD who are at the lower end of the spectrum with minimal or non-existent communication skills and mental retardation. Some of the other techniques that have been presented above are more likely to be working with this group, such as the circle of friends, social stories or small groups and dyad instruction. A quite promising intervention is social effectiveness training that consists of exposure and social skills training in both individual and group formats (Turner, Beidel, Cooley, Woody, and Messer, 1994).

# References

American Psychiatric Association. (1994). *Diagnostic and statistical manual of mental disorders* (4th ed.). Washington, DC: Author.

138 Efrosini Kalyva and Vlastaris Tsakiris

American Psychiatric Association. (2000). *Diagnostic and statistical manual of mental disorders* (4th ed-revised.). Washington, DC: Author.

Attwood, T. (1998). *Asperger's syndrome: A guide for parents and professionals.* Philadelphia: Kingsley.

Bellini, S. (2004). Social skill deficits and anxiety in high-functioning adolescents with autism spectrum disorders. *Focus on Autism and Other Developmental Disabilities,* 19, 78–86.

Bellini, S. (2006). The development of social anxiety in adolescents with autism spectrum disorders. *Focus on Autism and Other Developmental Disabilities,* 21, 138-145.

Biederman, J., Rosenbaum, J. F., Chaloff, J., and Kagan, J. (1995). Behavioral inhibition as a risk factor for anxiety disorders. In: J. S. March (Ed.), *Anxiety in children and adolescents* (pp. 61–81). New York: Guilford Press.

Butera, G. and Haywood, H. C. (1995). Cognitive education of young children with autism: An application of Bright Start. In: E. Schopler and G. B. Mesibov (Eds.), *Learning and cognition in autism.* New York: Plenum Press.

Cardaciotto, L. and Herbert, J. D. (2004). Cognitive behavior therapy for social anxiety disorder in the context of Asperger's Syndrome: A single-subject report. *Cognitive and Behavioral Practice,* 11, 75-81.

Gillott, A., Furniss, F. and Walter, A. (2001). Anxiety in high functioning children with autism. *Autism,* 5, 277–286.

Heimberg, R. G. and Becker, R. E. (2002). *Cognitive-behavioral treatment for social phobia: Basic mechanisms and clinical strategies.* New York: Guilford Press.

Heimberg, R. G., Holt, C. S., Schneier, F. R., and Leibowitz, M. R. (1993). The issues of subtypes in the diagnosis of social phobia. *Journal of Anxiety Disorders,* 7, 249–269.

Kalyva, E. (2010). Mutlirater congruence on the social skills assessment of children with Asperger Syndrome: Self, mother, father, and teacher Ratings. *Journal of Autism and Developmental Disorders,* 40, 1202–1208.

Kalyva, E. (2011a). *Autism: Educational and therapeutic approaches.* London: Sage.

Kalyva, E. (2011b). Peer interpersonal conflict resolution in children with and without disabilities. Hauppage, NY: Nova Science Publishers.

Kalyva, E. and Avramidis, E. (2005). Improving communication between children with autism and their peers through the Circle of Friends: A small-scale intervention study. *Journal of Applied Research in Intellectual Disabilities,* 18, 253–261.

Kessler, R. C., Stein, M. B. and Berglund, P. (1998). Social phobia subtypes in the National Comorbidity Survey. *American Journal of Psychiatry,* 155, 613–619.

Kim, J. A., Szatmari, P., Bryson, S. E., Streiner, D. L., and Wilson, F. J. (2000). The prevalence of anxiety and mood problems among children with autism and Asperger syndrome. *Autism,* 4, 117–132.

Kleinhans, N. M., Richards, T., Weaver, K., Johnson, C. L., Greenson, J., Dawson, G., and Aylward, E. (2010). Association between amygdala response to emotional faces and social anxiety in autism spectrum disorders. *Neuropsychologia,* 48, 3665–3670.

Koning, C. and Magill-Evans, J. (2001). Social and language skills in adolescent boys with Asperger syndrome. *Autism,* 5, 23–36.

Kuusikko, S., Pollock-Wurman, R., Jussila, K., Carter, A. S., Mattila, M. L., Ebeling, H., Pauls, D. L., and Moilanen, I. (2008). Social anxiety in high-functioning children and adolescents with autism and Asperger syndrome. *Journal of Autism and Developmental Disorders,* 38, 1697–1709.

Müller, E., Schuler, A. and Yates, G. B. (2008). Social challenges and supports from the perspective of individuals with Asperger syndrome and other autism spectrum disabilities. *Autism,* 12, 173-190.

Rubin, K. H. and Burgess, K. B. (2001). Social withdrawal and anxiety. In: M. W. Vasey and M. R. Dadds (Eds.), *The developmental psychopathology of anxiety* (pp. 435–458). New York: Oxford University Press.

Schultz, R. T., Romanski, L. M. and Tsatsanis, K. D. (2000). Neurofunctional models of autistic disorder and Asperger syndrome. In: A. Klin, F. R. Volkmar and S. S. Sparrow (Eds.), *Asperger syndrome* (pp. 172–209). New York: Guilford Press.

Stein, M. B., Torgrud, L. J. and Walker, J. R. (2000). Social phobia symptoms, subtypes, and severity: Findings from a community sample. *Archives of General Psychiatry,* 57, 1046–1052.

Tantam, D. (2000). Psychological disorder in adolescents and adults with Asperger syndrome. *Autism,* 4, 47–62.

Trepagnier, C. (1996). A possible origin for the social and communicative deficits of autism. *Focus on Autism and Other Developmental Disabilities,* 11, 170–182.

Turner, S. M, Beidel, D. C., Cooley, M. R., Woody, S. R., and Messer, S. C. (1994). A multicomponent behavioral treatment for social phobia: Social effectiveness therapy. *Behavior Research and Therapy,* 32, 381-390.

Turner, S. M., Beidel, D. C. and Townsley, R. M. (1992). Social phobia: A comparison of specific and generalized subtypes and avoidant personality disorder. *Journal of Abnormal Psychology,* 101, 326–332.

Vasey, M. W. and Dadds, M. R. (2001). An introduction to the developmental psychopathology of anxiety. In: M. W. Vasey and M. R. Dadds (Eds.), *The developmental psychopathology of anxiety* (pp. 3–26). New York: Oxford University Press.

In: Social Anxiety
Editor: Efrosini Kalyva

ISBN: 978-1-62808-396-5
© 2013 Nova Science Publishers, Inc.

*Chapter VIII*

# Social Anxiety and HIV/AIDS: Psychological Well-Being and Intervention Effectiveness

*Miltiadis Stefanidis,* * *Charilaos Liampas, Fotis Katimertzopoulos,*
*Vlad Dediu, Christina Zintro, Victoria Georgieva,*
*and Aleksandar Ilievski*
The International Faculty of the University of Sheffield,
CITY College, Thessaloniki, Greece

## Abstract

HIV affects millions of people every year. Although most think of the effects HIV
has on physical health, the psychological consequences are not to be taken lightly. In the
following chapter we look at how HIV impacts the mental state of the people who suffer
from it. More specifically, we will explore the links between HIV, anxiety and the other
co morbid symptoms that manifest with it. The chapter starts by introducing the reader to
the concept of stigma, how it can influence anxiety symptoms and then moves to describe
how people living with HIV are perceived in their social environment. It then explains
how social interactions affect the feelings of stigmatization. Later, we discuss how stress
also comes into play in affecting the behavior and psychological well-being of HIV
patients. Then we look at how support from within the family influences the feelings of
anxiety and depression, of HIV sufferers. The immediate social environment
(neighborhood) and economic status are also examined in relation to coping with the
illness. Finally, the chapter ends by presenting findings from a number of studies that
have evaluated the interventional programs designed to reduce social anxiety and stigma.
In absence of fully effective antitoxin remedies for HIV, factors such as safe-sex
practices, raising awareness and making people more knowledgeable about the disease

---

* Corresponding author: Miltiadis Stefanidis, E-mail: milts.stefs@gmail.com.

have been assessed to better understand how effective they are in helping people better cope with their illness.

**Keywords**: HIV/AIDS, stigma, social anxiety, mental health

# Introduction

Physical illness affects not only the biological, but also the psychological well-being of a patient. Although many diseases are often accompanied by psychological distress there are some that are particularly demanding psychologically, because of their aggressiveness, severity and stigma. A prominent example is the Human Immunodeficiency Virus (HIV) disease, with more than 34 million people suffering from it as of 2010. Moreover, around 3.4 million children were reported HIV positive, suggesting that HIV does not afflict only those engaging in unsafe sex or substance abusers. Prenatal contraction of the disease is a real threat that subjects people to a life of hardships, both medically and socially (Gonzalez, Zvolensky, Parent, Grover, and Hickey, 2012).

HIV/AIDS disease is associated with mental stress, stigma and psychiatric morbidity (Vyavaharkar, Moneyham, Corwin, Saunders, Annang, and Tavakoli, 2010). HIV infection is a developing illness that has various impacts on affected individuals. Individuals with HIV have to cope not only with the physical dysfunctions of the illness but also with its consequential psychological effects, including HIV-stigma factors and changes in psychological distress dimensions, both contributing to social anxiety (Kang, Rapkin, and DeAlmeida, 2006). A growing body of literature revealed that HIV symptom distress is significantly associated with anxiety sensitivity in relation to the symptomatology of panic disorder, social anxiety disorder and depression among people with HIV (Gonzalez et al., 2012). Further empirical evidence suggests that many individuals with HIV are exposed to stigmatizing attitudes, involving social rejection, negative self-worth, perceive interpersonal insecurity, sadness and anxiety (Chiu, Grobbelaar, Sikkema, Vandormoel, Bomela, and Kershaw, 2008; Kang et al., 2006). Research in South Africa has revealed that stigmatizing attitudes are further affected by social capital components, with components of trust and familiarities being crucial in the way community members treat HIV affected individuals (Chiu et al., 2008). It is suggested that building a sense of trust and safety may lead to positive social norms, which in turn may influence attitudes and behavior, thus minimizing stigma and HIV stigmatization (Chiu et al., 2008). This is further supported by research revealing that individuals with high - internalized HIV stigma (I.H.S.) tend to report that their families were less accepting of their illness (Lee, Kochman, and Sikkema, 2002). It is of great interest that individuals with positive HIV experience different degrees of stigma related to their illness, ranging from high I.H.S. to no stigma at all (Lee et al., 2002). This evidence clearly supports that stigmatization and the associated social anxiety is significantly impacted by the way individuals are treated and accepted by their social environment (Chen, Choe, Chen, and Zhang, 2007).

Individuals living with HIV/AIDS tend to show high rates of distress, which is associated with low emotional dysregulation related to psychological and disease-specific distress (Brandt, Gonzalez, Grover, and Zvolensky, 2012). Research supports that emotional dysregulation is significantly and positively related to HIV-symptom distress, depressive symptom, anxiety and pain-related anxiety (Brandt et al., 2012). Indeed, HIV infected individuals are challenged by the various psychosocial effects related to their disease. These psychosocial effects refer to negative affect symptom and emotional problems initially driven by biological responses to the infection (Brandt et al., 2012). These biological responses are caused by side-effects of the antiretroviral therapy (ART).

Furthermore, HIV individuals face negative social influences (i.e.: HIV related stigma) and distress linked to the disclosure of their HIV status (Brandt et al., 2012). All these parameters place HIV individuals at an elevated risk for psychological distress.

Depressive symptomatology is related to emotional dysregulation. Negative emotional experiences involve greater anxiety, depressive symptoms, and HIV related stress in HIV infected individuals.

In addition to that emotional dysregulation, being a changeable construct, is significantly influenced by psychological and social resources available to individuals. Psychological resources reflect individuals' ability to engage in positive coping behaviors when facing emotional distress, while social resources reflect the social support and acceptance provided by individuals' social context (Brandt et al., 2012).

The assumption that HIV/AIDS enhances vulnerability and increases risk of psychological distress, is clearly supported by the fact that depression and anxiety disorders are very common amongst HIV infected people (Brandt et al., 2012; Gonzalez et al., 2012). This is attributed to the fact that HIV infected individuals are exposed to more general and specific life stressors, while possibly having less resources to manage those emotional states. Furthermore, individuals with HIV may engage in more maladaptive health behavior and self-destructive behavior as a way to eliminate personal distress (Brandt et al., 2012). These behaviors are significant due to high rates of anxiety experience. This is related to statistics showing that suicide rates among HIV individuals are three times higher compared to the general population (Capron, Gonzalez, Parent, Zvolensky, and Schmidt, 2012).

Further evidence supports that one third of HIV individuals attempting to commit suicide present also an anxiety disorder. Suicidality among HIV individuals is significantly impacted by their experienced psychiatric, biological and social vulnerabilities. More importantly elevated risk of suicide among HIV infected individuals is influenced by the social stigma associated with living with HIV (Capron et al., 2012).

Stigma refers to a feeling of being rejected, disrespected or unappreciated by others. For example, it is relatively common for people to run away from individuals living with HIV/ AIDS, just because of the disease they have. This makes them feel ashamed, and in order not to be rejected by society, they hide their condition. Stigmatization arises from the understanding that there has been a violation of a set of a considered socially acceptable set of attitudes, beliefs, and values. The scientific consensus defines stigma as "an undesirable or discrediting attribute that an individual possesses, thus reducing that individual's status in the eyes of society" (Brown, Trujillo, and Macintyre, 2001).

There are three distinct types of stigma: a) stigmas of the body (such as blemishes or skin rashes) b) stigmas of character (e.g. people with mental health problems or criminals) and c) stigmas associated with social collectivities (racial or tribal) (Gilbert and Walker, 2010). Brown, Trujillo and Macintyre (2001) investigated the latter, that is social stigma and divided it into: a) *felt* or *perceived* stigma that referred to real or imagined fear of social reactions and potential discrimination that aroused from a particular undesirable attribute, disease (such as

HIV), or association with a particular group (like prostitutes or drug addicts) and b) *enacted* stigma, which was considered as the real experience of discrimination.

Sorsdahl, Mall, Stein and Joska 's (2011) study on social stigma based itself on this proto-theory, and with their research, they concluded that stigma may be experienced through three mechanisms, and not two: i) enacted stigma, ii) anticipated stigma, and iii) internalized stigma.

Enacted stigma referred to the extent to which people living with HIV/AIDS are actually being discriminated against by others because they have or are thought to have the disease. Anticipated stigma refers to the degree to which people with HIV/AIDS anticipated they will experience prejudice and discrimination. Internalized stigma refers to the degree to which people with HIV/AIDS endorse the negative beliefs and feelings thought to be associated with the disease. As victims of the stigma that this infection caries, people with HIV/AIDS isolate themselves from other communities and even from their own families. They feel anxious to interact with others because of the fear of being discriminated against or criticized. This is why it is common for people living with HIV/AIDS to feel insecure outside their home. Spending most of their time at home, people avoid any interaction with the outside world, which in psychology is referred to as social anxiety disorder. Even the idea of going outside of the house and facing people that might criticize them, if they know they suffer from that disease, make these people extremely anxious.

To examine the extent to which the three different mechanisms of stigma mentioned above are experienced by people living with HIV/AIDS, Sorsdahl, Mall, Stein and Joska (2011) measured the experience of stigma in the last three months among 400 HIV-positive respondents from the area of Western Province. The study resulted in numerous findings. Respondents reported overall low levels of both internalized and enacted stigma. The explanation the researchers gave for these results are that all the participants interviewed were already in HIV care and might be experiencing reduction in the levels of stigma due to interaction with care providers and other patients. Interpreting the results in terms of social anxiety it turns out that people in HIV care centers are less likely to experience stigma and therefore social anxiety. Communicating with other infected people and health care providers makes people with HIV/AIDS feel more comfortable and less anxious. However, internalized stigma was more often noticed than enacted stigma. This finding shows that the actual criticism people with HIV/AIDS receive from others is much less than the one they believe about themselves. Therefore, people suffering from social anxiety, resulted by the infection they have, do not feel comfortable communicating with others because they believe that negative beliefs about the disease they have are associated with them, even when the person they are communicating with does not show that. Second, male participants, young participants and those who had been living with HIV/AIDS longer were less likely to experience internalized stigma and along with that - social anxiety. Third, educated participants were more likely to experience internalized stigma than those with less education, showing that educated people might have more negative beliefs about themselves, an outcome of the disease they have, which makes them more anxious interacting with others and preferable to stay home in order to avoid being ashamed in public. The study also shows that if patients are predominantly only disclosing to their families, they may be less likely to experience social isolation, fear of contagion and verbal abuse.

When referring to these results, however, it is important to mention the limitations of the study. An important weakness of the study refers to the fact that HIV stigma has not been completely examined due to the use of a measure that does not include an element regarding perceived stigma. Also, because of the use of an adjusted sample, the findings of the study cannot summarize the extent to which all people with HIV/AIDS, living in the area of South Africa, experience the disease. Despite its limitations, the study is important for giving an idea of how these three mechanisms of stigma are experienced among people living with HIV and the way they are potentially related to social anxiety.

Other studies, like the one conducted by Earnshaw, Smith, Chaudior, Lee and Copenhaver (2012), are based on a stigma theory for HIV, following the HIV Stigma Framework, stating that HIV stigma is displayed among people at high risk for HIV via three distinct mechanisms: stereotypes, prejudice and discrimination. In order to understand how HIV stigma is associated with HIV-related behavior, such as HIV testing, it is important to differentiate those three mechanisms. Stereotypes are considered to be group-based beliefs about people living with HIV/AIDS that are often applied to individuals (for example: people with HIV are gay man, prostitutes and drug users). Prejudice refers to negative emotions, like disgust, towards people suffering from the disease. Discrimination reflects behavioral expressions of prejudice directed towards people living with HIV/AIDS. All these key mechanisms can affect the way people suffering from the disease perceive themselves. Being discriminated against or prejudiced are feelings that no one would like to experience and in this way people with HIV/AIDS may avoid situations, in which they can be judged. This is how we come back to the topic of social anxiety, experienced by people with HIV/AIDS. If we take stereotyping as an example, a woman may not want to disclose her infection in front of others, because she might be considered as a prostitute or a drug user by people, holding such beliefs about people suffering from the disease. Another reason why this woman would keep her ailment as a secret is because people might start behaving in a different way, considering her condition. As mentioned above, disgust is a common reaction towards people with HIV/AIDS, while some people might not want to stay close to the infected person in order to protect themselves from contamination. However, educated people seem to be less distant, knowing that it is absolutely impossible to be infected by touching, hugging or simply speaking to a person living with the disease. Stereotypes, prejudice and discrimination make people with HIV/AIDS feel ashamed, disgusted or guilty explaining thus why they avoid social interactions and find the home environment more comfortable, safe and relaxing.

Chiu's et al. (2008) study aimed to assess the relationship between HIV stigmatizing attitudes and individual perception of social capital in South Africa. Social capital was defined as the expected collective or economic benefits derived from the preferential treatment and cooperation between individuals and groups. A major advantage of the study is that it was the first study trying to explain the role of social capital on stigmatizing attitudes. Researchers define personal stigma as individual's own attitude toward people with HIV, while attributed stigma concerned the attitudes that individuals perceived as existing in their communities. This study revealed novel results in that social capital components exhibited strong relationship to perceptions of HIV stigma, both personal stigmatizing attitudes and attributed stigmatizing attitudes towards people with HIV. Furthermore, *"in line with existing research, it is clear that social capital components like trust, group participation, safety, and empowerment are not the only predictors of stigma"*(Chiu et al., 2008, p.527). Interesting results were drawn concerning who and how was affected by stigma. In specific, individuals who felt empowered to make changes had less personal stigma, while individuals who felt trust and safety in their community were less likely to attribute stigma to members of their community. Further on, perceptions of trust affected stigmatizing attitudes differently in those who were close to an HIV-infected person than those who were not, illustrating the importance of familiarity.

Despite the advantage of the study in using a novel sample on the field, there are some important sample limitations that need to be considered. Participants of the study involved indigenous Africans predominately of Sotho heritage, which may indicate that results may not apply cross-culturally, as regions of Republic of South Africa tend to have much higher HIV rates than most western countries (Chiu et al., 2008). This limitation is common in various studies on the effects of HIV, which need to be interpreted with caution (Myers, Sumner, Ullman, Loeb, Carmona, and Wyatt, 2009).

Familiarity with HIV- individuals has a significant impact on the way individuals treat and support infected individuals, while in turn this familiarity plays a crucial role in the way those infected individuals perceive their illness and their self worth in general. Research supports that individuals with HIV whose families were less supporting and less accepting of their illness tended to have higher rates of internalized HIV stigma (Lee et al., 2002). HIV stigmatization is not only associated with to lack of familiarity and adequate education, but also to strong links of depression, low self esteem and substance use to people with HIV (Myers et al., 2008). These negative experiences are likely to feed back to the stigma that HIV individuals may feel. Empirical evidence suggests that being HIV positive is associated with more depression and higher chronic burden. Depression on its own as a disorder is highly contributing to social anxiety. This occurs often in women, as they are more vulnerable to experience chronic stress in comparison to men, leading to higher rates of depression and social anxiety. These depressed feelings are especially reinforced when individuals with HIV are not accepted by their social environment, which in turn leads to enhanced stigmatization (Lee et al., 2002).

Psychosocial factors play a crucial role in the way vulnerable individuals with HIV deal with their illness (Myers et al., 2008). The degree and quality of interaction within individuals' support system is highly relevant to the psychological distress they experience (Myers et al., 2009). Psychological distress is often associated with higher levels of substance abuse among HIV individuals. Negative social interactions and social conflicts are perceived by individuals with HIV as criticism and excessive anger, which can lead to social undermining. Social undermining is particularly linked to social anxiety and psychological distress, while it is more prevalent among lower socio-economic status populations, possibly due to lower education on health issues. Although this is an appealing and promising research on the effects of social undermining on mental health affected individuals, further research needs to be conducted.

An additional role that highlights the importance of social surroundings, in experiencing anxiety and stigma, is the cultural factor. It is widely acknowledged that ethnic minorities (such as African Americans in the United States) deal with a lot more social, economic and cultural issues, such as racism, unemployment and certain types of homophobia from the community. Nevertheless, studies indicate that especially, African Americans tend to seek assistance from professional caregivers less than fellow white individuals (Broman, 1997; Snowden, 1998). Even though, ethnic minorities deal with more difficulties, stress, social stigma and anxiety, they cope with the distress more effectively (and religious coping) (Leserman, Perkins, and Exans, 1992). Kalichman, Heckman, Kochman, Sikkema and Bergholte (2000) designed a study in order to compare and characterize levels of life-stressors, ways of coping, social support, psychological distress among African American and white men living with HIV/AIDS, ranging from the age of 48 to 66 years old. Some of the features measured were the perceived level of social support and psychological distress, which are important factors contributing to social anxiety. The results of the study interestingly suggest that older African Americans express less hopelessness and seek less social support, and as a result felt more positive in social context and optimism for the future.

An interesting fact that should be mentioned is that even though African Americans had more family support (a valuable emotional, financial, tangible support) than social support, their level of anxiety, depressive symptoms and somatization were lower (Kalichman et al, 2000).

In, addition, in the US, HIV affects more African Americans children living in high-poverty neighborhoods and this social influence shapes the child's behavior and emotional state (Kohen, Brooks-Gunn, Leventhal, and Hertzman, 2002). Evidence suggests that people who move from a high-poverty neighborhood to low-poverty ones, report less stress and less anxiety, (Leventhal and Brooks-Gunn, 2003). Social relations and support in the neighborhood and availability to community resources play an important role in the child's behavior and psychological state, (Moore, Daniel, Gauvin, and Dube, 2009).

To further investigate the issue, a study was conducted by Wandersman and Nation (1998) who found that chronic environmental stressors affect children's coping and behaviors; (Foster and Brooks-Gunn, 2009; Kliewer, Parrish, Taylor, Jackson, Walker and Shivy 2006; Kliewer, Murrelle, Mejia de Torres, and Angold, 2001). Youths with prenatally HIV positive (PHIV+), who mostly lived in a high-poverty neighborhood and faced daily stressors, reported more impulsive behaviors, depressive symptoms and anxiety in social environments (Najman, Hayatbakhsh, Clavarino, Bor, O'Callaghan, and Williams, 2010). Being exposed to poverty in childhood and facing the stigma of HIV, make PHIV+ children experience depressive symptoms, anxiety and inferiority feelings in adolescence and young adulthood (Santiago, Wadsworth, and Stump, 2011).

In a similar study conducted in 2011, the relationship between exposure to neighborhood disorder and anxiety and depression and life stressors among PHIV+ and PHIV- youngsters, ranging from the age of 9 to 16 years old was observed. The results of the study suggest that the consequences of the environmental stress on anxiety and depression were explained by stressful life events that PHIV+ youths face (Malee et al., 2011). According to Ross, Reynolds, and Geis (2000), the experience of disadvantaged neighborhoods influence one's perception of hopelessness, control over life and perceived image of the inferior self; which in turn influence the possibility of experiencing social anxiety or depression later on.

It is widely suggested that efforts must be made to encourage family members as well as friends to get involved in HIV individuals' management of symptomatology (Vyavaharkar et al., 2010). Further research indicates that HIV/AIDS affected families are at increased risk for conflicts, threats to educational attainment, economic insecurity and generalized community stigmatization, which all feed back to affected individuals' social anxiety (Betancourt, Rubin-Smith, Beardslee, Stulac, Fayida and Safren, 2011). Researchers stress the importance of these findings when creating mental health assessments and planning HIV/AIDS interventions (Betancourt et al., 2011). This is further highlighted when considering the emotional and behavioral problems (possibly due to stigmatization) that are common among HIV individuals. Further research on HIV prevention reveals highly interesting outcomes. Worth-noting are results indicating that fear at a personal level was significantly associated with negative attitudes and unwillingness to interact with people with HIV, when controlling for accurate knowledge, inaccurate beliefs and self-perceived risk of HIV infection (Chen et al., 2007). This highlights the importance of education and familiarization in both minimizing and eliminating stigmatization, and thereby the social anxiety of affected individuals.

Having looked at the different links between HIV and social anxiety it is important to focus on and analyze what the field of practical research has shown us.

This following study is focused on how to help prevent HIV and social anxiety between homosexual and bisexual youth. People with social anxiety feel very uncomfortable and anxious when they are at the center of attention. People with observational anxiety feel uncomfortable performing tasks in public because they fear that they will be judged, so they will be less likely to perform well at any task. Reducing the spread of HIV and AIDS among people with social anxiety disorders is very important. Most people will not use a condom if their partner is against it or they will not discuss it with their partner out of fear that they might feel offended. For people with social anxiety disorders the fear of negative evaluation is enough to make them think twice about discussing the use of condoms with their partners. The hypothesis that this study focused on was whether people with social anxiety increase their tendency to have unprotected intercourse due to the decrease of communication about condom use. In this study there were 100 participants with the age raging from 16 to 21 and they had to state whether they were gay or bisexual. Parental informed consent was waved due to protected confidentiality because some participants were not open about their sexual orientation. All participants received $10 for their participation. They were measured using two scales the first one is a Social interaction anxiety scale (SIAS) and the second is the Social phobia scale (SPS) (Mattick and Clark, 1998). Both of these scales were designed to assess social anxiety in the general public. Examination stated that social anxiety continued to be associated with unprotected anal intercourse above and beyond the effects of communication about condom use and social support variables. Furthermore, findings suggested the need to consider the effect of social fears when designing HIV prevention interventions (Hart and Heimberg, 2005).

In view of the absence of an antitoxin or remedy for AIDS, it is of vital importance that the expansion of HIV be regulated through programs constructed to teach people to resist to exposure to HIV (Venier, Ross, and Akande, 1998). Young populations are mainly at risk because at the onset of their intense social life their attitudes and decisions are likely to predict their exposure. In areas of high prevalence rates of HIV, infection is most probable to occur during adolescence. Therefore, it is very important that young populations should become the main focus of prevention programs. It is noted that HIV prevention programs should not be solely informative, but they should also include education on practical skills that need to be applied in social situations in order to limit the risk of infection (Venier et al., 1998).

The main barrier when dealing with the spread of HIV is understanding people's attitudes towards the disease. Many studies have been conducted to assess people's awareness and beliefs; (Irwin et al., 1991; Lindan et al., 1991; Lwihula, Dahlgren, Killewo, and Sandstroem, 1993; Nicoll et al., 1993) they indicated that people's false beliefs should be challenged with more solid evidence than just a raw presentation of facts. Rather, soundness of factual information is required. Therefore, the significance of assessing a group's beliefs before structuring a program is highlighted (Venier et al., 1998).

Analyzing social anxiety is important when designing prevention programs in youngsters because their decisions are very much affected by social influences. Studies in the U.S (Kasen, Vaughan, and Waters, 1991) demonstrated that high school students are unsure about their ability to deny sex, ask sex partners about former risky sexual behavior, and use of condoms. Students with lower self-efficacy for refusing sex had double chances of engaging in sexual intercourse (Kasen et al., 1991). These results highlight the significance of investigating social skills and associated anxieties as hindrances to HIV prevention.

The AIDS Social Assertiveness Scale (ASAS), a measure of these social anxieties (anxiety associated with performing specific social skills), was used in two studies to assess adolescents' social anxieties in situations associated with HIV (Ross, Caudle, and Taylor, 1989). Specifically, the ASAS was used to assess participants' behavior in sex-related situations in five domains: a) condom interactions, b) refusal of risk, c) confiding in significant others, d) contact with people with HIV/AIDS, and e) general assertiveness (Venier et al., 1998). Ross, Caudle, and Taylor (1991) indicated that the factor structures of the ASAS in the two studies of the Australian high school students was identical and that social assertiveness is related with age, AIDS knowledge, and past sexual experience.

Taking these facts into consideration, Venier et al. (1998) conducted a study in three African countries to explore the social anxieties related to HIV in adolescents. All participants were black Africans and not diagnosed with any psychogenic disease. The results indicated that Kenyan students experienced less anxiety and this was attributed to the fact that AIDS had been known for a longer period of time and more prevention campaigns had taken place. Women reported lower anxiety regarding condom interactions and assertiveness but higher anxiety in confiding in others. Moreover, variances were evident between the countries. Finally, the findings of this study pose many implications about the design of HIV prevention programs. It is suggested that the programs should mainly focus on the five areas of social anxieties described in the ASAS. So, adolescents will be able to better behave against AIDS infection than they would by simply knowing about AIDS facts. Eventually, similar studies should be conducted in other places of the world with more representative samples so that the applicability of the suggested prevention programs can be tested in various cultural contexts.

Another route to HIV prevention is peer education (Population Council, 1999). Various studies have assessed the effectiveness of peer education with sex workers, showing positive results with the specific population (Asamoah-Adu, Weir, Pappoe, Kanlisi, Neequaye, and Lamptey, 1994; Ford, Wirawan, Suastina, Reed, and Muliawan, 2000; Luchters, Chersich, Rinyiru, Barasa, Kingola, and Mandaliya, 2008; Morisky, Stein, Chiao, Ksobiech, and Malow, 2006; Walden, Mwangulube, and Makhumula- Nkhoma, 1999; Welsh, Puello, Meade, Kome, and Nutley, 2001; Williams, Taljaard, Campbell, Gouws, Ndhlovu, van Dam, and Auvert, B, 2003; Wong, Chan, and Koh, 2004). Increases in knowledge and condom use, and sometimes reduced degrees of self-reported sexually transmitted infections (STIs), are the most usual positive results (Sarafian, 2012).

Studies have indicated a positive association between social support and HIV/STI in various populations (Bachanas, Morris, Lewis-Gess, Sarett-Cuasay, Sirl, and Ries, 2002; Gaede, Majeke, Modeste, Naidoo, Titus, and Uys, 2006; Naar-King, Wright, Parsons, Frey, Templin, and Ondersma, 2006; Nyamathi, Stein, and Swanson, 2000; Taylor-Seehafer, Johnson, Rew, Fouladi, Land, and Abel, 2007), but only few studies examined the relationship between social support and HIV/STI preventive attitudes for sex workers. Therefore, the likelihood of social anxiety standing as a hindrance to HIV/STI prevalence among those populations is highly possible. Moreover, other studies have demonstrated that low social support is negatively associated with condom use among (Dalla, Xia, and Kennedy, 2003; Dandona, Dandona, Gutierrez, Kumar, McPherson, Samuels, and the ASCI FPP Study Team, 2005; Hong, Fang, Li, Liu, and Li, 2008; Lippman, Donini, Díaz, Chinaglia, Reingold, and Kerrigan, 2010).

A study was carried out to assess peer education in a program that involved hotel-based sex workers in Dhaka, Bangladesh.

Social support was posed as a hypothetical groundwork to monitor the various activities accomplished by peer educators. Social support can be described as the operative composition of relationships separated into four kinds of supportive attitudes., with an estimation that most relationships will supply more than one type: informational support - advice and information an individual can use to forward problems - instrumental support - supplying services that immediately aid the person in need - appraisal support – supplying principles of self-evaluation - and emotional support (Heaney and Israel, 2008).

The participants were sex workers aged from 15 and above who were working for hotels that were involved in the study. The participants were evaluated in terms of socio-cognitive and behavioral variables. They were examined through baseline and follow-up assessments 23 weeks later. The procedure was appraised according to the composition of peer education sessions. The sessions were monitored and classified into ratings of social support types supplied by the peer educator to her listeners. Peer educators were allocated into three "social support profiles" depending on average ratings of emotional and informational support they administered. Encounters with more peer educators with a high informational support profile were associated with higher sex worker self-efficacy, self-reported STI symptoms and self-reported condom use. Additionally, higher emotional support profile encounters were positively related to treatment seeking. The main limitations of the study were low retention rates and lack of a comparison group.

In summary, this was the first study to investigate the verbal attitude of peer educators. The findings of the study establish fundamental evidence for the importance of using interspersed social support groundwork. Finally, the study emphasizes the significance of emotional support which was previously underestimated. Concluding, the link between social anxiety and HIV/STI infections can be further understood since it is demonstrated that different types of social support pose different positive effects towards HIV/STI prevention.

In a clinical study that took place in a public sector HIV/AIDS clinic South Africa, researchers tried to explore and analyze how the patients perceived and experienced social anxiety symptoms, and how it had shaped their behavior and their understanding of the disease (Gilbert and Walker, 2010). The participants were asked about anxiety, stigma, discrimination and the role of disclosure and ART (anti-retroviral therapy) at work, in the family and in any other social context. The findings suggested that the fear of stigma played a major role in their experience of the disease and their perceived anxiety, from the very early stages of testing and disclosure to the initiation and commitment to the antiretroviral therapy. It is also understood that the findings did differ among participants due to factors such as socioeconomic status, gender, work, age and most importantly family role (Gilbert and Walker, 2010).

Nonetheless, the main implications these procedures face are that they represent just a handful of countries. This is the main problem that needs to be adjusted for establishing a representative global picture. A paper that was published by Brown, Trujillo and Macintyre

(2001) tried to assess and evaluate 21 interventions that had strongly attempted to decrease HIV/AIDS stigma both in the developed and developing countries and 9 studies that aimed to decrease stigma related with other diseases. The studies selected met stringent evaluation criteria in order to draw common lessons for future development of interventions to combat stigma. In particular, this paper amounted and reported studies through comparison of audiences, types of interventions, and methods used to measure change (Brown, Trujillo and Macintyre, 2001).

These studies were gathered from places all over the world such as the US., Canada, Uganda, Israel, Zimbabwe, Scotland, Tanzania, Jamaica, and India among others. However, most of the reports come from developed countries and not from developing countries.

These intervention studies had to fulfill two criteria to be eligible for consideration: a) the study had to evaluate an intervention that included some component to reduce the stigma of AIDS or other diseases, and b) was a randomized experiment or quasi-experiment with at least a post-intervention test. Most of them had various strategies to adjust to the country stratifications to avoid bias and to increase significant findings. The types of intervention that were included were: a) information-based approaches, b) coping skills acquisition, c) counseling approaches and d) contact with affected groups (Brown, Trujillo, and Macintyre, 2001).

The major conclusion of these studies was that some aspects of stigma can be reduced and that adding an intervention strategy such as counseling or coping skills acquisition (based on Lazarus and Folkman's model of stress and coping, 1984) was overall highly effective in changing attitudes and behaviors. Nevertheless, there are some future research suggestions. Very few interventions have been conducted to reduce AIDS stigma in developing countries and in different cultural contexts. Furthermore, there is a need for programs that scale up efforts to fight stigma and social anxiety and for studies that measure the effect of mass media campaigns on social stigma and discrimination (Brown et al., 2001).

Taking into consideration all of the evidence above, one can understand that social and individualistic perception of HIV/AIDS is not only an essential public health issue, but also a significant social concern. Individuals' social network and social support to have important effects on their levels of stress and depression, which in turn act as mediators for alcohol use, drug dependence and suicide attempts (Myers et al., 2009). HIV-related stigma has been shown to have long-term detrimental consequences on an individual's well being (Kang et al., 2006). Psychological distress, stigmatization and social anxiety caused by HIV are less of a matter of individual coping, but rather a social learning process, importantly driven by social surroundings and stimuli (Chen et al., 2007). Future efforts to prevent HIV individuals' social anxiety should focus in enhancing education on the illness and increase familiarization of social supporting systems.

# References

Asamoah-Adu, A., Weir, S., Pappoe, M., Kanlisi, N., Neequaye, A., and Lamptey, P. (1994). Evaluation of a targeted AIDS prevention intervention to increase condom use among prostitutes in Ghana. *AIDS*, 8, 239-246.

Bachanas, P. J., Morris, M. K., Lewis-Gess, J. K., Sarett-Cuasay, E. J., Sirl, K., and Ries, J. K. (2002). Predictors of risky sexual behavior in African American adolescent girls: Implications for prevention interventions. *Journal of Pediatric Psychology,* 27, 519-530.

Betancourt, S. T., Rubin-Smith, J., Beardslee, W., Stulac, S., Fayida, I., and Safren. S. (2011). Understanding locally, culturally, and contextually relevant mental health problems among Rwandan children and adolescents affected by HIV/AIDS. *AIDS Care,* 23, 401–412.

Brandt, C., Gonzalez, A., Grover, K., and Zvolensky, M. (2012). The relation between emotional dysregulation and anxiety and depressive symptoms, pain-related anxiety, and HIV-symptom distress among adults with HIV/AIDS. *Journal of Psychopathology and Behavioral Assessment.* DOI: 10.1007/s10862-012-9329-y

Bronman, C. (1997). Race-related factors and life satisfaction among African Americans. *Journal of Black Psychology,* 23, 36-49.

Brown, L., Trujillo, L. and Macintyre, K. (2001). *Interventions to reduce HIV/AIDS stigma: What have we learned?* Horizons Program Tulane University.

Capron, D., Gonzalez, A., Parent, J., Zvolensky, M., and Schmidt, N. (2012). Suicidality and anxiety sensitivity in adults with HIV. *AIDS PATIENT CARE and STDs,* 26, 298-303.

Chen, J., Choe, K. M., Chen, S., and Zhang, S. (2007). The effects of individual- and community-level knowledge, beliefs, and fear of stigmatization of people living with HIV/AIDS in China. *AIDS Care,* 19, 666-673.

Chiu, J., Grobbelaar, J., Sikkema, K., Vandormoel, A., Bomela, B., and Kershaw, T. (2008). HIV-related stigma and social capital in South Africa. *AIDS Education and Prevention,* 20, 519-530.

Dalla, R. L., Xia, Y. and Kennedy, H. (2003). "Just give them what they want and pray they don't kill you": Street-level sex workers' reports of victimization, personal resources, and coping strategies. *Violence Against Women,* 9, 1367-1394.

Dandona, R., Dandona, L., Gutierrez, J. P., Kumar, A. G., McPherson, S., Samuels, F., and the ASCI FPP Study Team. (2005). High risk of HIV in non-brothel based female sex workers in India. *BMC Public Health,* 5, 87-97.

Earnshaw, V., Smith, L., Chaudior, S., Lee, I., and Copenhaver, M. (2012). Stereotypes about people living with HIV: Implications for perceptions of HIV risk and testing frequency among at-risk populations. *AIDS Education and Prevention,* 24, 574–581.

Ford, K., Wirawan, D. N., Suastina, W., Reed, B. D., and Muliawan, P. (2000). Evaluation of a peer education programme for female sex workers in Bali, Indonesia. *International Journal of STD and AIDS,* 11, 731-733.

Foster, H. and Brooks-Gunn, J. (2009). Toward a stress process model of children's exposure to physical family and community violence. *Clinical Child and Family Psychology Review,* 12, 71–94.

Gaede, B. M., Majeke, S. J., Modeste, R. R. M., Naidoo, J. R., Titus, M. J., and Uys, L. R. (2006). Social support and health behaviour in women living with HIV in KwaZulu-Natal. *Journal of Social Aspects of HIV/AIDS,* 3, 362-368.

Gilbert, L. and Walker, L. (2010). 'My biggest fear was that people would reject me once they knew my status...': Stigma as experienced by Patients in an HIV/AIDS clinic in Johannesburg, *South Africa. Health and Social Care in the Community,* 18, 139–146.

Gonzalez, A., Zvolensky, M., Parent, J., Grover, K., and Hickey, M. (2012). HIV symptom distress and anxiety sensitivity in relation to panic, social anxiety, and depression symptoms among HIV-positive adults. *AIDS Patient Care and STDs*, 26, 156-164.

Hart, T. and Heimberg, R. (2005). Social anxiety as a risk factor for unprotected intercourse among gay and bisexual male youth. *AIDS and Behavior*, 9, 505-512.

Heaney, C. A. and Israel, B. A. (2008). Social networks and social support. In: K. Glanz, B. K. Rimer and K. Viswanath (Eds.), *Health behavior and health education: Theory, research, and practice* (4th ed.). (pp. 189e210) San Francisco, CA: Jossey-Bass.

Hong, Y., Fang, X., Li, X., Liu, Y., and Li, M. (2008). Environmental support and HIV prevention behaviors among female sex workers in China. *STD*, 35, 662-667.

Irwin, K., Bertrand, J., Mibandumba, N., Mbuyi, K., Muremeri, C., Mukola, M., Munkolenkole, K., Nzilambi, N., Bosenge, N., Ryder, R., Peterson, H., Lee, N. C., Wingo, P., O'Reilly, K., and Rufo, K. (1991). Knowledge, attitudes and beliefs about HIV infection and AIDS among healthy factory workers and their wives, Kinshasa, Zaire. *Social Science and Medicine*, 32, 917-930.

Kalichman, S., Heckman, T., Kochman, A., Sikkema K., and Bergholte, J. (2000). Depression and thoughts of suicide among middle-aged and older persons living with HIV-AIDS. *Psychiatric Services*, 51, 903-907.

Kang, E., Rapkin, B. and DeAlmeida, C. (2006). Are psychological consequences of stigma enduring or transitory? A longitudinal study of HIV stigma and distress among Asians and Pacific Islanders living with HIV illness. *AIDS PATIENT CARE and STDs*, 20, 712-723.

Kasen, S., Vaughan, R. D. and Walter, H. J. (1992). Self-efficacy for AIDS preventive behaviors among tenth grade students. *Health Education Quarterly*, 19, 187 202.

Kliewer, W., Parrish, K., Taylor, K., Jackson, K., Walker, J., and Shivy, V. (2006). Socialization of coping with community violence: Influences of caregiver coaching, modeling, and family context. *Child Development*, 77, 605–623.

Kliewer, W., Murrelle, L., Mejia, R., de Torres, Y., and Angold, A. (2001). Exposure to violence against a family member and internalizing symptoms in Colombian adolescents: The protective effects of family support. *Journal of Consulting and Clinical Psychology*, 69, 971–982.

Kohen, D., Brooks-Gunn, J., Leventhal, T., and Hertzman, C. (2002). Neighborhood income and physical and social disorder in Canada: Associations with young children's competencies. *Child Development*, 73, 1844–1860.

Lazarus, R. S. and Folkman, S. (1984). Coping and adaptation. In: W. D. Gentry (Ed.), *The handbook of behavioral medicine* (pp. 282–325). New York: Guilford.

Lee, R., Kochman, A. and Sikkema, K. (2002). Internalized stigma among people living with HIV-AIDS. *AIDS and Behavior*, 6, 309-319.

Leserman, J., Perkins, D. and Exans, D. (1992). Coping with the threat of AIDS: The role of social support. *The American Journal of Psychiatry*, 149, 1514-1520.

Leventhal, T. and Brooks-Gunn, J. (2003). Moving to opportunity: an experimental study of neighborhood effects on mental health. *American Journal of Public Health*, 93, 1576–1582.

Lindan, C., Allen, S., Carael, M., Nsengumuremyi, F., van de Perre, P., Serufilira, A., Tice, J., Black, D., Coates, T., and Hulley, S. (1991) Knowledge, attitudes, and perceived risk of AIDS among urban Rwandan women: relationship to HIV infection and behavior change. *AIDS,* 5, 993-1002.

Lippman, S. A., Donini, A., Díaz, J., Chinaglia, M., Reingold, A., and Kerrigan, D. (2010). Social-environmental factors and protective sexual behavior among sex workers: the Encontros intervention in Brazil. *American Journal of Public Health,* 100, 216-223.

Luchters, S., Chersich, M. F., Rinyiru, A., Barasa, M. S., King'ola, N., Mandaliya, K. (2008). Impact of five years of peer-mediated Interventions on sexual behavior and sexually transmitted infections among female sex workers in Mombasa, Kenya. *BMC Public Health,* 8, 143-153.

Lwihula, G., Dahlgren, L., Killewo, J., and Sandstroem, A. (1993) AIDS epidemic in Kagera Region, Tanzania: the experiences of local people. *AIDS Care,* 5, 347-357.

Malee, K., Tassiopoulos, K., Huo, Y., Siberry, G., Williams, P., Hazra, R., Smith, R., Allison, S., Garvie, P., Kammerer, B., Kapetanovic, S., Nichols, S., Van Dyke, R., Seage, G., and Mellins, C. (2011). Mental health functioning among children and adolescents with perinatal HIV infection and perinatal HIV exposure. *AIDS Care,* 23, 1533–1544.

Mattick, R. and Clark, C. (1998). Development and validation of measures of social phobia scrutiny fear and social interaction anxiety. *Behaviour Research and Therapy,* 36, 455–470. Moore, S., Daniel, M., Gauvin, L., and Dube, L. (2009). Not all social capital is good capital. *Health and Place,* 15, 1071–1077.

Morisky, D. E., Stein, J. A., Chiao, C., Ksobiech, K., and Malow, R. (2006). Impact of a social influence intervention on condom use and sexually transmitted infections among establishment-based female sex workers in the Philippines: A multilevel analysis. *Health Psychology,* 25, 595-603.

Myers, H., Sumner, L., Ullman, J., Loeb, T., Carmona, J., and Wyatt, G. (2009). Trauma and psychosocial predictors of substance abuse in women impacted by HIV/AIDS. *Journal of Behavioral Health Services and Research,* 36, 233-246.

Naar-King, S., Wright, K., Parsons, J. T., Frey, M., Templin, T., and Ondersma, S. (2006). Transtheoretical model and condom use in HIV-positive youths. *Health Psychology,* 25, 648-652.

Najman, J., Hayatbakhsh, M., Clavarino, A., Bor, W., O'Callaghan, M., and Williams, G. (2010). Family poverty over the early life course and recurrent adolescent and young adult anxiety and depression: A longitudinal study. *American Journal of Public Health,* 100, 1719-1723.

Nicoll, A., Laukamm-Josten, U., Mwizarubi, B., Mayala, C., Mkuye, M., Nyembela, G., and Grosskurth, H. (1993). Lay health beliefs concerning HIV and AIDS: A barrier for control programmes. *AIDS Care,* 5, 231-241.

Nyamathi, A. M., Stein, J. A. and Swanson, J. M. (2000). Personal, cognitive, behavioral, and demographic predictors of HIV testing and STDs in homeless women. *Journal of Behavioral Medicine,* 23, 123-147.

Ross, C., Reynolds, J. and Geis, K. (2000). The contingent meaning of neighborhood stability for residents' psychological well-being. *American Sociological Review,* 65, 581-597.

Ross, M. W., Caudle, C. and Taylor, J. (1989). A preliminary study of social issues in AIDS prevention among adolescents. *Journal of School Health,* 59, 308-311.

Ross, M. W., Caudle, C. and Taylor, J. (1991). Relationship of AIDS education and knowledge to AIDS-related social skills in adolescents. *Journal of School Health,* 61, 351-354.

Santiago, C., Wadsworth, M. and Stump, J. (2011). Socioeconomic status, neighborhood disadvantage, and poverty-related stress: Prospective effects on psychological syndromes among diverse low-income families. *Journal of Economic Psychology,* 32, 218–230.

Sarafian, I. (2012). Process assessment of a peer education programme for HIV prevention among sex workers in Dhaka, Bangladesh: A social support framework. *Social Science and Medicine,* 75, 668-675.

Snowden, L. (1998). Racial differences in informal help seeking for mental health problems. *Journal of Community Psychology,* 26, 429–438.

Sorsdahl, K., Mall, S., Stein, D., and Joska, J. (2011). The prevalence and predictors of stigma amongst people living with HIV/AIDS in the Western Province. *AIDS Care,* 23, 680-685.

Taylor-Seehafer, M., Johnson, R., Rew, L., Fouladi, R. T., Land, L., and Abel, E. (2007). Attachment and sexual health behaviors in homeless youth. *Journal for Specialists in Pediatric Nursing,* 12, 37-48.

Venier, J. L., Ross, M. W. and Akande, A. (1998). HIV/AIDS-related social anxieties in adolescents in three African countries. *Social Science and Medicine,* 46, 313-320.

Vyavaharkar, M., Moneyham, L., Corwin, S., Saunders, R., Annang, L., and Tavakoli, A. (2010). Relationships between stigma, social support, and depression in HIV-infected African American women living in the rural Southeastern United States. *Journal of the Association of Nurses for AIDS Care,* 21, 144–152.

Walden, V. M., Mwangulube, K. and Makhumula-Nkhoma, P. (1999). Measuring the impact of a behaviour change intervention for commercial sex workers and their potential clients in Malawi. *Health Education and Research,* 14, 545-554.

Wandersman, A. and Nation, M. (1998). Urban neighborhoods and mental health. Psychological contributions to understanding toxicity, resilience, and interventions. *The American Psychologist,* 53, 647-656.

Welsh, M. J., Puello, E., Meade, M., Kome, S., and Nutley, T. (2001). Evidence of diffusion from a targeted HIV/AIDS intervention in the Dominican Republic. *Journal of Biosocial Science,* 33, 107-119.

Williams, B. G., Taljaard, D., Campbell, C. M., Gouws, E., Ndhlovu, L., van Dam, J., and Auvert, B. (2003). Changing patterns of knowledge, reported behaviour and sexually transmitted infections in a South African gold mining community. *AIDS,* 17, 2099-2107.

Wong, M. L., Chan, R. and Koh, D. (2004). Long-term effects of condom promotion programs for vaginal and oral sex on sexually transmitted infections among sex workers in Singapore. *AIDS,* 18, 1195-1199.

In: Social Anxiety
Editor: Efrosini Kalyva

ISBN: 978-1-62808-396-5
© 2013 Nova Science Publishers, Inc.

*Chapter IX*

# Barriers to Medication Adherence among Chronic Heart Failure Patients in Greece

*Paraskevi Theofilou[1,2]\* Konstadina Griva[3] and Sophia Zyga[4]*
[1]Sotiria Hospital for Thoracic Diseases, Athens, Greece
[2]Centre for Research and Technology, Department of Kinesiology, Health & Quality of Life Research Group, Trikala, Thessaly, Greece
[3]Department of Psychology, National University of Singapore, Singapore
[4]Nursing Department, University of Peloponnese, Sparta, Greece

## Abstract

Several studies have shown that non-adherence is a common and increasing problem regarding the individuals with chronic illnesses, including chronic heart failure (CHF) patients. The present study aimed to investigate the influence of psychological and sociodemographic variables on medication adherence among patients with CHF. A sample of 174 participants was recruited from five General Hospitals in the broader area of Athens, consisting of CHF patients. Measurements were conducted with the following instruments: the Medication Adherence Rating Scale (MARS), the Center for Epidemiologic Studies Depression Scale (CES-D), the Trait Anxiety Inventory (STAI 2) and the Multidimensional Health Locus of Control (MHLC). The results indicated that medication adherence was associated positively with the dimensions of internal health locus of control and doctors, measured by MHLC questionnaire. It was also related negatively to depression, measured by CES-D scale. No statistically significant correlation was observed between adherence and trait anxiety. Younger patients (<45 years) were significantly ($p<0.01$) more adherent than the elders (>45 years). Also, married patients presented significantly ($p<0.01$) higher scores of medication adherence in comparison to singles as well as divorced/widowed. The present study demonstrates

---

\* Corresponding author: Paraskevi Theofilou, Eratous 12, 14568, Athens, Greece. Tel. +30 6977 441502; +30 210 6221435; Fax +30 210 6221435; Email: theofi@otenet.gr.

the importance of psychological as well as sociodemographic features in understanding medication adherence of CHF patients.

**Keywords** Adherence, Medication, Chronic heart failure, Depression, Health locus of control, Trait anxiety

# Introduction

Chronic heart failure (CHF) is a major health problem, with an increasing incidence and a gloomy prognosis, that is often accompanied by restricted physical activity and severe complaints in several areas of quality of life (QoL) and mental health (Theofilou, 2011; Wielenga et al., 1997). Patients suffering from CHF experience a variety of symptoms as a result of the disease. The most frequent symptoms are fatigue, decreased exercise tolerance, swelling in the legs and ankles (edema), weight gain and difficulty in breathing (dyspnea) because of fluid accumulation. As a result, heart function is decreasing, the needs of oxygen in the tissues are unmeet and also cognitive impairment (memory loss, poor concentration) may occur. Consequently, the disease is significantly related to poor physical, psychological and social functioning (Jessup, 2003; Theofilou, 2012).

Furthermore, over 70 percent of heart failure patients are prescribed three or more medications solely for heart failure (Komajda, Follath & Swedberg, 2003), and greater than 50 percent of patients have concurrent conditions that warrant other drug therapies (Dargie, 2001; Gattis, 2000; Murray, Young & Morrow,2004; Poole-Wilson, Swedberg & Cleland, 2003). This often creates complex dosing regimens, resulting in decreased adherence rates (Osterberg & Blaschke, 2005).

Adherence to medications and treatments has been defined in several ways for patients with chronic diseases. One definition of adherence includes a person's behaviors concerning taking medication, following a diet, and making changes in lifestyle in accordance with health professional recommendations (Sabate, 2003). Another common definition is the extent to which people follow the instructions they are given for prescribed treatments (Haynes, Ackloo, Sahota, & McDonald, 2008). There are two types of medication non-adherent behaviors. Unintentional non-adherence occurs when patients forget or are unable to follow directions because of poor understanding, medication regimen complexity or physical disability (George, Vuong, Bailey, Kong, Marriott & Stewart, 2006; Rigby, 2007). Intentional non-adherence results when patients decide not to take medications because of adverse drug reactions and/or have self perceptions about the risk of harm and benefit of a medication (George et al., 2006; Rigby, 2007). Personal health beliefs and experiences contribute to intentional non-adherence in patients with chronic diseases.

Health Psychology offers a number of models that seek to help us understand the factors that influence an individual's adherence to a medical regime. One such model is Leventhal and colleagues' self-regulatory model (SRM) or health belief model, which suggests that attitudes and beliefs of individuals can explain health behavior. Important constructs of the model are perceived benefits and barriers about the health care regimen. Perceived benefits consist of the believed effectiveness of strategies designed to reduce the threat of illness; perceived barriers are the potential negative consequences that may result from taking particular health actions (Becker, 1974). Because barriers to certain health care behaviors are known to be highly related to non-adherence (Bennett, Milgrom, Champion & Huster, 1997), it is important that patients believe that it is possible to obtain control over the disease.

Therefore, it is obvious that a factor which contributes to the patient's self-management and hence medication adherence is health locus of control (HLOC) (Covic, Seica, Gusbeth - Tatomir, Gavrilovici & Goldsmith, 2004). HLOC reflects individuals' beliefs regarding the extent to which they are able to control or influence health outcomes. These beliefs are based on personal experience. They are also expected to develop and change over the course of illness and hence the experience of different treatments is likely to influence them (Covic, Seica, Gusbeth - Tatomir, Gavrilovici & Goldsmith, 2004). Recently it has been recognized that internal health locus of control, that is the patient is focused on his/her personal control on the disease management, is significantly and positively related to physical and social functioning, bodily pain, general health perception and the physical component score in haemodialysis (HD) and peritoneal dialysis (PD) patients (Covic, Seica, Gusbeth - Tatomir, Gavrilovici & Goldsmith, 2004). A higher personal control is also associated with lower emotional response, better understanding on behalf of the patient of his/her disease as well as higher medication adherence (Timmers, Thong & Dekker, 2008). The findings suggest that by identifying patients' beliefs about an illness and its treatment, it might be possible to obtain more insight into the (mal-)adaptive responses to the illness (Timmers et al., 2008).

Another psychological factor that relates to medication adherence is social anxiety. Several studies have shown the strong relation between these two factors like the impact of social phobia on alcoholism treatment adherence (Terra et al., 2006).

Finally, it has been indicated that better health-related quality of life (HRQoL) in chronic disease patients is associated with higher control beliefs, lower illness and treatment disruptiveness, lower consequences and less symptoms (Griva, Jayasena, Davenport, Harrison & Newman, 2009; Theofilou, 2012). In general, it is evident that an individual with internal locus of control may be more willing to follow treatment recommendations as he or she believes the path of disease progression may be controlled via personal ability and action; action in this sense referring to adherence (Cameron, 1996). The positive reinforcement maintaining behavior is derived from the belief that hard work and ability leads to desired positive outcomes (Marks, 1998). In contrast, individuals who believe that their fate is determined largely by chance or by other persons and not by their own actions may less likely to adhere to therapy, because they feel that their actions may not appreciably affect outcomes or (Kehoe, 1998). These individuals would attribute advances or declines in health to natural remission or progression of disease.

Past studies have shown that non-adherence is a common and increasing problem by those with chronic illnesses, including CHF patients (Bennett & Lane, 2005; Van Der Wal, 2007). These studies tended to examine non-adherence as a whole, including diet, fluid restriction, skipping treatments and medications. Because of the multiple medications that CHF patients need on a daily basis, a study of non-adherence directly related to medication-taking behavior was thought to be important for this population. Although a considerable number of articles on CHF have been published, there are a limited number of studies indicating the relation of medication adherence to depression, anxiety as well as health locus of control in these patients. Also, studies of health beliefs and adherence have produced mixed findings. Consequently, the assessment of this relation needs to be better understood and addressed more fully in CHF patients.

The purpose of the present study is a) to examine the association of medication adherence with mental health and health locus of control in CHF patients and b) to determine if there are potential influences of sociodemographic as well as clinical factors on medication adherence of these patients.

We mainly hypothesize that a high level of medication adherence is related to better mental health, indicating less symptoms of depression and anxiety, as well as internal and doctor-attributed health locus of control. Further, we hypothesize that chance or others-attributed locus of control are associated with less medication adherence.

# Method

## Participants

A sample of 180 patients was recruited from five General Hospitals in the broader area of Athens. Selection criteria included: > 18 years of age; ability to communicate in Greek; diagnosed with CHF  by clinical criteria, based on clinical data collected by a cardiology fellow; and satisfactory level of cooperation and perceived ability. The response rate was very high, reaching 99%. Thus, the total sample includes almost all patients of these five units, consisting of 103 males (59.2%) and 71 females (40.8%), with a mean age of 62.28 years ± 13.46. The remaining 6 patients were excluded having incomplete data because they decided during the interview to discontinue their participation. Individuals were Greek adults having signed a consent form for participation. All subjects had been informed of their rights to refuse or discontinue participation in the study according to the ethical standards of the Helsinki Declaration. Ethical permission for the study was obtained from the scientific committees of the participating hospitals. The study took place between October 2009 and September 2010. Full descriptive sociodemographic and clinical data of the sample are presented in tables 1 and 2.

# Measures

Measurements were conducted with the following instruments:

## 1) Medication Adherence Report Scale (MARS)

The *Medication Adherence Report Scale* (MARS) was developed for measurement of adherence to a wide range of medication regimens (Horne & Weinman, 2002). The five statements comprising the scale are: 'I forget to take my diabetes medicines', 'I alter the dose of my diabetes medicines', 'I stop taking my diabetes medicine for a while', 'I decide to miss out a dose of my diabetes medicine', 'I take less diabetes medicine than instructed'. The MARS was scored in accordance with standard practice with a maximum score of 25 by summing the score from the five questions, each with a five-point response scale (from 'always true' to 'never' - scored 1-5) (Horne & Weinman, 2002). The higher the score, the better the adherence (26). A cut-off point of <20 indicates an abnormal pattern of medication adherence while scores above 20 indicate a normal pattern of medication adherence among patients (Axelsson, 2011). The MARS has previously been used in samples with chronic disease and has shown good internal reliability (Grunfeld, Hunter, Sikka & Mittal, 2005; Mårdby, Åkerlind & Jörgensen, 2007; Ohm & Aaronson, 2006). The Cronbach's alpha values for the MARS ranged between 0.71 and 0.81. In the present study, the above questionnaire, which is under validation in Greek, was used in order to assess patients' adherence to medication that they take as a result of CHF.

**Table 1. Sociodemographic characteristics of the sample (N= 174)**

|  | **CHF patients** |
|---|---|
| Age (years) Mean (SD) | 62.28 (13.46) |
| Gender | |
| Male | 103 (59.2%) |
| Female | 71 (40.8%) |
| Total | 174 (100.0%) |
| Marital status | |
| Single | 37 (21.3%) |
| Married | 114 (65.5%) |
| Divorced/Widowed | 23 (13.2%) |
| Total | 174 (100.0%) |
| Education | |
| Elementary | 43 (24.7%) |
| Secondary | 61 (35.1%) |
| University | 70 (40.2%) |
| Total | 174 (100.0%) |
| Work status | |
| Unemployed | 0 (00.0%) |
| Employee | 14 (8.0%) |
| Freelancer | 13 (7.5%) |
| Pensioner/housewives | 147 (84.5%) |
| Total | 174 (100.0%) |

SD, Standard Deviation; CHF, Chronic Heart Failure.

## 2) Center for Epidemiologic Studies Depression Scale (CES-D)

One of the most common screening tests for helping an individual to determine his or her depression quotient, the *Center for Epidemiologic Studies Depression Scale* (CES-D) was originally developed by Lenore Radloff of Utah State University. The Center for Epidemiologic Studies Depression Scale (CES-D) (Hann, Winter & Jacobsen, 1999; Radloff, 1977) is a 20-item self-report measure of depressive feelings and behaviors during the past week. Four of the items are worded in a positive direction to control for response bias.

Subjects are asked to rate each item on a scale from 0 to 3 on the basis of "how often you have felt this way during the past week": 0 = rarely or none of the time (less than 1 day), 1 = some or a little of the time (1–2 days), 2 = occasionally or a moderate amount of time (3–4 days), and 4 = most or all of the time (5–7 days). CES-D scores range from 0 to 60; higher scores indicate more severe depressive symptoms. Total severity is calculated by reversing scores for items 4, 8, 12, and 16 (the items that control for response bias), then summing all of the scores. Scores range from 0 to 60, with higher scores indicating more symptoms of depression. CES-D scores of 0 to 15 are considered indicative of not depressive symptomatology, 16 to 26 are considered indicative of mild depression and scores of 27 or more indicative of severe depression (Ensel, 1986; Zich & Attkisson, 1990). These classifications have been used in a number of studies (Geisser, Roth & Robinson, 1997; Logsdon, McBride & Birkimer, 1994).

Internal consistency as measured by Cronbach's alpha is high across a variety of populations (generally around 0.85 in community samples and 0.90 in psychiatric samples). Split-half reliability is also high, ranging from 0.77 to 0.92. Test-retest reliability studies ranging over 2–8 weeks show moderate correlations ($r = 0.51$–$0.67$), which is desirable for a test of symptoms that are expected to show change over time.

**Table 2. Clinical characteristics of the sample (N= 174)**

|  | CHF patients |
|---|---|
| **Duration of CHF treatment** (years) (M±SD) | (6.45 ± 5.41) |
| <4 years | 100 (57.5) |
| >4 years | 74 (42.5) |
| Total | 174 (100.0%) |
| **Pattern of adherence** (M±SD) | (22.58 ± 2.69) |
| Normal (20-25 score) | 130 (74.7%) |
| Abnormal (<20 score) | 44 (25.3%) |
| Total | 174 (100.0%) |
| **Degree of depression** (M±SD) | (28.91 ± 8.24) |
| No depression (0-15) | 0 (00.0%) |
| Mild depression (16-26) | 69 (39.7%) |
| Severe depression (>26) | 105 (60.3%) |
| Total | 174 (100.0%) |
| **Degree of anxiety** (M±SD) | (35.56 ± 8.95) |
| Non-anxious (<40) | 144 (82.8%) |
| Anxious (>40) | 30 (17.2%) |
| Total | 174 (100.0%) |
| **Health Locus of Control dimensions** | |
| Internal (M±SD) | (27.22 ± 3.06) |
| Chance (M±SD) | (23.89 ± 5.98) |
| Doctors (M±SD) | (15.89 ± 2.53) |
| Others (M±SD) | (12.91 ± 3.61) |

SD, Standard Deviation; CHF, Chronic Heart Failure.

## 3) The Trait Anxiety Inventory (STAI 2)

The STAI 2 consists of 20 items referring to self-reported trait anxiety (Liakos & Giannitsi, 1984; Spielberger, 1970). Trait anxiety denotes "relatively stable individual differences in anxiety proneness" and refers to a general tendency to respond with anxiety to perceived threats in the environment (Spielberger, 1970). This assessment is administered to participants ages 18-85 years old. It uses ratings on a 4-point scale: 1-Almost never, 2-Sometimes, 3-Often, 4-Almost always. Higher scores mean that patients are more anxious. Before the study, a cut off point of scores >40 was selected for trait anxiety (Spielberger, 1970). Internal-consistency reliabilities estimated by Cronbach's (1951) alpha were higher than .90

## 4) The Multidimensional Health Locus of Control (MHLC)

The MHLC is a self-report tool measuring a patient's beliefs about control over health outcomes. Health locus of control is one of the widely used measures of individuals' health beliefs and has been designed to determine whether patients are internalists or externalists. It includes three orthogonal dimensions (namely internal, chance, powerful others). A revised form of the MHLC further subdivides the powerful others scale into two separate scales: doctors and others (Wallston, Stein &, Smith, 1994). The brief description of the theory explores the fact that health locus of control is a degree to which individuals believe that their health is controlled by internal or external factors. Whether a person is external or internal is based on a series of statements. The statements are scored and summed to find the above. Externals refer to belief that one's outcome is under the control of powerful others (i.e., doctors) or is determined by fate, luck or chance. Internals refers to the belief the one's outcome is directly the result of one's behavior (Wallston & Wallston, 1976; Wallston, Wallston & DeVellis, 1978). The 4 categories are not mutually exclusive and scores may weight in a particular direction. Higher scores indicate stronger presence of the specific dimension of beliefs. In the present study, the above questionnaire was used in order to assess patients' locus of control related to CHF. Internal consistency as measured by Cronbach's alpha is ≥70.

# Procedure

After the approval of the clinics' directors, two health psychologists selected the data using the relevant psychometric tools in the context of an interview at clinic which lasted for 20-25 minutes. Concerning the selection of the patients, we were mainly based on the medical staff's advice about the level of cooperation of each patient. So,

180 patients accepted to participate in the present study. CES-D and STAI 2 questionnaires have been validated in Greek populations. MARS and MHLC questionnaires have been translated into Greek and are under validation.

# Statistical Analysis

Kolmogorov-Smirnov tests were performed in order to check whether the values of the sample would fall within a normal distribution. Next, the analyses performed aimed to:

a) Investigate differences between patients with a normal and those with an abnormal pattern of medication adherence with respect to depressive symptoms, anxiety and health locus of control. Thus, independent-Samples T Test was performed.
b) Investigate differences between patients with mild depressive symptoms as well as patients with severe depressive symptoms with regards to medication adherence and health locus of control. Thus, independent-Samples T Test was performed.
c) Investigate differences between anxious and non-anxious patients with regards to medication adherence and health locus of control. Thus, independent-Samples T Test was performed.

Also, statistical analyses were performed with the use of Independent-Samples T Test and One - Way ANOVA in order to investigate potential effects of sociodemographic factors on medication adherence. The variables of gender, age, education, marital status and work status, in order to be included in the analyses, were recoded in the below categories:

a) Gender (males, value 1), (females, value 2)
b) Age (younger <45, value 1), (older >45, value 2)
c) Education (primary, value 1), (secondary, value 2), (university, value 3)
d) Marital status (single, value 1), (married, value 2), (widowed/divorced, value 3)
e) Work status (individuals who are employees, value 1), (individuals who are freelancers, value 2), (individuals who are pensioners/housewives, value 3)

Finally, statistical analysis was performed with the use of Independent-Samples T Test in order to check differences between patients who recently commenced treatment (< 4 years) and those on long term treatment (> 4 years). A cut - off period of 4 years of treatment was agreed upon because it was considered that a period of 3-4 years is required for patient adjustment to the diagnosis and treatment of a chronic illness (Ginieri - Coccossis, Theofilou, Synodinou, Tomaras & Soldatos, 2008; Theofilou, 2012).

A p - value of 0.05 or less was considered to indicate statistical significance. All analyses were performed with the Statistical Package for the Social Sciences (SPSS 13.0 for Windows).

# Results

The values of the total cohort were found to pass the normality distribution test. Investigating the differences between CHF patients with a normal and those with an abnormal pattern of medication adherence, the results indicated that patients, who adhered more to medication, showed less *depressive* symptoms (p=0.00). They also presented higher scores on *internal* and *doctors* locus of control (p=0.00) as well as lower scores on *others*-attributed locus of control (p=0.01) (table 3). On the other hand, there were no statistically significant differences between CHF patients with a normal pattern of adherence and those with an abnormal with regards to the variable of trait anxiety (p=0.16) (Table 3).

Furthermore, the results of independent-Samples T Test analysis in relation to the differences between patients who present mild depressive symptoms as well as patients with severe depressive symptoms, indicated that patients with severe depressive symptomatology were less medication adherent (p=0.00) and less focused on *doctors* (p=0.02) and *others*-attributed health locus of control (p=0.00) (table 3). Concerning the groups of anxious and non-anxious patients, there were no statistically significant differences in relation to medication adherence (p=0.21).

In order to assess the associations between adherence, locus of control, depressive symptoms, anxiety and duration of treatment, intercorrelations were used. Medication adherence was associated positively with *internal* locus of control (p=0.44) as well as *doctors* (p=0.26) and negatively with *depressive symptoms* (p=-0.42) and duration of treatment (p=-0.43) (Table 4). Further, duration of treatment was related positively to *internal* locus of control (p=0.21) and *depressive symptoms* (p=0.43) and negatively to the dimension of *others* locus of control (p=-0.22) (Table 4).

Regarding the effects of sociodemographic and clinical variables on medication adherence, the results indicated that younger patients (<45 years), patients who had their own family and those who were freelancers, were more adherent (p=0.00) (Tables 5, 6). Married patients showed more medication adherence in comparison to singles as well as divorced/widowed patients (p=0.00) (table 6). There were no statistically significant differences with regards to the variables of gender (p=0.25) and level of education (p=0.48). Finally, patients on long term CHF treatment (>4 years) presented lower scores of medication adherence (p=0.00) as well as more depressive symptoms (p=0.00) (table 3). There were no statistically significant differences between CHF patients on long term treatment and those with less years of treatment with regards to the variable of trait anxiety (p=0.99) (table 3).

# Discussion

In the present study we demonstrated high adherence rates in medication taking (74.7%) in this CHF population. Evangelista et al. (Evangelista, Berg & Dracup, 2001; Evangelista, Doering, Dracup, Westlake, Hamilton & Fonarow, 2003) also found a high medication adherence. From other studies, it is known that medication adherence in CHF patients can range from 10% as reported by Monane et al. (46) to 93% as reported by Artinian et al. (Artinian, Magnan, Sloan & Lange, 2002).

The present study shows strong associations of medication adherence with depressive symptoms as well as health locus of control in CHF patients. Concerning the relation between the dimensions of health locus of control and the variable of medication adherence in the sample, CHF patients, who focus on themselves in order to face their problems related to the disease, present a higher level of medication adherence. These results correspond to previous findings showing that a higher personal control is associated with better understanding of chronic disease as well as higher adherence to medication. Specifically, Theofilou (2012) has

Table 3. Mean scores ± SD of Depression, Anxiety, Medication Adherence and Health Locus of Control dimensions. Independent-Samples T Test showing differences between patients with an abnormal and normal pattern of adherence, the two categories of duration of treatment as well as patients with mild and severe depression

| | (N=44) CHF patients with an abnormal pattern of adherence (<20) M ± SD | (N=130) CHF patients with a normal pattern of adherence (20-25) M ± SD | p-value |
|---|---|---|---|
| CES-D - Depression | 35.47 ± 6.02 | 26.69 ± 7.70 | $p < 0.01$ |
| STAI 2 - Trait Anxiety | 33.93 ± 7.71 | 36.11 ± 9.29 | 0.16 |
| Health Locus of Control dimensions | | | |
| Internal | 24.90 ± 3.28 | 28.00 ± 2.56 | $p < 0.01$ |
| Chance | 22.97 ± 2.20 | 24.20 ± 6.78 | 0.07 |
| Doctors | 14.25 ± 2.87 | 16.44 ± 2.14 | $p < 0.01$ |
| Others | 13.66 ± 1.27 | 12.66 ± 4.08 | 0.01 |
| | (N=100) CHF treatment (<4 years) M ± SD | (N=74) CHF treatment (>4 years) M ± SD | p-value |
| MARS - Medication Adherence | 23.27 ± 2.23 | 21.66 ± 3.00 | $p < 0.01$ |
| CES-D - Depression | 25.60 ± 5.06 | 33.39 ± 9.53 | $p < 0.01$ |
| STAI 2 - Trait Anxiety | 35.57 ± 9.01 | 35.55 ± 8.92 | 0.99 |
| Health Locus of Control dimensions | | | |

| | (N=44) CHF patients with an abnormal pattern of adherence (<20) M ± SD | (N=130) CHF patients with a normal pattern of adherence (20-25) M ± SD | p-value |
|---|---|---|---|
| Internal | 26.51 ± 3.64 | 28.19 ± 1.62 | p < 0.01 |
| Chance | 24.18 ± 7.47 | 23.50 ± 2.98 | 0.41 |
| Doctors | 15.83 ± 2.52 | 15.97 ± 2.55 | 0.71 |
| Others | 14.24 ± 2.60 | 11.12 ± 4.00 | p < 0.01 |
| | (N=69) CHF patients with mild depression (16-26) M ± SD | (N=105) CHF patients with severe depression (>26) M ± SD | p-value |
| MARS - Medication Adherence | 23.59 ± 1.37 | 21.92 ± 3.12 | p < 0.01 |
| Health Locus of Control dimensions | | | |
| Internal | 27.01 ± 2.22 | 27.36 ± 3.51 | 0.42 |
| Chance | 23.08 ± 6.94 | 24.42 ± 5.23 | 0.17 |
| Doctors | 16.37 ± 1.63 | 15.57 ± 2.93 | 0.02 |
| Others | 13.85 ± 2.30 | 12.29 ± 4.15 | p < 0.01 |

N=174

**Table 4. Intercorrelations between Medication Adherence, Health Locus of Control dimensions, Depression, Anxiety & Duration of CHF treatment**

| | MARS - Medication Adherence | MHLC - Internal | MHLC - Chance | MHLC - Doctors | MHLC - Others | CES-D - Depression | STAI 2 - Anxiety | Duration of CHF treatment |
|---|---|---|---|---|---|---|---|---|
| MARS - Medication Adherence | - | 0.44** | 0.05 | 0.26** | -0.07 | -0.42** | 0.05 | -0.43** |
| MHLC - Internal | - | - | -0.29** | 0.42** | -0.13 | 0.12 | 0.00 | 0.21** |
| MHLC - Chance | - | - | - | 0.40** | 0.07 | 0.00 | 0.05 | -0.07 |
| MHLC - Doctors | - | - | - | - | 0.28** | 0.07 | 0.16* | 0.05 |
| MHLC - Others | - | - | - | - | - | -0.26** | 0.01 | -0.22** |
| CES-D - Depression | - | - | - | - | - | - | 0.08 | 0.43** |
| STAI 2 - Anxiety | - | - | - | - | - | - | | -0.03 |
| Duration of CHF treatment | - | - | - | - | - | - | | - |

*p<0.05
**p<0.01; N=174

indicated the positive relation of internal health locus of control to medication adherence in patients undergoing HD treatment. One of the only studies conducted concerning locus of control (LOC) and HIV medication adherence found that high internal LOC was one of several variables that predicted greater adherence (Molassiotis, Nahas-Lopez, Chung, Lam, Li CK & Lau, 2002). A study conducted by Hong et al sought to illustrate the role of LOC as a moderating factor between medication barriers and anti-hypertensive medication adherence (Hong, 2006).

**Table 5. Mean scores ± SD of Medication Adherence. Independent-Samples T Test demonstrating differences between the two categories of age**

| MARS | (N=28)<br>Age (<45 years)<br>M ± SD | (N=146)<br>Age (>45 years)<br>M ± SD | p-value |
|---|---|---|---|
| Medication Adherence | 24.50 ± 0.51 | 22.22 ± 2.79 | $p < 0.01$ |

N=174

**Table 6. Mean scores ± SD of Medication Adherence. One-Way ANOVA showing differences among the three categories of marital and work status**

| MARS | (N=37)<br>Single<br>M ± SD | (N=114)<br>Married<br>M ± SD | (N=23)<br>Divorced/Widowed<br>M ± SD | p-value |
|---|---|---|---|---|
| Medication Adherence | 22.54 ± 2.30 | 23.36 ± 2.10 | 18.38 ± 2.42 | $p < 0.01$ |
| | (N=14)<br>Employees<br>M ± SD | (N=13)<br>Freelancers<br>M ± SD | (N=147)<br>Pensioners/housewives<br>M ± SD | p-value |
| | 24.50 ± 0.51 | 25.00 ± 0.04 | 21.92 ± 2.77 | $p < 0.01$ |

N=174

Internally-oriented patients seek information, see themselves as responsible for maintenance or improvement of their physical health, know more about conditions that cause poor health, and are more likely to take steps to improve or maintain their health (Lau, 1982), engage in health-protective behaviors (Strickland, 1978), stop smoking (Coan, 2001), and lose excess weight (Balch, 2005). Carlise-Frank (1991) posited that the relationship between locus of control and health-facilitating behaviors as a whole point to an internal locus of control as a mediating factor for any action taken to prevent health problems. Internally-oriented patients are more likely to engage in positive health behaviors and generally have good health, engage in preventive health care activities, cope adequately with illness, and have good adherence to a medical regimen. Persons with an internal LOC believe the consequences of their actions are a result of hard work, effort, or ability (Myers & Myers, 1999). The positive reinforcement maintaining behavior is derived from the belief that hard work and ability leads to desired positive outcomes (Myers & Myers, 1999).

With respect to the relation of medication adherence to external LOC, high powerful others have been shown to be independently related to better adherence (Christiansen, Wiebe, Benotsch & Lawton, 1996; Sensky, Leger & Gilmour, 1996). In a study of renal dialysis patients, those who reported high powerful other LOC had the best adherence (Azlin, Hatta, Norzila & Sharifa Ezat, 2007). Azlin et al. have shown in their research regarding LOC among non-adherent hypertensive patients undergoing pharmacotherapy that respondents with external locus of control ('doctors') have better drug adherence (Azlin, Hatta, Norzila & Sharifa Ezat, 2007). Also, Howat, Veitch and Cairns found that people who scored highly on powerful others LOC, generally believed that health professionals could control one's health outcomes. Therefore those with high powerful others LOC scores were more adherent to medication instructions (O' Hea Grothe, Bodenlos, Boudreaux, White & Brantley, 2005). O' Hea et al. also found that individuals who believe their health control lies with their physicians will be more likely to follow their physicians' instructions (Marks, 1998). In our study, CHF patients who are more adherent focus on the medical staff and less on other people.

As far as depressive symptomatology is concerned, the findings have demonstrated the negative association between level of medication adherence and depressive symptoms. Patients with depressive symptoms report greater feelings of hopelessness, compromising cognitive abilities. Hopelessness, cognitive distortions and fatigue produce negative expectations of the future that may affect individual ability to carry out prescribed therapies and lead to inadequate fluid and dietary adherence behaviors (Christensen & Ehlers, 2002; Theofilou, 2011). Evangelista et al. (2001) found similar results; CHF patients with better mental health were more adherent with diet, fluid restriction, and exercise.

There are also relative findings about the relationship between depressive symptoms and fluid, dietary as well as medication adherence in patients with chronic kidney disease (CKD). Sensky et al. (1996) found that younger depressed patients had higher predialysis serum potassium levels. Akman et al. found double the likelihood of dietary non adherence in depressed CKD patients when compared to patients without depression (Akman, Uyar & Afsar, 2007). Studies from other chronic diseases reveal that psychological stress and depressive symptoms may be associated with poor adherence, and it is logical that these factors may impact adherence to medications in patients with CKD and receiving dialysis (Browne & Merighi, 2010).

Also, based on the results of the present study, patients with severe depressive symptomatology are presented less focused on external factors with regards to locus of control, that is doctors and others. These findings are in agreement with the findings of other studies which have shown that belief in powerful others is associated with lower scores of depression in older people (Harris et al., 2003). Further, Meyers has indicated in a study concerning religiosity and health locus of control as predictors of depression and anxiety in women with breast cancer that a significant negative correlation was found between powerful others locus of control and level of depression (Meyers, 2002).

Regarding sociodemographic features and specifically the relation between age and medication adherence, findings are controversial. While some investigators have found older patients to have better adherence, others have shown younger patients to be more successful adherers (Granger et al., 2009). Monane et al. (46) and Evangelista et al. (2008) found old age to be independently associated with better adherence, and reported that older participants (85 and 65 years old, respectively) had 'no difficulty' in adhering to medications when compared with younger patients. In contrast, in a study of heart failure patients over 85 years of age, DeGeest et al. (2003) found that the elderly were less able to perform self care behaviors and were less adherent to a medication regimen. Bohari et al. (1989) in their study found that age had no influence on adherence. However, Aziz et al. (1999) in their study found that older age group was statistically significant to be non-adherer to the prescribed medication. In this study there was a significant association between age and adherence, with the majority of the respondents of the older age group (45 years and above) was noted to be non-adherent to the prescribed medication. This could be explained by the fact that in advanced age health problems are different and multiple. As it has been already mentioned, over 70 percent of heart failure patients are prescribed three or more medications solely for heart failure (Komajda et al., 2003) and greater than 50 percent of patients have concurrent conditions that warrant other drug therapies (Dargie, 2001; Gattis, 2000; Murray et al., 2004; Poole-Wilson et al., 2003). This often creates complex dosing regimens, resulting in decreased adherence rates (Osterberg & Blaschke, 2005).

Further, the elderly have memory problem and become forgetful, complexity of drug regimen and have encountered more medication side effects. Forgetfulness is a widely reported factor that causes non-adherence to medication (Benner, Glynn & Mogun, 2002; Cooper, Carpenter & Katona, 2005; Jeste, Patterson & Palmer, 2003; Kiortsis, Giral & Bruckert, 2000; Lindberg, Ekstrom & Moller, 2001; Okuno, Yanagi & Tomura, 2001). A Japanese study in elderly home-care recipients found an interesting association between meal frequency and adherence. Patients having less than 3 meals per day were less adherent than patients having 3 meals a day. It suggested that meal frequency was an effective tool to remind the patient to take drugs (Lertmaharit, Kamol-Ratankul & Sawert, 2005). Further, written instructions are better than oral advice for reminding patients to take medication.

Several studies attempted to venture other plausible reasons too for poorer adherence among elderly patients. Elderly patients may have problems in vision and hearing. In addition, they may have more difficulties in following therapy instructions due to cognitive impairment or other physical difficulties, such as having problems in swallowing tablets, opening drug containers, handling small tablets, distinguishing colors or identifying markings on drugs (Balbay, Annakkaya & Arbak, 2005; Caspard, Chan & Walker, 2005; Choi-Kwon, Kwon & Kim, 2005; Fodor, Kotrec & Bacskai, 2005; Hertz, Unger & Lustik, 2005). On the contrary, older people might also have more concern about their health than younger patients, so that older patients' non-adherence is non-intentional in most cases. As a result, if they can get the necessary help from healthcare providers or family members, they may be more likely to be adherent to therapies.

With regards to gender, in many studies retrieved related to this factor, the results are contradictory. Female patients were found by some researchers to have better adherence (Ghods & Nasrollahzadeh, 2003; Horne & Weinman, 1999; Senior, Marteau & Weinman, 2004; Spikmans, Brug & Doven, 2003; Sung, Nichol & Venturini, 1998; Vic, Maxwell & Hogan, 2004), while some studies suggested otherwise (Kaona, Tuba & Siziya, 2004; Stilley, Sereika & Muldoon, 2004; Yavuz, Tuncer & Erdogan, 2004). In the present study, there is no relationship between gender and adherence. This finding is in agreement with other studies' results (DiMatteo, 1995; Kyngas & Lahdenpera, 1999; Turner, Wright & Mendella, 1995; Wai, Wong & Ng, 2005). This is also consistent with another literature review on adherence in seniors that concluded that gender has not been found to influence adherence (Adisa,

Fakeye & Fasanmade, 2011). Gender may not be a good predictor of non-adherence because of the inconsistent conclusions.

The effect of education on non-adherence was equivocal in many articles which focused on the impact of educational level as they used different criteria for "higher" and "lower" education. Several studies found that patients with higher educational level might have higher adherence (Cummings, Kirscht & Binder, 1982; Kelloway, Wyatt & Adlis, 1994). In the present study, there is no association between education and adherence. This finding corresponds to other studies' results (Hernandez-Ronquillo, Tellez-Zenteno & Garduno-Espinosa, 2003; Ponnusankar, Surulivelrajan & Anandamoorthy, 2004). Intuitively, it may be expected that patients with higher educational level should have better knowledge about the disease and therapy and therefore be more adherent. However, DiMatteo found that even highly educated patients may not understand their conditions or believe in the benefits of being adherent to their medication regimen (DiMatteo, 1995). Other researchers showed that patients with lower education level have better adherence (Kyngas & Lahdenpera, 1999; Turner et al., 1995). A UK study group found that patients without formal educational qualifications had better adherence to cholesterol-lowering medication (Turner et al., 1995). Patients with lower educational level might have more trust in physicians' advice. From these results, it seems that educational level may not be a good predictor of medication adherence.

Further, marital status might influence patients' adherence to medication positively (Adisa et al., 2011; Cummings et al., 1982). In our study, patients who are married seem to adhere better than the singles and the divorced or widowed. This is a finding which is in agreement with other studies' results (Kelloway et al., 1994). The help and support from a spouse could be the reason why married patients are more adherent to medication. Other studies have shown that divorced/widowed patients undergoing haemodialysis, compared to singles and married, indicate a more compromised quality of life (QoL), reporting poorer physical health and social relations, more negative perception of their environment, as well as poorer overall QoL/health (Theofilou, 2011). Further, they evaluate less favourably their mental health and report a higher level of depression with suicidal thoughts (Theofilou, 2011). On the basis of these findings, married patients seem to experience a better QoL. Similar evidence in the literature indicates that the status of marriage in HD patients may be significantly correlated to an enhanced physical and emotional well-being as well as better medication adherence (Chiang, Peng, Chiang, Yang, He & Hung, 2004). The general findings showed that patients who had emotional support and help from family members or friends were more likely to be adherent to the treatment (DiMatteo, 2004; Feinstein, Keich & Becker-Cohen, 2005; Kyngas, 2001; Kyngas & Rissanen, 2001; Loffler, Kilian & Toumi, 2003; Seo & Min, 2005). The social support helps patients in reducing negative attitudes to treatment, having motivation and remembering to implement the treatment as well.

Moreover, findings have demonstrated that pensioners and housewives are less adherent to medication treatment. Perhaps, this relates to the fact that pensioners are the older patients who have shown that they are not so good adherers. This finding may also be associated with pensioners' as well as housewives' lower income in comparison to the income of those patients who have the ability to work and are still productive. The demographic parameter of income is very important because it brings to the surface the matter of cost. Cost is a crucial issue in patient's adherence especially for patients with chronic disease as the treatment period could be life-long (Connelly, 1984; Ellis, Erickson & Stevenson, 2004; Ponnusankar, Surulivelrajan & Anandamoorthy, 20041; Shaw, Anderson & Maloney, 1995). Healthcare expenditure could be a large portion of living expenses for patients suffering from chronic disease. Cost and income are two interrelated factors. Healthcare cost should not be a big burden if the patient has a relatively high income or health insurance. A number of studies found that patients who had no insurance cover (Choi-Kwon, Kwon & Kim, 2005; Kaplan, Bhalodkar & Brown, 2004; Swett & Noones, 1989), or who had low income (Apter, Reisine & Affleck, 1998; Benner, Glynn & Mogun, 2002; Berghofer, Schmidl & Rudas, 2002; Hernandez-Ronquillo, Tellez-Zenteno & Garduno-Espinosa, 2003; Mishra, Hansen & Sabroe, 2005) were more likely to be non-adherent to treatment.

With respect to the variable of duration of treatment, acute illnesses are associated with higher adherence than chronic illnesses (Gascon, Sanchez-Ortuno & Llor, 2004). In addition, longer duration of the disease may adversely affect adherence (Farmer, Jacobs & Phillips, 1994; Frazier, Davis-Ali & Dahl, 1994). Similarly, a longer duration of treatment period might also compromise patient's adherence (Dhanireddy, Maniscalco & Kirk, 2005). In one trial that compared 6-month and 9-month treatment of tuberculosis, adherence rates were 60% and 50% for the two regimens, respectively (Combs, O'Brien & Geiter, 1987). In another study comparing preventive regimens of 3, 6 and 12 months, adherence rates were 87%, 78% and 68% for the three regimens, respectively (International Union Against Tuberculosis Committee on Prophylaxis, 1982). Other studies have indicated that HD patients on long term of treatment had increased deficits in physical, social and environmental QoL, mental health as well as medication adherence (Ginieri – Coccossis et al., 2008; Theofilou, 2012). However, some studies about chronic diseases found that longer duration of the disease resulted in good adherence (Garay-Sevilla, Nava & Malacara, 1995; Sharkness & Snow, 1992), and newly diagnosed patients had poor adherence (Caro, Salas & Speckman, 1999). This may indicate that adherence is improved because patient's attitude of denying the disease is reduced and they accepted treatment after years of suffering from the disease.

Limitations in this study warrant mention. First, there is a need for future research to use prospective and longitudinal study designs to examine the interaction between adherence to medication and mental health as well as health locus of control in patients with CHF. At this moment, it is unclear whether there is a causal relationship between depression and adherence and, therefore, this relationship needs to be further explored. Another methodological issue relates to the sample representativeness. Studies on the broader CHF population and recruiting even larger samples to enable effective multi-group analysis should be pursued in future research.

Further, measuring medication adherence in the CHF population can be impacted by numerous other factors besides medications (such as adherence to diet, fluid restriction and exercise), comorbid conditions, nutritional status or type of treatment. In future studies, the above variables should be examined using in this way consistent and standardized measures of adherence.

Finally, as it has already been indicated, the relation of medication adherence to social anxiety is very crucial. Coles et al. (2004) analyzed the treatment course for patients with social anxiety disorder (SAD) from the initial telephone contact to the beginning of treatment. A total of 395 people made an initial telephone call; of these people, only 60 began treatment. Thus, 85% of the patients who made initial contact with the clinic did not begin treatment. Hofmann and Suvak (2006) also investigated 133 patients with SAD who sought group behavioral therapy or group cognitive behavioral therapy (CBT) in a center for anxiety at Boston University. Of the 133 patients, 34 (25.6%) dropped out of treatment. Studies which will investigate the association of medication adherence with social anxiety in CHF patients need to be conducted.

Despite its limitations, the present study demonstrates the importance of psychosocial factors in understanding medication adherence of patients with CHF. It is important for health professionals to identify and attempt to remove their patients' barriers to medication self-management and optimal medication adherence. Staff in hospitals can impact patient satisfaction with care and include patients as active team members in order to identify barriers to medication adherence and to create individualized care plans for patients.

# Acknowledgments

The author would like to thank the patients for their participation in the study and acknowledge the support given by the health professionals and the administration personnel of the participating units. Further, the author confirms that there were no grants and funds in support of this study and there is no conflict of interest.

# References

Adisa, R., Fakeye, T. O., & Fasanmade, A. (2011). Medication adherence among ambulatory patients with type 2 diabetes in a tertiary healthcare setting in southwestern Nigeria. *Pharmacy Practice, 9,* 72-81.

Akman, B., Uyar, M., & Afsar, B. (2007). Adherence, depression and quality of life in patients on a renal transplantation waiting list. *Transplant International, 5,* 1-6.

Apter, A. J., Reisine, S. T., & Affleck, G. (1998). Adherence with twice-daily dosing of inhaled steroids. Socioeconomic and health-belief differences. *American Journal of Respiratory Critical Care Medicine, 157,* 1810-1817.

Artinian, N. T., Magnan, M., Sloan, M., & Lange, M. P. (2002). Self-care behaviors among patients with heart failure. *Heart Lung, 31,* 161-172.

Axelsson, M. (2011). *Personality and adherence to medication treatment.* Sweden: Intellecta Infolog AB.

Aziz, A. M. A., & Ibrahim, M. I. M. (1999). Medication non compliance - A thriving problem. *Medical Journal of Malaysia, 54,* 192-198.

Azlin, B., Hatta, S., Norzila, Z., & Sharifa Ezat, W. P. (2007). Health locus of control among non-compliance hypertensive patients undergoing pharmacotherapy. *Malaysian Journal of Psychiatry, 16,* 20-39.

Balbay, O., Annakkaya, A. N., & Arbak, P. (2005). Which patients are able to adhere to tuberculosis treatment? A study in a rural area in the northwest part of Turkey. *Japanese Journal of Infectious Diseases, 58,* 152-158.

Balch, P. N. (2005). *Physician's guide to compliance in antiretroviral therapy.* Westpoint, PA: Merck & Co. Becker, M.H. (1974). *The Health Belief Model and Personal Health Behavior.* Thorofare, NJ: Charles B Slack Inc.

Benner, J. S., Glynn, R. J., & Mogun, H. (2002). Long-term persistence in use of statin therapy in elderly patients. *Journal of the American Medical Association, 288,* 455-461.

Bennett, S. J., Milgrom, L. B., Champion, V., & Huster, G. A. (1997). Beliefs about medication and dietary compliance in people with heart failure: an instrument development study. *Heart Lung, 26,* 273-279.

Bennett, S., & Lane, K. A. (2005). Medication and dietary compliance beliefs in heart failure. *Western Journal of Nursing Research 27,* 977-993.

Berghofer, G., Schmidl, F., & Rudas, S. (2002). Predictors of treatment discontinuity in outpatient mental health care. *Social Psychiatry and Psychiatric Epidemiology, 37,* 276-282.

Bohari, H., Ahmad, D. A. R., & Abdullah, M. Y. (1989). Compliance towards anti-h treatment in Besut District, Hospital Terengganu. *Journal Perubatan UKM,* 12, 139-145.

Browne, T., & Merighi, J. R. (2010). Barriers to adult hemodialysis patientsâeuro (TM) self-management of oral medications. *American Journal of Kidney Diseases, 56,* 547-557.

Cameron, C. (1996). Patient compliance: recognition of factors involved and suggestions for promoting compliance with therapeutic regimens. *Journal of Advanced Nursing, 24,* 244-250.

Carlise-Frank, P. (1991). Examining personal control belief as a mediating variable in health-demanding behaviors of substance use: An alternative approach. *Journal of Psychology, 125,* 381-397.

Caro, J. J., Salas, M., & Speckman, J. L. (1999). Persistence with treatment for hypertension in actual practice. *Canadian Medical Association Journal, 160,* 31-37.

Caspard, H., Chan, A. K., & Walker, A. M. (2005). Compliance with a statin treatment in a usual-care setting: retrospective database analysis over 3 years after treatment initiation in health maintenance organization enrollees with dyslipidemia. *Clinical Therapy, 27,* 1639-1646.

Chiang, C. K., Peng, Y. S., Chiang, S. S., Yang, C. S., He, Y. H., & Hung, K. Y. (2004). Health-related quality of life of haemodialysis patients in Taiwan: a multicenter study. *Blood Purification, 22, 490-498.*

Choi-Kwon, S., Kwon, S. U., & Kim, J. S. (2005). Compliance with risk factor modification: early-onset versus late-onset stroke patients. *European Neurology 54,* 204-211.

Christiansen, A., Wiebe, J., Benotsch, E., & Lawton, W. (1996). Perceived health competence, health locus of control, and patient adherence in renal dialysis. *Cognitive Therapy and Research, 20,* 411-421.

Christensen, A., & Ehlers, S. (2002). Psychological factors in end-stage renal disease: an emerging context for behavioral medicine research. *Journal of Consulting and Clinical Psychology, 70,* 712-724.

Coan, C. N. (2001). Compliance in HIV/AIDS therapy: Why don't patients take their pills? *Canadian Medical Association Journal, 160,* 64-65.

Coles, M. E., Turk, C. L., Jindra, L., & Heimberg, R. G. (2004). The path from initial inquiry to initiation of treatment for social anxiety disorder in an anxiety disorders specialty clinic. *Journal of Anxiety Disorders, 18,* 371–383.

Combs, D. L., O'Brien, R. J., & Geiter, L. J. (1987). Compliance with tuberculosis regimes: results from USPHS therapy trial 21. *American Review of Respiratory Diseases, 135,* 138.

Connelly, C. E. (1984). Compliance with outpatient lithium therapy. *Perspectives in Psychiatric Care, 22,* 44-50.

Cooper, C., Carpenter, I., & Katona, C. (2005). The AdHOC study of older adults' adherence to medication in 11 countries. *American Journal of Geriatric Psychiatry, 13,* 1067-1076.

Covic, A., Seica, A., Gusbeth – Tatomir, P., Gavrilovici, O., & Goldsmith, D. J. (2004). Illness representations and quality of life scores in haemodialysis patients. *Nephrology Dialysis Transplantation, 19,* 2078-2083.

Cummings, K. M., Kirscht, J. P., & Binder, L. R. (1982). Determinants of drug treatment maintenance among hypertensive persons in inner city Detroit. *Public Health Reports, 97,* 99-106.

Dargie, H. J. (2001). Effect of carvedilol on outcome after myocardial infarction in patients with left-ventricular dysfunction: the CAPRICORN randomised trial. *Lancet, 357,* 1385-1390.

De Geest, S., Scheurweghs, L., Reynders, I., Pelemans, W., Droogne, W., Van Cleemput, J., Leventhal, M., & Vanhaecke, J. (2003). Differences in psychosocial and behavioral profiles between heart failure patients admitted to cardiology and geriatric wards. *European Journal of Heart Failure, 5,* 557-567.

Dhanireddy, K. K., Maniscalco, J., & Kirk, A.D. (2005). Is tolerance induction the answer to adolescent non-adherence? *Pediatric Transplantation, 9,* 357-363.

DiMatteo, M. R. (1995). Patient adherence to pharmacotherapy: the importance of effective communication. *Formulary, 30,* 596-605.

DiMatteo, M. R. (2004). Social support and patient adherence to medical treatment: a meta-analysis. *Health Psychology, 23,* 207-218.

Ellis, J. J., Erickson, S. R., & Stevenson, J. G. (2004). Suboptimal statin adherence and discontinuation in primary and secondary prevention populations. *Journal of General Internal Medicine, 19,* 638-645.

Ensel, W. (1986). *Measuring depression: The CES-D Scale.* New York: Academic Press.

Evangelista, L. S., Berg, J., & Dracup, K. (2001). Relationship between psychosocial variables and compliance in patients with heart failure. *Heart Lung, 30,* 294-301.

Evangelista, L., Doering, L. V., Dracup, K., Westlake, C., Hamilton, M., & Fonarow, G. C. (2003). Compliance behaviors of elderly patients with advanced heart failure. *Journal of Cardiovascular Nursing, 18,* 197-206.

Evangelista, L. S., Moser, D. K., Westlake, C., Pike, N., Ter Galstanyan, A., & Dracup, K. (2008). Correlates of fatigue in patients with heart failure. *Progress in Cardiovascular Nursing, 23,* 12-17.

Farmer, K. C., Jacobs, E. W., & Phillips, C. R. (1994). Long-term patient compliance with prescribed regimens of calcium channel blockers. *Clinical Therapy, 16,* 316-326.

Feinstein, S. Keich, R., & Becker-Cohen, R. (2005). Is noncompliance among adolescent renal transplant recipients inevitable? *Pediatrics, 115,* 969-973.

Fodor, G. J., Kotrec, M., & Bacskai, K. (2005). Is interview a reliable method to verify the compliance with antihypertensive therapy? An international central-European study. *Journal of Hypertension, 23,* 1261-1266.

Frazier, P. A., Davis-Ali, S. H., & Dahl, K. E. (1994). Correlates of noncompliance among renal transplant recipients. *Clinical Transplantation, 8,* 550-557.

Garay-Sevilla, M. E., Nava, L. E., & Malacara, J. M. (1995). Adherence to treatment and social support in patients with non-insulin dependent diabetes mellitus. *Journal of Diabetes Complications, 9,* 81-86.

Gascon, J. J., Sanchez-Ortuno, M., & Llor, B. (2004). Treatment compliance in hypertension study group. Why hypertensive patients do not comply with the treatment: results from a qualitative study. *Family Practice, 21,* 125-130.

Gattis, W. A. (2000). Practical issues in the treatment of patients with heart failure. *Pharmacotherapy, 20,* 385S-391S.

Geisser, M. E., Roth, R. S., & Robinson, M. E. (1997). Assessing depression among persons with chronic pain using the Center for Epidemiological Studies Depression Scale and the Beck Depression Inventory: a comparative analysis. *Clinical Journal of Pain, 13,* 163-170.

George, J., Vuong, T., Bailey, M. J., Kong, D. C., Marriott, J. L., & Stewart, K. (2006). Medication regimen complexity and adherence in patients at risk of medication misadventure. *Journal of Pharmacy Practice and Research 36,* 99-102.

Ghods, A. J., & Nasrollahzadeh, D. (2003). Noncompliance with immunnosuppressive medications after renal transplantation. *Experimental and Clinical Transplantation, 1,* 39-47.

Ginieri – Coccossis, M., Theofilou, P., Synodinou, C., Tomaras, V., & Soldatos, C. (2008). Quality of life, mental health and health beliefs in haemodialysis and peritoneal dialysis patients: Investigating differences in early and later years of current treatment. *BMC Nephrology,* 9, 1-9.

Granger, B.B., Ekman, I., Granger, C.B., Ostergren, J., Olofsson, B., Michelson, E., McMurray, J .J. V., Yusuf, S., Pfeffer, M. A., & Swedberg, K. (2009). Adherence to medication according to sex and age in the CHARM programme. *European Journal of Heart Failure, 11,* 1092-1098.

Griva, K., Jayasena, D., Davenport, A., Harrison, M., & Newman, P. S. (2009). Illness and treatment cognitions and health related quality of life in end stage renal disease. *British Journal of Health Psychology, 14,* 17-34.

Grunfeld, E. A., Hunter, M. S., Sikka, P., & Mittal, S. (2005). Beliefs among breast cancer patients taking tamoxifen. *Patient Education and Counseling, 59,* 97-102.

Hann, D., Winter, K., & Jacobsen, P. (1999). Measurement of depressive symptoms in cancer patients: Evaluation of the Center for Epidemiological Studies Depression Scale (CES-D). *Journal of Psychosomatic Research, 46,* 437-443.

Harris, T., Cook, D., Victor, C., Rink, E., Mann, A., Shah, S., Dewilde, S., & Beighton, C. (2003). Predictors of depressive symptoms in older people – a survey of two general practice populations. *Age and Ageing, 32,* 510-518.

Haynes, R., Ackloo, E., Sahota, N., & McDonald, H. (2008). Interventions for enhancing medication adherence. *Cochrane Database of Systematic Reviews, 2,* CD000011.

Hernandez-Ronquillo, L., Tellez-Zenteno, J. F., & Garduno-Espinosa, J. (2003). Factors associated with therapy noncompliance in type-2 diabetes patients. *Salud Publica de Mexico, 45,* 191-197.

Hertz, R. P., Unger, A. N., & Lustik, M. B. (2005). Adherence with pharmacotherapy for type 2 diabetes: a retrospective cohort study of adults with employer-sponsored health insurance. *Clinical Therapy, 27,* 1064-1073.

Hofmann, S. G., & Suvak, M. (2006). Treatment attrition during group therapy for social phobia. *Journal of Anxiety Disorders, 20,* 961–972.

Hong, T. B. (2006). Medication barriers and anti-hypertensive medication adherence: The moderating role of locus of control. *Psychology, Health & Medicine, 11,* 20-28.

Horne, R., & Weinman, J. (1999). Patients' beliefs about prescribed medicines and their role in adherence to treatment in chronic physical illness. *Journal of Psychosomatic Research, 47*, 555-567.

Horne, R., & Weinman, J. (2002). Self-regulation and self-management in asthma: exploring the role of illness perceptions and treatment beliefs in explaining non-adherence to preventer medication. *Psychology & Health, 17*, 17-32.

Howat, A., Veitch, C., & Cairns, W. A. (2006). Descriptive study comparing health attitudes of urban and rural oncology patients. *Rural and Remote Health, 6*, 563.

Jessup, M. L. (2003). Understanding the syndrome of heart failure. In M. L. Jessup & E. Loh (Eds). *Heart Failure: A clinician's guide to ambulatory diagnosis and treatment.* Totowa, New Jersey: Humana Press.

Jeste, S. D., Patterson, T. L., & Palmer, B. W. (2003). Cognitive predictors of medication adherence among middle-aged and older outpatients with schizophrenia. *Schizophrenia Research, 63*, 49-58.

International Union Against Tuberculosis Committee on Prophylaxis. (1982). Efficacy of various durations of isoniazid preventive therapy for tuberculosis: five years of follow-up in the IUAT trial. *Bull World Health Organ, 60*, 556-564.

Kaona, F. A., Tuba, M., & Siziya, S. (2004). An assessment of factors contributing to treatment adherence and knowledge of TB transmission among patients on TB treatment. BMC Public Health, 29, 68.

Kaplan, R. C., Bhalodkar, N. C., & Brown, E. J. (2004). Race, ethnicity, and sociocultural characteristics predict noncompliance with lipid-lowering medications. *Preventive Medicine, 39*, 1249-1255.

Kehoe, W. A., & Katz, R. C. (1998). Health behavior and pharmacotherapy. *Annual Pharmachotherapy, 32*, 1076-1086.

Kelloway, J. S., Wyatt, R. A., & Adlis, S. A. (1994). Comparison of patients' compliance with prescribed oral and inhaled asthma medications. *Archives of Internal Medicine, 154*, 1349-1352.

Kiortsis, D. N., Giral, P., & Bruckert, E. (2000). Factors associated with low compliance with lipid-lowering drugs in hyperlipidemic patients. *Journal of Clinical Pharmacy and Therapeutics 25*, 445-451.

Komajda, M., Follath, F., & Swedberg, K. (2003). The EuroHeart Failure Survey programme -a survey on the quality of care among patients with heart failure in Europe. Part 2: treatment. *European Heart Journal, 24*, 464-474.

Kyngas, H., & Lahdenpera, T. (1999). Compliance of patients with hypertension and associated factors. *Journal of Advanced Nursing, 29*, 832-839.

Kyngas, H. (2001). Predictors of good compliance in adolescents with epilepsy. *Seizure, 10*, 549-553.

Kyngas, H., & Rissanen, M. (2001). Support as a crucial predictor of good compliance of adolescents with a chronic disease. *Journal of Clinical Nursing, 10*, 767-774.

Lau, R. C. (1982). Origins of health locus of control beliefs. *Journal of Persian Social Psychology 42*, 322-334.

Lertmaharit, S., Kamol-Ratankul, P., & Sawert, H. (2005). Factors associated with compliance among tuberculosis patients in Thailand. *Journal of Medical Association of Thailand, 88*, 149-156.

Liakos, A., & Giannitsi, S. (1984). Reliability and validity of the Greek State-Trait Anxiety Inventory of Spielberger. *Egephalos, 21,* 71-76.

Lindberg, M., Ekstrom, T., & Moller, M. (2001). Asthma care and factors affecting medication compliance: the patient's point of view. *International Journal of Quality Health Care, 13,* 375-383.

Loffler, W., Kilian, R., & Toumi, M. (2003). Schizophrenic patients' subjective reasons for compliance and noncompliance with neuroleptic treatment. *Pharmacopsychiatry, 36,* 105-112.

Logsdon, M. C., McBride, A. B., & Birkimer, J. C. (1994). Social support and postpartum depression. *Research in Nursing & Health, 17,* 449-457.

Mårdby, A. C., Åkerlind, I., & Jörgensen, T. (2007). Beliefs about medicines and self-reported adherence among pharmacy clients. *Patient Education and Counseling, 69,* 158-164.

Marks, I. (1998). Deconstructing Locus of Control: Implications for Practitioners. *Journal of Counseling & Development, 76,* 251.

Meyers, K. R. (2002). Religiosity and health locus of control as predictors of depression and anxiety in women with breast cancer. *ETD Collection for Fordham University.* Paper AAI3056149 http://fordham.bepress.com/dissertations/AAI3056149.

Mishra, P., Hansen, E. H., & Sabroe, S. (2005). Socio-economic status and adherence to tuberculosis treatment: a case-control study in a district of Nepal. *International Journal of Tuberculosis Lung Diseases, 9,* 1134-1139.

Molassiotis, A., Nahas-Lopez, V., Chung, W. Y., Lam, S. W., Li, C. K., & Lau, T. F. (2002). Factors associated with adherence to antiretroviral medication in HIV-infected patients. *International Journal of STD and AIDS, 13,* 301-310.

Monane, M., Bohn, R. L., Gurwitz, J. H., Glynn, R. J., & Avorn, J. (1994). Noncompliance with congestive heart failure therapy in the elderly. *Archives of Internal Medicine, 154,* 433-437.

Murray, M. D., Young, J. M., & Morrow, D. G. (2004). Methodology of an ongoing, randomized, controlled trial to improve drug use for elderly patients with chronic heart failure. *American Journal of Geriatric Pharmacotherapy, 2,* 53-65.

Myers, L., & Myers, F. (1999). The relationship between control beliefs and self-reported adherence in adults with cystic fibrosis. *Psychology, Health & Medicine, 4,* 387-391.

O' Hea Grothe, K. B., Bodenlos, J. S., Boudreaux, E. D., White, M. A., & Brantley, P. J. (2005). Predicting medical regimen adherence: The interactions of health locus of control beliefs. *Journal of Health Psychology, 10,* 705-717.

Ohm, R., & Aaronson, L. S. (2006). Symptom perception and adherence to asthma controller medications. *Journal of Nursing Scholarship, 38,* 292-297.

Okuno, J., Yanagi, H., & Tomura, S. (2001). Is cognitive impairment a risk factor for poor compliance among Japanese elderly in the community? *European Journal of Clinical Pharmacology, 57,* 589-594.

Osterberg, L., & Blaschke, T. (2005). Adherence to medication. *New England Journal of Medicine, 353,* 487-497.

Ponnusankar, S., Surulivelrajan, M., & Anandamoorthy, N. (2004). Assessment of impact of medication counseling on patients' medication knowledge and compliance in an outpatient clinic in South India. *Patient Education and Counseling, 54,* 55-60.

Poole-Wilson, P. A., Swedberg, K., & Cleland, J. G. (2003). Comparison of carvedilol and metoprolol on clinical outcomes in patients with chronic heart failure in the Carvedilol Or Metoprolol European Trial (COMET): randomised controlled trial. *Lancet, 362*, 7-13.

Radloff, L. S. (1977). The CES-D scale: A self-report depression scale for research in the general population. *Applied Psychological Measurement, 1*, 385-401.

Rigby, D. (2007). Adherence assessment tools: drugs don't work when they are not taken. *Austalian Journal of Pharmacy, 88*, 32-33.

Sabate, E. (2003). *Adherence to long-term therapies: Evidence for action.* Geneva: World Health Organization.

Senior, V., Marteau, T. M., & Weinman, J. (2004). Self-reported adherence to cholesterol-lowering medication in patients with familial hypercholesterolaemia: the role of illness perceptions. *Cardiovascular Drugs Therapy, 18*, 475-481.

Sensky, T., Leger, C., & Gilmour, S. (1996). Psychosocial and cognitive factors associated with adherence to dietary and fluid restriction regimens by people on chronic haemodialysis. *Psychotherapy and Psychosomatics, 65*, 36-42.

Seo, M. A., & Min, S. K. (2005). Development of a structural model explaining medication compliance of persons with schizophrenia. *Yonsei Medical Journal, 46*, 331-340.

Sharkness, C. M., & Snow, D. A. (1992). The patient's view of hypertension and compliance. *American Journal of Preventive Medicine, 8*, 141-146.

Shaw, E., Anderson, J. G., & Maloney, M. (1995). Factors associated with noncompliance of patients taking antihypertensive medications. *Hospital Pharmacy 30*, 201-207.

Spielberger, G. O. (1970). *The State-Trait Anxiety Inventory.* California: Consulting Psychologists Press.

Spikmans, F. J., Brug, J., & Doven, M. M. (2003). Why do diabetic patients not attend appointments with their dietitian? *Journal of Human Nutrition Dietetics, 16*, 151-158.

Stilley, C. S., Sereika, S., & Muldoon, M. F. (2004). Psychological and cognitive function: predictors of adherence with cholesterol lowering treatment. *Annual of Behavioral Medicine, 27*, 117-124.

Strickland, B. R. (1978). Internal-external expected and health related behaviors. *Journal of Consulting Clinical Psychology, 46*, 1192-1211.

Sung, J. C., Nichol, M. B., & Venturini, F. (1998). Factors affecting patient compliance with antihyperlipidemic medications in an HMO population. *American Journal of Managed Care, 4*, 1421-1430.

Swett, C.Jr., & Noones, J. (1989). Factors associated with premature termination from outpatient treatment. *Hospital Community Psychiatry, 40*, 947-951.

Terra, M. B., Barros, H. M., Stein, A. T., Figueira, I., Athayde, L. D., Spanemberg, L., de Aguiar Possa, M., Filho, L. D., & da Silveira, D. X. (2006). Does co-occurring social phobia interfere with alcoholism treatment adherence and relapse? *Journal of Substance Abuse Treatment, 31*, 403-409.

Theofilou, P. (2011). Sleep and quality of life in patients with chronic heart failure. *Journal of Sleep Disorders & Therapy, 1*, 1-2.

Theofilou, P. (2011). Non - compliance with medical regimen in haemodialysis treatment: a case study. *Case Reports in Nephrology*, 1-4.

Theofilou, P. (2011). Depression and anxiety in patients with chronic renal failure: The effect of sociodemographic characteristics. *International Journal of Nephrology*, 1-6.

Theofilou, P. (2012). Evaluation of quality of life in Greek patients with heart failure: the role of health cognitions before and after participation in an exercised - based rehabilitation program, *Journal of Clinical Trials, 2*, 1-5.

Theofilou, P. (2012). Quality of life and mental health in hemodialysis and peritoneal dialysis patients: the role of health beliefs. *International Urology and Nephrology, 44*, 245-253.

Theofilou, P. (2013). Medication adherence in Greek hemodialysis patients: The contribution of depression and health cognitions. *International Journal of Behavioral Medicine, 20*, 311-318.

Timmers, L., Thong, S. Y. M., & Dekker, W. F. (2008). Illness perceptions in dialysis patients and their association with quality of life. *Psychology & Health, 23*, 679-690.

Turner, J., Wright, E., & Mendella, L. (1995). Predictors of patient adherence to long-term home nebulizer therapy for COPD. *Chest, 108*, 394-400.

Van Der Wal, M. H. (2007). Unraveling the mechanisms for heart failure patients, beliefs about compliance. *Heart lung; 36*, 253-261.

Vic, S. A., Maxwell, C. J., & Hogan, D. B. (2004). Measurement, correlates, and health outcomes of medication adherence among seniors. *Annual Pharmacotherapy, 38*, 303-312.

Wai, C. T., Wong, M. L., & Ng, S. (2005). Utility of the Health Belief Model in predicting compliance of screening in patients with chronic hepatitis B. *Alimentary Pharmacology and Therapeutics, 21*, 1255-1262.

Wallston, K. A., Stein, M. J., & Smith, C. A. (1994). Form C of the MHLC scales: A condition-specific measure of locus of control. *Journal of Personality and Assessment, 63*, 534-553.

Wallston, B. S., & Wallston, K. A. (1976). The development and validation of the health related locus of control (HLC) scale. *Journal of Consulting and Clinical Psychology, 44*, 580-585.

Wallston, B. S., Wallston, K. A., & DeVellis, R. (1978). Development of the multidimensional health locus of control (MHLC) scale. *Health Education Monographs, 6*, 160-170.

Wielenga, R. P., Erdman, R. A. M., Huisveld, I. A., Bol, E., Dunselman, P. H., Baselier, M. R., & Mosterd, W. L. (1997). Effect of exercise training on quality of life in patients with chronic heart failure. *Journal of Psychosomatic Research, 45*, 459-464.

Yavuz, A., Tuncer, M., & Erdogan, O. (2004). Is there any effect of compliance on clinical parameters of renal transplant recipients? *Transplantation Proceedings 36*, 120-121.

Zich, J. M., & Attkisson, C. C. (1990). Screening for depression in primary care clinics: the CES-D and the BDI. *International Journal of Psychiatry in Medicine, 20*, 259-277.

In: Social Anxiety
Editor: Efrosini Kalyva

ISBN: 978-1-62808-396-5
© 2013 Nova Science Publishers, Inc.

*Chapter X*

# Social Anxiety Disorder: The Role of Cognitive Behavioral Therapy

*Stavros Simitsis\*, Klearchos Konstantinos Stamatoulakis,*
*Valeria Strigkou, Kyriaki Avramidou,*
*Nikolaos Drouboulas-Theodoridis and Pagona Papadimitriou*
The International Faculty of the University of Sheffield, CITY College,
Thessaloniki, Greece

## Abstract

Among the many treatment options that are available for individuals with social anxiety disorder or social phobia is cognitive behavioral therapy. This chapter introduces the reader to the different kinds of cognitive behavioral therapies that can be delivered either face-to-face or online, using a critical perspective. The techniques that therapists use are described in detail together with evidence of their effectiveness. This chapter is very useful not only for a novice reader who wants to gain a general understanding of the basic principles of cognitive behavioral therapy, but also for experts in the area who want a comprehensive and critical review of the existing literature on cognitive behavioral therapy and social anxiety disorders.

**Keywords:** Cognitive behavioral therapy, social anxiety disorders, social phobia, effectiveness, internet

## Cognitive Behavioral Therapy

Behavioral therapy was first introduced in 1963, with the official founding of the first relevant journal "Behavior: Research and Therapy". However, it has changed substantially

---

\* Corresponding author: Stavros Simitsis, ssimitsis@gmail.com.

over time. Behavioral therapy was studied explicitly by examining the process of behavior; meaning associations between incentives and reactions, and also theories regarding learning methods. Nowadays behavioral therapy focuses on cognition, having adapted principles based on altering the way a psychological event is comprehended and experienced by individuals (Hayes, Villatte, Levin, & Hildebrandt, 2011).

Behavioral psychologist John B. Watson was the first to separate the concept of "mind" from the primary focus of psychology, as well as "soul searching" from the established methods of examination. This notion was an effort to steer psychology both as a profession and as a research subject to more scientific pathways, where definitions and methods that cannot be operationalized and objectively observed, were of no use. The strictness that characterized behavioral examination –although at a great percentage useful- was first rejected by B. F. Skinner who believed that objectivity should not define only what can be observed by the many, but it should be accounted as a moderator of both public and private observations.

The evolution of behavior therapy into cognitive behavioral therapy (CBT) was possible due to the influence from cognitive psychology and computer science. The overall simplistic logic of cause-effect perspective (of behavioral therapy) was significantly enhanced by the more sophisticated and adaptive reasoning rooted in theories of information processing. Still, hard science was a difficult achievement, especially when one wished to remain within the field of behaviourism. Thus, CBT was largely practiced in clinical settings, where accesses to means for examining the single source of non-vague behavioral patterns –the brain- were available. Under such circumstances, the CBT objective was no longer an effort to adjust the components of a behavior, but an adjustment of the patterns of cognition and emotion that exerted the behavior (Hayes et al., 2011).

CBT treatment methods were developed initially as a means of countering specifically depression and anxiety (Beck, 2005). The main focus of the intervention was the malfunctioning process of information interpretation on the patients' part. Additionally, the therapy aimed to hinder avoidance and helplessness in order to enhance the willingness and active participation of the patients. Later modifications, fostered compatibility between CBT and other disorders, such as substance abuse, eating, personality and in some cases bipolar and schizophrenia (Wright, 2006).

According to Wright (2006), patients undergoing CBT treatment are trapped in a vicious circle that is based on their experience, evaluating skills and emotional and cognitive interpretation. This circle comprises of the main traumatic event, the cognitive appraisal, the evoked emotion and the resulting behavior. Since cognition and behavior are interrelated, CBT therapy aims at interrupting the vicious circle by taping on the three cognitive levels of the patient; (1) consciousness, (2) automatic thoughts and (3) schemas.

Consciousness represents the decision making process, executed in the state of situational awareness. Automatic thoughts are the constant "trains-of-thought" – cognitions that exist right under the stream of consciousness- and rarely attract much attention (Longmore & Worrell, 2006). Still, they distort heavily the patient's mind set, self esteem, effectiveness as well as perceived discrepancies between the stressful situation requirements and his own abilities. Schemas are a significant factor in determining one's self worth and defence mechanisms. They act as place holders of information acquired throughout the developmental stages and the general life experience of each person (Wright, 2006).

CBT treatment is characterized by a constructive collaboration between the therapist and the patient during which actions are taken towards the identification and reconfiguration of problematic behaviors and cognitions (Longmore et al., 2006; Lowinger & Rombon, 2012; Wright, 2006). The purpose of these methods is to aid patients to become aware of their problems as well as to develop useful skills in managing them. The treatment process includes several vital factors that are instrumental for the patient's progress.

First, the defining of the way and conditions under which therapeutic progress will be achieved. This process is done by the patient and the help of the therapist. It is during this phase that social, religious, interpersonal and biological sub-factors must be taken into account. Second, psychoeducation is a very important asset in the whole procedure. The therapist can take advantage of an emotional breakdown during practice, to encourage the patient to record the streaming automatic thoughts and then share information regarding their nature as well as coping strategies. Psychoeducation is useful because it serves as a "double agent" that provides tactical information on the enemy's (e.g.: anxiety) plans; this information can be used to strengthen the patient and make him able to thwart the progress of his condition. Third, the development of homework assignments is an important component of CBT therapy, because it serves as a link between sessions further ensuring the patient's commitment. Furthermore, they serve as a stepping stone for the mastering of skills learned in practice. Last but not least, homework assignments are the basis for the patient's gradual transition from the safe therapeutic environment to the greater world (Wright, 2006).

Since CBT focuses on both cognitive and behavioral processes, several relevant techniques have been developed for an effective intervention. Two of the most vital cognitive techniques are the Socratic questioning and the guided discovery (Wright, 2006). The first technique challenges the patient in an effort to find solutions to specific questions relevant to his condition. The second technique aims to encourage the patient to think in ways that will make him actively question his maladaptive cognitive process. Both Socratic questioning and guided discovery constitute reconfigurative efforts of the patient's distorted thinking.

Another cognitive technique is known as imagery; the process of creating meaningful mental images based on pieces of information regarding life experiences recalled from memory (Weinberg & Gould, 2007). It is almost identical to other sensory experiences, such as seeing or hearing, with the only difference that imagery occurs completely in the mind. Imagery is a useful asset of psychotherapy since it aids the patient in several ways. First, it improves concentration. Simply by imagining how a patient wants to react in a certain situation he can train his mind to block automatic thoughts. Second, through imagery the patient can develop new skills, practice and/or correct them. For example, the patient can use imagery as a pre-phase of gradual exposure (mentioned below). Additionally, imagery is found to enhance motivation and also build confidence – something that can be very useful with patients suffering from depression (Weinberg et al., 2007).

In a similar manner, techniques that focus on the behavioral modification of the patient include the development of a schedule comprised of physical and mental activities as well as pleasurable events. The purpose of these weekly schedules is to complete the amount of included activities, in an effort to counter the patient's inactivity and flat affect. These schedules can later be modified based on the rating of the activity experience gained by the patient (Wright, 2006). Another technique is the graded task assignment. This technique is particularly useful with patients suffering from anxiety. It is a method of reducing the perceived inability at the face of a difficult situation by breaking the problem into smaller pieces and developing a management plan that will aid in the solution of the problem while influencing the patient's perceptions –and ultimately behavior- in the process. Finally, a behavioral technique, effective in cases where the patient has to overcome a traumatic experience such as a railway accident for example, is the gradual exposure to the negative stimulus. In this method, the patient undergoes systematically increased exposures to the traumatic event, up to the point where anxiety symptoms are effectively controlled or disappear. Gradual exposure is always paired with relaxation techniques that ensure the psychological and physical safety of the patient - especially in the early stages (Wright, 2006).

There are several research studies indicating the usefulness and effectiveness of CBT in the treatment of psychological disorders. In one such study, Scheeringa, Sallonn, Arnberger, Weens, Amaya-Jackson, and Cohen (2007) tested this therapy with young children with post-traumatic stress disorder (PTSD). Their 12-session intervention included psychoeducation regarding PTSD symptomatology, its self-identification and rating and various relaxation techniques (1-4 sessions). The fifth session was devoted to recitation of PTSD experiences by the children. Four sessions (6-10) recommended exposure exercises and the last two sessions were focused on relapse prevention and overall review respectively. Results showed that even though the young participants were in their middle development stages, their cognitive capacities and their concept of self allowed for a motivated and willing cooperation towards improvement. This study by Scheeringa et al. (2007) underlined the fact that CBT is an effective treatment for children with PTSD, specifically regarding relaxation and exposure exercises and progress prevention from external factors (i.e. parental anxiety).

Yet another modified version of CBT treatment is the combination of CBT with spiritual and religious elements. According to Hook, Worthington, Davis, Jennings and Gartner (2009), there is a strong association between religion and mental equilibrium in the views and beliefs of many individuals, who regard religious beliefs as a significant source of psychological strength. The main difference between spiritualized CBT and standard CBT treatments is that the first is conducted with spiritual components and a religious context that suits the client. The development of this particular technique, however, is thwarted by various factors. First, the process and nature of psychotherapy is sometimes misunderstood by religious patients and such an impression often results in withholding their beliefs during the session. Second, many mental health professionals do not come from a religious background; thus, their lack of knowledge and experience in assessment or approach results in the total avoidance of the subject. Third, there is a profound lack of practical foundation on the matter as most treatment cases refer to outpatients.

Nevertheless, research indicates that spiritualized CBT treatment might be more effective compared with standard treatment (Hook et al., 2009). Rosmarin, Anerback, Bigda-Payton, Bjorgvinsson, and Levendusky (2011) developed a pilot treatment in order to fill the specific gaps in the literature. The treatment outcome was more than encouraging as the vast majority of participants (almost 50%), evaluated the effort to impart religion in psychological treatments most positive. Last but not least, a quarter of the participating patients recommended that this treatment method be available to larger groups and more frequently.

# CBT Compared to Other Therapies Addressing Social Anxiety

The most widely used technique for the treatment of Social Anxiety Disorder (SAD) is CBT. Lately, however, a group format of CBT, CBGT, has started being used with successful results. In CBGT, Exposure therapy has been integrated with CBT. Except for CBGT, two more approaches to the therapy of SAD will be explored; Social Skills Training (SST)- that focuses mostly on the problematic aspects of social life patients with SAD face, and Social Effectiveness Therapy (SET) that is mainly a form of psychoeducation. All of these therapeutic techniques have been used in different categories of SAD patients and in different formats; adolescent patients, patients with perfectionism, brief modes and extended ones.

In their paper, Herbert, Rheingold, and Goldstein (2002) are exploring the effectiveness of Cognitive Behavioral Group Therapy (CBGT) on Social Anxiety Disorder patients. They are presenting some other treatments for SAD such as, exposure based treatment, where the patient is gradually faced with the stressor; cognitive intervention, where the patient's "faulty" cognitions are targeted and reformed; self-instructional treatment, that involves self-talk as a means of becoming covert; social skills training, usually with the use of different possible scenarios that the patient has to act out in order to build up their social skills; and relaxation techniques, that include breathing or muscle-relaxation exercise that will help the patient relax and be more functional in different situations. They conclude, though, that the most widely used is the CBGT, developed by Heimberg and colleagues (1991, as cited in Herbert et al., 2002). It is a combination of Exposure therapy with Cognitive therapy. Although it is the most widely used and researched mode for treating SAD, the mechanism behind it is quite unclear. However, it is considered that the cognitive aspect of the model is the one responsible for the therapeutic result. A meta-analysis conducted by Taylor (1996) showed that the combination of Exposure Therapy and Cognitive Therapy has higher effect sizes than Exposure Therapy alone. On the other hand, there were other studies (Feske & Chambless, 1995 as cited in Herbert et al., 2002) arguing that there is no evidence that Cognitive Therapy adds to Exposure Therapy. More recently, Hoffman (2000) claims the issue unresolved, but at the same time suggests there is little evidence of the additive effect of Cognitive Therapy over Exposure. CBGT is organized with groups of 6-8 individuals, with two co-therapists and it lasts for 12 weekly sessions. It uses exposure techniques and exercises and also cognitive reconstruction. In their study, Herbert et al. (2002) are using a brief version of the CBGT, that lasts for 6 weeks and proved that an intensive version of the brief CBGT can have similar results to the extended one (lasting 12 weeks). The therapeutic influence was still in progress for 6 weeks over completion and the effect of it was maintained for 3 months. Despite the limitations (limited sample; not direct comparison between the brief and the extended model; lack of behavioural assessment) the results are considered valid and promising in terms of effectiveness of the CBGT. In addition the nature of SAD- it is chronic and without remission- and the results of patients in waiting lists (no improvements) also support the validity of these results.

Herbert et al. (2002) and Franklin et al. (2001) have provided positive results of integrating Social Skills Training into CBGT. Based on their results Herbert et al. (2005) have conducted their research on 65 participants diagnosed with SAD. It involved 65 participants diagnosed with SAD. They were divided into groups of four to six people. The participants were randomly assigned to treatment with or without Social Skills Training (SST). The SST included a) speech content, b) paralinguistic features of speech and c) non-verbal behavior and it was modified to fit the specific needs of each participant. In order to fit the SST into the program, the time of the Cognitive Therapy was minimized. However, it still occupied the larger part of treatment. Each group received weekly group therapy for 12 weeks. The results showed that in the group of combined modes, the improvement was significantly higher, while the results of the non integrative group were similar with other studies.

Clark, Ehlers, Hackmann, McMagnus, and Fennell, (2006) present in their paper the model used by Clark and Wells (1995) in order to develop a new cognitive therapy program. The processes that are highlighted in the model are: "(a) increased self-focused attention and a linked decrease in observation of other people and their responses,(b) use of misleading internal information (feelings and images) to make excessively negative inferences about how one appears to others, (c) extensive use of overt and covert safety behaviors, and (d) problematic pre- and post event processing" (Clark et al., 2006, p. 568). One of the issues raised is the argument by Mortberg et al. (2006) that individual CBT is more effective than the intensive 3-week CBGT, therefore a group setting might not be as effective as an individual format in specific cases. In a meta analysis of other studies they found that the results from Exposure Therapy versus CBT showed no convincing differences; six of the studies showed no differences at all, one stated the superiority of the CBT on a minority of patients and one study provided inconsistent differences in the results; one measure supported the effectiveness of CBT, while some other measures the effectiveness of exposure therapy. In sum, research evidence suggests that CBT is more effective than Exposure Therapy. In SAD, the area of the patients' life that is the most affected, researched and targeted during treatment is their social life. However, there are other traits that can be connected to SAD, such as Perfectionism, that are not researched in depth (Asbaugh, Antony, Liss, Summerfeldt, McCabe, Swinson, 2007). Perfectionists with SAD, will be more stressed when they have to present their work in public; their work must be perfect and to add to that, "people will judge". In their research they present the argument that perfectionism can have a negative effect on treatment, based on the work of Blatt et al. (1995) who suggested that those with higher levels of perfectionism before the treatment showed lower effective results in short-term treatment than the rest of the participants. However, the reasons why perfectionism had an effect in that research are not clearly specified. In general, the research on perfectionism and treatment outcome is quite limited.

After discussing different aspects of SAD for the adult population, it is interesting to review the research conducted with adolescents. The onset of SAD is approximately the age of 15.5 (Herbert et al., 2009). Adolescents with SAD tend to have fewer friends and limited activities beside school that have difficulty attending. SAD is also related with selective mutism, school refusal and there is comorbidity with depressive, anxiety, somatoform and substance abuse disorders. Given that adolescence is a difficult period for most individuals, the extra burden of social anxiety adds up and can lead to long-term problems in function. There is limited research on children and adolescents with SAD and the interventions available are modified models for adult treatments, that are targeting anxiety disorders in general, and they are used individually. More specifically, there are few researched treatments focusing on SAD. The most commonly used programs are CBGT and Social Effectiveness Therapy (SET)- there is also another model, the "coping cat" model, that is also a behavior therapy program but it is for general anxiety disorders and not specifically for SAD. The CBGT and the Social Effectiveness Therapy are used for groups and share the same strategies; psychoeducation-where the participants had discussions with the therapists about different topics of SAD, but they were not provided with specific advice and problem-solving skills, exposure, coping skills, like relaxation techniques, and homework based on individual needs, to apply the theoretical aspect of training in everyday situations in the real world.

Research in the last decade has shown that CBGT is the best option to treat SAD. In different experiments and interventions, researchers used CBT in different forms, either group or individual, and in comparison with other models of treatment such as Social Skills Training (Herbert, Gaudiano, Rheingold, Myers, Dalrymple, & Nolan, 2005), Exposure Therapy alone or Exposure Therapy along with Applied Relaxation (Clark et al., 2006), and Psychoeducational-Supportive Psychotherapy (Herbert et al., 2008). The results always support the CBT group, which can help alleviate some comorbid disorders, such as depression (Cardaciotto & Herbert, 2004) and perfectionism (Asbaugh et al., 2007). All in all, CBT, and mostly CBGT has better recovery rates than any other model of therapy for individuals with SAD.

# Interned Delivered CBT

In this section, the form of Internet Delivered Cognitive Behavioral Therapy (CBT-ID) will be explored. The definition of the term Internet Delivered Treatment proves to be ambiguous due to the plethora of opinions and perspectives on the matter. Internet can be used in multiple ways and for numerous purposes, including communication between two or more individuals, as well as research via browsing web pages to find the information in question. Consequently, as far as cyber intervention is concerned, it is understood that it can be achieved in various ways using the aforementioned tools provided by the Internet, as well as through the use of certain interactive platforms that do not require input from a licensed clinician. It is worth mentioning that there is a difference between interned based treatment and computer based treatment. The difference lies in the fact that when the individual is receiving computerized treatment, he usually has to use a particular computer, while internet delivered treatment can be conducted via the individual's computer in his private environment (Marks, Mataix-Cols, Kenwright, Cameron, Hirsch, & Gega, 2003; Proudfoot, Goldberg, Mann, Everitt, Marks, & Gray, 2003).

Nowadays, especially in industrialized societies, the internet has become embedded in the every day life of the vast majority of the planet's population and this phenomenon is continuously and rapidly increasing. The internet has become a popular activity even among groups that are not accustomed to the use of information technologies (IT) such as women, the elderly and also people belonging to minority groups (Lamerichs, 2003). Regarding CBT, there is significant debate on whether Internet Delivered Treatment can have a positive outcome (Cook & Doyle, 2002).

According to Knaevelsrud and Maercker (2007), internet based treatments and therapeutic alliance tend to create a strong bond between each other, although they are not strongly connected with the outcome. The Internet Delivered Treatment (IDT) consists of two types; the guided and the non-guided treatment. Marks, Cavanagh, and Gega (2007) proposed that any computerized intervention should instruct at least a legitimate amount of therapy decisions to the computer. Anderson et al. (2007) have proposed that a therapy which relies on self-help books and is led by a certified therapist who is able to give feedback, answer to queries posed by the client, and also have some scheduled sessions, is very similar to face to face treatment. Such a treatment could also include some interactive online features; for instance questions set to retrieve passwords in order to receive access to different modules that may concern them individually. Watkins and Clum (2008) have suggested that, in research, when self-help is mentioned it usually refers to treatment that is taking place with very little or no help from a professional. When an IDT is guided from a specialist, it could be safely stated that it is an approach which contains the advantage of scheduled self-help materials which are easy to obtain via the internet. In addition, it should be emphasized that the most important role in Guided IDT is played by an identified therapist who will provide the client with support, encouragement and direct therapeutic activities via email exchange (Postel, De Haan, & De Jong, 2008).

Research on self-help techniques and subsequently in CBT-ID therapy provided with knowledge extensively applied on anxiety disorder patients. It is remarkable that many people suffering from anxiety disorders never seek help or if they do it is after many years of suffering (Clark, 1999). There are two ambivalent sides on whether or not CBT-ID has a positive effect on people with Social Anxiety Disorder (SAD). According to Erwina, Turk, Heimberg, Frescoa and Hantula (2004), it is possible that instead of diminishing their avoidance symptoms (such as crowd exposure), it reinforces them.

In contrast, it is argued that CBT-ID could be more beneficial than traditional therapy for individuals with SAD, who may feel "safer" in a familiar environment. So, it may be easier for them to go through the necessary psycho-educational phase of CBT. In reality however, systematic exposure and behavioral modification, are part of the effectiveness of this treatment. Furthermore, researchers who support CBT-ID state that many individuals with social anxiety have managed to break their own boundaries and consciously and wilfully expose themselves to their fears under the guidance of a self help program and the online support of a mental health professional (Andersson, 2009).

Humans, on a daily basis, are exposed to numerous negative stimuli of varying degrees, which evoke social anxiety. Fear and anxiety are some of the symptoms experienced in situations when a person is exposed to public evaluation and consequently, feedback. Rhetoric skills are highly rated in higher education. Consequently, this exerts extra pressure – an additional obstacle for young adults with SAD. Researchers have mentioned that SAD is one of the most prevailing anxiety disorders in western societies, reaching rates of about 10% (Furmark, 2002; Mancini, Van Ameringen, Bennett, Patterson, & Watson, 2005). According to Rapee and Spence (2004) SAD should be regarded as a major health issue, and especially for young people who have not yet sought treatment, as there are many resulting risks, varying from low academic performance school dropouts, to low employability in later life. As mentioned earlier, most young people who suffer from social anxiety disorder do not receive any treatment. It is assumed that the reason for this is mainly because the symptoms are misinterpreted as shyness which will eventually subside with time.

Cognitive Behavioral Therapy is an effective treatment for anxiety disorders. On the other hand, CBT-ID has more advantages for both the client and the therapist. Individuals suffering from any psychological problem tend to find internet usage easier for them in order to receive help and the same technique may be preferred by the therapist in offering his guidance, due to the anonymity and accessibility of the internet. Many individuals who have received help via the internet are able to avoid being stigmatized by their social circles (Gega, Marks, & Mataix-Cols, 2004). Carlbring et al. (2005) found that Internet Based Self help, accompanied with an expert's help, has been proved to be at least equally effective with the traditional CBT. Additionally, three recent mental analyses on CBT-ID for people with anxiety and/or depression have been published (e. g., Andersson et al., 2009). According to the results, the outcomes were stable and the patients participating found internet CBT to be satisfying.

# Additional Therapies

Social Anxiety is a prevalent condition that might cause significant functional impairments on the sufferers so ever since Social Anxiety got included in the DSM –III a large body of research on how to treat this disorder has been conducted over the last two decades (Rowa & Antony, 2005).

Throughout the bibliography there are several empirically supportive treatments for Social Anxiety Disorder and Social Phobia including psychological combined with psychosocial treatments. Most treatments based on evidence for social phobia include exposure therapies, applied relaxation, social skills training techniques and cognitive treatments. Furthermore, research attention has been paid recently on the use of interpersonal psychotherapy supportive psychotherapy, Attentional Focus Training and mindfulness treatment strategies.

Although cognitive behavioral treatment is the most widely used psychological treatment for social phobia, interpersonal psychotherapy is the second most frequent treatment for this kind of phobia. Furthermore, it is estimated that social anxiety could be addressed more effectively within the context of the individual's interpersonal functioning (Alden & Taylor, 2004; Neal & Edelmann, 2003).

## Interpersonal Psychotherapy

Interpersonal psychotherapy was originally developed for the treatment of depression by Klerman, Weissman, Rounsaville, and Chevron (1984) and it is considered as an alternative form of treatment for Social Anxiety Disorder as well. It is an individual time-limited approach with treatment goal to target any modified interpersonal patterns in the central problem areas of role transitions, role disputes, and role insecurity/role deficits. Interpersonal psychotherapy treatment seeks to improve the client's symptoms by specifically targeting the individual's interpersonal problems. The therapist's interventions include clarification, exploration, encouragement of emotional expression, communication analysis, encouragement of social activity, and the use of the therapeutic relationship (Lipsitz, Gur, Miller, Forand, Vermes, & Fyer, 1997). During the Interpersonal psychotherapy treatment procedure Social Anxiety Disorder sufferers report past traumatic parenting experiences, developmental peer difficulties and high levels of stressful life events. Most often they are unmarried or they usually report marital difficulties such as difficulties in family and peer relationships (Wenzel, 2002). Interpersonal psychotherapy treatment is considered as an effective short-term treatment for Social anxiety patients because it improves various relational factors in the patients' life. Therapists usually apply Interpersonal psychotherapy on these patients because based on their fear of negative evaluation by others it is estimated that they suffer from interpersonal issues that need to be resolved as well. Interpersonal psychotherapy treatment is beneficial for Social Anxiety and most of the time it demonstrates positive results with most of the patients showing significant improvement of their symptoms (Lipsitz, Markowitz, Cherry, & Fyer, 1999). Lastly, it is suggested that Interpersonal psychotherapy treatment could be more efficient if it is combined with other proven therapies such as Cognitive Behavioral Treatment and Exposure treatment.

## Supportive Psychotherapy

Supportive psychotherapy is another approach for the treatment of social phobia. The initial idea originated from the Freudian psychodynamic therapy, where it has a more precise meaning. Basically, based on the theory of psychoanalytic psychotherapy combined with the supportive, it is assumed that most of our feelings result from past wishes and impulses that arise out of conscious mental activity. So, psychological symptoms usually derive from conflicting impulses or from conflicts between impulses and the demands of reality.

In summary, it indicates that a person's present behavior, emotions and personal relationships are influenced by her repressed childhood experiences. An effective supportive psychotherapy should include helpful caring, encouraging and sympathetic approach by the therapist. Essentially, the main goal of the supportive therapy is to lighten client's emotional dysfunctions by promoting conscious control or past repressed feelings, memories and impulses. Supportive therapy is considered in general as a beneficial treatment but in comparison with Cognitive Behavioral Treatment it appears to be inferior. Heimberg et al. (2000) compared group Cognitive Behavioral Treatment with a supportive group psychotherapy and indicated that while both groups showed improvement at post treatment and follow-up, the participants who completed group Cognitive Behavioral Treatment improved more than those in the supportive group, and they maintained improvements at 5-year follow-up (Cottraux, Note, Albuisson, Yao, Note, & Mollard, 2000).

## Attentional Concentration Training

Attentional concentration training also called Task Concentration Training and mindfulness training are considered as innovative treatment strategies and are still evaluated by researchers. In Task Concentration Training social anxiety sufferers are taught to allocate their attention away from themselves and concentrate toward external objectives starting with neutral stimuli and progressing to anxiety-provoking stimuli (Bogels, Sijbers, & Voncken, 2006). The treatment procedure requires several individual sessions and it is divided into tree different phases. Mulkens, Bogels, & Jon (1999) described this procedure as:1) becoming aware of self-focused attention, 2) focusing attention outward in non threatening situations, and 3) focusing attention outward in threatening situations. For example, clients could be encouraged to concentrate on sounds in the room or the sound of the therapist's voice instead of focusing on the therapist's physiological status. Lastly, individuals start Task Concentration Training treatment in the therapist's office and practice at home before using these skills in social situations. Furthermore, the effectiveness of this kind of treatment is still questioned because based on current case studies, there are several difficulties in order to define whether patients were using a combination of exposure and TCT or either a component in isolation that was most helpful for the client. In an effort to address this question, Mulkens, Bogels, Jong & Louwers (2001) conducted a randomized trial that compared in vivo exposure with Task Concentration Training in patients with fears of blushing. Results indicated that, although Task Concentration Training appeared to have some small advantages at post treatment (6-week follow-up), later on (1 -year follow-up) the same treatment revealed no significant differences between groups in effectiveness.

## Mindfulness Treatment

Mindfulness treatment strategy is another novel treatment for social phobia. Mindfulness is basically a form of meditation that derived from Buddhist spiritual practices and has been employed in various clinical psychological practices, including mindfulness-based stress reduction (Kabat-Zinn, 1990).

Furthermore, while it was initially developed for other disorders, such as depression (preventing relapse in depression) research evidence suggested that mindfulness-based strategies could be effective for social phobia as well. It is actually another form of attention training that provides systematic training with mindfulness meditation as a self-regulatory approach to facilitate the individual adapt to mental illness, reduce the stress that she is experiencing and manage her emotions (Anderson et al., 2007 ).

## Exposure Treatments

Exposure treatments have become more and more effective over time for social phobia sufferers and they usually include systematic desensitization, in vivo (real-life) exposure and in vivo flooding to feared objects (Kring, Johnson, Davison, & Neale, 2010). It is estimated that exposure-based interventions are the most effective strategies for treating a range of anxiety disorders including social phobia.

Exposure therapy is rooted in behaviorism and it was designed to treat fears, anxiety and negative emotions by exposing or introducing the client to situations that might cause the above feelings under carefully controlled exposure conditions.

## Systematic Desensitization

Systematic desensitization is among the most empirically supported therapies for social anxiety and it is usually popular among clients according to Head and Gross, 2008 (as cited in Corey, 2013). It is a behavior therapy procedure that it is based on the principle of classical conditioning developed by Joseph Wolpe (1990). The main goal of the therapy is to accomplish desensitization of the clients for future anxiety-arousing situations that they might encounter in their lives. After several sessions, clients should be able to imagine successively more anxiety-arousing situations and by the same time they should engage in a behavior that competes with anxiety. The procedure is in general time consuming and plenty of homework tasks are administered to the clients and follow-up is an essential component of successful desensitization (Corey, 2013).

## In Vivo Exposure and Flooding

Additionally, in vivo exposure and flooding are two variations of traditional systematic desensitization that involve exposure to real life situations. In vivo exposure therapy includes the client's exposure only to the actual anxiety-evoking events rather than simple imagining these situations. Treatment begins with a functional analysis of objects or situations that the sufferer avoids or fears. Then the therapist in cooperation with the client set a hierarchy for the client to confront beginning from the bottom of the hierarchy (Corey, 2013). Among the therapy sessions clients are frequently required to carry-out self-directed exposure exercises and they usually have home practice in order to achieve progress. Finally, in some cases the therapist might accompany the client in the confrontation of feared situations.

## Flooding

Flooding is another form of exposure therapy that contains either imaginal or in vivo exposure to anxiety-arousing stimuli for a long period of time. In vivo flooding basically includes intense and long-term exposure to the actual anxiety-producing stimuli. With the above procedure the client is remaining exposed to feared stimuli for a prolonged period of time without trying to adjust any anxiety-reducing behaviors because they are prevented to do so in order to avoid engaging in any maladaptive responses (Corey, 2013). The general outcome is that the anxiety will decrease on its own and quite rapidly also. Imaginal flooding is typically based on the same procedure with in vivo flooding but the main difference is that the exposure only occurs in the client's imagination instead of in daily life situations. The biggest advantage of the imaginal flooding though is that there are no potential harmful risks for the clients due to the fact that it is an imaginary procedure.

There is a widespread concern about the legal risks that might be associated with these therapeutic techniques. Several clinicians have characterized those treatments as inhuman, potentially dangerous or even intolerable for clients. It is very important that the behavioral therapist will adequately inform the client about the intense and log-term exposure therapy before consenting to participate because exposure techniques usually require crucial attention. Clients should primarily understand that by choosing this kind of treatment, they will elect a therapy that will induce their fears and anxiety initially before reducing them and that the procedure would be most likely unpleasant (Corey, 2013).

## Applied Relaxation

Applied relaxation is considered to be a popular and very promising therapy about the somatoform symptoms of the social phobia sufferers. In general, it aims to combat the physiological effects of the disorder in order to aid the patients. Relaxation training is required to address problems that are related to anxiety and stress because these patients usually lack the ability to relax their body and mind but they can be trained through therapy (Conrad, Isaac, & Roth, 2008).

Progressive Muscle Relaxation (PMR) was developed by Edmund Jacobson in 1938 and the procedure was based on the idea that muscle relaxation can lead to mind relaxation as well. Ever since it has been refined and modified and nowadays behavioral therapists frequently combine it with a number of other techniques such as systematic desensitization, self-management programs, hypnosis, meditation etc.

Relaxation procedures involve explicit guidance by the therapist. Initially a set of specific instructions is given to the client that teaches her how to relax. Clients are instructed to take a relaxed position in a quite comfortable environment while alternately contracting and relaxing their muscles (Corey, 2013). The therapist guides them to actually feel and experience the tension that is building up and notice their muscles getting tighter. They are suggested to study this tension and also to hold and fully experience the tension because it is extremely important that the client can experience the difference between a tense and a relaxed state. Later the client would be trained on how to relax all the muscles of her body by visualizing the various parts of the body but more specifically the facial muscles. It is very important that the client would have deep and regular breathing in order to achieve a state of calmness and peacefulness.

## Social Skills Training (SST)

SST is another type of psychotherapy that is used to improve a person's social skills and it is most likely addressed in people who are dealing with social anxiety disorder because they lack of ability to behave in a positive way is social situations. Although it is recognised as a very helpful technique, it is extremely rare to implement alone and it is usually combined with Cognitive Behavioral Therapy (CBT).

Social skills training include several behavioral techniques such as psychoeducation, modelling, behavior rehearsal and feedback. Sergin, 2007 (as cited in Corey 2013) identified the key elements of social skills training which contain a collection of techniques such as: assessment (setting the goals), direct instruction and coaching, modeling, role-playing, feedback and homework assignments.

As with any other type of psychotherapy it is necessary to establish some goals in the beginning of the therapy. So the therapist will help the client to identify the skill or skills that she wants to change and develop the treatment goals. Once the goals will be skills-specific the therapist will model the skill that the client is focusing on so that she can identify exactly what she needs to do before attempting to do it by herself. Role-playing is a very important aspect of the SST, the client is asked to role-play and rehearse the skill many times in an effort to be able to use it with confidence in real life situations. Meanwhile, the client will receive feedback after each session that concerns about her strengths and weaknesses. The therapist will provide her with directions of what she need to work on and practice and she will set homework challenges that the client would be required to practice until the next session.

After the completion of the therapy, trainees will be able to communicate with others effectively and appropriately in various social situations, to change selected behaviors and to increase their self-esteem. Although there is research evidence that Social Skills Training is in general helpful for social anxiety, it is questionable whether the patients' positive outcomes will be maintained over a long-term follow-up (Rowa et al., 2005). It is also unclear whether SST is more helpful than placebo conditions. Although SST may show some evidence for effectiveness in SP, this does not confirm that people with the disorder have significant social skills deficits. In fact, research suggests that SST may work by encouraging the use of underused social skills or by facilitating exposure to social situations through role-plays and real-life practices but it could be less helpful alone than as part of a combination protocol.

## Individual Differences and Social Phobia

Individual differences are very important in psychology in order to help clinicians understand why a specific theory might not apply to every individual. Colin Cooper (1998) suggested that psychological theories are made based on the belief that people are all same in terms of generalizations about behavioral characteristics; however Cooper argued that this assumption is not objective because of the different experiences that each of us has in our everyday lives. For that reason, Cooper assumed that the approach of the individual differences is an important element for psychologists, not only for the assumption that all people differ, but for a better understanding of the complexities of different behaviors that exist at any topic or area in psychological framework (Maltby, Day & Macaskill, 2010).

Psychologists proposed two major concepts that make humans distinct from one to another, intelligence and behavior (Eysenck, 1994). Different personality types are one of the main concepts in the identification of individual differences. The concept of individual differences was one of the main concerns of Darwin in 1895, in his theory of evolution. More specifically, Darwin suggested that individuals adapt different strategies for their survival, which are explained by the different biological and psychological mechanisms that they acquire during their life span.

Intelligence can be defined as the ability to think and to reason well and also is the ability that includes several forms of creative and practical thinking and reasoning (Eysenck, 1994). However, sometimes intelligence is not a proper indicator of how individuals differ intellectually because sometimes prejudice might affect the interpretation of IQ scores where ethnicity and culture play a fundamental role. This is one of the reasons why most psychologists believe that personality is the strongest indicator of individual differences among humans. Child (1968) gave a clear definition which captures more or less what most of the psychologists mean by personality. More specifically, according to Child (1968, p. 83) personality is "more or less stable, internal factors that make one person's behavior consistent from one time to another and different from the behavior other people would manifest in comparable situations". For the identification of specific personality traits that are most likely to be found in people with social phobia, one study have shown that people with Generalized

Social Phobia (GSP) had significant lower scores in extraversion (one of the five personality traits) and higher neuroticism (neuroticism is another type of personality trait) scores compared to healthy volunteers (Van Velzen, Emmelkamp & Scholing, 2000).

Exploring individual differences among humans is very beneficial to mention two basic models proposed by Cooper (1998) and Lubinski (2000). More specifically, Cooper (1998) and Lubinski (2000) suggested that the nature of individual differences has to be separated into two basic concepts; the structural and the process model (Maltby et al., 2010). The structural model answers the question of "how" individuals differ and more specifically, what personality factors such as optimism make people differ from one to another, also experiences, societal constructs and/or people's cognitive capacities. The second model is the process one, which answers three basic questions regarding individual differences; the "why", "when" and "where" people differ, which according to Cooper (1998) gives us a deeper understanding of "how" individuals differ and also what causes these differences, and what are the consequences of these differences among individuals.

Eysenck's theory of personality contains three different personality traits; neuroticism (worry and anxiety), extraversion (optimism and positive thinking) and psychoticism (egocentric and antisocial personality traits). In addition, coping refers to individuals' effective cognitive processes in order to adapt to stressful and difficult events in their lives (Maltby et al., 2010). There are two different coping styles; the problem-focused coping and the emotion-focused coping. Let's assume that a neurotic person (as it mentioned above in the study of Van Velzen et al. (2000); people with social phobia (tend to score higher on neurotic) usually focuses on his/her emotions (e.g. anxious feelings), which might be an indicator that this person under stressful events would use the emotion-focused coping style, and the extraverted one the problem-focused coping. To conclude, by combing different theories, better adaptations to several cognitive and emotionally difficulties could be suggested by psychologists/clinicians during the therapeutic process where individual differences have been identified initially (Maltby et al., 2010).

Because of all the individual differences that have been reported so far, (personality traits, intelligence and/or different coping styles, and the structural and the process model) it is obvious that all these could possibly influence the outcome of the Cognitive Behavioral Treatment (CBT) for social phobia. More specifically, relevant research proposed that few patients with social phobia achieve high-functioning state after the end of the treatment process (Moscovitch, 2008). For this reason, it is crucial to identify what are the main reasons influencing the outcome of the CBT, and under which conditions therapists and clinicians could develop ways to maximize the efficiency of CBT. For that reason, an important clinical goal should be to consider- the differences between individuals- that might affect the outcome of the therapeutic process. More specifically, Moscovitch (2008) proposed that clinicians should adequately conceptualize patients' core fears in order to create an individualized patient profile that will focus mainly on each individual and thereby create specific treatment strategies. Each patient's anxiety symptom profile should be assessed in the early stages of therapy where clinicians should gather precise information concerning patient's anxious feelings, thoughts and behaviors covered by four questions: (a) the perceived feared stimulus, (b) the perceived feared consequences, (c) the fear triggers and contexts and (d) the feared avoidance, escape, and safety behaviors. All the four above questions should be answered in order for the clinician to create an adequate 'anxiety symptom profile' and thus, be more able to help his patients adequately.

Previous research on social phobia showed that depression could be an important indicator for the final outcome of CBT for social phobia. More specifically, clients who scored higher on the Beck Depression Inventory were found to be less likely to be treated by CBT for social anxiety because depression is strongly linked with interpersonal problems which are one of the core problems of social phobia (Chambless & Tran, 1997). This could be explained by the fact that depressive subjects have shown greater propensity to recall negative experiences in social situations as stable, global and internal. In addition researchers suggested that the avoidant personality trait associated with social isolation, which leads to depression could predict the presence of social phobia in individuals with these characteristics. Another important finding on the correlation of individual differences and the outcome of treatment for social anxiety showed that clients who, at the beginning of the sessions showed more optimism and reported higher expectancy for benefit from the treatment outcome were found to be more likely to be cured and remain well functioning at the end of the therapeutic process comparing to those with less expectancy of benefits.

In addition, a study conducted in 47 clients with social anxiety disorder showed that maladaptive beliefs such as negatively biased, inaccurate and inflexible thoughts play a key role for the outcome of CBT. Results of this study showed that client's maladaptive beliefs reduce the possibility for the completion of treatment; maladaptive beliefs are strongly associated with social anxiety disorder. However, researchers found that during treatment, treatment-related reductions in maladaptive interpersonal beliefs could be reduced and also being cured after the application of CBT for social phobia (Boden, John, Goldin, Werner, Heimberg & Gross, 2012). Another study conducted on 25 patients who completed 12 sessions of group CBT and who were measured at pre-, mid-, and post treatment sessions have shown that self-reported judgment biases could be reduced at the end of the therapeutic process. More specifically, patients' judgment biases could be reduced by the use of emotional regulation coping strategies and thus the early acquisition of these reappraisal skills showed at the end of the 12 sessions an overall reduction of symptoms of social phobia and much support for the efficiency of CBT for social anxiety disorders (Moscovitch et al., 2012).

Despite individual's traits and beliefs, research on this field has shown that biological factors could also predict the sense of perceived danger by individuals with social phobia. More specifically, genetic influence is an important indicator to anxious symptomatology, because patients' threat appraisal might be genetically mediated (Rapee & Heimberg, 1997). Twin research on the genetic influence has shown that individuals with social phobia are more likely to have first relatives with this type of disorder rather than panic or other type of anxiety disorders. Additionally, researchers suggest that the genetic influence of social phobia is indicated by the tendency that people show to perceive environmental cues, such as being more or less threatening (Rapee et al., 1997).

Factors such as parenting styles, modeling and restricted exposure suggest that family contributes to the anxious symptomatology of social phobia. Over-controlling or over-intrusive parenting style is strongly associated with the symptoms of anxiety. This could be explained by the negative evaluations and the excessive control that they receive from their parents regularly (Rapee et al., 1997). Moreover, modeling may also be influential to the development of social phobia, because of the verbal and nonverbal messages that the offsprings receive from their parents at the very early ages. Finally, research on the family factors of the symptomatology of social phobia has shown that people with social phobia are more likely to state that their parents did not encourage their or family's social life (Rapee et al., 1997).

Finally, cultural differences should also be considered because different ethnic groups have different ways of experiencing, expressing, and reporting their social fears. More specifically, one study (Furmark, 2002) has shown that 'the reported prevalence for social phobia is markedly lower in the few studies that have been conducted in South-East Asian countries (Korea and Taiwan) than in Western cultures'. Regarding gender differences, epidemiological studies have shown that females are more likely to report signs of social phobia comparing to males. These findings are contradicted with findings in clinical populations, where males report social anxiety more frequently than women, in many societies (Rapee & Spence, 2004).

# References

Alden, L. E., & Taylor, C. T. (2004). Interpersonal processes in social phobia. *Clinical Psychology Review, 24*, 857–882.

Anderson, N. D., Lau, M. A., Zindel, V., Segal, R., & Bishop, S. R. ( 2007). Mindfulness-Based Stress Reduction and Attentional Control. *Clinical Psychology and Psychotherapy, 14*, 449-463.

Andersson, G. (2009). *Using the Internet to provide cognitive behavior therapy.* Department of Behavioral Sciences and Learning, Swedish Institute for Disability Research.

Asbaugh, A., Antony, M. M., Liss, A., Summerfeldt, L. J., McCabe, R. E., & Swinson, R. P. (2007). Changes in perfectionism following cognitive-behavioral treatment for social phobia. *Depression and Anxiety, 24*, 169-177.

Beck, A. T. (2005). The current state of cognitive therapy: A 40-year retrospective. *Archives of General Psychiatry, 62*, 953-959.

Boden, M. T., John, O. P., Goldin, P. R., Werner, K., Heimberg, R. G., & Gross, J. J. (2012). The role of maladaptive beliefs in cognitive behavioral therapy: Evidence from social anxiety disorder. *Behavioral Research and Therapy, 50,* 287-291.

Bogels, M. S., Sijbers, M. V. F. G., & Voncken, M. (2006). Mindfulness and task concentration training for social phobia: A pilot study. *Journal of Cognitive Psychotherapy: An International Quarterly, 20*, 33-44.

Cardaciotto, L., & Herbert, J. D. (2004). Cognitive behavior therapy for social anxiety disorder in the context of Asperger's Syndrome: A single-subject report. *Cognitive and Behavioral Practice, 11*, 75-81.

Carlbring, P., Nilsson-Ihrfelt, E., Waara, J., Kollenstam, C., Buhrman, M., Kaldo, V., Soderberg, M., Ekselius, L., & Andersson, G. (2005). Treatment of panic disorder: Live therapy vs. self-help via the Internet. *Behavior Research and Therapy, 43,* 1321–1333.

Chambless, D. L., & Tran G. Q. (1997). Predictors of response to cognitive behavioral group therapy for social phobia. *Journal of Anxiety Disorders, 11*, 221-240.

Clark, D. M. (1999). Anxiety disorders: why they persist and how to treat them. *Behavior Research and Therapy, 37*, S5–S27.

Clark, D. M., Ehlers, A., Hackmann, A., McMagnus, F., & Fennell, M. (2006). Cognitive therapy versus exposure and applied relaxation in social phobia: A randomized controlled trial. *Journal of Consulting and Clinical Psychology, 74*, 568-578.

Clark, D. M., Wells, A. (1995). A cognitive model of social phobia. Social phobia; diagnosis, assessment, and treatment. *New York: Guilford Press*, 69-93.

Conrad, A., Isaac, L., & Roth, W. (2008). The psychophysiology of generalized anxiety disorder: Effects of applied relaxation. *Psychophysiology, 45*, 377–388.

Cook, J. E., & Doyle, C. (2002). Working alliance in online therapy as compared to face-to-face therapy: preliminary results. *Cyberpsychology & Behavior, 5*, 95–105.

Cooper, C. (1998). *Individual differences*. London: Arnold.

Corey, G. (2013). *Theory and practice of counseling and psychotherapy* (9th ed.). New York: Brooks and Cole.

Cottraux, J., Note, I., Albuisson, E., Yao, S., N., Note, B., & Mollard, E. (2000). Cognitive behavior therapy versus supportive therapy in social phobia: A randomized controlled trial. *Journal of Psychotherapy and Psychosomatics, 69*, 37-46.

Erwina, B. A., Turk, C. L., Heimberg, R. G., Frescoa, D. M., & Hantula, D. A. (2004). The Internet: home to a severe population of individuals with social anxiety disorder? *Journal of Anxiety Disorders, 18*, 629–646.

Eysenck, M. W. (1994). *Individual differences.* Cornwall, UK: International Ltd.

Furmark, T. (2002). Social phobia: Overview of community surveys. *Acta Psychiatrica Scandinavica, 105*, 84–93.

Gega, L., Marks, I. &Mataix-Cols, D. (2004). Computer-aided CBT self-help for anxiety and depressive disorders: experience of a London clinic and future directions. *Journal of Clinical Psychology, 60*, 147–157.

Hayes, S., Villatte, M., Levin, M., & Hildebrandt, M. (2011). Open, aware and active: Contextual approaches as an emerging trend in the behavioral and cognitive therapies. *Annual Review of Clinical Psychology, 7*, 141-168.

Herbert, J. D., Gaudiano, B. A., Rheingold, A. A., Moitra, E., Myers, V. H., Dalrymple, K. L., & Brandsma, L. L. (2009). Cognitive behavior therapy for generalized social anxiety disorder in adolescents: A randomized controlled trial. *Journal of Anxiety Disorders, 23*, 167-177.

Herbert, J. D., Gaudiano, B. A., Rheingold, A. A., Myers, V. H., Dalrymple, K., & Nolan, E. M. (2005). Social skills training augments the effectiveness of cognitive behavioral group therapy for social anxiety disorder. *Behavior Therapy, 36*, 125-138.

Herbert, J. D., Rheingold, A. A., & Goldstein, S. G. (2002). Brief cognitive group therapy for social anxiety disorder. *Cognitive and Behavioral Practice, 9*, 1-8.

Hook, J., Worthington, E., Davis, D., Jennings, D., & Gartner, A. (2009). Empirically supported religious and spiritual therapies. *Journal of Clinical Psychology, 66*, 46-72.

Kabat-Zinn, J. (1990). *Using the wisdom of your body and mind to face stress, pain, and illness.* New York, NY: Delacorte Press.

Klerman, G. L., Weissman, M. M., Rounsaville, B. J., & Chevron, E. (1984). *Interpersonal psychotherapy of depression.* New York: Basic Books.

Knaevelsrud, C., & Maercker, A. (2007). Internet-based treatment for PTSD reduces distress and facilitates the development of a strong therapeutic alliance: a randomized controlled clinical trial. *BMC Psychiatry, 7*, 13-19.

Kring, M. A., Johnson, L. S., Davison, C. G., & Neale, M. J. (2010). *Abnormal psychology* (11th ed.). New York: John Wiley and Sons.

Lamerichs, J. (2003). Discourse of support: exploring online discussions on depression. Dissertation: Wageningen University.

Lipsitz, J. D., Gur, M., Miller, N., Forand, N., Vermes, D., & Fyer, A. J. (1997). An open pilot study of interpersonal psychotherapy for panic Disorder (IPT-PD). *Journal of Nervous Mental Disorder, 194*, 440–445.

Lipsitz, J. D., Markowitz, J. C., Cherry, S., & Fyer, A. J. (1999). An open pilot study of interpersonal psychotherapy for social phobia. *American Journal of Psychiatry, 156*, 1814–1816.

Longmore, R., & Worrell, M. (2006). Do we need to challenge thoughts in cognitive behavior therapy? *Clinical Psychology Review, 27*, 173-187.

Lowinger, R. J., & Rombon, H. (2012). The effectiveness of cognitive behavioral therapy for PTSD in New York City transit workers: A preliminary evaluation. *North American Journal of Psychology, 14*, 471-484.

Lubinski, D. (2000). Scientific and social significance of assessing individual differences: "Sinking shafts at a few critical points." *Annual Review of Psychology, 51*, 405-444.

Maltby, J., Day, L., & Macaskills, A. (2010). *Personality, individual differences, and intelligence* (2nd ed.). Essex: Pearson Education.

Mancini, C., Van Ameringen, M., Bennett, M., Patterson, B., & Watson, C. (2005). Emerging treatments for child and adolescent social phobia: A review. *Journal of Child and Adolescent Psychopharmacology, 15*, 589–607.

Marks, I. M., Cavanagh, K., & Gega, L. (2007). *Hands-on help*: *Maudsley monograph.* Hove: Psychology Press.

Marks, I. M., Mataix-Cols, D., Kenwright, M., Cameron, R., Hirsch, S. & Gega, L. (2003). Pragmatic evaluation of computer-aided self-help for anxiety and depression. *British Journal of Psychiatry, 183*, 57–65.

Mortberg, E., Karlsson, A., Fyring, C., & Sundin, O. (2006). Intensive cognitive-behavioral group treatment (CBGT) of social phobia: A randomized controlled study. *Journal of Anxiety Disorders, 20*, 646-660.

Moscovitch, D, A. (2008). What is the Core Fear in Social Phobia? A new model to facilitate invidualized case conceptualization and treatment. *Cognitive and Behavioral Practice, 14*, 1-12.

Moscovitch, D. A., Gavric, D. L., Senn, J. M., Santesso, D. L., Miskovic, V., Schmidt, L. A., McCabe, R. E., & Antony, M. M. (2012). Changes in judgment biases and use of emotion regulation strategies during Cognitive-Behavioral Therapy for Social Anxiety Disorder: Distinguishing treatment responders and non responders. *Cognitive Therapy Research, 36*, 261-271.

Mulkens, S., Bogels, S. M., & Jong, P. J. (1999). Attentional focus and fear of blushing: A case study. *Journal of Behavioural Cognitive Psychotherapy, 27*, 153-164.

Neal, J. A., & Edelmann, R. J. (2003). The etiology of social phobia: Toward a developmental profile. *Clinical Psychology Review, 23*, 761–786.

Padesky, C. (1993). Socratic questioning: Changing minds or guiding discovery? *European Congress of Behavioral and Cognitive Therapies, 19*, 3-6.

Postel, M. G., de Haan, H. A., & De Jong, C. A. (2008). E-therapy for mental health problems: a systematic review. *Telemedicine and e-Health, 14*, 707–714.

Proudfoot, J., Goldberg, D., Mann, A., Everitt, B., Marks, I. & Gray, J. A. (2003). Computerized, interactive, multimedia cognitive behavioral program for anxiety and depression in general practice. *Psychological Medicine, 33*, 217–227.

Rapee, R. M., & Heimberg, R. G. (1997). A Cognitive-Behavioral model of anxiety in social phobia. *Behavioral Research Therapy, 35*, 741-756.

Rapee, R. M., & Spence, S. H. (2004). The etiology of social phobia: Empirical evidence and an initial model. *Clinical Psychology Review, 24*, 737-767.

Rapee, R. M., & Spence, S. H. (2004). The etiology of social phobia: Empirical evidence and an initial model. *Clinical Psychology Review, 24*, 737–767.

Rosmarin, D., Auerbach, R., Bigda-Peyton, J., Björgvinsson, T., & Levendusky, P. (2011). Integrating spirituality into cognitive behavioral therapy in an acute psychiatric setting: A pilot study. *Journal of Cognitive Psychotherapy: An International Quarterly, 25*, 287-303.

Rowa, K., & Antony M. (2005). Psychological treatment for social phobia. *Canadian Journal of Psychiatry, 50*, 308-316.

Scheeringa, M., Salloum, A., Arnberger, R., Weems, C., Amaya-Jackson, L., & Cohen, J. (2007). Feasibility and effectiveness of cognitive–behavioral therapy for posttraumatic stress disorder in preschool children: Two case reports. *Journal of Traumatic Stress, 40*, 631–636.

Van Velzen, C. J. M., Emmelkamp, P. M. G., & Scholing, A. (2000). Generalized social phobia versus avoidant personality disorder: Differences in psychopathology, personality traits, and social and occupational functioning. *Journal of Anxiety Disorders, 14*, 395-411.

Watkins, P. L., & Clum, G. A. (2008). *Handbook of self-help therapies.* New York: Routledge.

Weinberg, R. S., & Gould, D. (2007). *Foundations of sport and exercise psychology* (4th ed.). Champaign, IL: Human Kinetics.

Wenzel, A., (2002). Characteristics of close relationships in individuals with social phobia: A preliminary comparison with non-anxious individuals. In: J. H. A. Wenzel (Ed.), *A clinician's guide to maintaining and enhancing close relationships* (pp. 193-213). Mahwah, NJ: Laurence Erlbaum Associates.

Wolpe, J. (1990). *The practice of behavior therapy* (4th ed.). New York: Pergamon Press.

Wright, J. (2006). Cognitive behavior therapy: Basic principles and recent advances. *Focus: The Journal of Lifelong Learning in Psychiatry, 4*, 173-178.

# Index

## #

21st century, 46

## A

abuse, vii, 3, 40, 91, 92, 93, 94, 95, 97, 98, 99, 102, 104, 110, 111, 116, 117, 119, 121, 122, 126, 144
academic performance, 127, 190
access, 32, 37, 76, 107, 131, 190
accessibility, 191
accommodation, 73, 85
adaptation, 101, 153
adaptations, 197
Adherence, vi, 157, 158, 160, 166, 167, 168, 169, 174, 176, 177, 179, 180
adjustment, 68, 70, 85, 116, 125, 164, 184
administrators, 66
adolescent adjustment, 67, 68
adolescent boys, 138
adolescent development, 67
adolescent drinking, 124
adolescent problem behavior, 67
adulthood, 3, 33, 34, 66, 97, 98, 100, 111, 116, 121, 128, 147
adults, 2, 6, 9, 16, 31, 32, 34, 40, 45, 49, 50, 52, 54, 63, 64, 66, 75, 76, 77, 116, 117, 118, 130, 139, 152, 153, 160, 176, 177, 179
advancements, 109
adverse effects, 74, 114
affective disorder, 46, 72
African American women, 155
African Americans, 146, 147, 152
age, 7, 8, 9, 10, 11, 12, 13, 14, 16, 17, 33, 34, 42, 50, 52, 54, 55, 70, 78, 80, 93, 97, 98, 99, 101, 110, 120, 124, 125, 130, 135, 147, 148, 149, 150, 160, 164, 169, 170, 177, 188

aggression, 55, 64, 65
aggressiveness, 142
agoraphobia, 2, 35, 87
AIDS, v, viii, 92, 141, 142, 143, 144, 145, 147, 148, 149, 150, 151, 152, 153, 154, 155, 175, 179
Albania, 91, 126
Alcohol, 44, 91, 111, 112, 113, 114, 115, 116, 117, 118, 119, 120, 121, 123
alcohol abuse, 73, 111, 119
alcohol consumption, 99, 105, 108, 118, 124
alcohol dependence, 100, 103
alcohol problems, 114, 119
alcohol use, 34, 44, 48, 91, 92, 94, 98, 100, 103, 108, 109, 110, 111, 112, 113, 114, 115, 116, 117, 119, 120, 121, 122, 123, 124, 125, 151
alcoholics, 124
alcoholism, 73, 115, 117, 119, 122, 123, 159, 180
alternative hypothesis, 52
ambassadors, 132
American Psychiatric Association, 15, 34, 43, 93, 101, 112, 137, 138
American Psychological Association, 66, 68, 70
amygdala, 130, 138
anger, 16, 79, 146
ankles, 158
ANOVA, 164, 169
Anticipated stigma, 144
antisocial personality, 197
antitoxin, 141, 148
APA, 3, 4, 72, 112, 129
Applied relaxation, 195
appointments, 180
appraisals, 24, 25, 56, 68, 118
arousal, vii, 19, 20, 21, 22, 23, 24, 25, 26, 29, 121
assertiveness, 137, 149
assessment, 2, 6, 12, 15, 16, 17, 18, 27, 81, 109, 113, 114, 118, 138, 155, 159, 163, 178, 180, 186, 187, 195, 200

assessment tools, 180
asthma, 178, 179
athletes, 39, 135
at-risk populations, 152
attachment, 64, 73, 85, 89
attentional bias, 20, 22
Attentional concentration training, 192
attentional training, 82
attitudes, 43, 109, 111, 136, 137, 142, 143, 145, 148,
    149, 150, 151, 153, 158, 178
Austria, 19
authority, 102
autism, viii, 127, 128, 129, 138, 139
Autism spectrum disorders, 127
Automatic thoughts, 184
autonomic nervous system, 6
autonomy, 53, 70, 75, 76, 79, 81, 83, 84, 97
aversion, 130
avoidance, 2, 5, 7, 18, 26, 34, 38, 41, 50, 52, 55, 58,
    61, 72, 73, 76, 77, 78, 101, 104, 105, 107, 112,
    114, 118, 184, 186, 190, 197
Avoidance, 4, 5, 13, 58
avoidance behavior, 73, 77
awareness, 19, 20, 22, 23, 25, 28, 29, 33, 38, 39, 130,
    141, 148, 184

**B**

Bangladesh, 67, 150, 155
barriers, 40, 42, 44, 158, 169, 174, 177
base, 89
Beck Depression Inventory, 177, 198
behavior rehearsal, 195
behavior therapy, 16, 45, 81, 84, 86, 138, 184, 189,
    193, 199, 200, 201, 202
Behavioral inhibition, 2, 17, 138
behavioral medicine, 153, 175
behavioral models, 20
behavioral problems, 147
behaviorism, 193
belief systems, 41
benefits, 36, 41, 47, 80, 83, 93, 145, 158, 172, 198
benign, 2
bias, 25, 28, 54, 55, 77, 78, 86, 87, 103, 118, 122,
    151, 161
binge drinking, 126
biological responses, 143
bladder cancer, 92
body weight, 98
Bosnia, 67
bowel, 2
brain, 92, 184
brain cancer, 92

Brazil, 13, 18, 154
breakdown, 185
breast cancer, 170, 177, 179
breathing, 158, 187, 195
bronchitis, 92
browsing, 189
Bulgaria, 99

**C**

calcium, 176
calcium channel blocker, 176
campaigns, 149, 151
cancer, 177
candidates, 11
cannabis, 91, 92, 93, 94, 100, 101, 102, 103, 104,
    107, 109, 110, 111, 113, 114, 116, 121, 123
cardiac activity, 23
cardiovascular system, 22
caregivers, 10, 130, 146
caries, 144
case studies, 193
case study, 109, 180, 201
category b, 72
causal relationship, 173
causality, 21, 100
Census, 54, 70
CFI, 57, 58, 59, 60, 61
challenges, 128, 129, 131, 132, 139, 185, 196
chemical, 116
CHF, 157, 158, 159, 160, 161, 162, 163, 164, 165,
    166, 167, 168, 170, 173, 174
Chicago, 1
child abuse, 92
Child Behavior Checklist, 11, 13, 14, 55, 57
child development, 68
childhood, 2, 15, 16, 17, 44, 47, 51, 52, 53, 54, 65,
    67, 69, 75, 82, 84, 85, 86, 88, 89, 90, 116, 131,
    147, 192
childrearing, 51, 52, 88
China, 67, 152, 153
cholesterol, 172, 180
chronic diseases, 158, 170, 173
chronic heart failure, viii, 157, 179, 180, 181
Chronic heart failure, 158
chronic illness, 157, 159, 164, 173
chronic renal failure, 180
cigarette smoke, 100
cigarette smokers, 100
cigarette smoking, 92, 95, 96, 99, 112, 118, 119, 121
CIS, 8
City, 201
CKD, 170

classes, 41, 127
classical conditioning, 193
classification, vii, 2, 3, 6, 120
classroom, 127
clients, 9, 81, 155, 179, 192, 193, 194, 198
clinical disorders, 27
clinical interventions, 65
clinical presentation, 123
clinical psychology, 85
close relationships, 32, 202
clusters, 3
cocaine, 99, 119, 120
coding, 14
cognition, 28, 30, 95, 138, 184
cognitive abilities, 170
Cognitive affective theories, 93
Cognitive behavioral therapy, 124, 183
cognitive behavioral training, viii
cognitive biases, 73
cognitive capacities, 186, 197
cognitive function, 180
cognitive impairment, 107, 158, 171, 179
cognitive level, 184
cognitive models, 23
cognitive process, 20, 25, 103, 185, 197
cognitive psychology, 184
cognitive skills, 41
cognitive style, 77, 85
cognitive tasks, 75
cognitive theory, 112, 114
cognitive therapy, 81, 137, 188, 199
cognitive-behavioral therapy, 41, 44, 85, 109
coherence, 21, 22, 26, 132
collaboration, 41, 185
college students, 3, 18, 96, 98, 103, 114, 115, 116, 117, 118, 119, 120, 121, 123, 125
colleges, 40
Colombia, 67
combined effect, 109, 113
commercial, 155
commercials, 96
communication, 36, 39, 74, 82, 83, 84, 129, 131, 132, 133, 135, 136, 137, 138, 148, 176, 189, 191
communication patterns, 84
communication skills, 82, 83, 133, 136, 137
communist countries, 96
communities, 144, 145
community, 1, 10, 12, 13, 16, 33, 34, 46, 47, 48, 49, 50, 53, 69, 72, 76, 81, 85, 86, 88, 94, 100, 121, 125, 139, 142, 145, 146, 147, 152, 153, 155, 162, 179, 200
comorbidity, 42, 44, 45, 46, 72, 84, 87, 89, 100, 108, 109, 110, 111, 115, 121, 122, 123, 124, 129, 188

Comorbidity, 46, 72, 87, 91, 138
comparative analysis, 177
compatibility, 184
compensation, 36
complexity, 158, 171, 177
compliance, 174, 175, 176, 177, 178, 179, 180, 181
complications, 76
composition, 150
computer, 36, 41, 184, 189, 190, 201
conceptual model, 27, 69
conceptualization, 122, 201
conduct disorder, 103, 128
confidentiality, 148
conflict, vii, 49, 51, 52, 53, 56, 58, 59, 61, 63, 64, 65, 67, 68, 70, 174
conflict of interest, 174
conformity, 93, 105, 107, 115, 120, 126
confounding variables, 103
confrontation, 20, 194
congestive heart failure, 179
Congress, 201
congruence, 2, 27, 138
conscientiousness, 99, 100
consciousness, 119, 184
Consciousness, 12, 184
consensus, 15, 72, 97, 98, 112, 143
consent, 160
construct validity, 2, 9, 10, 17, 56
consumption, 97, 108, 112, 116
containers, 171
contamination, 145
contemporary societies, vii
content analysis, 44
contingency, 38, 82, 83
control group, 14, 75, 78, 83, 130
controlled exposure, 193
controlled trials, 16
controversial, 170
conversations, 133, 137
cooperation, 33, 135, 145, 160, 163, 186, 194
Coparenting, 66, 79
COPD, 181
coping strategies, 44, 82, 94, 109, 152, 185, 198
correlation(s), 57, 58, 157, 170, 162, 198
cost, 36, 45, 47, 93, 172
counseling, 121, 151, 179, 200
craving, 101, 114
criminals, 143
criticism, 40, 100, 144, 146
cross-sectional study, 45, 77, 78
cues, 22, 23, 128, 133, 134, 198
Cultural, 45, 71, 121
cultural beliefs, 73

cultural differences, 102, 111, 199
cultural norms, 43
cultural stereotypes, 32
cultural values, 43
culture, viii, 43, 111, 196
Cyprus, 8
cystic fibrosis, 179

## D

dance(s), 132, 134
danger, 24, 26, 198
data collection, 54, 57
database, 175
deaths, 91
defence, 184
deficiencies, 31
deficit, 130
delinquency, 97
Department of Health and Human Services, 125
Depression, 10, 12, 13, 15, 44, 45, 47, 87, 88, 113,
    122, 146, 153, 157, 158, 161, 166, 168, 177, 180,
    198, 199
depressive symptomatology, 162, 165, 170
depressive symptoms, 35, 52, 53, 63, 105, 143, 147,
    152, 162, 164, 165, 170, 177
depth, 101, 102, 106, 188
desensitization, 40, 193
detection, 2, 20, 22, 29, 42
detoxification, 120
developed countries, 151
developing countries, 92, 98, 151
developmental disorder, 5, 129
developmental factors, 18
developmental milestones, 98
developmental psychopathology, 17, 139
diabetes, 160, 177
diabetic patients, 180
Diagnostic and Statistical Manual of Mental
    Disorders, 34, 129
dialysis, 159, 170, 175, 177, 181
diet, 158, 159, 170, 173
diffusion, 155
directors, 163
disability, 72, 131, 158
disclosure, 36, 37, 40, 76, 88, 143, 150
discomfort, 38, 72
discontinuity, 175
discrimination, 22, 143, 144, 145, 150, 151
disease progression, 159
diseases, 92, 142, 151, 158
disgust, 145
dissatisfaction, 1

distortions, 73, 170
distress, 20, 34, 50, 53, 72, 73, 76, 79, 101, 102, 105,
    124, 128, 142, 143, 146, 151, 152, 153, 200
distribution, 164
diversity, 107, 136
doctors, 157, 163, 164, 165, 170
DOI, 152
Dominican Republic, 155
dosing, 158, 171, 174
drawing, 40
dream, 136
drug addict, 144
drug dependence, 94, 112, 151
drug reactions, 158
drug treatment, 176
drugs, 91, 94, 99, 113, 116, 122, 171, 178, 180
Drugs, 119, 180
DSM, vii, 191
DSM-IV-TR, 4, 15, 43, 112
dyslipidemia, 175
dyspnea, 158
dysthymia, 117

## E

East Asia, 120, 199
eating disorders, 5
economic status, 102, 141, 146, 179
edema, 158
education, 54, 81, 102, 121, 127, 138, 144, 146, 148,
    149, 150, 151, 152, 154, 155, 164, 172
educational attainment, 54, 70, 147
educators, 39, 150
elders, 157
elementary school, 8
e-mail, 133
emission, 8
emotion, 6, 16, 18, 86, 94, 118, 184, 197, 201
emotion regulation, 18, 94, 201
emotional distress, 51, 52, 99, 101, 121, 143
emotional experience, 22, 29, 143
emotional problems, 143
emotional state, 143, 147
emotional well-being, 172
emotionality, 17, 100
empathy, 130, 134
emphysema, 92
empirical studies, viii, 91, 110
employability, 190
employees, 164
employment, 1, 72, 98, 102
empowerment, 145
Enacted stigma, 144

encouragement, 36, 78, 190, 191
end stage renal disease, 175, 177
environment, 38, 43, 76, 77, 86, 88, 130, 141, 145, 163, 172, 185, 189, 190, 195
environmental factors, 154
environmental stress, 147
environments, 33, 40, 96
enzyme, 98
epidemic, 154
epidemiologic, 46, 89, 116, 122
epidemiology, 86, 87, 121
epilepsy, 178
epistemology, 73
equilibrium, 186
equity, 120
esophagus, 92
ethanol, 115
ethical standards, 160
ethnic background, 43
ethnic groups, 199
ethnicity, 118, 121, 178, 196
etiology, 50, 51, 73, 84, 88, 91, 92, 101, 108, 110, 201, 202
Europe, 6, 178
everyday life, 16
evidence, 2, 3, 18, 19, 20, 21, 22, 23, 25, 35, 37, 55, 71, 77, 80, 84, 85, 88, 92, 96, 97, 99, 100, 109, 114, 115, 129, 130, 142, 143, 146, 148, 150, 151, 172, 183, 187, 188, 191, 193, 196, 202
evolution, 184, 196
examinations, 51
exclusion, 65
exercise, 21, 23, 28, 135, 158, 170, 173, 181, 187, 202
expertise, 38
exposure, 24, 34, 38, 41, 75, 76, 77, 81, 82, 83, 101, 108, 125, 137, 147, 148, 152, 154, 185, 186, 187, 188, 189, 190, 191, 193, 194, 196, 198, 200
Exposure therapy, 187, 193
external locus of control, 170
externalizing behavior, 68
externalizing disorders, 5, 72
extraversion, 17, 40, 99, 100, 197

**F**

face-to-face interaction, 36, 133
facial expression, 123, 133
facial muscles, 195
false belief, 148
families, vii, 13, 40, 49, 50, 53, 54, 55, 66, 69, 74, 77, 78, 87, 93, 96, 107, 115, 142, 144, 146, 147, 155

Family, v, 17, 44, 45, 46, 49, 51, 52, 55, 57, 60, 61, 66, 67, 68, 69, 70, 71, 74, 80, 84, 85, 86, 87, 88, 89, 90, 120, 121, 122, 124, 152, 154, 177
family behavior, 83
family conflict, 74
family environment, 74, 78, 84, 85, 87, 89, 135
family factors, vii, 49, 50, 65, 71, 74, 80, 88, 198
family functioning, 51, 71, 73, 74, 82, 84, 85
family history, 119
family income, 70
family interactions, 73, 107
family life, 54
family members, 42, 54, 73, 136, 147, 171, 172
family relationships, vii
family support, 81, 147, 153
family system, 51, 67, 73
family therapy, 69, 86
family violence, 70
fasting, 135
feelings, 25, 29, 32, 36, 37, 39, 50, 52, 63, 64, 83, 131, 133, 134, 136, 141, 144, 145, 146, 147, 161, 170, 188, 192, 193, 197
financial, 147
five-factor model, 120
flavor, viii
flooding, 193, 194
Flooding, 194
fluid, 158, 159, 170, 173, 180
focus groups, 32
food, 116, 132
football, 136
Ford, 149, 152
formal education, 172
formation, 23, 25, 92
foundations, 53, 112
freedom, 96, 97, 112
friendship, 40, 47, 125
functional analysis, 194
funds, 54, 174

**G**

gender differences, 48, 63, 102, 111, 113, 124, 125, 199
gender equality, 96
gender gap, 99
gender role, 98
general practitioner, 83
generalizability, 3, 103
generalized anxiety disorder, 5, 36, 82, 128, 200
Generalized Anxiety Disorder, 7
genetic factors, 73, 74
Germany, 35, 67

grades, 50, 53, 57
grants, 174
Greece, vi, viii, 127, 135, 141, 157, 183
group activities, 136
group therapy, 16, 109, 177, 188, 199, 200
group treatment, 89, 109, 201
grouping, 3
growth, 57, 61, 65
guidance, 132, 134, 135, 190, 191, 195
guilty, 145

# H

habituation, 28
happiness, 79
harassment, 68, 133
harmony, 70
health, 1, 18, 32, 34, 35, 36, 37, 42, 43, 45, 46, 84,
    91, 96, 110, 111, 113, 115, 118, 125, 126, 143,
    144, 146, 152, 153, 154, 157, 158, 159, 160, 163,
    164, 165, 169, 170, 171, 172, 173, 174, 175, 177,
    178, 179, 180, 181, 190
Health and Human Services, 92
health care, 1, 32, 37, 42, 43, 45, 144, 158, 169
health care professionals, 43
health education, 153
health effects, 91
health information, 32, 36, 37, 46
health insurance, 173, 177
health locus of control, 157, 159, 160, 163, 164, 165,
    169, 170, 173, 175, 178, 179, 181
Health locus of control, 158, 163, 174
health problems, 169, 171
health services, 37
heart disease, 92
heart failure, 157, 158, 171, 174, 175, 176, 177, 178,
    181
heart rate, 6, 21, 23, 24, 27, 28, 29
heavy drinking, 10, 92, 118, 119, 123
helplessness, 184
hemodialysis, 175, 181
hepatitis, 181
heroin, 99, 116, 119
high school, 7, 97, 98, 112, 116, 121, 126, 149
higher education, 172, 190
history, 112, 119
HIV, v, viii, 124, 141, 142, 143, 144, 145, 146, 147,
    148, 149, 150, 151, 152, 153, 154, 155, 169, 175,
    179
HIV test, 145, 154
HIV/AIDS, v, viii, 141, 142, 143, 144, 145, 147,
    149, 150, 151, 152, 154, 155, 175
homes, 74

homework, 137, 185, 189, 194, 195, 196
hopelessness, 147, 170
hostility, vii, 49, 51, 52, 53, 55, 56, 57, 58, 60, 61,
    63, 64, 67
hotel(s), 150
household income, 54
human, 34, 69, 112, 133
human agency, 112
human development, 69
Hunter, 161, 177
husband, 56
hyperactivity, 9
hypertension, 175, 177, 178, 180
hypnosis, 195
hypothesis, 22, 36, 63, 68, 75, 77, 94, 102, 103, 106,
    115, 119, 125, 131, 148

# I

ID, 189, 190
identification, vii, 6, 42, 72, 185, 186, 196
identity, 31, 52, 97, 116
ideology, 99
illicit drug use, 119
imagery, 17, 45, 46, 185
image(s), 35, 41, 44, 89, 147, 188
imagination, 194
imitation, 95
impairments, 39, 128, 191
impersonal living environments, vii
implicit memory, 104
improvements, 82, 83, 187, 192
impulses, 192
impulsive, 147
impulsivity, 99
in transition, 125
in vivo, 81, 193, 194
In vivo exposure, 194
inattention, 9
incidence, 158
income, 54, 153, 155, 172
independence, 52, 64, 78, 97
India, 67, 151, 152, 179
indirect effect, 124
individual development, 69
individual differences, 22, 61, 86, 123, 163, 196,
    197, 198, 201
individual perception, 145
individuation, 36
Indonesia, 152
induction, 176
industrialized countries, 92
industrialized societies, 189

infancy, 88
infants, 74, 78, 130
infection, 142, 143, 144, 145, 148, 149, 153, 154
inferences, 188
inferiority, 16, 147
infertility, 92
inflation, 54
information processing, 73, 77, 184
informed consent, 148
inhibition, 2, 17, 34, 51, 65, 67, 69, 73, 78, 85, 87, 130, 138
initiation, 91, 93, 95, 96, 97, 98, 99, 150, 175
injury, 128
insecurity, 50, 63, 142, 147, 191
instrumental support, 150
integration, 6, 27
intelligence, 196, 197, 201
intercourse, 148, 153
interdependence, 63
internal consistency, 2, 7, 8, 9, 10, 11, 12, 13, 14
Internalized stigma, 144, 153
internalizing, 50, 52, 53, 55, 57, 58, 60, 61, 63, 65, 68, 69, 72, 128, 130, 153
Internalizing, 61
International Classification of Diseases, 128
Internet, 16, 36, 37, 44, 45, 189, 191, 199, 200
Interoceptive accuracy, 20
interparental conflict, 67, 68, 69
interpersonal communication, 134
interpersonal conflict, 127, 130, 138
interpersonal interactions, 103
Interpersonal psychotherapy, 191, 200
interpersonal relations, 93, 130, 131
interpersonal relationships, 93, 130, 131
interpersonal skills, 130
intervention, viii, 3, 18, 38, 40, 41, 45, 68, 72, 83, 84, 87, 89, 100, 109, 123, 132, 137, 138, 151, 154, 155, 184, 185, 186, 187, 189, 190
Intervention, v, 15, 141
Intrapersonal, 97
introvert, 32, 39, 47
IQ scores, 196
Ireland, 71
irony, 133
isolation, vii, 128, 129, 144, 193, 198
isoniazid, 178
Israel, 44, 45, 150, 151, 153
issues, 66, 68, 85, 107, 108, 111, 131, 138, 146, 154, 177, 188, 192

**J**

Jamaica, 151

Japan, 11, 112, 117
Jordan, 43, 44, 99, 123

**K**

Kenya, 154
kidney, 92, 170
kill, 152
Korea, 199

**L**

language skills, 138
larynx, 92
later life, 190
lead, 3, 6, 24, 25, 34, 35, 76, 121, 128, 129, 130, 131, 133, 137, 142, 146, 170, 188, 195
Leahy, 15
learning, 5, 32, 37, 39, 79, 93, 98, 104, 112, 113, 128, 130, 184
learning disabilities, 112, 113
legs, 158
leisure, 39, 102, 124
lens, 65
level of education, 165
life course, 154
life expectancy, 91
life experiences, 38, 88, 185
life satisfaction, 152
lifetime, 67, 111
light, 25
Likert scale, 7, 8, 9, 10, 11, 12, 13, 14
linear model, 124
linear modeling, 124
literacy, 37, 44, 45, 46
lithium, 175
living environment, vii
locus, 44, 51, 158, 159, 160, 163, 164, 165, 169, 170, 174, 177, 181
Longitudinal, 3, 49, 109, 122, 124, 125
longitudinal study, 17, 78, 80, 121, 153, 154, 173
love, 116
lung cancer, 92

**M**

magnitude, 3, 103
major depression, 117
major depressive disorder, 2, 36
majority, 25, 35, 84, 97, 123, 171, 186, 189
Malaysia, 174
man, 99, 145

management, 38, 41, 82, 83, 84, 93, 95, 104, 106,
    107, 123, 124, 147, 159, 174, 175, 178, 186, 195
manipulation, 21, 22, 27
MANOVA, 55
marijuana, 3, 113, 114, 117
marital conflict, vii, 49, 51, 52, 53, 54, 56, 57, 58,
    59, 60, 61, 63, 64, 65, 66, 67, 68, 73
Marital conflict, 51, 68
marital quality, 52
marital status, 54, 164, 172
marketing, 96, 112
marriage, 98, 172
masculinity, 99, 120
mass, 98, 132, 151
mass media, 151
materials, 37, 190
matter, 126, 151, 172, 186, 189
maturation process, 98
measurement, vii, 1, 2, 4, 6, 16, 107, 160
measurements, 108
media, 96
median, 54
medical, 158, 163, 169, 170, 176, 179, 180
medication, viii, 37, 41, 94, 102, 103, 104, 114, 115,
    119, 120, 122, 124, 157, 158, 159, 160, 164, 165,
    169, 170, 171, 172, 173, 174, 175, 176, 177, 178,
    179, 180, 181
medication compliance, 179, 180
medicine, 160
memory, 25, 26, 28, 77, 126, 131, 158, 171, 185
memory loss, 158
memory performance, 28
mental activity, 192
mental disorder, 15, 32, 33, 34, 43, 44, 45, 46, 112,
    137, 138
mental health, 15, 32, 33, 35, 37, 38, 39, 40, 42, 44,
    46, 47, 80, 81, 83, 97, 113, 121, 135, 142, 143,
    146, 147, 152, 153, 155, 158, 160, 170, 172, 173,
    175, 177, 181, 186, 190, 201
mental health professionals, 42, 186
mental illness, 120, 193
mental image, 185
mental representation, 25
mental retardation, 137
mental state, 141
messages, 40, 198
meta-analysis, 21, 28, 52, 53, 69, 70, 75, 88, 113,
    117, 118, 120, 176, 187, 188
methadone, 116
methodology, 108
Mexico, 177
Mindfulness treatment, 193
miniature, 135

minorities, 146
minority groups, 189
mission, 33
misuse, 72, 101, 111, 117
modelling, 195
models, 2, 19, 39, 57, 67, 73, 94, 95, 96, 103, 106,
    110, 114, 115, 118, 124, 130, 139, 158, 188, 189,
    197
moderates, 69, 119, 124, 126
modifications, 184
modules, 190
monoamine oxidase inhibitors, 41, 108
mood disorder, 36, 100, 125
morbidity, 46, 47, 89, 115, 119, 122, 124, 125
mortality, 113, 116
motivation, 30, 35, 44, 93, 109, 112, 172, 185
MR, 58, 59, 60, 62
multidimensional, 17, 113, 181
multimedia, 202
multiple factors, 73
multivariate analysis, 55
muscle relaxation, 41, 195
muscles, 195
music, 136
myocardial infarction, 176
myopia, 123

## N

naming, 81
National Institute of Mental Health, 34, 46, 66
National Survey, 46, 55, 70
nebulizer, 181
negative affectivity, 105, 121
negative attitudes, 148, 172
negative consequences, 92, 158
negative effects, 22, 24, 107, 109
negative emotions, 79, 87, 145, 193
negative experiences, 146, 198
negative mood, 21, 118
negative outcomes, 93, 94, 105
negative reinforcement, 94, 104, 112
negative relation, 105, 106
negative stimulus, 186
negative valence, 23
neglect, 51, 92
Nepal, 179
nervousness, 50, 63
Netherlands, 14
neurobiology, 86, 122
neuroscience, 117
neutral, 41, 192
New England, 46, 179

New Zealand, 46, 47, 86, 121
nicotine, 46, 94, 107, 113, 118, 119, 121
Nigeria, 174
non-insulin dependent diabetes, 176
nonverbal cues, 134
norepinephrine, 41
normal children, 77
normal distribution, 164
North America, 123, 201
Norway, 112
novelty seeking, 99
nuisance, 133
nutritional status, 173

**O**

objectivity, 184
observational learning, 95
obstacles, 34
old age, 170
openness, 35
opportunities, 65, 76, 127, 130, 131
optimism, 147, 197, 198
organize, 40
outpatient, 121, 175, 179, 180
outpatients, 7, 11, 13, 178, 186
overlap, 6, 43, 129
oxygen, 158

**P**

Pacific, 153
Pacific Islanders, 153
pain, 118, 143, 152, 159, 177, 200
pairing, 40
Panic, 5, 7, 121
panic attack, 36
panic disorder, 2, 23, 26, 35, 75, 88, 100, 142, 199
parallel, 38, 131
parasympathetic activity, 6
parental authority, 79
parental control, 38, 75, 76, 99
parental involvement, 79, 80, 83, 89
parental participation, 81, 82
parental smoking, 119
parenting, 50, 51, 52, 53, 61, 63, 64, 65, 66, 67, 69,
    70, 71, 75, 76, 80, 81, 83, 84, 87, 88, 89, 96, 119,
    123, 191, 198
parenting styles, 69, 76, 80, 88, 89, 198
parents, vii, 32, 33, 38, 42, 45, 49, 51, 52, 53, 54, 56,
    57, 64, 65, 66, 67, 68, 73, 74, 75, 76, 77, 78, 79,
80, 81, 82, 83, 84, 88, 89, 90, 96, 97, 116, 121,
    126, 127, 130, 132, 135, 136, 138, 198
paroxetine, 108
participants, 3, 11, 21, 22, 24, 33, 35, 37, 39, 94,
    103, 106, 108, 109, 131, 132, 133, 144, 148, 149,
    150, 157, 163, 170, 186, 187, 188, 189, 192
passive-aggressive, 65
pathology, 3
pathways, vii, 19, 21, 25, 71, 73, 79, 184
peer group, 93, 97, 104, 107
peer influence, 96, 112, 114, 126
peer rejection, 2, 52, 131
peer relationship, 68, 73, 88, 120, 125, 192
peer support, 82
pensioners, 164, 172
perceived control, 70
perceived norms, 119
percentage of fat, 98
perfectionism, 5, 187, 188, 189, 199
performance appraisal, 24
perinatal, 154
permission, 54, 160
personal benefit, 93
personal control, 159, 165, 175
personal relations, 98, 192
personal relationship, 98, 192
personal responsibility, 98
personality, 18, 41, 89, 93, 97, 99, 100, 101, 112,
    115, 117, 118, 119, 120, 121, 123, 124, 125, 139,
    184, 196, 197, 198, 202
Personality, 15, 16, 17, 27, 29, 46, 47, 68, 88, 99,
    117, 118, 121, 122, 123, 124, 125, 174, 181, 201
personality characteristics, 18, 93, 97, 99, 100, 101
personality disorder, 89, 125, 139, 202
personality factors, 197
personality traits, 99, 100, 115, 118, 123, 196, 197,
    202
personality type, 196
pharmacotherapy, 170, 174, 176, 177, 178
phenotype, 3
phenotypes, 20
Philadelphia, 138
Philippines, 154
phobia, 3, 5, 15, 17, 18, 27, 33, 36, 44, 46, 66, 72,
    73, 74, 75, 76, 79, 80, 81, 83, 84, 85, 86, 87, 88,
    89, 104, 122, 128, 138, 139, 148, 191, 193, 197,
    198, 199, 200
Physical, 5, 142
physical abuse, 73
physical activity, 158
physical aggression, 51, 64
physical characteristics, 98
physical health, 122, 141, 169, 172

physicians, 170, 172
Physiological, 5, 21, 24
physiological arousal, 19, 20, 21, 22, 23, 24, 25, 26,
    27, 128, 130, 131
physiology, 87
pilot study, 44, 47, 89, 199, 201, 202
placebo, 47, 111, 196
plasticity, 124
playing, 136, 195
pleasure, 108, 118, 136
poor performance, 78, 129
population, vii, 17, 26, 31, 33, 37, 40, 42, 44, 46, 70,
    84, 112, 116, 120, 121, 128, 129, 143, 149, 159,
    165, 173, 180, 188, 189, 200
positive attitudes, 42
positive emotions, 16, 118
positive reinforcement, 159, 169
positive relationship, 105
postpartum depression, 179
posttraumatic stress, 202
post-traumatic stress disorder, 2, 186
potassium, 170
poverty, 54, 147, 154, 155
preferential treatment, 145
prejudice, 144, 145, 196
premature death, 92
preschool, 202
preschool children, 202
preschoolers, 2
preterm delivery, 92
prevention, 87, 105, 109, 110, 112, 147, 148, 149,
    150, 151, 152, 153, 154, 155, 176, 186
principles, 132, 150, 183, 184, 202
proactive behavior, 83
probability, 22, 94, 97
probe, 20
problem behavior(s), 67, 69, 70
problem drinking, 118, 120
problem solving, 64, 74, 75, 82, 83
problem-focused coping, 197
problem-solving, 39, 74, 189
problem-solving skills, 189
professionals, 138, 170, 174
prognosis, 35, 158
programming, 67, 121
project, 1, 52
protective factors, 65, 99
prototype, 99
psychiatric disorders, 6, 45, 87, 113, 117, 119, 122
psychiatric morbidity, 142
psychiatric patients, 39, 43
psychiatry, 16, 85
Psychoeducation, 185

Psychological control, 70
psychological distress, 142, 143, 146, 147
psychological problems, 94
psychological stress, 170
psychological well-being, 141, 142, 154
psychologist, 184
psychology, 30, 87, 122, 144, 184, 196, 201, 202
psychometric properties, 3, 15
psychopathology, 23, 32, 50, 68, 69, 71, 73, 77, 78,
    79, 80, 81, 84, 85, 87, 88, 124, 128, 129, 139, 202
Psychopathology, 69, 79, 86, 89, 125, 152
psychosis, 3, 12, 15
psychosocial factors, 174
psychotherapy, 37, 40, 108, 185, 186, 191, 192, 195,
    200, 201
psychotic symptoms, 5
psychoticism, 100, 197
PTSD, 186, 200, 201
public health, 32, 123, 151
public sector, 150

## Q

qualifications, 172
quality of life, 18, 31, 37, 72, 84, 91, 94, 123, 127,
    158, 159, 172, 174, 175, 176, 177, 180, 181
Quality of life, 177, 181
questioning, 185, 201
questionnaire, 20, 36, 54, 55, 56, 113, 157, 161, 163

## R

race, 54, 125
racism, 146
rating scale, 15, 16
reactions, 27, 94, 143, 184
reactivity, 18, 20, 22, 26, 28, 29, 67, 113
reading, 33, 40
real time, 6
reality, 32, 190, 192
reasoning, 23, 24, 26, 184, 196
recall, 88, 198
recalling, 131
receptors, 121
reciprocal relationships, 70
recognition, 35, 37, 46, 175
recommendations, vii, 31, 35, 36, 38, 40, 42, 43,
    158, 159
reconstruction, 187
recovery, 28, 189
recreational, 74, 99, 131
recruiting, 173

regions of the world, 92
rehabilitation, 181
rehabilitation program, 181
reinforcement, 39, 75
rejection, 65, 69, 75, 76, 80, 82, 88, 142
Rejection, 75
relatives, 198
relaxation, 82, 93, 108, 132, 135, 186, 187, 189, 191, 195, 200
Relaxation, 189, 195
relevance, 16, 51, 52, 96
reliability, 5, 6, 7, 9, 10, 13, 14, 16, 161, 162
relief, 94
religion, 134, 135, 186
religiosity, 170
religious beliefs, 186
remission, 159, 187
replication, 65, 67
representativeness, 173
requirements, 184
researchers, 2, 3, 20, 35, 41, 42, 72, 73, 75, 77, 78, 79, 82, 131, 144, 150, 171, 172, 189, 190, 192, 198
resilience, 119, 155
resistance, 35
resolution, 127, 130, 138
resources, 24, 32, 143, 147, 152
response, 4, 6, 17, 23, 24, 30, 54, 56, 76, 96, 98, 103, 123, 138, 159, 160, 161, 199
response format, 56
restructuring, 41, 82, 108, 109, 137
retention rate, 150
rewards, 81
rhythm, 22
rights, 127, 131, 160
risk factors, 47, 72, 73, 76, 80, 85, 87, 123, 125
RMSEA, 57, 58, 59, 60, 61
role-playing, 133, 135, 137, 195
romantic relationship, 102
routines, 73, 75, 129, 135

## S

sadness, 142
safety, 39, 142, 145, 186, 188, 197
SAS, 7, 8
scarcity, 108
schema(s), 3, 184
schemata, 77
schizophrenia, 178, 180, 184
school, 3, 5, 8, 15, 17, 45, 50, 53, 54, 55, 57, 61, 65, 66, 68, 72, 73, 74, 102, 127, 133, 188, 190
school activities, 127

school performance, 72, 102
science, 69, 184
scripts, 132, 135
search terms, 1
security, 51, 68
selective mutism, 188
selective serotonin reuptake inhibitor, 108
self esteem, 146, 184
self help, 190
self-awareness, 26, 118, 135
self-concept, 96
self-confidence, 52, 53
self-consciousness, 51
self-definition, 97
self-destructive behavior, 143
self-efficacy, 75, 81, 95, 108, 149, 150
self-enhancement, 121
self-esteem, 99, 102, 120, 137, 196
self-evaluations, vii, 19, 26
Self-medication, 114, 122, 124
self-monitoring, 20
self-perceptions, 21, 24, 25
self-presentation, 122
self-reports, 21, 129
self-worth, 142
seminars, 40
sensations, vii, 19, 21, 25, 26
sensitivity, vii, 19, 20, 23, 26, 27, 29, 65, 69, 76, 77, 105, 142, 152, 153
sensitization, 122
sensory experience, 185
serotonin, 41
serum, 170
services, 35, 43, 47, 150
SES, 102
sex, 92, 98, 116, 121, 134, 141, 142, 149, 150, 152, 153, 154, 155, 177
sexual abuse, 73
sexual behavior, 115, 116, 149, 152, 154
sexual behaviour, 119, 122
sexual health, 155
sexual intercourse, 122, 149
sexual orientation, 148
sexually transmitted diseases, 92
sexually transmitted infections, 149, 154, 155
shame, 2, 35
showing, 63, 109, 130, 143, 144, 149, 165, 166, 169, 192
shyness, 2, 33, 34, 36, 40, 44, 51, 72, 74, 78, 86, 89, 190
Shyness, 36, 39, 43, 44, 45, 46, 47
siblings, 33, 67, 79, 81, 87, 136
side effects, 171

signals, 22

signs, 76, 88, 199

Singapore, 120, 155, 157

skills training, 195, 200

skin, 143

smoking, 34, 46, 92, 93, 94, 95, 96, 99, 100, 103, 107, 109, 111, 112, 113, 115, 116, 117, 118, 119, 120, 121, 123, 125, 169

Smoking, 92, 112, 117, 119, 120, 124

smoking cessation, 100, 117, 118

sociability, 78, 84, 132

social acceptance, 34, 101

social activities, 40, 74, 75, 77, 132, 137

social adjustment, 31

social anxiety disorder, vii, 2, 3, 4, 5, 15, 16, 17, 18, 27, 31, 32, 34, 38, 42, 43, 44, 45, 46, 47, 67, 72, 73, 87, 100, 101, 102, 103, 112, 114, 116, 117, 120, 122, 123, 125, 129, 137, 138, 142, 144, 148, 173, 175, 183, 190, 195, 198, 199, 200

social behavior, 78, 88, 111, 132

social capital, 142, 145, 152, 154

Social capital, 145

social change, 99

social circle, 191

social competence, 68, 69

social conflicts, 146

social consequences, 92

social context, 63, 96, 128, 143, 147, 150

social desirability, 78

social environment, 40, 122, 141, 142, 146, 147

social events, 101, 135

social group, 95, 105

social influence(s), 93, 96, 97, 105, 143, 147, 149, 154

social interactions, 6, 25, 31, 37, 40, 50, 76, 83, 101, 128, 129, 130, 131, 132, 134, 136, 141, 145, 146

social learning, vii, 91, 93, 95, 99, 102, 104, 105, 106, 110, 123, 124, 151

social life, 148, 187, 188, 199

social network, 47, 125, 133, 151

social norms, 96, 99, 104, 105, 122, 142

Social phobia, 17, 18, 27, 44, 46, 72, 84, 85, 86, 89, 122, 138, 139, 148, 200

social problems, 52

social psychology, 30

social relations, 34, 50, 52, 63, 65, 66, 118, 172

social relationships, 34, 50, 52, 63, 65, 66

social resources, 143

social roles, 98

social rules, 136

social situations, 20, 22, 27, 34, 39, 72, 76, 78, 85, 96, 103, 105, 106, 108, 114, 129, 135, 137, 148, 193, 195, 196, 198

social skills, 26, 40, 41, 44, 49, 50, 63, 65, 68, 73, 76, 82, 89, 93, 95, 99, 108, 129, 130, 131, 132, 135, 137, 138, 149, 154, 187, 191, 195, 196

social skills training, 41, 89, 108, 137, 187, 191, 195, 200

social status, 105

social stigmatization, 131

social stress, 20, 103, 135

social support, 36, 72, 79, 82, 102, 114, 143, 147, 148, 149, 150, 151, 153, 155, 172, 176

social support network, 82

social withdrawal, 72, 78, 129, 130

socialization, 36, 47, 50, 51, 73, 74, 77, 98, 125

socially acceptable behavior, 34

society, 92, 111, 143

socioeconomic status, 150

Socratic questioning, 185, 201

solitude, 33, 136

solution, 22, 186

somatization, 147

South Africa, 67, 142, 145, 146, 150, 152, 155

South America, 6

SP, 196

Spain, 7, 13, 123

speech, 20, 22, 23, 27, 29, 95, 101, 103, 110, 188

spending, 36, 135

spirituality, 135, 202

stability, 34, 63, 68, 154

standard deviation, 57, 128

state, vii, 3, 6, 19, 20, 21, 22, 23, 24, 26, 29, 136, 147, 148, 184, 190, 195, 197, 199

states, 18, 20, 35, 36

State-Trait Anxiety Inventory for Children, 5

statin, 174, 175, 176

Statistical Package for the Social Sciences, 164

statistics, 57, 143

stereotypes, 145

stereotyping, 145

steroids, 174

stigma, 35, 99, 141, 142, 143, 144, 145, 146, 147, 150, 151, 152, 153, 155

Stigma, 143, 145, 152

stigmatized, 191

stimulus, 197

stomach, 92

stream of consciousness, 184

stress, 7, 10, 12, 16, 22, 27, 28, 48, 93, 94, 95, 100, 102, 103, 104, 113, 115, 119, 121, 122, 123, 125, 132, 134, 135, 137, 141, 142, 143, 146, 147, 151, 152, 155, 193, 195, 199, 200, 202

stress response, 94, 102, 122

stressful events, 197

stressful life events, 147, 191

stressors, 79, 143, 147
stroke, 133, 175
structural equation modeling, 2, 53, 57
structure, 17, 69, 105, 120, 132, 135
structuring, 148
style, vii, 78, 80, 82, 86, 88, 98, 132, 197, 198
Styles, 7
subjective experience, 20
substance abuse, 3, 5, 40, 100, 109, 112, 113, 119,
    120, 123, 128, 142, 146, 154, 184, 188
substance use, vii, 17, 34, 35, 45, 46, 48, 91, 92, 93,
    94, 95, 96, 97, 98, 99, 100, 101, 102, 103, 104,
    105, 106, 107, 108, 109, 110, 111, 115, 116, 117,
    118, 119, 120, 121, 122, 123, 124, 125, 146, 175
Substance use, 91, 92, 110, 115, 122, 123, 126
suicidal ideation, 128
suicide, 72, 92, 94, 116, 122, 143, 151, 153
suicide attempts, 72, 115, 151
suicide rate, 143
supervision, 97
Supportive psychotherapy, 192
suppression, 16, 118
survival, 196
susceptibility, 98
sustainability, 132
Sweden, 174
swelling, 158
sympathetic nervous system, 29
symptomology, 3
syndrome, 14, 92, 128, 129, 130, 136, 137, 138, 139,
    178
synthesis, 118
systematic desensitization, 109, 193, 194, 195

## T

tactics, 64, 65
Taiwan, 175, 199
tamoxifen, 177
Tanzania, 151, 154
target, 81, 84, 132, 137, 191
target behavior, 81
task conditions, 19, 20
task difficulty, 20
teachers, 32, 39, 42, 54, 66, 118, 127, 132, 133, 134,
    136
team members, 174
techniques, viii, 41, 64, 81, 109, 132, 135, 137, 183,
    185, 186, 187, 189, 190, 191, 194, 195
technologies, 189
telephone, 37, 173
temperament, 43, 45, 65, 68, 69, 73, 78, 130
Temperament, 9, 124, 130

tension, 94, 95, 102, 103, 104, 106, 111, 119, 195
test anxiety, 121
testing, 103, 109, 118, 150, 152
test-retest reliability, 7, 8, 9, 11, 13, 14
textbook, 69
Thailand, 178
therapeutic approaches, 138
therapeutic process, 197, 198
therapeutic relationship, 191
therapist, 81, 185, 190, 191, 192, 194, 195
therapy, 28, 39, 40, 43, 44, 45, 47, 67, 80, 81, 82, 83,
    85, 87, 88, 89, 90, 109, 124, 139, 143, 150, 159,
    171, 172, 173, 174, 175, 176, 177, 178, 179, 181,
    183, 184, 185, 186, 187, 188, 189, 190, 192, 193,
    194, 195, 196, 197, 199, 200, 201, 202
thoughts, 6, 42, 52, 64, 83, 101, 104, 107, 117, 153,
    172, 184, 185, 197, 198, 201
threats, 104, 105, 147, 163
time constraints, 54
tissue, 98
tobacco, 3, 34, 91, 95, 99, 116, 120, 125, 126
tobacco smoke, 125
tobacco smoking, 99
toddlers, 69
toxicity, 155
toys, 135
traditions, 47
trainees, 196
training, viii, 81, 82, 83, 88, 108, 132, 133, 134, 135,
    137, 181, 189, 192, 193, 195, 199
trait anxiety, 23, 29, 157, 163, 165
Trait anxiety, 158, 163
traits, 100, 117, 130, 188, 197, 198
transition period, 63
transition to adulthood, 125
translation, 14
transmission, 79, 88, 90, 178
transplant, 176, 181
transplant recipients, 176, 181
transplantation, 174, 177
transportation, 131
Treatment, i, iii, v, 1, 31, 35, 36, 71, 108, 113, 131,
    177, 180, 189, 192, 193, 194, 197, 199
treatment methods, 111, 184
trial, 4, 16, 81, 82, 84, 86, 89, 118, 122, 173, 175,
    176, 178, 179, 180, 193, 200
triangulation, 49, 51, 52, 56, 58, 67, 68
triggers, 197
tuberculosis, 173, 174, 175, 178, 179
Turkey, 174
two-parent families, vii, 49, 50, 54, 66
type 2 diabetes, 174, 177

## U

UK, 116, 118, 125, 172, 200
unconventionality, 100
United, 6, 32, 33, 45, 47, 54, 67, 87, 93, 101, 111, 117, 146, 155
United States, 6, 32, 33, 45, 47, 54, 67, 87, 93, 101, 111, 117, 146, 155
univariate analyses of variance, 54
urban, 125, 154, 178
USA, 43, 112, 115, 121, 124

## V

valence, 2, 6
validation, 15, 16, 38, 40, 115, 154, 161, 163, 181
variables, 27, 54, 55, 61, 84, 100, 101, 103, 106, 110, 115, 123, 148, 150, 157, 164, 165, 169, 173, 176
variations, 194
victimization, 51, 67, 70, 152
victims, 144
Vietnam, 120
violence, 92, 152, 153
violent crime, 116
vision, 171
vulnerability, 2, 34, 53, 68, 112, 114, 118, 119, 143

## W

war, 176
Washington, 7, 15, 66, 68, 70, 137, 138

water, 98, 133
weakening family ties, vii
weakness, 144
web, 45, 189
web pages, 189
websites, 37, 39
weight gain, 158
well-being, 34, 47, 50, 51, 52
wells, 40, 47
Western Europe, 111
wetting, 135
WHO, 123
wilderness, 135
withdrawal, 64, 92, 110, 139
workers, 149, 150, 152, 153, 154, 155, 201
workforce, 99
workplace, 92
World Health Organization, 3, 91, 123, 126, 180
worldwide, 92, 110
worry, 5, 56, 128, 197

## Y

young adults, 31, 32, 33, 34, 35, 37, 38, 40, 41, 42, 43, 45, 46, 47, 48, 91, 97, 101, 106, 113, 119, 120, 125, 190
young people, vii, 31, 46, 96, 121, 131, 190

## Z

Zimbabwe, 151